Praise for *Sweet Charity?*

"Anyone who has ever coordinated a school food drive, or even tossed a few boxes of macaroni into a donation bin at the supermarket, is likely to be taken aback by *Sweet Charity?*, a no-holds-barred critique of America's emergency food system. Poppendieck convincingly argues that food programs are a Band-Aid solution to hunger, assuaging liberal guilt and at the same time reinforcing the benighted conviction that private charity is an adequate response to the problem. . . . A powerful work."
—*Chicago Tribune*

"There's a great deal of information in *Sweet Charity?*, but it's the stories that stay with you. Poppendieck's well-written, passionately argued book proves that seriousness does not have to be dull, that you can inform and still tell a good story. She raises difficult questions for many people of this country—the ones who are still outraged by hunger and poverty in the midst of plenty. *Sweet Charity?* is truly food for thought."
—*San Jose Mercury News*

"Experienced caregivers across the country have been shouting about these problems for years. It's great to have such a well-researched book available that's shouting about them, too."
—*The Dallas Morning News*

"A book that reads not like a leaden opus from a serious academic but refreshingly like the work of a bright friend and good listener who knows a lot about an important topic . . . Laudably evenhanded."
—*San Francisco Chronicle*

"The special genius of *Sweet Charity?* is Poppendieck's ability to combine insight into systemic failings with profound respect for individual moral commitments. She moves us to seek out ways that the impulse toward charity can be instructed by wisdom and transformed into a quest for justice."
—*The Christian Science Monitor*

"What is the meaning of charity—speci⟨...⟩ ⟨...⟩grams— in a wealthy society in which hunger co⟨...⟩ will? Janet Poppendieck explores this ⟨...⟩ an unusual depth of understanding, a⟨...⟩ those providing sustenance. *Sweet Ch⟨...⟩ able, and wise exploration of altruis⟨...⟩ social policy in contemporary America."
—Ruth Sidel, author of *Keeping Women and Children Last*

"In *Sweet Charity?*, Jan Poppendieck addresses the central dilemma of American food assistance: how the drive for food donations to meet the immediate needs of the poor tends to divert private citizens from demanding decent public policies that would prevent hunger in the first place. This is a beautifully written, deeply compassionate work that breaks new ground in understanding the emotional basis—as well as the history and economics—of public and private food assistance programs in the United States today. This is an instant classic that should influence thinking about welfare and hunger issues for years to come."
—Marion Nestle, Ph.D., M.P.H., Professor and Chair of the Department of Nutrition Food Studies, New York University

"*Sweet Charity?* is a profoundly disturbing, soul-searching analysis of the nation's emergency food network. Our 'emergency' response to hunger has become an institutional fixture, and Poppendieck argues that, laudable as it is, it plays into the hands of those who want to abandon governmental responsibility for ending hunger and poverty. Whether you agree or not, she has written a book that deserves to trigger a national debate. The first readers should be those at every food bank, soup kitchen, and food pantry."
—Art Simon, Founder, Bread for the World

"*Sweet Charity?* provides a brilliant and timely critique of the futility of emergency food programs and the need for a broader vision to obliterate poverty. Beautifully written and powerfully argued, Poppendieck speaks with great authority about the seductions of charity for many Americans at the same time she shows a wide range of people speaking for themselves. This important book needs to be read by anyone concerned about hunger and the harmful effects of ending welfare."
—Lynn S. Chancer, Assistant Professor, Department of Sociology, Barnard College

"*Sweet Charity?* bears important messages for volunteers and organizations fighting against hunger. An insightful, balanced, yet compassionate analysis, it argues persuasively that solutions to hunger and to other symptoms of inequality depend on transforming unjust into just societies."
—David G. Gill, Professor of Social Policy, Director, Center for Social Change, Brandeis University

PENGUIN BOOKS

SWEET CHARITY?

Janet Poppendieck is a professor of sociology at Hunter College of the City University of New York and director of its Center for the Study of Family Policy. She is the author of *Breadlines Knee Deep in Wheat: Food Assistance in the Great Depression*.

SWEET CHARITY?

Emergency Food and
the End of Entitlement

Janet Poppendieck

PENGUIN BOOKS

PENGUIN COMPASS
Published by the Penguin Group
Penguin Group (USA) Inc., 375 Hudson Street, New York, New York 10014, U.S.A.
Penguin Group (Canada), 90 Eglinton Avenue East, Suite 700, Toronto,
    Ontario, Canada M4P 2Y3 (a division of Pearson Penguin Canada Inc.)
Penguin Books Ltd, 80 Strand, London WC2R 0RL, England
Penguin Ireland, 25 St Stephen's Green, Dublin 2, Ireland (a division of Penguin Books Ltd)
Penguin Group (Australia), 250 Camberwell Road, Camberwell,
    Victoria 3124, Australia (a division of Pearson Australia Group Pty Ltd)
Penguin Books India Pvt Ltd, 11 Community Centre, Panchsheel Park, New Delhi – 110 017, India
Penguin Group (NZ), cnr Airborne and Rosedale Roads,
    Albany, Auckland 1310, New Zealand (a division of Pearson New Zealand Ltd)
Penguin Books (South Africa) (Pty) Ltd, 24 Sturdee Avenue,
    Rosebank, Johannesburg 2196, South Africa

Penguin Books Ltd, Registered Offices: 80 Strand, London WC2R 0RL, England

First published in the United States of America by Viking Penguin,
a member of Penguin Putnam Inc, 1998
Published in Penguin Books 1999

11 12 13 14 15 16 17 18 19 20

THE LIBRARY OF CONGRESS HAS CATALOGED THE HARDCOVER AS FOLLOWS:
Poppendieck, Janet, date.
Sweet Charity?: emergency food and the end of entitlement/Jane Poppendieck.
p.   cm.
Includes bibliographical references and index.
ISBN 0-670-88020-5 (hc.)
ISBN 0 14 02.4556 1 (pbk.)
1. Food relief—United States.   2. Food relief—United States—Evaluation.
3. Charities—United States.
4. Voluntarism—United States.   I. Title.
HV696.F6P663   1998
363.8'83'0973—dc21   98–18325

Printed in the United States of America
Set in New Caledonia

For Woody Goldberg

Acknowledgments

MANY PEOPLE have contributed to this book. First and foremost, I want to thank those whom I interviewed and observed at their work in the course of my research: the soup kitchen and food pantry volunteers and staff, the food bankers, the food rescuers, and the staff members in local and national advocacy organizations. Their generosity with time and their candor went far beyond what I had any right to expect. I am particularly grateful to Foodchain for permitting me to attend a national gathering on short notice, and to the staff at Second Harvest for sharing both their own histories and their perceptions of issues and trends, for providing access to national conferences, and for arranging an opportunity to interview board members. The participant observation aspect of this work has been enormously gratifying to me. It is not an exaggeration to say that I have spent some of the happiest hours of my adult life in the company of emergency food providers; their hospitality and their good humor as well as their creativity and dedication have left me full of admiration.

Purposely, I interviewed relatively few clients in this research. We have, on the whole, a great deal more information about poor people in such settings than we do about more privileged staff and volunteers, and I believe that we need to know more about the latter in order to understand how our society has made the transition from entitlements to charity that is explored in this book. Those clients whom I did interview, however, and others with whom I had brief conversations or shared meals, were singularly gracious and forthcoming.

Interviews would be of limited use were it not for careful transcription of tapes, and I had the assistance of several extraordinarily talented people in this task. Laura Konigsburg brought to the work of transcription not only her patience and skill, but also a lively interest in the subject, informed by her own research on services for homeless people in London and by years of volunteer work with a shelter and food pantry. She not only transcribed; she identified themes, provided annotations, and shared ideas. This project would not have been the same without her. Lynn du Hoffman also brought both great skill and real interest to bear and enriched the final product with her insights.

I could not have afforded the transcription, nor the trips to observe and interview in locations outside the New York area, had it not been for the generous support of the Aspen Institute Nonprofit Sector Research Fund and the Professional Staff Congress–City University of New York Faculty Research Award program. I am grateful to these funders, to the anonymous reviewers whose efforts make such funding possible, and to the staff of the CUNY Research Administration, especially Bob Buckley, for help in securing and administering these grants.

These funds also allowed me to obtain able research assistance from two particularly talented students, Rebecca Bergmann and Maureen Lane. I am grateful for their efforts on my behalf, as I am for those of librarians at Hunter College, Brooklyn College, the National Archives and Records Service, the New York Public Library, and the Brooklyn Public Library.

For almost the entire time I worked on this book, I served as director of the Hunter College Center for the study of Family Policy, and I want to thank all of its staff, particularly Elena Georgiou, who encouraged this project in every conceivable way and took on many tasks that would normally fall to a center director. I thank Professor Christina Taharally for her excellent leadership of the Center during my sabbatical leave, a gift of time from Hunter College that contributed a great deal to this project.

Numerous colleagues and friends read partial drafts or discussed the central ideas of this work with me and provided helpful feedback. I am grateful to Mimi Abramovitz, Lynn Chancer, Elena Georgiou, David Gil, Dick Goebel, Sarah Greenblatt, Susan Hanson, Ken Hecht, Barbara Howell, Melinda Lackey, Ester Madriz, Suzanne Michael, Graham Riches, Danny Ripps, Rich Ryan, Ruth Sidel, Hans Spiegel, David Tobis, Dee Unterbach, and Sara Zug. I especially want to thank Ruth Sidel, not only for unfailingly good advice and encouragement all along the way, but for the example of her own work, and the clear pleasure she takes in carrying it out, which inspired me to take on this project in the first place. I thank Elizabeth Danto for the question mark in my title and Department of Sociology chair Pam Stone for her sharp eyes at a crucial juncture. I'm grateful to Professors Phil Kasinitz and Naomi Kroeger and the students in their qualitative methods courses for a receptive hearing for this work and several sets of revealing field notes. Jason Black, then at World Hunger Year, read the entire manuscript with care and provided numerous helpful suggestions for which I cannot thank him enough.

Colleagues in the Association for the Study of Food and Society, and those in the Agriculture, Food and Human Values Society have listened with thoughtful attention to papers prepared along the way. I'm especially grateful to Jeff Sobal and Donna Maurer for encouraging me to explore the social constructionist perspective, to Barbara Gordon for hospitality early in my research and encouragement throughout, and to Kate Clancy and Jean Bowering for getting me involved in research on emergency food in the first place. A faculty seminar on philanthropy and diversity at the CUNY Graduate Center, directed by Professor Kathleen McCarthy and sponsored by the W. K. Kellogg Foundation, helped me to clarify some of my ideas about charity, as did the meetings of the Association for Research on Nonprofit Organizations and Voluntary Action. I'm thankful to the W. K. Kellogg Foundation for introducing me to the network of Kellogg fellows and to fellows Jackie Lundy and Bill Bolling, without whose input this project would never have been launched.

The possibility of this book first occurred to me as I watched the staff and fellow board members of the Community Food Resource Center in New York City struggle with the challenges posed by the project that grew into the Community Kitchen of West Harlem. Many of my ideas about the relationship between advocacy and direct service were forged in discussions with CFRC director Kathy Goldman, staff members Agnes Molnar and Liz Krueger, and CFRC board members, especially Jeff Ambers, Hiji Bailey, Fran Barrett, Jane Sujen Bok, Jesse Cagen, Alan Levine, Rosalie Stutz, and Mabel Wilson. I am also grateful to Diane Ward and the staff of the kitchen for their responsiveness to requests for information, and to the whole CFRC staff for working so hard to create a society in which soup kitchens won't be necessary.

I want to thank the dedicated staff and my fellow board members of the Saint John's Bread and Life Program, as well. I have learned a great deal from the program's director, Hossein Sadaat, and I am indebted to board chair Father Jim Maher and members Neil Sheehan and Bill Di-Fazio for their forthright exploration of the issues central to this book.

My agent, Beth Vesel at Sanford Greenburger Associates, was instrumental in encouraging me at a crucial point in this process and helping me understand what would be needed to take my work beyond the academic audience. My editors at Viking Penguin, Mindy Werner and Susan Hans O'Connor, have been unfailingly patient when patience was required, and have provided an occasional nudge when one was needed. I thank them especially for their skill in helping me to reduce an unwieldy manuscript to a manageable size. I am grateful to Kristine Puopolo for her gracious adoption of this project in its final stages.

Finally, my family has supported this work in all imaginable ways. My father-in-law, Saul Goldberg, accompanied me on one of my research trips and proved an able collaborator as well as a thoughtful reader. My sister-in-law Jill Cutler and her partner, Jeremy Brecher, read material and offered useful suggestions. My parents, Robert and Trudy Poppendieck, and my sister, Trudie Prevatt, clipped relevant items from the local newspapers, read drafts of chapters, offered hospitality during research trips, and provided both sound advice and general moral support. My daughter, Amanda Goldberg, has offered her own unique brand of encouragement. And through it all, my husband, Woody Goldberg, has been there, intellectually, emotionally, and in a host of practical ways: the first sounding board for half-baked ideas and the reader of last resort, the willing receptacle of anxieties and complaints, the fellow traveler prepared to substitute a research trip for a vacation. He has lent me his extraordinary sense of humor when mine has worn thin, and all the while he has continued his own demanding day-to-day work on behalf of New York City's hungry and homeless people. This book is dedicated to him.

Contents

Introduction

IT SNOWED IN BROOKLYN the night before I was scheduled to begin my research at the soup kitchen. When I awoke, the feeling of embarking on an adventure was heightened by what I saw outside my window. Several inches had already fallen, and it was coming down hard. Snow is not the rarity in Brooklyn that it is in, say, Atlanta, but it is infrequent enough to transform an ordinary day into something special. It evokes childhood memories of unscheduled days off from school, and it puts a new face on familiar surroundings. I decided to leave my car parked at home and walk the mile or so to the site. I bundled up, extra layers because the wind was blowing, and set out for the low red-brick building located in an area of warehouses and light industry where I would be helping to prepare and serve a hot meal for several hundred impoverished people.

Trudging through the snow, I found myself humming, and tried to identify the song. Over the years, I've learned that the lyrics to the melodies that circulate in my brain are often clues to my interior state, if only I can recall them. What was this uninvited tune, why couldn't I remember its words? It seemed somehow connected to the snow, but it wasn't anything as obvious as "Winter Wonderland."

I laughed when I got it. Of course: "Good King Wenceslas." Good King Wenceslas, whose journey through the snow bearing food and fuel to the poor is celebrated in a familiar Christmas carol. A secular social scientist on the way to a research site, I was surprised to realize how much of the song I recalled: the king, looking out the window on the evening of a feastday, spies a poor man gathering fallen branches for fuel, despite the deep snow and cruel, frigid temperature. The king summons a page and inquires about this subject, out on such a night, and learns that he lives "a good league hence." Then Wenceslas calls for flesh and wine and pine logs and announces to the skeptical page, "thou and I will see him dine, when we bear them thither." Page and monarch set out through the "rude wind's wild lament" to deliver their gifts, and when the page grows faint of heart, he learns the true power of his master's goodness as he finds heat emanating from the king's footsteps. It was the last four lines of the last verse, however, memorized perhaps thirty years earlier, that resounded in my brain:

> Therefore, Christian men, be sure,
> Wealth or rank possessing
> Ye who now will bless the poor,
> Shall yourselves find blessing.

This book is about a group of modern-day Wenceslases, not kings or queens, but men, women, and children from all walks of life who provide food for hungry people through "emergency food" programs: soup kitchens, food pantries, food banks, and food rescue operations. It is about the blessings, or in more contemporary language, the gratifications, that these emergency food providers find in their work. It is about the functions that this activity serves, not primarily for the destitute who use charitable food programs, but for the rest of us. And it is about the price that our society is paying for these blessings, about the ways in which "feeding the hungry" distracts us from the urgent challenges of deteriorating economic security and accelerating inequality.

Emergency Food

Emergency food as we know it is largely a product of the last decade and a half. Such programs did not suddenly begin in 1980, of course. Soup kitchens, food pantries, and food banks all existed in the United States before the decade began, but they were generally small in size and relatively few in number. Then, in the early 1980s, a series of factors converged to bring about a sudden, dramatic expansion of private charitable food programs. A sharp recession, widely regarded as the deepest since the Great Depression, arrived to accelerate a long-term trend toward increasing unemployment and decreasing job security. This destruction of livelihoods coincided with steep cutbacks in federal social spending which aggravated a long-term decline in the purchasing power of public assistance. Homeless people became visible in many of the nation's large cities, and the "New Poor" turned to their churches and union locals for help. Existing kitchens and food pantries found themselves with ever longer lines at their doors, and new programs were hastily established to help meet this need. The term "emergency food," which had originally designated programs designed to respond to a "household food emergency," now took on the connotation of a societal emergency, a time-limited, urgent need for help, and Americans responded, as they always do, with energy and compassion. In New York City one hundred new emergency food programs opened their doors in 1983 alone. Food banks, which receive donations of unsalable food from corporations and pass them along to frontline kitchens and pantries, multiplied from about two dozen in 1980 to more than a hundred by the middle of the decade. Food rescue programs, which redistribute perishable and prepared foods, were not even invented until City Harvest in New York City came up with the idea in the early 1980s; by the end of the decade, there were enough such programs to form a national association called Foodchain.

When the economy improved for some Americans, it left behind a layer of people who continued to rely upon this private charitable assistance to get by. Emergency food programs did not wither away. Through upturns and downturns, expansions and contractions, accelerations and recessions, they grew in number and capacity, and gradually they invested in equipment, warehouses, trucks, computers, the whole infrastructure of provision. Today there are tens of thousands of emergency food programs in the United States, providing assistance, at least occasionally, to nearly a tenth of the population. In 1994, Second Harvest, the national organization of food banks, projected that programs affiliated with its member banks had provided food to some 25,970,000 "unduplicated" clients in the previous year, most of it through kitchens and pantries.

Literally millions of Americans support these programs with contributions of food, money, time, and effort. They bring bags of rice and jars of peanut butter to collection points in the church sanctuary or the local library, or drop a can in the barrel just outside the supermarket door. They pack grocery bags at food pantries. They prepare and serve meals at soup kitchens and deliver sandwiches to encampments of homeless people. They organize canned goods drives in their schools and Sunday schools, and send their youth groups and scout troops to help sort the proceeds at the food bank. They pick up leftovers from caterers and restaurants, from corporate dining rooms and campus cafeterias, and rush them in special thermal containers to soup kitchens and shelters. They "check out hunger" at their local supermarket counters and "dine out to help out" with their American Express cards. They "tee off against hunger" on their golf courses, and run against hunger in their marathons. It is an outpouring of compassion, both organized and individual, that would be the envy of most societies in human history: a "kinder, gentler nation" indeed.

Kinder, Less Just

Unfortunately, this kindness comes with a price tag. "I have found the world kinder than I expected, but less just," Samuel Johnson is said to have remarked. The same might be said of the popular response to poverty and hunger in America. It, too, is kinder but less just, not merely less just than I hoped or expected it would be, but less just than it was two decades ago. Poor people have lost—have been deprived of—rights to food, shelter, and income that were theirs twenty years ago. The Personal Responsibility and Work Opportunity Reconciliation Act of 1996 (PRWORA) and the end of welfare as we know it are only the culmination of a long, dreary process that has undermined the nation's fragile safety net. The erosion of the value of the minimum wage, a reduction in the purchasing power of public assistance, the decline in job security, and wave after wave of cutbacks in food assistance, housing subsidies, and welfare benefits have all reduced the overall share of income going to the bottom layers of our society, and curtailed the legally enforceable claims that people in need may make upon the collectivity. Measurable inequality is more pronounced now than it has been at any point since World War II.

The growth of kindness and the decline in justice are intimately interrelated. In one direction, the relationship is obvious. Visit nearly any soup kitchen or food pantry in America and you will find its staff and volunteers gearing up to cope with the sharp increases in need that they anticipate as the PRWORA—"welfare reform"—gradually takes effect. The cutbacks and reductions in public assistance benefits, along with declining wages at the bottom of the pay scale, increasing shelter costs, and a growing reliance on layoffs and downsizing to increase profitability are reducing people to destitution and sending them to the food lines. These changes are causing the hunger to which kindhearted people are responding with pantries and kitchens.

It works the other way too, however, and this is less obvious. The resurgence of charity is at once a *symptom* and a *cause* of our society's failure to face up to and deal with the erosion of equality. It is a symptom in that it stems, in part at least, from an abandonment of our hopes for the elimination of poverty; it signifies a retreat from the goals as well as the means that characterized the Great Society. It is symptomatic of a pervasive despair about actually solving problems that has turned us toward ways of managing them: damage control, rather than prevention. More significantly, and more controversially, the proliferation of charity *contributes* to our society's failure to grapple in meaningful ways with poverty. My argument, in short, is that this massive charitable endeavor serves to relieve pressure for more fundamental solutions. It works pervasively on the cultural level by serving as a sort of "moral safety valve"; it reduces the discomfort evoked by visible destitution in our midst by creating the illusion of effective action and offering us myriad ways of participating in it. It creates a culture of charity that normalizes destitution and legitimates personal generosity as a response to major social and economic dislocation.

It works at the political level, as well, by making it easier for government to shed its responsibility for the poor, reassuring policymakers and voters alike that no one will starve. By harnessing a wealth of volunteer effort and donations, it makes private programs appear cheaper and more cost effective than their public counterparts, thus reinforcing an ideology of voluntarism that obscures the fundamental destruction of rights. And, because food programs are logistically demanding, their maintenance absorbs the attention and energy of many of the people most concerned about the poor, distracting them from the larger issues of distributional politics. It is not an accident that poverty grows deeper as our charitable responses to it multiply.

If emergency food were only a kindly add-on to an adequate and secure safety net of public provision, I would have no problem with it. It would reach some poor people who are ineligible for public programs, or unwilling or unable to avail themselves of such welfare provisions. It would provide a few extras for people whose wages or pensions or public assistance payments leave them little margin for error or enjoyment. It would serve as an invitation and inducement to people to seek the help of programs designed to meet more complex needs—to provide education, job training, health care screening, or mental health services, for example—and it would reduce the operating costs of congregate meal programs for senior citizens and the food expenditures of day-care centers, freeing resources for enrichment programs. It would tide people over in the unpredictable emergencies that can strike anyone without warning, and assist whole communities confronted with floods, hurricanes, and other natural disasters. And it would provide constructive outlets for food that might otherwise go to waste, both government surpluses and corporate products. As a supplement to a robust array of constructive public provisions, emergency food (renamed community food security, or supplemental food) would clearly be a net social gain, and we could all rejoice in the energy and compassion of the volunteers and the generosity of donors that make possible a kinder, gentler society.

If, however, as I believe, charity food is increasingly substituting for adequate public provision, both in the benefits obtained by individuals and at the overall level of social policy, then it is time to take a closer look at the costs of kindness. What accounts for the dramatic expansion and enduring popularity of emergency food programs? Why do people use them, and why do other people provide the resources to support them? How did this phenomenon get started, and what keeps it growing? How does it affect the people who use it, and what is its impact upon the larger culture and society? Does it constitute an additional resource for poor people, or does it contribute to the erosion and destruction of the public safety net, substituting for rather than expanding upon public provisions? These are the questions that this book tries to answer, and by doing so, to understand the larger dynamic by which we have allowed ourselves to be diverted from the task of eliminating hunger and reducing inequality.

The emergency food phenomenon is indicative of a larger social trend. A growing reliance on small-scale, local, grassroots, voluntary programs is not restricted to poverty. It has characterized recent response to a host of other social ills, as well: AIDS, battered women, illiteracy, and child abuse come readily to mind as examples. There are undoubtedly others, because the same frustrations with government and the same despair over the potential for humane, effective public policy underlie civic response to many pressing problems. I am not claiming that these vernacular efforts are the only responses, but that these are the responses that have captured the public imagination, and, as the April 1997 "Summit" on volunteering reveals with startling clarity, these are the approaches that are being promoted by the nation's official leaders—presidents, generals, and the like. At first glance, many of these projects are heartwarming expressions of neighborly solidarity, compassion, and caring. They are not problematic, in and of themselves. They become problematic when we use them in place of the basic social provisions that any complex industrial or postindustrial society needs. Tutoring programs are good, but they are not a substitute for good schools. Friendly visitors for AIDS patients are good, but they are no substitute for medical care or access to pharmaceuticals. Volunteer advocates for abused children are good, but they can not replace adequately staffed and accountable systems of foster care, and should not replace social supports that enable families to stay together in times of stress and crisis.

Why Study Emergency Food?

The problem of poverty is broader than hunger, of course, and the grassroots charitable responses to it have embraced not only food programs but also a variety of approaches to shelter—Habitat for Humanity, for example, and the myriad "private" shelters in churches and synagogues—as well as other basic needs. This book, however, focuses specifically upon hunger and charitable food programs. There are several compelling reasons for using emergency food as the primary lens to explore the larger trend from entitlements to charity.

Rapid Growth

First, the growth of emergency food has been so significant as to demand explanation. In fifteen years, Second Harvest ascended from obscurity to become one of the nation's largest recipients of charitable contributions; it has been among the top five in each of the past five years, bringing in more in the value of donations than the American Red Cross or Harvard University. This is big charity, and it merits some scrutiny. Similarly, the sheer numbers of soup kitchens and food pantries are large enough to deserve attention, and their proliferation has been both extraordinarily rapid and remarkably sustained. There is no national baseline data; we really don't know how many of these organizations there were *before* 1980, and we don't know exactly how many there are now. Figures from New York City, however, are startling. The Food and Hunger Hotline, which was organized in 1979, reports that there were 30 emergency food providers known to the Hotline before 1980. The number had grown to 487 in 1987 and 600 by the end of the decade. The 1991 tally was 730, and by 1997, the Food For Survival Foodbank was serving nearly a thousand pantries and kitchens. The growth in New York is probably more extreme than that in most areas, but large cities around the country report similar growth curves. In 1993, there were more than 36,000 emergency food programs receiving food from the 185 food banks affiliated with Second Harvest. If we could count the pantries and kitchens that are affiliated with the several dozen food banks that are not Second Harvest members, and the kitchens and pantries that are not members of a food bank at all, either because they are located in areas not served by any existing bank or because they have been suspended for failure to comply with the rules—or find the food bank not worth the effort—the numbers would be much greater, but no one knows how much. Bread for the World, a Christian anti-hunger activist organization, uses a figure of 150,000 kitchens and pantries, but even if there are "only" one-half that number, this is a phenomenon that merits investigation.

Widespread Participation

Second, the structure of emergency food programs has permitted a very wide diffusion of participation in this project. Millions of Americans of all ages support emergency food programs in small ways, with an occasional donation of food or time or money, so the emotional and psychic side effects are widespread. This wide participation is partly a reflection of the ease and convenience of contributing, but it also reflects the deep feelings that many people have about food, and consequently, about hunger. Hunger is a form of poverty that makes us intensely uncomfortable. The "moral safety valve" function of charitable programs, relieving the discomfort of the privileged and thus the pressure for more fundamental action, is especially characteristic of programs and activities that are emotionally gratifying and respond to those aspects of poverty about which we have strong feelings.

The emotional salience inherent in hunger is intensified in emergency food programs because these programs have a dual function in our society. They not only feed the hungry; they also prevent waste of food. Much of the food that flows through the emergency food system is food that would otherwise go to waste, whether dented cans or corporate mistakes cycled through food banks or the leftovers from Donald Trump's wedding rescued by City Harvest. Thus these programs offer a moral relief bargain.

Charity versus Entitlement

Finally, emergency food programs illustrate the retreat to charity especially well because they offer such pronounced contrast to the food assistance policies and politics of the previous two decades. In the late 1960s, this country experienced a "rediscovery" of hunger in America. It began when a U.S. Senate committee decided to hold hearings on the operation of federal anti-poverty programs in Mississippi. Civil rights worker Marian Wright (now Marian Wright Edelman), who would later go on to found and direct the Children's Defense Fund, convinced some of the visiting senators, among them Bobby Kennedy, to accompany her on a tour of the back roads and empty cupboards of the Mississippi Delta. Many counties in the Delta had recently switched from the distribution of federal surplus commodities, which were free, to the newly revived Food Stamp Program which required the purchase of stamps. Delta sharecroppers, unneeded and unemployed as the mechanical cotton picker took over their jobs, were unable to scrape together the cash to purchase the stamps, and without the commodities, they were slowly starving. In fact, civil rights activists charged that the changeover to food stamps had been undertaken precisely to drive economically obsolete but politically aroused blacks out of the Delta. The senators encountered hunger and malnutrition in their starkest forms. In 1967, nearly anything Bobby Kennedy did was news, and hunger in Mississippi became news in America.

Hunger might have disappeared, as quickly as it had come, however, had not a group of civil rights and anti-poverty activists seized on the issue as a possible means to revitalize a flagging national commitment to the war on poverty. The Field Foundation immediately dispatched a team of physicians to Mississippi to assess the nutritional status of children there, and various citizens groups and church agencies undertook studies of their own. Congress continued its investigations, establishing a U.S. Senate Select Committee on Nutrition and Human Needs.

People were shocked at the discovery of hunger, first in Mississippi and then in many parts of the nation, and angry that Americans should be going hungry when the primary preoccupation of government agricultural policy seemed to be storing and disposing of huge farm surpluses. Today we have become so accustomed to portrayals of hunger in our midst that it is no longer news. It is hard to remember how innocent we were as a society, how unaware, and to recall the resulting sense of outrage. Senator George McGovern, writing in 1969, captured the spirit of the reaction to revelations of hunger and malnutrition among America's poor:

> Hunger is a unique issue in contemporary American politics in that it has only been "discovered" in the late 1960's. Until recently, most Americans assumed that hunger and malnutrition are the afflictions of Asia and other faraway places. How could anyone really be hungry in the world's richest nation—a nation endowed with an agricultural productivity so vast that it has accumulated troublesome surpluses? . . .
>
> Hunger is unique as a public issue not only because it is newly recognized but because it exerts a special claim on the conscience of the American people. It is the cutting edge of the problem of poverty. Somehow, we Americans are able to look past the slum housing, the polluted air and water, the bad schools, the excessive population growth, and the chronic unemployment of our poor. But the knowledge that human beings, especially little children, are suffering from hunger profoundly disturbs the American conscience. There is a sense, too, in which it outrages the Puritan ethic to have billions spent to stop food from being grown and finance surplus storage while other Americans languish under the blight of malnutrition.

In the aftermath of the hunger revelations of the late 1960s, an anti-hunger movement emerged, and it proved particularly adept at using the tools of legislation, litigation, and community organization to bring pressure on Congress to reform federal food assistance programs. In the late 1960s and early 1970s the "hunger lobby," as the anti-hunger network was quickly labeled, scored victory after victory, reforming existing food assistance programs and devising new ones. Federal expenditures on food assistance grew, in real (inflation adjusted) dollars, by 500 percent in the decade following the rediscovery of hunger. When this decade of achievement began, it was not immediately obvious to all that food stamps were preferable to surplus commodities. After all, it was the purchase requirement in food stamps that accounted for the severest malnutrition exposed in the Mississippi Delta. Gradually, however, as purchase requirements were reduced—and eliminated for the poorest households—and benefits were increased to ensure access to a nutritionally adequate if minimal diet, the advantages of food stamps became clear. They eliminated much of the hardship and inconvenience of the commodity program, in which recipients often had to carry home a month's supply at a time—a month's supply of whatever happened to be in surplus at the moment. Food stamps permitted their recipients to shop with the same convenience and almost the same degree of consumer choice as their non-poor neighbors. In a society in which the consumer role is of paramount importance, they "mainstreamed" participants, making their lives, or at least their grocery shopping trips, as much as possible like those of their non-poor neighbors.

To me, these characteristics made food stamps good social policy, not only from an efficiency and cost-effectiveness standpoint, but also because the program promoted social integration. It helped to bring us together, to make us one society. I was taken aback, therefore, when soup kitchens and food pantries began to proliferate in the early 1980s. They looked to me like a great leap backward. In the first place, they seemed to embody approaches to hunger that were precisely the opposite of those that had animated the anti-hunger agenda of the seventies. They were a retreat from the effort at mainstreaming and inclusion, however imperfect, represented by food stamps to programs that separated and segregated poor people. They were a retreat from the convenience and consumer choice of stamps and vouchers to the predetermined menu of provisions in kind. They were a retreat from national standards to haphazard local provision. Most important, they were a retreat from rights to gifts. Poor people might be, and often are, very well treated in charitable emergency food programs, but they have no rights, at least no legally enforceable rights, to the benefits that such programs provide. In a very real sense, emergency food seemed to threaten not only a reversal of the hard-won victories of the anti-hunger movement of the sixties and seventies but also a retreat to the reliance on private charity that characterized American society before the New Deal.

Reflections of the Great Depression

In the early 1980s, when the rapid expansion of emergency food began, social conditions were frequently the subject of unflattering comparisons with the Great Depression of the 1930s. The overall national unemployment rates were the highest that they had been since that difficult period, and whole industries were shutting down their U.S. operations, leaving some communities in the Rust Belt with staggering rates of unemployment and social dislocation. The federal government's decision to distribute surplus farm products in the form of cheese and butter further aggravated the comparison. The mass distribution of cheese, a food bank director told a congressional committee, "painfully recalls the sorrow of breadlines in the depression," while another called it a "substitution of cheese lines in 1983 for bread lines in 1933." The primary factor in these comparisons, however, was probably the reappearance of soup kitchens: "America has become a 'soup kitchen society,' a spectre unmatched since the bread lines of the Great Depression," declared the Physician Task Force on Hunger in America. "Soup kitchens and bread lines, thought to be an occurrence limited to the Depression era, have become almost commonplace," noted the Food Research and Action Center. For me these comparisons had an almost surreal quality, for I was then writing *Breadlines Knee Deep in Wheat: Food Assistance in the Great Depression*, a book that traced the development of Depression-era food programs and the downstream consequences of New Deal food assistance policy. At the point that contemporary soup kitchens caught the attention of the media, I was focusing my research on the Hoover years, during which soup kitchens and "breadlines" had played an important role in the nation's confused and hesitant response to the Depression.

Several aspects of the Hoover era shaped my perspective as I read newspaper accounts of a rebirth of soup kitchens. One was the nearly universal rejection and condemnation of soup kitchens and breadlines, first by social workers and relief professionals, and later by the public and the members of Congress who voted for appropriations for cash relief and then for work relief and social insurance. Serving meals and handing out groceries are ways of helping the poor that were regarded as old-fashioned, inadequate, and demeaning when the Depression first struck, in part because they deprived recipients of the consumer choice that had already become a hallmark of American life. To relief professionals, they appeared a throwback to the nineteenth-century welfare reformers who had argued, successfully, for providing relief "in kind," both to make it less attractive than cash wages and to protect the poor from the lures of the grog shop and the gaming table. Writing in the 1970s, Helen Hall recalled the Depression as she had experienced it from her vantage point as director of New York's famous Henry Street Settlement House: "our depression had really brought us back to the breadbasket, the grocery order, the commissary, welfare cafeterias, and the scrip commissaries . . . all humiliating forms of warding off starvation . . . that seemed to promise economies to the community but not security to the unemployed."

It was not just the humiliation, however, that worried the social workers. They were also concerned that the visibility of the food programs obscured the extent of need and gave a false sense of security to the comfortable. To relief professionals, breadlines were evidence of unmet need, but to the casual observer, whose contribution to the community's annual fund-raising appeal was urgently needed, the breadlines might be taken as evidence that the hungry were being fed. As Louis Adamic, a contemporary observer of what he called the "bread line situation" put it, "many of the wealthy already were contributing to the maintenance of one or more bread lines. Others, seeing new bread lines frequently formed, and reading about them in the newspapers, believed that, with all this food being handed out, the needy were receiving adequate relief."

As I watched the proliferation of the new breadlines of the 1980s, I wondered what had become of the conviction that food programs were an inappropriate response. The emergency food epidemic of the 1980s occurred in a society that had long ago rejected the soup kitchen/food pantry approach to meeting human need on the grounds that it segregated, stigmatized, and demeaned the poor, and that it was wasteful and inefficient. What had changed in our society to make this sort of charity, once so thoroughly discredited, acceptable once again? Might the emergency food programs springing up around me help to convince the affluent that the need was being met, the problem was being solved? By planting the idea that hunger *could be* effectively addressed by voluntary programs, might these charitable projects eventually lead to diminished support for public provisions such as food stamps? Would the emergency food programs be a true addition to the existing array of public food assistance programs, or would they gradually undermine public sector commitments? Would they increase the adequacy of available help, or would they become a substitute for adequate assistance? While I knew that these grassroots charitable efforts were not intended by their creators to *replace* such major social supports as food stamps, I worried that they might lull the public into complacency about the cuts being proposed by the Reagan administration and enacted by Congress.

With all this historical perspective, however, I didn't really decide to study emergency food providers until I began to meet them. In part, this happened through an assessment of food program use, prepared for the Bureau of Nutrition of the New York State Department of Health, in which I assisted colleagues at Syracuse University. The project involved site visits and interviewing at dozens of soup kitchens and food pantries, and as I began visiting these programs, I realized that they both confirmed and challenged my assumptions. They were, in short, kinder and gentler than I had expected, and I began to wonder if my concerns about the rise of emergency food were misplaced.

Methodology

This book is the product of a multiple research strategy which includes participant observation, both brief and in-depth interviews, and analysis of documents such as annual reports, press coverage, and research studies. I conducted many hours of participant observation at soup kitchens and food pantries, food banks and food rescue programs in nine states scattered around the nation; I generally combined such observation with interviews with staff members, clients, volunteers, and sometimes with board members, donors, government officials or other observers. I interviewed many more emergency food providers and anti-hunger advocates and other knowledgeable observers when they gathered at national conferences of Second Harvest, of Foodchain, and of the Food Research and Action Center, so that the interviews represent emergency food providers operating in eighteen states and the District of Columbia. The interviews were taped and then transcribed, and with one exception requested by an interviewee, actual names have been used and identities have not been disguised. All quotations, unless otherwise attributed, are from my transcripts, and except for eliminating hesitations, I have not altered or "cleaned up" these quotations. I want the real voices of emergency food providers to come through as clearly as possible.

I began my research with an extended observation at a soup kitchen near my home in Brooklyn, but many of my subsequent visits were brief—a day or two—and I am aware that I have captured particular programs at particular points in time. This is a serious caveat; in those programs that I had an opportunity to revisit after a substantial interval, things had always changed, sometimes quite dramatically. And since this research has engaged me for much of the last seven years, things have almost certainly changed and changed again in many of these programs.

In addition to the on-site research described above, I conducted historical research, some of it archival, some of it in newspapers and periodicals, and some of it through oral history techniques. It was my familiarity with the history of public food assistance in the United States that first drew my attention to the significance of the return of private food programs, and that earlier research is also reflected here and there in this book.

When I began my research, I worried that emergency food providers would be alienated by the implicit criticism in my perspective. Instead, I found that they are often their own most perceptive critics, that they recognize and are troubled by the inherent limitations of emergency food, and that many of them feel trapped, unwilling to deprive the poor of the help that these programs provide, but increasingly unconvinced that their work can contribute to solving the basic problems. Soup kitchen and food pantry staff and volunteers, food bankers and food rescuers were extraordinarily candid with me, and many of them share the underlying values that inform this book. What I have heard, as these people have shared their experiences, hopes, and frustrations with me has both inspired and distressed me. I have heard a degree of caring and a capacity for innovation that are cause for celebration. The commitment, good will, and creativity that are poured into this system are surely inspiring. But I have heard another message as well, one that worries me: that we are becoming attached to our charitable food programs and increasingly unable to envision a society that wouldn't need them. We are so busy building bigger, better programs to deliver food to the hungry, and to raise the funds and other resources necessary to continue and expand our efforts in response to the rising need, that we are losing sight of both the underlying problem and its possible solutions.

The Wenceslas Syndrome

Throughout this research, I found my mind returning now and again to King Wenceslas, and finally, I went to the library and looked him up. The famous carol that tells his story was written by a British clergyman, John Neale, in the early 1800s; the events it depicts are fictional, but there was a real King Wenceslas. The historical Wenceslas, whose statue towers over Prague's Wenceslas Square, was the ruler of Bohemia in the early tenth century. For most of his brief reign, he was engaged in a struggle against a group of nobles, led by his brother, Duke Boleslaw. Wenceslas wanted to establish peaceful relations with neighboring states, even if this involved paying tribute; the nobles wanted to remain independent, even at the price of continuous warfare. Religion was another issue; Wenceslas had been raised as a Christian by his grandmother and father; his brother and the other nobles resented his efforts to convert the peasants, perhaps because the new religion gave them less power over the poor than had traditional pagan beliefs. After a few years on the throne, Wenceslas was ambushed and murdered by his brother's companions, and the rule of Bohemia passed to Boleslaw. While he lived, however, Wenceslas is credited with efforts to control the ruthless and exploitative practices of the nobles and to establish rights for the poorest of his subjects. After his death, Wenceslas was quickly elevated to sainthood, and his story became part of the hagiography of the Roman Catholic Church and the national identity of Czechoslovakia.

Children's stories depict Wenceslas as a hero and martyr who tried to protect the poor from warlords who used pagan superstitions to extract wealth from the labors of the humble peasants and then squandered it in feasting and fighting. The carol depicts him as a brave, generous, kindly monarch whose personal charity is rewarded by signs of God's favor: "heat was in the very sod, which the Saint had printed." For the past century and a half, the carol, with its simple portrayal of direct, individual charity, has probably been more influential than the complex historical reality. It is the carol that has entered our culture.

Suppose, for a moment, that the good king of the carol enjoys his visit to the hungry peasant. "[A]s it is always pleasing to see a man eat bread, or drink water," Ralph Waldo Emerson noted in his famous essay on gifts, "so it is always a great satisfaction to supply these first wants. Necessity does everything well." It *is* pleasing to watch a hungry person consume a meal. "I feel so good leaving here, knowing I've helped someone," a volunteer at a soup kitchen in Maine told me. "It's almost like a high." Suppose King Wenceslas, too, finds a high in his charitable forays, becomes attached to them. Suppose he neglects certain urgent problems facing his domain. Suppose he fails to notice that formerly prosperous craftspeople are now foraging for food and fuel, reduced to destitution by foreign competition, and excluded from the forests nearest their homes by the decrees of greedy nobles. Suppose he is so distracted by the logistical challenges of getting that flesh and wine and fuel through the snow to the hungry that he doesn't notice the wealthy feasting more and more sumptuously, consuming an ever larger share of his kingdom's resources. Imagine, in fact, that although temperate himself, a conservationist at heart, he begins to look forward to their lavish feasts as a source of leftovers to carry to the growing numbers of poor peasants. Finally, suppose he is so consumed by his labors on behalf of the destitute, that he fails to perceive the growing threat to his fragile rule of law, his hard-won protections for the poorest in his domain. Suppose that he so exhausts himself in efforts to secure and deliver food for the hungry that he fails to heed warnings of the smoldering plot against him, and when the decisive ambush comes, he is too tired to defend himself.

He ends up a saint, a point of light, and the poor of Bohemia end up poorer and hungrier than ever.

There is a little of Wenceslas in most of us. We, too, "find blessing" in exerting ourselves on behalf of the poor, especially if we can simultaneously prevent waste. And we, too, have become distracted by these labors from challenges that urgently require our attention. This is what might be called the "Wenceslas syndrome," the process by which the joys and demands of personal charity divert us from more fundamental solutions to the problems of deepening poverty and growing inequality, and the corresponding process by which the diversion of our efforts leaves the way wide open to those who want more inequality, not less. The Wenceslas syndrome is not just something that happens to individuals and groups that become deeply involved in charitable activity; it is a collective process that affects our entire society as charity replaces entitlements and charitable endeavor replaces politics.

I believe that it is time to reevaluate our headlong plunge into emergency food programs, to take a closer look at how all this good will and effort affect the fabric of social life in our society. Shall we keep on perfecting our means of acquisition, transportation, and delivery of charity food until the protections—and the underlying sense of equity and fairness—that might have kept people from becoming poor and destitute in the first place are completely destroyed?

And if not, if we want to make sure that our children are neither eating in soup kitchens nor serving soup twenty years from now, what can we do? And what role can the existing network of kitchens and pantries, and the vast reservoir of good will upon which it draws, play in bringing about a future in which "emergency food" can be reserved for true emergencies? I hope that this book will clarify the dynamics and effects of emergency food and reveal the essential functions of the retreat to charity, and in so doing, provoke discussion of our common future.

CHAPTER ONE

Charity for All

"ALL WEEK LONG I have been hearing about how they are going to go from door to door and that they hope lots of people give lots of food so they can collect. They are very much into it." Marge, the mother of two Cub Scouts, is filling me in on the home front side of the Boy Scouts' Scouting for Food canned goods drive as we sort and pack donated foods at sturdy tables set up in the parking lot of the Ciba-Geigy company cafeteria. It is warm and sunny, extraordinarily pleasant weather for New Jersey in November, so I have opted for the outdoor operation, but most of the packing is taking place inside the cafeteria, a long, low building on Ciba-Geigy's corporate campus in Toms River, New Jersey. Toms River is also home to the Jersey Shore Council of the Boy Scouts of America, which covers Ocean, Atlantic, and parts of Burlington and Cape May Counties. Each November since 1988, the Jersey Shore Council has sponsored one of the nation's most successful drives. The Scouts distribute empty bags, preprinted with an explanation and a list of needed food items, door-to-door on a Saturday in early November and pick up the filled bags and bring them to central collection points a week later. Marge has brought three of her children to help with the sorting and repacking. There are two sons who are Webelos, the last stage of Cub scouting before they become full-fledged Boy Scouts, and her daughter, aged seven, who, according to her mom, "is just packing her little heart away."

"This is their fifth year doing it," she explains. "I think they look forward to it. As an incentive, Great Adventure [a nearby amusement park] has a big rally where they give them a day at the park for free. . . . It gets them geared up for it." Six Flags Great Adventure not only hosts the pep rally; for the remainder of the season, it offers half-price tickets to anyone donating a can. This year the weather has been unusually sunny and warm and business has been good; the haul from Great Adventure is larger than usual. The food collected will go to food pantries and prepared-meal programs throughout the four counties.

I ask Marge if her children understand where the food is going. "I think so," she replies. "They hear very often on TV about the homeless. This brings it more to light. They realize that people are in need, especially for the baby food. My son asked me about all this baby food. 'Don't the mamas have money?' and I had to explain to him that 'no, not everybody is as fortunate as we are, to give their children the things they need.' " She goes on to articulate a feeling that I have heard from other parents who make special efforts to involve their children in emergency food projects, the hope for an antidote to the selfishness that sometimes seems built into their children's lives: "I think it is unfortunate that it is all give-me, give-me, give-me, and this gives them a sense of perspective. A lot of more fortunate kids, they have money and everything they ask for is suddenly given to them." The Scouting for Food drive, she feels, gives them a chance to give something back.

The 20,000 pounds from Great Adventure are just the tip of the iceberg. The logistics of this particular drive are impressive, to say the least. Ten thousand scouts and nearly three thousand adult leaders in more than two hundred scouting units are involved. Ten collection points around the four-county area are equipped with truck trailers, loaned for the occasion by a local hardware company that also supplies three rigs and drivers to haul the filled containers to the central collection point at Ciba-Geigy. A communications company lends cellular phones so that volunteers can alert a dispatcher when a particular container is nearing capacity, and a rig can be detailed to bring it in, dropping off an empty replacement where the volume warrants. Meanwhile, Scout troops and Cub packs located near the Ciba-Geigy campus can take their collections directly to the company cafeteria. A uniformed Scout directs station wagons, minivans, and pickup trucks to one side of the cafeteria parking lot; the other is reserved for the eighteen-wheelers.

There is only one loading dock for the cafeteria building, so a Ciba-Geigy executive has designed an ingenious system for unloading the large trucks. A forklift equipped with a platform lifts several Scouts with empty shopping carts, loaned for the weekend by a supermarket chain whose president is the drive's honorary chairperson, to the level of the truck. The boys empty the bags into the shopping carts; when the carts are full, the forklift operator lowers the platform to ground level, and the boys and their companions hustle the filled carts into the cafeteria while a new team of Scouts begins emptying bags into a new set of shopping carts. Special ramps have been provided by a moving company to ease the carts down the three or four widely spaced steps between the parking lot and the cafeteria entrance.

Inside the cafeteria, a growing pandemonium drowns out the background music. Many of the people who come by to drop off food stay to help with the packing. At long tables pushed end to end, volunteers sort the goods into predetermined categories: "Veggies and Soups," "Fruits and Juices" and "Meat/Fish/Prepared Foods," and pack them into boxes, assembled and labeled early that morning and stacked in precarious towers around the edges of the room. The plan calls for culling out any products in less durable containers—rice, pasta, and the glass jars that show up every year despite the requests to the contrary—and any baby foods or other specialized items, for separate packing. The atmosphere is festive, with an undertone of controlled chaos. Shouts of "We need more boxes," and "Where does tomato paste go?" surface among the general din of shopping carts clanking, misplaced children crying, and a pile of boxes collapsing as a very short Scout pulls ones from the bottom. "It is kind of overwhelming," one volunteer suggests. "There is just so much work going on, so many people in a room which is probably too small for all the goings-on, but then to see that there are this many people willing to donate their time and do stuff, it makes you feel that there are still some good people left." By midmorning, the good people number in the hundreds, not only Boy Scouts, but grandparents,

parents, siblings, whole families, and unaffiliated helpers as well. The Scouts conduct the drive, but the packing is obviously a community affair. Ciba-Geigy is providing refreshments for all comers, and as the morning progresses, the smell of burgers and franks begins to overwhelm that of coffee and doughnuts.

Once the cans are sorted and boxed by category, pallets, each containing about two dozen boxes of a single type of food, are assembled, covered with shrink-wrap, and transferred to a warehouse, also on the Ciba-Geigy campus, where they will be stored and distributed as needed to area food pantries and meal programs. Local pantries will come to the warehouse to pick up food when they need it, take it back to their own headquarters, unpack it, sort it into their own categories, and repack it into pantry bags for needy families to take home. I plan to leave Ciba-Geigy at sunset, but I understand that the packing fest often continues until nearly midnight and sometimes resumes the next day. "Last year we came around the same time," a father told me at midmorning, "as soon as our immediate food drive was done. . . . We were here until eight or nine o'clock that night. Every time we were getting ready to leave, another tractor trailer would come in, so they would ask those who could to stay. So we did. My son had a blast. He thought it was a lot of fun and he felt he was helping people and he wanted to come back this year."

The Jersey Shore Council's Scouting for Food drive has all the ingredients for success. It has committed, experienced leaders with a finely tuned understanding of the project's complex logistics. It has highly visible corporate sponsors that lend credibility among potential donors as well as necessary material support. It has the active participation of the local media for the essential publicity. It asks the Scouts to do something that is well within their capability, and provides them with the ingredients they need—preprinted flyers and bags and adult transportation—to do it. It has the cooperation of other civic organizations and the good will of the populace. Further, it has roles for the minimally involved donor and the casual volunteer. People who simply fill up their bags and get them to their doorsteps by 9:00 A.M. can share in the sense of community solidarity, and someone who wakes up on the morning of the second Saturday in November with the urge to help can wander over to Ciba-Geigy and lend a hand—no advance commitment necessary. An estimated three hundred community volunteers helped with the sorting and packing, adding their efforts to those of the nearly thirteen thousand Scouts and Scout leaders who participated in various phases of the project. Beginning with the pep rally at Great Adventure and continuing through the music and refreshments at Ciba-Geigy, it creates an upbeat, festive atmosphere that makes good deeds fun. And it is the quintessential good cause: food for the hungry. The drive netted more than 280,000 pounds of donated food.

A National Pastime

Fighting hunger has become a national pastime. Millions of Americans are involved. Early in 1992, a polling firm hired by Kraft General Foods, on behalf of the sponsors of the Medford Declaration to End Hunger in America, conducted a survey of 1,000 randomly selected voters to assess public attitudes toward hunger in the United States. The results were clear: three-fifths of those surveyed thought that hunger was a "very serious" problem in the United States, and 90 percent agreed that "there are significant numbers of people in the United States who are hungry and don't have enough to eat." The study's clients welcomed the overall findings, which included not only the widespread perception that hunger is a serious problem but also the belief that it is solvable, and the willingness to pay additional taxes in order to eliminate it. Possibly the most significant finding, however, was one that drew only limited attention: 79 percent of those interviewed answered "yes" to a question that asked "Have you, personally, done anything to help those people who don't have enough to eat in your community such as being a volunteer at a soup kitchen, contributing food to a distribution center and so forth?"

This is a remarkable finding, whether we believe it or not. Either an extraordinarily high percentage of registered voters in this country has contributed something to the support of a local food program, or an extraordinarily high percentage of respondents felt sufficiently strongly that they *ought* to have done so that they were willing to lie to an anonymous pollster on the telephone. We have known for a long time that Americans contribute a great deal of time and money to voluntary-sector activities, but for nearly four-fifths of respondents to indicate that they had tried to do something about one particular problem seemed, well, incredible.

When we begin to consider the myriad opportunities to contribute, however, the credibility quotient goes up. All our respondent has to have done, after all, is contribute to a food drive—by leaving a bag on the doorstep for the Boy Scouts in the fall, or the letter carriers in the spring, or by dropping a can in a convenient barrel outside the grocery store. Or perhaps our respondent has "rounded up for hunger" at the supermarket checkout counter—rounded up her bill to the next nearest dollar with the change going to help an anti-hunger organization—or "checked out hunger" at a supermarket of another denomination. Maybe the respondent's child has asked for a can or two to contribute to a collection at school or Sunday school. Or a neighbor's teenager has walked in a hunger walkathon and our respondent has agreed to be a sponsor. Perhaps there was a drive at the office in conjunction with a holiday party. Or maybe the respondent just used her American Express card between Thanksgiving and Christmas, automatically joining the Charge Against Hunger, whether she meant to or not. Giving to food charities has been made so easy, so convenient, that it is probable that a very large number of Americans has contributed in some way. As an American Express advertisement put it just after Christmas, "You may have helped and not even know it."

You may even have had fun doing it. Like the Boy Scouts' trip to Great Adventure, elements of recreation have been added to many anti-hunger projects. Bikers can pedal against hunger, film buffs can attend a Canned Film Festival, concertgoers can secure reduced-price admission by bringing a can, and gourmets can Dine Out to Help Out. In more than a hundred communities across the country, you can help the hungry by attending a Taste of the Nation buffet, at which top-ranked chefs offer samples of their work; the chefs donate their time and food, and the price of admission goes to Share Our Strength (SOS) which raises and dispenses funds for anti-hunger activity on a national—in fact, an international—scale. In 1994, Taste of the Nation raised $3.7 million for hunger relief. A spin-off called Taste of the NFL invites people attending the Super Bowl to sample the fare of the chefs of the host city, again for a hefty contribution; players participate by doing promotions, and both chefs and fans join the long list of food program supporters. Last year's Taste of the NFL raised $400,000. If your recreations are more literary, another SOS production, Writer's Harvest, sponsors readings by well-known authors in communities and on college campuses across the country. Writers are not yet as popular as chefs: last year's harvest raised $40,000 in 150 cities and towns. This list could continue at great length, because fund-raising for hunger has elicited the talents of some exceptionally creative people. They have made it extraordinarily easy and rewarding to do something about hunger in America.

Not all participants opt for the easy or glamorous roles, of course. Some of the people who answered "yes" to the pollster's survey may have been among the million or more Americans who actively volunteered in a soup kitchen or food pantry. The emergency food system is dependent upon volunteer labor. A recent survey in New York City, for example, found that more than four-fifths of the people working in soup kitchens and food pantries were volunteers, who accounted for just over two-thirds of the hours worked. The median pantry in the Second Harvest National Research Study conducted in 1993 had twelve volunteers during the year, who gave an average of a bit over fifty-two hours each. Soup kitchens are more labor intensive than pantries, and the kitchens in the survey had a median of forty volunteers over the course of the year, who reported an average of about twenty-five hours apiece. Such averages, of course, reflect not only the regulars who come week after week and month after month, but also the casual volunteer who helps out once a year to serve Thanksgiving dinner or put up new shelves in the pantry. But casual volunteers, like occasional donors, contribute to the overall size of the phenomenon and its capacity to touch the life of the larger society.

The significance of all this giving and volunteering extends far beyond the generic celebration of voluntarism and compassion to which politicians so frequently give voice. It is this widespread diffusion of involvement, however limited, that allows the emergency food phenomenon to function as a "moral safety valve," to relieve the discomfort that people feel when confronted with evidence of privation and suffering amid the general comfort and abundance, thus reducing the pressure for more fundamental action. The sheer magnitude of community anti-hunger activity, and the widespread publicity essential to such efforts, create images of food drives and fund-raisers, of kitchens and pantries and food banks and food rescue programs, that permeate the culture. These images reassure us that no one will starve in our community, that the problem is being addressed. Few of us stop to assess the size of the problem or measure the sufficiency of the response; the illusion of effective community action lingers, long after the canned goods are depleted. The specific dynamics of pervasive involvement merit explanation and help to illuminate the safety valve process. Why has the emergency food phenomenon been so successful in eliciting the effort and contributions of so many Americans? Why do so many volunteer?

Something for Everyone

The pastor of a church in Maine explained how his food pantry obtained its supplies from the food bank, which was located several hours away. A regional supermarket chain, Shop and Save, picks up supplies for area pantries at the Good Shepherd Food-Bank in Lewiston and brings them to the local store, and "as soon as the food gets there they give us a call and we blast over there with old men and pickup trucks and load it and bring it back over here. That's a great phenomenon—the old men with pickup trucks." It is a scenario that is repeated, with endless local variations, all over the nation, every day. The newspaper image of an emergency food volunteer depicts a person preparing food or dishing it up in a soup kitchen or packing bags in a food pantry, but the emergency food system offers many others avenues of participation as well. Food must be procured—or even produced—and transported as well as prepared and served, and the space in which all this occurs must be equipped and maintained. Funds must be raised, bills must be paid, and other volunteers must be coordinated. As one volunteer at a soup kitchen in Immokalee, Florida, put it, "There is something for everybody." And kitchens and pantries, food banks and food rescue programs have an extraordinary capacity to absorb and put to use whatever a volunteer has to offer. You may start out by washing the dishes and end up doing the books. As Ken Hecht, a food policy advocate in California, recounted:

> I am a lawyer, and I spent twenty-five years litigating cases in a number of different poverty areas.... Then I went to work in a foundation and was there for three or four years. When I left there I wanted to do something that was exactly the opposite of working in a foundation where you were working behind somebody who was working behind somebody who was several layers removed from anybody who looked like he needed any help, and a friend of mine suggested that I walk down the hill from my house and go to a soup kitchen. And about a month after I left the foundation I walked down the hill and went to a soup kitchen and did onions. So I'm now good at onions. It absolutely satisfied everything I wanted to do at that moment, and as time went on I became more and more involved in the work in the soup kitchen and obviously had some experience that could be useful to them in terms of stabilizing, organizing their work, so I became just as involved in the administration and fund-raising parts of the program as well, and still am.

Hecht's experience illustrates several of the factors that help to make soup kitchens and food pantries such magnets for participation. In the first place, there are few barriers to entry. You do not need a lengthy training course to become a volunteer in a soup kitchen or food pantry, and in many places, you don't need an appointment, either. A prospective volunteer can just walk down the hill and start doing onions, or drop by Ciba-Geigy and help sort the donations. Everything you need to know, you learned in kindergarten: carrying chairs, pouring juice, setting the table, peeling carrots. Since little training or orientation is needed, a volunteer can easily try it out on an experimental basis. "Word of mouth is our best advertisement. People who come here and enjoy it tell somebody else. And they come and see what it's like and then they'll stay," Joyce Hoeschen, one of the founders of the Bath Area Food Bank Soup Kitchen, described her volunteer recruitment to me. Her husband and cofounder chimed in: "They might be a little skittish to begin with, but by the end of the day, they say 'I'm hooked! Can't I come more often?'"

For those who find the experience rewarding, there are always new tasks and new opportunities to contribute. Hecht's work in the Haight-Ashbury Kitchen led to the idea of forming the San Francisco Anti-Hunger Coalition, for which he helped to prepare first a concept paper and then a grant application. You don't have to be a lawyer, however, or a foundation insider, to put your cumulative work experience and life history to work on behalf of an emergency food program. One of the biggest boosts to Hecht's efforts to initiate a coalition was an idea from a seafood purveyor, convicted of dealing illegally in abalone, who was doing his "community service" sentence at the Haight-Ashbury Kitchen. Noting the kitchen's constant search for sources of protein, he told the director that there was always leftover fish at the piers at the end of the week. Often, the market value of frozen seafood did not justify the cost of freezing the fish, and it could not be kept over the weekend as a fresh product, so it was dumped. Hecht and his colleagues began collecting the leftover seafood and distributing it to other kitchens; for Hecht, it was an organizing tool:

> The other thing we did that stimulated the coalition's coming into existence was to take advantage of a supply of excess fish that was coming into the piers. We've been using that in our program, expanding the pick-up of fish, and started using the fish all over town, demonstrating without having to say it that there's a lot of advantage to working together. I have no doubt that that was, and remains, an inducement to working together.

When some of the kitchens proved reluctant to accept the free seafood because their volunteer cooks were unaccustomed to preparing fish in quantity, Hecht and his associate, Ed Bolen, recruited seafood chefs from some of San Francisco's leading hotels and restaurants to demonstrate the art of large-volume seafood preparation. Chowder has become a staple on the San Francisco soup kitchen circuit, and seafood purveyors, fishing boat captains, and seafood chefs have become part of the network of donation and participation that sustains emergency food in San Francisco.

A Network of Supply

San Francisco may be unique, but it is not alone. Nearly every kitchen and pantry, and absolutely every food bank and food rescue program, is the focal point of a web of participation, with its own network of suppliers, supporters, contributors, and volunteers. The supply end of the emergency food chain provides an enormous variety of opportunities for volunteer work and donation. Some people literally produce food for soup kitchens and food pantries—children's gardening programs in or outside schools, gardens tended by the inmates of correctional facilities, community gardens, camp gardens, church gardens. The Food Bank of Western Massachusetts runs a 63-acre organic farm with the help of volunteers and members of its Community Supported Agriculture project. The American Garden Writers Association, a professional organization of journalists with an estimated combined audience of 78 million people, has recently undertaken a campaign called Plant a Row for the Hungry, and has enlisted a seed company to offer a free packet of vegetable seeds to each participating gardener. In Mount Carmel, Connecticut, Bill Liddell grows 49,000 pounds of vegetables each year on the three-quarter-acre plot that he farms intensively, assisted by donated seeds and volunteer labor, specifically for the purpose of supplying food for the hungry of Connecticut.

More typical, however, are donations of food that was originally intended for other purposes—for the market, for home consumption, even for decoration. Gleaners in Miami harvest citrus from trees planted at race tracks and golf courses for Miami's Daily Bread Food Bank, and many gleaning groups will bring ladders and buckets and harvest the fruit in your backyard if you invite them. By the end of the eighties, Project Glean in Concord, California, was harvesting a quarter of a million pounds annually of vegetables, including onions, eggplants, tomatoes, and corn, and fruits, including plums, oranges, tangerines, lemons, limes, grapefruits, nectarines, and pomegranates. A core group of thirty regular volunteers was supplemented by the efforts of Scout troops, church youth groups, mother-daughter teams from the National Charity League, senior citizens organizations, people from drug rehabilitation centers, and offenders doing court-ordered community service. Beth Coulter is a slim, energetic woman who volunteers as a cook at the soup kitchen run by the Bath Area Food Bank in Bath, Maine. The food bank is actually a pantry, established before the terminology sorted itself out; the soup kitchen is a subsidiary project and is run on Mondays, Wednesdays, and Fridays at the Knights of Columbus Hall. Ms. Coulter was cooking the day I visited, but she took the time to tell me about her experience with gleaning because she was so excited about the outcome:

> Last summer I contacted a couple of farmers in the area . . . after they had picked their crops, we asked if we could go in and glean the fields . . . it's a domino theory. It looks like we're taking leftovers and pretty soon the farmer's saying "Could you use a couple of bushels of tomatoes? Could you use a bushel of cucumbers?" We went up to get a few tomatoes and ended up with fourteen kinds of produce from one farm. We went to other farms and, when it was time for frost to set in, they said "Come and dig all the carrots you want." We ended up with eighteen bushels of carrots.

I asked how they could handle so many, and learned that one form of participation can elicit another.

> We move it because we've got great ladies . . . one lady made pickles; I made pickled beets. We froze carrots; we blanched and froze, we canned, we did all kinds of things. Peeling the carrots and cleaning them was a major chore. It was the end of September or the beginning of October and we brought them to an elementary school and the fifth grade took it on as a project to wash the carrots and peel them for us. It was incredible. . . . We often talk about the poor people and the hungry and homeless, and we burden a lot of children with this kind of information, and what can they do about it, except be sad. But this was a hands-on thing the children could do.

Old and Young and Everything in Between

Hands-on things that children can do, the availability of work that entire families can do together or that school and religious groups can undertake, is another factor that helps to account for the tremendous appeal of emergency food programs. Ginna Lockie was coordinating the volunteers on behalf of the North Naples United Methodist Church on one of the days that I visited the kitchen at Immokalee; "my kids . . . have actually all been out here to the soup kitchen on days when they don't have school," she reported. "They really enjoy it. They are learning, at a very early age, that we need to help other folks outside our home." For individual families, as well as for organized groups like the Boy Scouts, emergency food programs create opportunities for teaching compassion.

Of course the same characteristics that make the work suitable to newcomers and children might also tend to make it, eventually, boring—not in a once-a-year event like the Boy Scouts drive, but on a regular basis. Even the simplest and most routine tasks, however, can be made enjoyable by social interaction, and this is a common characteristic of almost all of the emergency food volunteer work I observed. Packing bags in a food pantry or preparing a soup kitchen meal or labeling boxes at Ciba-Geigy provides a fine opportunity to catch up on local news, to discuss sports, to talk a little politics, or a little theology. The more repetitious the task, the more conducive it seems to be to humor, banter, teasing.

The sociability factor is also a characteristic of much of the volunteer work available one notch up the emergency food ladder, at the food bank. A significant portion of the food that is donated to food banks is what food bankers and grocers call "salvage": dented cans, products with some cosmetic problem on the packaging, products that have been slightly crushed or torn. The new scanning technology permits grocers to obtain credit for such unsalable products by culling them from the shelves and sending them to a reclamation center, where their bar codes are scanned and credit is assigned to retailers from the manufacturers. At the reclamation centers, leaking containers are generally pulled out, but the rest is simply boxed, and if the manufacturer designates, shipped to a food bank, where it must of course be further sorted to remove any hazardous items. Sorting salvage is one of the primary tasks to which food bank volunteers are set. The sorting process does require some training, and it lacks the variety characteristic of work at the kitchen or pantry level, but it makes up for that in camaraderie. It is also the sort of activity for which whole groups from schools, churches, or businesses can be recruited. Bill Bolling is the founder and director of the Atlanta Community Food Bank, one of the oldest and most respected in the nation; he described the volunteers who come to the bank to help with sorting as well as with warehouse and office tasks:

> Old, young and everything in between. We use students, we use senior citizens and retirees during the day, because everybody else is working, we use professionals in the evening—at least four nights a week we have groups till nine at night. We have people come in their BMWs and three-piece suits and come in and change clothes into their blue jeans and work a two-hour shift, three-hour shift after work. And they mostly come as groups, not individuals. We use a lot of church and synagogue religious communities on weekends and for specialized kinds of food drives. We're seeing now, and this is real precedent-setting in Atlanta, we're seeing companies send employees on company time down as a group with their department managers, and they come down and volunteer.

The organized group participation phenomenon is visible in the fund-raising and food procurement aspects of the emergency food system as well as in the sorting and packing and processing. A pantry that can enlist the support of a civic organizaiton, youth program, school, church, or business is likely to obtain far more than it would from simply deploying collection barrels, however strategically placed. In tiny Benson, Arizona, a town of a few thousand not far from Tombstone, the food pantry, which goes by the name of the Benson Food Bank, has nurtured all of these relationships. The vice president of the organization, Jan Olsen, explains her strategy:

> In November, I go to the mayor and I ask him to declare November "Food Bank Month," which he does. We've got the certificate up on the wall. I divide the month into separate categories, like one week will be church collections, one week will be civic collections, another one will be the Scouts, the other one will be the school children. And I target in on those and make special arrangements for those people to have special collections during that month . . . food and/or money.

The schools have proven especially responsive; the local elementary school sponsors a contest among classrooms to see which room can bring in the most food. The contest is a big hit with the kids, even though the principal has ruled that they may not collect prizes for their winning efforts: "We want them to give from their hearts, not for an award," Olsen told me. One of the biggest sources in tiny Benson came as a surprise to the food pantry board. The local branch of Arizona Electric Power Company called up one day to see if the pantry could send someone to pick up "a few items." The utility had held a contest among its departments and produced three station-wagon loads of food; "That was three station wagons . . . filled right to the roof."

Facilities and Equipment

Soup kitchens, food pantries, and food banks all require facilities and equipment, and the creation and maintenance of space offers another whole arena for participation. Hawley Botchford, the director of the Harry Chapin Food Bank of Southwest Florida, succeeded in eliciting thousands of dollars' worth of donated plumbing, carpentry, and the like from skilled craftspeople, and thousands of dollars' worth of equipment and supplies from local businesses when the food bank rehabilitated an old building to serve as its office and warehouse. His story of how the building came to be painted is typical of his experience. He had canvassed the local paint distributors for a paint donation with no success, but he had succeeded in talking a representative of Sherwin-Williams into "just coming over to see if our numbers were right on what we thought we were going to need to paint the building." Meanwhile, Sherwin-Williams had the contract to supply paint for a church that was being refurbished nearby. As Botchford recounts:

> Well, we firmly believe, being good Presbyterians, that while the guys were mixing the paint, God smacked one of their hands and they dumped too much of one color into the mix and the church refused it because it was not the color they had picked. All of a sudden, Sherwin-Williams had fifty-five gallons of exterior premium

paint, and they called and said, "Are you fussy about what color the outside of your building's going to be?" and I said, "Not a bit." So they said, "All right, we've got your exterior paint," and we had the audacity to say "What about the inside?" And, sure enough, they came through. Now we've got the paint and I figured we could get volunteers to paint the inside, the outside's a little trickier. So we went over to where they were painting the church . . . and started talking to them. We said, "Look—your equipment—and the color's so close you wouldn't even have to wash it out, just pour our paint into it and do our building." And they did it. They came over and started here one day and they were finished by lunch. And they primed it and painted the entire building—it was a painting contractor—no charge for that.

Botchford's ability to corral contributions of labor and materials is probably exceptional, but all over the country emergency food programs have been the beneficiaries of building materials, refrigeration and storage capacity, kitchen equipment, and the like. Soup kitchens and food pantries, after all, are unlikely to be choosy about the appearance of their equipment. Have almond and avocado gone out of style for appliances, replaced by black and chrome? It doesn't matter much in the church basement. And since donations of equipment often come with the skilled time and effort required to install them, they draw another group of people into the web of participation and create another group with a sense of ownership in the project, another group of people who could have answered "yes" to the pollster's survey.

We will probably never know just how much has been given to the emergency food system when time and talent and the use of specialized skills and tools are factored into the equation. We have difficulty even with gifts of food. If you are a large corporation donating a truckload of breakfast cereals to a food bank, you may find it well worth the trouble to record the donation and file for a tax deduction, and the food bank will happily provide you with all the verification you need. If you are a backyard gardener who has responded to the American Garden Writers Association's plea to Plant a Row for the Hungry, or simply an amateur who has nurtured an overabundance of zucchini, you may or may not think it appropriate and worthwhile to seek a record of your donation for tax purposes. Certainly, few of the millions of people who Check Out Hunger at the local supermarket or contribute canned goods to the Boy Scouts drive itemize these contributions in their tax returns. IRS data, therefore, are not a very good source of information about donations to emergency food programs. Neither are the surveys of giving, most of which do not collect much information on gifts in kind. Nor are the programs themselves, many of which are small-scale, grassroots, low-budget operations that can barely get the dishes washed and the head counts turned in to the food bank. Since the vast majority of these programs are affiliated with religious institutions, they are exempt from the reporting requirements with which many other nonprofits must comply; they are not required to file the Form 990s from which much of the data in the National Taxonomy of Tax Exempt Organizations is derived. Like many nonprofit organizations, they may provide donors who request them with blank receipt forms to be filled in with the donors' estimate of the value of goods contributed, but they are unlikely to keep extensive records of their own. Clearly, we do not know how much has been given to these organizations in the form of money, food, supplies, and time, but we know it is a lot.

Cash versus Food

Cash donations are more likely to be recorded than gifts in kind, and cash has other advantages as well. After all, cash replaced barter precisely because cash conferred vastly increased flexibility. You can readily convert cash into other inputs you might need—electricity, for example, or the services of an accountant or an exterminator—but you cannot readily convert donated foods into such services. And even when the donor specifies that the gift be used for food, donating cash may be a more productive strategy. Joyce Jacobs at the Harry Chapin Food Bank of Southwest Florida in Fort Myers has a set of glossy photos that show what you could purchase for donation to a food program with ten dollars spent at the grocery store, and what the same ten dollars, spent at the food bank, could provide. The second picture is much, much larger than the first, because the food in the food bank is essentially free, except for the handling fee, generally called "shared maintenance." At a shared maintenance rate of fourteen cents a pound, the food bank can provide more than seventy-one pounds of food for a ten-dollar donation. For one dollar, which would buy the average panhandler two cups of coffee on the streets of New York, a donor can expect somewhere between seven and ten pounds of food from the food bank for a recipient kitchen or pantry. Cash is giving canned goods a good run for the money.

If convenience and efficiency were the only operant principles, cash would certainly have the edge over canned goods, but these are clearly *not* the only considerations. Donations of actual food have several advantages over collections of money. In the first place, they serve symbolic functions. Offerings of "first fruits" are traditional in many religions, and they are laden with deep ritual significance. It is not uncommon for offerings of canned goods to be brought to the altar in congregations that support pantries or kitchens. Some churches collect for the month or so before Thanksgiving and then decorate the chancel with a display of donated food. This is precisely the sort of historically and emotionally significant activity in which congregants of all ages can participate with understanding. The medium is the message.

The same characteristic helps to explain the attraction of emergency food activities for youth-serving organizations and civic groups. Donations of money may be easier to handle and more efficient, but canned food drives provide a visceral connection between the general abundance of the society and the needs of poor families. They educate as they collect. "We are very interested in getting the food collected because there are people out there, kids and older people particularly, and whole families that are going hungry. . . . Beyond that, we are in the business of training youth. One of our goals is, through this project, to make youth aware that hunger is a problem in the community and then to give them an outlet to help do something about hunger," explained Jere Williams, the executive director of the Jersey Shore Council of the Boy Scouts of America. The BSOA could send its troops out to collect money door-to-door, but it just wouldn't have the same educational impact on the Scouts.

They probably wouldn't get as much, either. Some people prefer giving cans to giving cash. Giving food assures the donor that food is what the recipient will receive. Many people who are generous with their time and treasure on behalf of emergency food programs are highly skeptical of the motivations and skills of the beneficiaries of their largesse. By giving food, they believe that they are making sure that the gift will enhance nutrition and well-being, not end up as a pint of Night Train or a pair of trendy sneakers. Further, they can make sure that the gift is a nutrient-dense commodity such as peanut butter or beans, not a frivolous snack. "We watch for nutrition," the director of the Willcox, Arizona, food pantry told me. "We want to make sure that they get balance in their bodies. Sure, we've got cake mix in there, cookies, candy. Sure, those are all things they can have, that you should have, but they've also got the basics. Everybody gets a bag of beans."

It is not just a lack of faith in the culinary skills or spending priorities of recipients, however, that explains the heavy reliance on food donations in the emergency food system. Emergency food programs do not see—or portray—themselves as solutions to the problem of poverty. They are, very specifically, responses to hunger. Many feel they have done their job if they relieve urgent hunger, and they invite others to join them in that specific and manageable task by contributing food. Critics of the food drive approach recognize this as well. "I hate canned food drives," Hawley Botchford told me. "I really do, because it lets people off the hook. It gives them a warm, fuzzy feeling to give you a little bag of cans which, in the whole scope of the things, is meaningless. It's an easy way out. I don't want people to have the easy way out. I want them to look at the whole problem and what are we really dealing with. . . . I want to know why people are in need, and why they continue to be in need." Botchford went on to lay out one of the persistent dilemmas of the emergency food project, the tension between pursuing more fundamental solutions to poverty and meeting the immediate need. "In the meantime, we've got little kids that are growing up and, if they are going to reach their potential, if they're going to learn, if they're going to become productive parts of the system, they need to be fed, they need decent diets . . . and when we throw away as much as we do, then we're missing the boat there."

The Appeal of Hunger

Botchford would find many who would argue with his critique of food drives, but he would find few who would disagree with the idea that we are missing the boat if we allow children to go hungry while we throw away food. At its heart, the success of the emergency food project in attracting resources rests on the emotional and ethical impact of hunger as an issue. No amount of convenience or ease of access or leveraging of gifts would elicit the outpouring of donations and volunteer efforts that characterizes this phenomenon if the cause itself were not compelling. George McGovern said it well three decades ago in the excerpt quoted in the introduction. "Hunger . . . is the cutting edge of the problem of poverty. . . . the knowledge that human beings, especially little children, are suffering from hunger profoundly disturbs the American conscience."

The sensitivity of the nation's tender conscience is undoubtedly heightened by religious teachings. Hunger is probably the most common evocation of poverty and injustice found in either testament. Remember Isaiah's description of an acceptable fast: "Is it not to share your bread with the hungry?" Or the New Testament evocation of the Last Judgment in which Jesus welcomes to eternal reward those to whom he can say "I was hungry and you gave me food." Questioned by the righteous about just when they had found him hungry and fed him, he gives the memorable reply, quoted to me by emergency food providers all over the country: "Truly, I say to you, as you did it to one of the least of these my brethren, you did it to me." Religious people in the Judeo-Christian tradition are instructed, obligated to feed the hungry.

Further, the call to feed the hungry is reinforced by ritual as well as morality. As the Christian anti-hunger organization Bread for the World explained in a recent publication, "Food produced, prepared, shared, and consumed has a spiritual dimension and has thus always been a central part of religious observance. The filled stomach and the shared table dwell close to the heart and hearth of religious imagery, liturgy, and practice. Religious communities, therefore, have taken the lead in responding to hunger."

In fact, virtually all of the world's major religions make reference in their scriptures to the obligation to alleviate suffering in general, and to "feed the hungry" in particular. June Tanoue, a practicing Buddhist who is director of the Island Food Bank in Hawaii, which was started under the auspices of the social ministry of the Roman Catholic Church, explained it this way: "Everybody can get behind hunger and ending it. No matter what religious persuasion you are, or what economic background you are, you can get behind that."

There are secular arguments, however, that are similarly powerful. Everyone who has ever taken an introductory psychology course knows that hunger is at the very base of Maslow's hierarchy of human needs, that a hungry child cannot learn, that adequate nutrition is a prerequisite to optimal performance. The enormous success of the WIC Program (the Special Supplemental Nutrition Program for Women, Infants and Children) in obtaining bipartisan support in Congress suggests something of the potential of the hunger issue to appeal to conservatives as well as liberals. Preventing malnutrition is a prudent investment in human capital. Fighting hunger is the nonpartisan, ecumenical, inclusive goal upon which we can nearly all agree: "everybody . . . can get behind that."

Ellen Teller is an attorney whose work at the Food Research and Action Center in Washington, D.C., puts her at the heart of the anti-hunger advocacy community and in frequent touch with emergency food providers. She attributes the broad appeal of the hunger issue to the common everyday experiences that make the term immediately meaningful for almost everyone. "I think the reason we have such an incredibly diverse network," she explained, "the reason you get the whole spectrum of people involved in this, is because it's something that is real basic for people to relate to. You know, you're busy, you skip lunch, you feel hungry. On certain levels, everyone has experienced some form of feeling hungry."

I suspect that the emotional power of hunger has deep roots in our development as human organisms. Even those of us who now graze through the day to avoid that hungry feeling were hungry enough as infants to give the cry that brought the breast or bottle. "There is no question," psychiatrist Willard Gaylin has written, "that the feeding process is the dominant event in both the biological existence of the child and its earliest psychological and social life. It is the primary factor in the communication between the infant and that person who, he quickly learns, supports his life-style as well as his life. There develops therefore a fusion—and confusion—between food and security that often lasts throughout life." In the feeding situations of infancy lie the sources of our enduring tendency, widely remarked in the literature on dieting, to equate food and security, food and well-being, food and love. Gaylin goes on to explain that

> feeding is more than the squirting of nutrients into a gastrointestinal tract, either in bottle or breast feeding. While it is now fashionable to state that we are what we eat, what we eat early in life is predictable and relatively constant. The variable is actually the process and milieu of eating. It is a situation of embrace, pressure, contact, fondling, cooing, tickling, talking, stroking, squeezing; it is the warmth of the body, the pulsation of the parent's heart, the brushing of her lips, the smell of her secretions. This extended environment reinforces the child's fused image of security and food. . . .

No wonder food is a highly charged, emotion-laden part of life for most of us. No wonder it has such power. And if food is intensely cathected, then it makes sense that imagining people without food makes us intensely uncomfortable, and that providing food for people who lack it is intensely satisfying.

There is another side to the feeding experience of infancy, that of the parent. The perpetuation of the human species has depended to a great extent upon maternal willingness to feed hungry infants. Our bodies are designed to lactate after pregnancy, and nature has made sure that we will figure out what to do by building in a letdown reflex that moves milk toward the nipples, a reflex that can be triggered by a child's cry, or even the thought of nursing. Further, nature has predisposed us to keep on nursing our young by making the experience mutually gratifying. Perhaps this gratification is all the explanation we need for why mothers feed infants, but it does not seem to me far-fetched to imagine that natural selection favored the genes of mothers who fed their infants well and often, nor to imagine that in those genes might be a predisposition to be distressed by the cry—or idea—of a hungry child, or more broadly, by the suffering of others. Women are certainly overrepresented in the emergency feeding system, as they are in food-related roles throughout our culture. Perhaps it is in our genes, the urge to feed people.

The childhood roots of the emotional power of hunger as an issue do not end with the salience of the infant feeding experience, however. They extend throughout childhood as the growing child learns the fundamentals of ethics—at the family table. Of all the childhood and youthful memories I heard, none was more powerful than the recollection of family meals. The director of Channels, a food rescue program in Harrisburg, Pennsylvania, put it simply: "I come from a large family, and I think the importance of the family meal cannot be overstated. That is where you learn to deal with other people." I agree. Share and share alike. Leave something on the platter in case someone else wants it. Don't take too much, even if it's your favorite, until everyone else has had a chance. The norms for sharing food and paying attention to the needs of others are taught, in many American households, at the family table and very early in life, but they extend beyond the family. Don't eat in front of playmates unless you are willing to share. Offer food and drink to visitors. And the earlier the lesson, the more powerful, according to most child-rearing experts and developmental psychologists. Food is one of the first media through which we learn our notions of being good.

Sharing is not the only food-related lesson that Americans learn in childhood. Questioned about family food rules, an extraordinary number of people mentioned admonishments to "clean their plates" or avoid food waste. "I grew up with a Jewish grandmother who made me a member of the Empty Plate Club," Ellen Teller recalls. "I would have to eat everything on my dish. . . . I was brought up that it was a *shanda* to have waste. That was the word that my grandmother always used. And it is, I mean, that goes against people's grain. Throwing food out just goes against everyone's grain."

Herein lies the particular genius of emergency food. Much of the food distributed by the emergency food system is food that would otherwise go to waste. Food rescue programs take food that would literally go into the garbage, despite the fact that there is nothing wrong with it, and many corporate donations to the food banking system would otherwise end up in the landfill. Although much of the food currently contributed by the U.S. Department of Agriculture is not, technically, surplus food, agricultural surpluses purchased by the federal government in price-support programs played an important role in the establishment and institutionalization of the emergency food network, as we shall see in chapter 3. But even those sources, like the Scouting for Food program, that do not involve food that would otherwise be wasted are suffused with a halo effect from the system's overall reputation as a waste prevention measure.

This is important in explaining the success of emergency food, because it expands the constituency for feeding projects far beyond the traditionally liberal supporters of expanded public food assistance. The waste prevention factor pulls in a whole additional group. "It wasn't an idealistic vision of saving the hungry or anything like that," the student director of SPOON—the Stanford Project on Nutrition—told me, explaining how he had become involved in the campus food rescue project when his cooperative house had too many leftovers to fit in the freezer. "I just looked at it as, here's good food that would go to waste if something wasn't done about it, and there are people who could use it." Thinking back, he said he had become sensitized to the enormity of waste in America while visiting his mother's relatives in India: "They don't have garbage cans, and it's only when we go there that they actually need garbage cans." The emergency food phenomenon attracts the efforts of people who are primarily motivated by prevention of waste, as well as those of anti-hunger activists, and allows emergency food providers to craft messages that appeal to a much broader audience of potential donors and supporters.

Some of us, of course, were brought up to connect food waste directly to the plight of starving people—usually starving children—elsewhere. "Always clean your plate, there are starving chidren in India," food banker Andy Cohen remembers hearing. "Oh, we had to eat everything because of the starving kids in China. And just think, if you didn't eat, then they would starve, so eat everything up," Amelia McKenny told me. McKenny, who helped to start a food pantry in Deer Isle, Maine, and undertook a cross-country bicycle trip with her husband to raise funds for the project, talked about the enduring power of such childhood lessons: "Somehow or other, something gets planted in your subconscious," she asserted, "and you can't leave it alone."

I was struck by the clarity with which First Lady Hillary Rodham Clinton recalls her own clean plate milieu in her recent book, *It Takes a Village*:

> I grew up in the "clean plate" era. Today I look back at my family table, circa 1959—the pot roast and potatoes piled high and spilling over the edges of our plates—and see a catastrophe of calories, whose consequences my brothers and I avoided during childhood by walking or biking back and forth to school and around town and playing hours and hours of sports. We were expected to eat all of whatever we were served. If we balked, we heard, like a broken record, stories about starving children in faraway lands who would gladly eat what we scorned. My brother . . . Tony offered to mail his food to any country my father named. In the end, we ate whatever we had to in order to be "excused" from the table.

I was subject to the same admonitions about clean plates; in my case, it was usually Armenians who were mentioned, although it had been many years since their plight was an international issue. For decades afterward, I thought my mother had simply been engaging in a particularly blatant form of guilt-tripping, since it was never clear to me how my stuffing myself was going to benefit those in need. Recently, however, I have learned that for mothers—like my own—who were homemakers during and after World War II, the connection was real. The primary strategy by which the United States government tried to obtain food to meet its famine relief commitments in the aftermath of the war was a voluntary food conservation campaign. Housewives were exhorted to reduce household waste in order to free grains and fats for people starving in Europe and Asia. Many people now in adulthood grew up with the idea that cleaning our plates was an important contribution to feeding the hungry, so of course we hate to throw food in the garbage and feel guilty when we do. It is no wonder, therefore, that programs that prevent food waste by the ton and the truckload are a potent antidote to guilt.

Food waste is not the only way in which food taps into the human capacity for guilt. For many people, in fact, food consumption is riddled with guilt, and control of our own food intake is an unrelenting struggle for virtue. We are constantly being told that we eat too much, or too little, or the wrong things. A great deal has been written about this by psychologists and other behavioral scientists, but I am more interested in the pervasiveness of the popular associations between food and guilt. Weight Watchers calls its line of frozen desserts Sweet Temptations. Cookbooks routinely include some recipe associating chocolate with sin. I own a cookbook (*The Seven Chocolate Sins: A Devilishly Delicious Collection of Chocolate Recipes*) that is completely devoted to such matters; the fact that the authors could think up close to two hundred recipe titles that reflect that theme is testimony in itself. And sweets are only the most obvious category of "forbidden" food pleasures. The overall dynamic is to define some foods—or some quantities of some foods—as "illicit," and then feel guilty about consuming them.

What better way to work off that guilt than by participation in an activity that feeds the hungry, even better, one that feeds the hungry, prevents waste, and celebrates fitness? Columnist Dennis Hamill began a *New York Daily News* piece on the "Run Against Hunger," a fund-raising project of the St. John's Bread and Life Soup Kitchen, with a direct appeal to guilt about overeating: "Here's a perfect way to ease your guilty conscience in advance for pigging out and overspending in the upcoming holidays—Run Against Hunger." Readers who were already registered for the New York City Marathon were invited to dedicate their run to ending hunger by finding sponsors to donate to Bread and Life, which serves 1,100 meals a day to poor people in Brooklyn's Bedford-Stuyvesant. More sedentary readers were invited to call in their pledges of a dollar figure for every mile completed by the kitchen's board chairman, Father Jim Maher, or other participating runners. Hamill deftly linked overeating to other forms of consumption, commenting that "Tens of thousands of people will show up for the marathon this year, wearing the most expensive of sneakers, their bodies honed on healthful diets, having trained for the big run in the leisure time of the economically comfortable before carbo-loading the night before the event."

A group called Dieters Feed the Hungry has institutionalized the connection between hunger and guilt-inducing consumption. It invites overeaters to channel funds that they would normally spend on sweet and fatty snacks into programs for hungry people. "We founded this to resolve a glaring paradox—that millions of people are dieting while many others don't have enough food to make it through the month," declared the group's founder, Ronna Kabatznick, in an article in *Prevention* magazine. "Helping others who are in need gives dieters an outlet for feelings of emptiness that may drive them to overeat."

The connection to overeating at the individual level is mirrored by a contrast between hunger and abundance at the national level. At its core, the American fondness for hunger-fighting is not so much about guilt or waste as about plenty. George McGovern was right again. It *does* outrage Americans to think of people going hungry in the midst of our nation's legendary abundance. Andy Cohen, the president of the board of directors of the Food Bank of the Virginia Peninsula in Newport News, grew up in Teaneck, New Jersey, an affluent suburb of New York City. He told me about his own personal discovery of hunger in America.

> One thing that happened to me that opened my eyes to the depth of the problem was when I was in high school, and I went down to Washington, D.C., to visit. I had gone to the Capitol and was two or three blocks from the Capitol and there were people sitting on their front steps with their kids and they were asking for money to buy some food for the kids, literally in the shadow of our nation's capitol. Anybody who has gone to school in this country has heard the stories about the purple mountain's majesty and the fruited plains and how this is the greatest country in the world and how we are the breadbasket of the world and yet right there in the shadow of the Capitol were people who weren't getting enough to eat.

This is an appeal to a different sort of ethical principle, not that the food would go to waste if we did not feed it to the poor, or that we will become fat and unattractive if we eat it ourselves, but that the suffering inherent in hunger is preventable and unnecessary in a society well supplied, oversupplied with food.

I have always been particularly partial to this line of argument about hunger for three reasons. First, it implies that we are indeed members of some commonality, fellow travelers in a common vessel. It hints at our interdependence and reflects a notion that, apart from issues of individual performance or merit, people have moral claims on the collectivity. The supply of the whole is relevant to the needs of the individual. Second, at some fundamental level it suggests limits to our appetite for inequality. The contrast is too great. It bothers us. We find it distasteful. We are moved to pity by the plight of the hungry in famine-ridden countries across the ocean, but we feel a sense of anger at such needless suffering on our own doorsteps, in sight of our own overflowing granaries and supermarkets. It violates some shared sense of decency. "Hunger in the world is an obscenity," singer and songwriter Harry Chapin used to say, "but hunger in America is the ultimate obscenity." And finally, the argument that we must feed the hungry because we have the wherewithal to do so connotes activism, not passivity, in the face of human suffering. This is one evil that we can remedy. "Hunger has a cure" is the slogan recently adopted by Second Harvest in conjunction with the development of an Advertising Council campaign. It appeals to something pragmatic in the American psyche. Don't just stand there! Do something!

A Moral Bargain

The extensive participation that has become a hallmark of the emergency food system reflects a simple equation. The two halves of this equation—the general ease of involvement with emergency food and the high degree of gratification that it provides—constitute what might be called a "moral bargain." That is, emergency food activities provide a visceral feeling of doing good and being good, a means to comply with the dictates of one's conscience or the obligations of one's religion, with a minimum of inconvenience. The opportunities to contribute are ubiquitous, and many of them require little effort and almost no disruption of other activities. Some are downright recreational. In decision-theory terms, the "opportunity costs" of participating, the other things one might have accomplished with the same investment of time or resources, are low, while the rewards—

gratification, moral relief, a sense of belonging—are high. The moral power of the hunger issue, and the immediacy of the "payoff" combine to deliver a big return on a small contribution. As Joyce and Jerome Hoeschen put it when I asked them why their volunteers keep coming, "Because it feels so good. Because you see the results right away. Someone comes in that door hungry and you give him something to eat. That's what it is."

Of course not all roles are low cost. There are volunteers and staff who exhaust themselves on behalf of the hungry in kitchens and pantries and food banks and food rescue programs all over the country, and there are approaches, like the Boy Scouts' food drive, which require an enormous amount of planning, coordination, and effort. Even these projects, however, are a rational choice from the sponsoring organization's point of view, since they contribute so much to the achievement of the organization's fundamental mission. From the recipient's point of view, however, there might be simpler, more dignified ways to achieve the same ends. I was moved by the energy and concentration with which even the smallest scouts and their siblings attacked the monumental task of sorting and packing 280,000 pounds of food in Toms River, New Jersey. But I was also haunted, as I watched these logistically complicated, labor-intensive efforts, by a memory from the "No Nukes" movement of the seventies. Describing the enormously complex, risky, and demanding technology of a nuclear reactor, activists were fond of asking, "And do you know what all of this equipment is for?" The reply was startling: "to boil water." That is, the reactor would heat water to create steam to drive steam turbines to generate electricity. I feel a little bit the same way about the Boy Scouts' food drive and its counterparts across the nation. This enormous outpouring of effort is needed to get a can of carrots or a jar of baby food into the hands of a hungry family, a result that could probably be accomplished far more simply by raising the food stamp allotment, or the minimum wage. The next chapter explores the role of low wages, along with that of unrealistic food stamp allotments and other factors, in bringing people to the food pantry and soup kitchen door.

CHAPTER TWO

Who Eats Emergency Food?

IT IS EARLY on a Thursday morning, and the tiny vestibule of the Yorkville Common Pantry is jammed with people. For a few minutes, they are all here together: the newly unemployed relying on pantry bags for a few months until another job is found, the chronically underemployed supplementing meager wages with a handout, the welfare mothers, the disabled, and the aged, trying to stretch public benefits that don't provide enough to pay real New York City rents and utility charges, and the homeless denizens of the neighborhood and the upper reaches of Central Park, themselves a diverse group including perpetual panhandlers and the marginally employed, youngsters "aged out" of foster care, a couple of displaced recent immigrants, a few hardy, aging "bag ladies," and an assortment of people ejected by the families and friends with whom they have been "crashing." It is a microcosm of hunger as it presents itself daily to emergency food providers across the country.

Emergency food programs are fundamentally a grassroots phenomenon; many programs are small and lack resources for extensive collecting and reporting of data. How do we know who uses them? Hundreds of state and local hunger studies have been conducted by emergency food providers and their allies since the early 1980s in efforts to understand who these people are, and what brings them to our doorsteps. Some of these studies are little more than tabulations of data from applications, while others have employed elaborate sampling designs and interviews in great depth. Local emergency food populations, like local conditions, vary, of course, but nutritionists Marion Nestle and Sally Guttmacher, who reviewed state-level studies in the early 1990s, found the results depressingly easy to summarize. Taken as a group, these studies

> found the individuals most at risk of hunger to include women, children, and the elderly, many of them members of minority groups. They attributed the cause of food insufficiency in these groups to poverty, and they laid the blame for poverty on unemployment or underemployment, the high costs of housing and other basic needs, and inadequate welfare and food assistance benefits.

Who Are the Hungry?

The ad hoc character and local auspices of emergency food programs make national figures on program users and their needs difficult to obtain. For more than a decade, as state and local studies piled up, no national overview was available. Then, in 1993, Second Harvest remedied the situation with an extensive National Research Study carried out by a consulting firm, the VanAmburg Group, in conjunction with 34 of Second Harvest's 185 member food banks, which projected results from this substantial sample to the whole system. Like the state and local studies, the national overview found women, children, and members of racial and ethnic minority groups overrepresented in comparison with their numbers in the general population. This will come as no surprise to anyone who has paid attention to the issue of poverty in the United States: these are precisely the groups who are most likely to be poor. In 1993, the year when Second Harvest's data were collected:

- 62.9% of adult poor people were women, and 60.9% of adult emergency food users were women; women were more than two thirds of adult pantry clients, while men outnumbered women three to two in the soup kitchens;
- 40% of all poor people and 42.9% of emergency food clients were children, as compared with just above a quarter of the general population.
- Just over 48% of all poor people, and just under 48% of all pantry

clients were (non-Hispanic) whites, as compared with three quarters of the U.S. population. White diners were underrepresented in the soup kitchens, where they constituted only about 30% of the clients.

- A little over 54% of both pantry and kitchen households with children were single parent households; 52.7% of all poor families with children were single parent households. Under one fifth of all families in the U.S. were single parent households.
- Persons 65 years old or older, who constituted 11.9% of the general population, and under a tenth of the officially poor, were 22% of kitchen clients, but only 7.1% of clients in pantry households.
- Among racial and ethnic minority groups, the patterns diverge a bit. African Americans constituted just over a quarter of the poor, a little over a third of pantry users, and more than two fifths of kitchen users. People of Hispanic origin were about 18% of the poor, but only 13.5% of pantry users, and just over a fifth of kitchen users.

In short, the national figures confirm the summary portrait presented above, and mirror with remarkable fidelity the national profile of Americans in official, statistical poverty. The answer to our question is almost too simple for words. Who eats emergency food? Poor people, and people very much like them.

The fact that the bleak national pattern of poverty is reproduced so faithfully in the emergency food system is no surprise. At its root, the official federal poverty line is derived from an estimate of what it costs to eat. In the mid 1950s, a USDA household food consumption survey showed that the typical American household spent about a third of its income on food. Looking around for an efficient way to measure poverty when it became a major social issue in the early 1960s, Mollie Orshansky, a staff member at the Social Security Administration, reasoned that if households tended to spend a third of their income on food, then any household that could not afford to purchase a nutritionally adequate diet by allocating a third of its income to food purchase would be poor. She obtained from the Department of Agriculture its Economy Food Plan, a subsistence diet developed for short-term use, and calculated a series of poverty income thresholds set at three times the cost of the Economy Food Plan, later replaced by the Thrifty Food Plan, for various household sizes. If people are officially poor, then, by definition, they do not have the money to purchase a nutritionally adequate diet in the marketplace (unless their non-food expenses are unusually low); if they are not getting some form of food assistance, they stand a good chance of going hungry.

Perhaps this will become clearer if we translate these figures into everyday shopping terms. The 1996 poverty income threshold for a family of four in the forty-eight contiguous states and the District of Columbia is $15,600. (It's higher in Hawaii and higher still in Alaska.) Since the poverty line assumes a third of income allocated to food, divide by three to find the total annual allocation for food: $5,200. None of us shops for a year at a time, however, so divide by 52 to get the weekly food budget: $100. For four people, this is $25 per person, $3.57 a day. Figuring three meals, $1.19 a meal. No snacks. If you buy a cup of coffee for $.60, you have spent half a meal's food allowance.

The poverty line does not somehow mysteriously give you $1.19 per person, per meal. It is not an expense account. It's just a measurement tool, an operational definition of poverty. It says that if you cannot, by allocating one-third of your income to food, afford to spend the munificent sum of $100 a week on food for a family of four, then you are not one of the 39 million officially poor Americans. "For the poor, poverty thresholds are income ceilings," Winifred Bell wrote in a memorable effort to dispel one of the most common misconceptions about poverty. There is no guarantee that the incomes of poor people will equal, or even approach, the poverty line. In fact, many poor people live far below the cutoff. Statisticians call the amount by which households fall *below* their appropriate poverty income thresholds *income deficits*. For 1993, the year that Second Harvest studied emergency food program users, the mean family income deficit was $5,960, or $1,671 per capita, and the average income deficit for what the Census Bureau calls "unrelated individuals," that is, people living alone or with a non-relative, was $3,541. While there were 399,000 poor families whose incomes were within $500 of their poverty threshold, more than two-fifths of poor people, including 3,387,000 families, lived below *half* their respective poverty lines!

There are many problems with the poverty line. It uses *pretax* income, for example, but poor people must pay their taxes anyway, so in fact, most have even less disposable income than the amounts suggested above. On the other hand, the poverty line does not take into account the value of non-cash income, such as housing subsidies or food stamps, so poor people receiving these benefits have more than the figures above imply. The biggest problem with the line, however, is that it is obsolete. The assumptions upon which it is based become more unrealistic every day. Back when the line was created, and people were spending a third of their income on food, they were typically spending a quarter of their income or less on housing. Jeans and sneakers were cheap. The subway fare in New York City was one-tenth of its current cost ($.15 a ride instead of $1.50 a ride). Medical procedures that are now routine had not yet been invented. There were no VCRs or faxes or PCs. It was much easier, much more realistic, to expect poor families to allocate a third of their income to food than it is today.

For most people in the society, for people leading "normal" lives, necessities constitute a smaller part of total expenditure than they once did. The average household no longer spends anywhere near a third of its income on food; in fact, by the early 1990s, the mean food expenditure was only one-fifth of household expenses. This is what is meant by a rising standard (as opposed to cost) of living. The poverty line is updated annually to reflect changes in the *cost* of living, but it has never been adjusted to reflect changes in the *standard* of living. As a result, the officially poor, even those with incomes at the *top* of the poverty range, right at or just under the cutoff, are farther from the norm than they were five or ten or twenty years ago. When the poverty line was first created, it constituted just under one-half the median household income; now it is down to about one-third.

At the same time, however, that non-poor households have been adding more and more non-necessities to our consumption patterns, all households, especially the poor, have been spending more on shelter and other fuel-related necessities. Rent, utility, and transportation costs, which began rising sharply in the aftermath of the oil crisis of the early 1970s, claim an increasing share of income, leaving less for food.

The implications of this falling standard of poverty for soup kitchens and food pantries are substantial. On the one hand, it means that the officially poor are poorer than ever in real terms, and more likely to turn to emergency food providers for help as ever-increasing shares of their limited incomes go for other necessities: the "heat or eat" dilemma that has captured attention from the press. If free food is available, for example, and free heating oil is not, then a poor household is likely to use its available cash for heating oil and turn to the food pantry for the makings of dinner. On the other hand, it means that more and more of the not-quite-poor experience household food emergencies. The pool of people who might realistically find themselves in need is much larger than the number of officially poor. Most food programs that have income eligibility criteria set them well above the official poverty level, which is widely regarded as unrealistically low by organizations and individuals who work with people in need on a daily basis. Cutoffs at 150 percent of poverty or even 185 percent of poverty, which is the eligibility ceiling for the federal government's WIC program, are common. The Second Harvest study used the 150 percent figure to collect and process its income data; it found that 92 percent of pantry clients and 86.7 percent of kitchen clients have incomes at or below 150 percent of poverty. In order to understand why the not-quite-poor have joined the officially poor in the food lines, and why only some of the officially poor are emergency food users, we need to take a closer look at why people turn to emergency food programs for help.

Why Are They Hungry?

The Second Harvest study asked respondent agencies to list the top three reasons that clients in their programs seek emergency food assistance. Recent unemployment was the reason cited more often than any other, by 55 percent of food pantries and 34 percent of kitchens. Long-term unemployment, cited by half the kitchens and two-fifths of pantries, came next, followed by "Working/Need More Money," a category included among the top three by more than half the pantries and 37 percent of kitchens. "Emergency/crisis" came next, a term that can cover anything from eviction or the sudden death of a breadwinner in an individual household to a flood or hurricane that devastates an entire community. Then came a series of reasons that can be fairly accurately summarized by saying that income, from whatever source, was inadequate to meet the high cost of being poor. And then a category labeled "bureaucratic hassles" that seemed to embrace various problems with public assistance. Because public food assistance programs, especially food stamps, were originally designed to prevent much of the chronic need now addressed by emergency food, the inadequacies of food stamps have come in for special mention, and sometimes detailed exploration, in many of the studies. Let us look at each of these broad categories—employment-related factors, high costs, public assistance problems, and inadequacies of food stamps—in turn.

Employment-Related Reasons

Employment-related factors—unemployment and low wages—head the list of explanations for emergency food use for many reasons. In the first place, they are among the most common given by applicants. Data from Second Harvest's client survey confirmed what agency directors had reported. The study found that nearly two-thirds of the network's clients are in the workforce, that is, they are working (18.3 percent) or unemployed (44.1 percent). A third of all emergency food recipient households had someone working either full or part time at the time of the interview; a quarter reported a job as the household's largest source of income in the previous month. Among the unemployed users of the network, those with relatively recent work histories predominate. More than half had been unemployed for less than a year, and almost half of those for less than three months.

Underlying economic conditions lend credibility to the agency directors' emphasis on unemployment as a primary factor in need. Average unemployment rates have been rising for the last quarter-century in virtually all western industrialized nations. Our overall rate in the United States averaged 4.6 percent in the 1968–1973 period and 7.2 percent in the 1980–1989 period. Globalization of the labor market has put U.S. workers in competition with workers around the world earning lower wages, and the relatively secure, high-wage industrial jobs with comprehensive fringe benefits that many American workers grew up expecting to occupy are disappearing. Food pantries first came to national attention, as we shall see, in a steep recession of the early 1980s, and the images in the press featured formerly prosperous manufacturing workers in Rust Belt and Oil Patch states who had lost their jobs and were struggling to keep their homes. Many food pantries were originally set up to aid the victims of plant closings or industry shutdowns. Another recession in the early nineties hit white-collar occupations, especially office workers and the wholesale and retail sales force, with particular force. This one was concentrated on the coasts, rather than in the heartland; California and the Northeast were especially hard hit.

It doesn't take a recession, however, to create job loss; it happens every day as firms close or downsize. In fact, a high rate of layoffs, despite overall economic vigor and moderate to low overall unemployment, appears to be an emerging trend. After reviewing newly released Labor Department figures, *New York Times* reporter Steve Lohr concluded that "layoffs have become a durable fixture of today's economy, occurring steadily in good times and bad. Three-quarters of all American households have seen a family member, friend, relative, or neighbor lose a job since 1980." Meanwhile, the proportion of the unemployed covered by unemployment compensation has been dropping. While over half of the unemployed in the seventies collected benefits, the average proportion fell to only around a third in the late eighties and rose to only about two-fifths in the recession of the early nineties, the lowest figure ever recorded for a recession. Job security has been declining, and the safety net has been fraying, at the same time.

Unemployment sends families to the food pantry—and sometimes to the soup kitchen—by a variety of routes. In the first place, workers earning modest wages may find themselves in need as soon as their regular income stops. They have barely been getting by on their earnings, and there is no cushion. "We had a fish factory here, a sardine packing plant that employed seventy men and women, which closed last year," Jim Jamison, one of the founders of a community pantry in Deer Isle, Maine, told me. I asked if they saw the results at the pantry. "Absolutely," he said, "right away, because they just said, 'Well, we're closing next week,' and they went out of business." Some of the laid-off sardine workers may have found new employment when a lobster company bought the facility and hired about two dozen workers, but many of the laid-off sardine packers had little to fall back on. "There are people here who are illiterate," Jamison continued. "How are they going to do much except menial work? When there were clams it was fine, but the clams are going, so they're just on the fringe, all the time."

Even workers with a far more ample salary scale than sardine packers may find themselves in need very soon. Unemployment compensation, on average, pays only about 40 percent of your earnings. Household expenses, however, do not necessarily decrease. The mortgage payments do not go down, nor the bus fare, nor your property taxes. Almost no one plans to become unemployed, and savings have become a relic of the past or a wistful fantasy in many American households. In the aftermath of downsizing or corporate relocation, many formerly middle-income families have learned what poor people have known for decades—that food is often the most flexible item in the family budget, the place where you can economize, and the easiest kind of help to get. People who expect to live on reduced earnings for the long term may act decisively to reduce spending—move to cheaper housing, sell off assets. People who hope that their displacement is temporary, however, are reluctant to take such drastic actions. Food pantries help a certain proportion of the formerly affluent while they try to put their lives back together.

It is not only their prevalence among clients, however, that accounts for the prominence of the recently unemployed in the literature on emergency food use. These are the quintessential "worthy poor," and they are using emergency food in the way that the programs' founders intended. Even programs that were not specifically created to respond to layoffs were designed for short-term or occasional, rather than chronic, use. Furthermore, the recently unemployed in particular, and temporary users in general, are popular with food program directors because they are good publicity. They help to combat the charge that such programs are creating dependency, and they reassure the staff and volunteers that their efforts are really helping people get back on their feet. Clients who turn to a food pantry after a layoff and then become volunteers or donors at the pantry when work and income are restored are among the "heroes" of the emergency food story. They give the pantry a good name and help to keep donations flowing. Nearly every annual report or fund-raising brochure I read contained some such account.

When unemployment drags on and on, the recently unemployed become the long-term unemployed. Long-term unemployment, defined as unemployment for a period of a year or more, was listed by more than two-fifths of both pantry and kitchen clients in the Second Harvest client study. For people who have never experienced prolonged unemployment before, the next steps after compensation runs out can come as a surprise. Testifying before a congressional committee, the director of a Los Angeles information and referral service pictured a typical caller who had never had to turn to public assistance before: "[They] knew nothing about what it was going to take to apply for public assistance. Finally got down to their last few dollars and decided they better apply. . . . Went in to apply and found that it was going to take from 30 to 45 days to get food stamps and they have nothing for the interim period." In such a situation, food pantries and soup kitchens may be the only safety net for those who do not have family to whom they can turn.

Eventually, most laid-off workers find new jobs, but usually not jobs at comparable remuneration. Of those who lost full-time jobs in 1991 or 1992, for example, 35 percent had obtained a comparable or better job by the beginning of 1994. A quarter had taken a full-time job at lower pay; nearly another quarter were still unemployed or had left the workforce; 8 percent were working part-time, and another 8 percent were self-employed. Those who take jobs below their skill levels, and those who take less than full-time jobs join the underemployed, who are often, also, the underpaid. Low wages, part-time schedules, seasonal employment account for another whole segment of soup kitchen and food pantry clients. These range from the down-sized former manager, earning 60 percent of his former salary, who is trying desperately to hold on to a home and turns to a food pantry because all he can earn must go to the bank or mortgage company, to the members of the vast army of people working twenty hours a week or less for companies that don't want to provide health insurance. In Searsport, Maine, Stanis Laycock, the founder of Waldo County

Project Hope, summed up this situation: Many local employers were hiring people for just twenty hours a week, she said, "so they don't have to pay any medical. Medical is a major problem, and there aren't enough of those twenty-hour-a-week jobs for everybody to have two. That makes it real hard on people, and the minimum wage doesn't go anywhere!" The image of a town where everyone hopes for two half-time jobs so that employers can be spared paying health insurance struck me as an emblem for a great deal that has been happening at the bottom levels of the American economy.

Seasonal work is another precursor to emergency food use. The Deer Isle, Maine, fishermen who can't get work in the winter have their counterparts in the south Florida sales clerks and bank tellers whose work is drastically cut back in the warmer months when the snowbirds—retired people who spend the winter in Florida—go back up north to spend the summer in cooler surroundings. I got a short course in the economics of seasonal employment from Father John Lindel, the founder and director of St. Matthew's House, a residential treatment program, soup kitchen, and food pantry in the wealthy Florida Gulf Coast town of Naples. "I mean, what happens to the lady that's got two kids that works at the garden center at Wal-Mart and they cut her down to fifteen hours a week in the summer?" Father Lindel asked. "When all the Town Cars are gone, . . . what the hell is she supposed to do? What is she supposed to do in August when her kids are getting ready to go back to school and Jimmy's two sizes bigger than he was and he wants a new set of Nikes, . . . what is she supposed to do?" She comes to the food pantry at St. Matthew's House, and he gives her a box of food, but neither one of them feels very good about it. "I call it underemployment," he continues. "It's the people who check out your groceries that get down to twenty or twenty-five hours a week. . . . The Barnett Bank advertises for tellers for ten bucks an hour. And if that was a forty-hour week, I'd say 'Praise God,' but it's three hours a day, five days a week. They take home $137 and change, so I don't say 'Praise God.' It's a rush-hour teller. They get enough training where everyone else can go to lunch and when everybody's back from lunch, you go home. You got no bennies, okay? You got nothing."

If you detect a hint of anger in Father Lindel's words when he

talks about limited hours and the absence of "bennies," fringe benefits, you are right. All across the country, people who run soup kitchens and food pantries are angry about what is happening to the
working poor. It just doesn't seem right that someone who tries so
hard, who gets up every morning and goes to work, and then goes out
and looks for a second job, should have to eat at a soup kitchen or line
up for handouts at a food pantry. But this is the reality for a significant segment of America's workforce. A job is just not what it used to
be. Real wages, adjusted for inflation, dropped by more than an
eighth in private nonagricultural employment between 1973 and
1993, and adjusted average weekly earnings declined by nearly a fifth
in the same period. The decline in purchasing power has been especially steep at the bottom. Despite increases in 1990 and 1991, and
again in 1995, the minimum wage has not kept pace with the cost of a
poverty-level life-style. Throughout most of the 1960s and 1970s, the
income earned by a person working full-time at a minimum-wage job
was sufficient to keep a family of three out of official poverty. By
1994, a minimum-wage job, forty hours a week, fifty-two weeks a year
would not even keep a household of two above the poverty threshold;
figured on the more typical thirty-five hours a week, the minimum
wage does not now pay enough to keep a single individual above the
poverty line.

Such hard-earned poverty has been the reality for a long time for
some segments of the workforce, especially migrant agricultural laborers. Across Collier County from St. Matthew's House in Naples, is
the Guadalupe Center in Immokalee, Florida, the home base of the
East Coast migrant stream. Immokalee has had substantial experience with seasonal, part-time, and low-wage labor. Immokalee, in
fact, was the scene of congressional hunger investigations in the late
1960s, when Senators George McGovern and Bob Dole brought the
Senate Select Committee on Nutrition and Human Needs to south
Florida to investigate charges that local officials were blocking much
needed federal assistance to the hungry in the form of federal surplus
agricultural commodities. Local officials argued that the migrants
were not Collier County citizens, and thus not their responsibility:
"These are federal people," declared a county commissioner. Eventu-

ally, federal commodities came into Immokalee, followed by food stamps, but the fundamental inequities of the migrant labor economy remain intact. Desperate people take whatever work they can get and crowd together in overpriced temporary housing. The desperate people are different now—fewer native-born whites, African Americans, and Puerto Ricans, more Mexicans, Haitians, and Guatemalans— than they were thirty years ago. But the new migrant farmworkers face the old problems: wages too low, and prices too high.

I asked Sister Judy Donher, the director of the Guadalupe Center, if she foresaw an end to the need for the soup kitchen that the Center runs five days a week. She did not hesitate: "I think as long as we have migrants, as long as we have an industry that is not twelve months, we are going to have poor people. We are going to have hungry people. . . . If harvesting is going well, there won't be many. We may see seventy-five, eighty, a hundred. . . . Today, it's raining. They will not be out in the field . . . right now, we're between crops. They've planted a second crop of tomatoes, but they're not ready. They'll be ready in another two, three, maybe four weeks. So we're going to have a down time now. So with the rain today and people not working in the fields right now, we'll probably have a hundred fifty. If we would have a freeze down here, we'd see three or four hundred a day." Sister Judy went on to make clear that people did not come to the kitchen simply because they had nothing better to do. Migrants do not get paid for the days when they cannot work. "And it may be their only meal during the day."

Hunger in Immokalee, however, is not just a product of low farm wages, unpredictable work, disability, or other factors that limit income. It is also an outcome of an exploitative housing market. Tom Lockie, a volunteer at the soup kitchen from the North Naples Methodist Church, expressed his frustration with overall national policy: "We don't get too much national policy that allows for taking care of people in a more meaningful fashion . . . people need to eat and they need to find some meaningful work and be a productive person in society." He went on to identify what he called "a different set of problems down here," specific to Immokalee. "No one has really gotten hardnosed and addressed the fact that some pretty large agricultural conglomerates are treating people incredibly poorly. The housing I see around here I would liken to pre-1920 days. . . . Sometimes I think that the agricultural conglomerates are just allowing other people to pick up the slack that they should be doing by providing a little more meaningful housing and better wages so that people can eat and get medical treatment." Much of the housing in Immokalee consists of high-rent, low-amenity shacks and trailers and apartment buildings that look like rundown motels or barracks. Since rents generally run $150 to $200 a week, and farmworkers are lucky to make more than $30 a day, far less if they are undocumented, the result is often dense crowding. As Sister Judy explained, "If there are ten men living in a trailer that's costing them two hundred dollars a week to rent and they are taking turns sleeping, they can't get to a kitchen. So they need a hot meal." Even when access to a kitchen is not a problem, however, such rents almost always require too much of the household's income, leaving too little for other expenses, including food. High shelter costs interact with low income to produce the demand for emergency food.

High Shelter Costs

It would be bad enough if Immokalee were somehow an aberration. But it is not; it is the extreme that makes visible the pervasive reality. Poor people pay too much for housing, not only in Immokalee, but almost anywhere in the United States. What do I mean by "too much"? For starters, there is the poverty line again. When Americans were spending an average of a third of their income for food, they were also spending about 30 percent for shelter. Thus the fundamental assumption involved in calculating poverty presumed that one-third for food, and another third for rent and utilities left a third for other necessities: school expenses, transportation, medical care, clothing, recreation. But rents and utilities charges have risen dramatically in the last two decades. A steep rise in shelter costs, triggered by the fuel crisis of the early 1970s and intensified by a wave of frenzied speculation in urban real estate in the 1980s, has affected all segments of our society, but it has been most burdensome for the poor. In 1980, the federal government established a benchmark of 30 percent of family income as the target ceiling for rents; anything higher was defined as excessive. By 1985, a Census Bureau survey found 22 million families paying rents in excess of that standard. Among the officially poor, the figures were shocking: 45 percent of all households with incomes below the poverty line were spending 70 percent or more of their income for rent and utilities. No wonder they could not afford to purchase adequate food! As studies of the growing demand at soup kitchens and food pantries have piled up, excess shelter costs have turned out to be a primary explanation for the emergency food needs of low-income households, both the working poor and those supported by public income transfers.

When shelter costs become unmanageable, people become homeless. That is, they fail to pay their rent, are evicted, and are unable to find new housing. It stands to reason that if you were unable to scrape together the month's rent in your old place, you are unlikely to have the deposit necessary for a new one. There are other routes to homelessness besides eviction, of course: fires still burn people out, people leave because of family quarrels or violence or the threat of violence. Mentally impaired people leave treatment centers and adult homes without authorization. But whatever the route to homelessness, once a person becomes homeless, he or she almost automatically joins the ranks of the hungry—or at least the ranks of those dependent upon soup kitchens and other providers of emergency food. Without access to cooking facilities, there is little hope of eating economically, and no place to store groceries, so eating becomes a meal-to-meal challenge; for many, it becomes the primary concern that structures the day. In large cities, publications like New York City's *Street Sheet*, a listing of soup kitchens, with their days and hours of service, on a laminated sheet impervious to rain, help the homeless find their way to available meals. Some 18.1 percent of the clients interviewed in the Second Harvest study reported themselves to be homeless—without any residence at all, living in a shelter or mission, living in a car or van, or living in an abandoned building. An additional 5.4 percent were living in what the study termed "potentially marginal housing"—doubled up with family or friends, or renting a room without access to a kitchen. With the "homeless" constituting a significant portion of the "hungry," or course, nearly anything that contributes to homelessness can be identified as a cause of hunger. The factors that contribute to homelessness have been the subject of many studies, with different scholars emphasizing different explanations, but the list almost always includes, in addition to rising housing costs and shrinking housing subsidies, the destruction of single-room occupancy (SRO) units, epidemics of drug and alcohol abuse, deinstitutionalization of the mentally ill, declining public assistance payments, and of course the same increases in unemployment and decreases in wages described above.

Inadequate Public Assistance

Public assistance is an important source of income for people who use soup kitchens and food pantries. Like wages, however, public assistance payments have declined in their ability to keep families fed and housed. Until recently, there have been three general categories of public assistance frequently used by people who seek help from soup kitchens and food pantries: General Assistance (GA), Supplemental Security Income (SSI), and Aid to Families with Dependent Children (AFDC). The Personal Responsibility and Work Opportunity Reconciliation Act (PRWORA) of 1996 has changed the contours of public assistance and replaced AFDC with Temporary Assistance to Needy Families (TANF). These changes will certainly affect the demand for emergency food, but it is too soon for most of the impact to have shown up in systematic studies. The public assistance problems that are reflected in the literature on emergency food use, and those that I encountered in my research, were those that existed before the recent legislation. Most emergency food providers expect such problems to intensify under the PRWORA.

General Assistance (GA), which goes by a variety of names in the different states, is a state/local program that provides assistance to destitute people who are not eligible for any of the federally supported cash income programs. Many states failed to adjust GA benefits to account for inflation in the decade that began in the early eighties, so by 1992, GA benefits in the median state were 20 percent lower than they had been a decade earlier. These benefits, almost never adequate to cover food and shelter, have hovered around a third of the poverty line in the median state in the 1990s. Even these meager benefits, however, have become a popular target for state budget cutters. In the 1991–1992 recession, twenty-two of the twenty-eight states that had statewide GA programs reduced benefits, restricted eligibility, or terminated their programs altogether. Of course, many states never had a GA program at all, or had one that restricted eligibility to the disabled. In an effort to understand the causes of homelessness in the eighties, Martha Burt of the Urban Institute studied factors associated with homelessness in 147 cities. She found that cities with no General Assistance program had the highest rates of homelessness; cities with programs restricted to the disabled had the next highest incidence, and the lowest rates were found in cities where GA benefits were also available to able-bodied people. The level and availability of GA benefits is a crucial determinant of homelessness, and thus of hunger and reliance upon emergency food.

Supplemental Security Income (SSI) is the federal program for aged and disabled poor people; its benefits are indexed—that is, they are adjusted automatically to cope with the impact of inflation, and they are more adequate than General Assistance, but they have never been ample. SSI or some combination of SSI and Social Security is the primary income source for many of the elderly clients of emergency food. The proportion of clients who are elderly varies tremendously from program to program, but the picture painted by emergency food providers of the situation of their elderly recipients is remarkably similar. In Benson, Arizona, Elaine Owens explained the economics of retirement:

> Take a normal budget for an elderly person. I know how much they get on SSI. You know, there's no place in Benson for less than $250 to rent, utilities run about $100. That gives us maybe about $100 left. . . . I would go through their budget, go through and go through with them, to try to help them stretch. . . . You pay your rent, you pay your utilities, you pay half your medicine. They never paid the full medicine, only half, because they can't afford it. They skimp on food.

Across the country in Deer Isle, the majority of the pantry users are elderly. "I think 58 percent of our people, clients, neighbors, whatever they want you to call them, are elderly. We're helping a tremendous number of elderly people," Jim Jamison said, and described a woman whose story was on television the day before because she owed Bangor Hydro $316 and they were getting ready to cut off her electricity. "Her income is $450 and she pays $350 a month rent, so that leaves her $100 for everything else, for everything else! And this is true here on the Island. There are a lot of these older people that are just living, just existing." His wife went on to explain that elderly residents are often shy about asking for help; the pantry "gets called by people who say 'I have tea and I have crackers. But it's four days till I get my check and that's all I have to eat. Do you think I could have anything at all?' "

In some communities a senior nutrition program eases some of the stress on limited incomes, but everywhere I went, people described seniors—and disabled people—on such limited incomes that an additional medication or a sudden hike in fuel prices could throw their budgets completely out of whack. "You are feeding seniors who might have to make a choice between a medication and a meal," the president of the board of the Food Bank of the Virginia Peninsula told me. "I know some people snickered when Bill Clinton was running for president and he met a couple and the media jumped on it and said 'here is a couple that had to make a decision, are they going to take their medicine or are they going to eat.' Some people thought it was staged. It wasn't staged. It happens every day."

You don't have to be elderly to need medication, of course, and both food pantries and soup kitchens see an extraordinarily high prevalence of chronic diseases and disabilities among clients. Health problems play a major role in the patterns of income loss that lead people to emergency food providers in the first place, and the need to care for family members in ill health keeps some clients out of the workforce. In the Second Harvest study, almost two-fifths of pantry households and more than a third of soup kitchen households reported that at least one person in the household was in poor health. More than two-fifths reported that they had unpaid medical bills, and a similar percentage reported that they were putting off medical care that they could not afford. Even without careful studies, however, I think that nearly anyone who spends much time in a kitchen or pantry would list health problems among the most obvious and distressing causes—and complications—of need. Just go and look.

The Second Harvest Study did not collect information on the HIV status of clients, but the link between AIDS and emergency food is more than incidental. Not only is an AIDS diagnosis a crucial step in the patterns of job and shelter loss that lead people to emergency food, but a substantial number of emergency food programs have been created specifically for people with AIDS. Some, like God's Love We Deliver in New York City, deliver meals to AIDS patients who are homebound or have limited mobility. Others serve meals or provide food packages that emphasize the nutrient density so important to preserving the health of HIV positive people. For those people with AIDS who must rely upon public assistance, especially, emergency food programs can provide a crucial margin of nutritional protection.

Up until the passage of the PRWORA, the third category of public assistance relied upon by emergency food clients was AFDC. Like GA, the AFDC benefit levels had been declining for some time. After adjusting for inflation, the average monthly AFDC benefit in 1989 was worth only about two-thirds of what it had been in 1970. Even when the federal "guarantee" of support for dependent children and their parents was still in force, each state set its own benefit level. In 1995, no state paid benefits as high as the poverty line, and one set AFDC grant levels as low as 14 percent of the poverty threshold. The median grant for a three-person family in 1990 represented 44 percent of the poverty line. AFDC has not been sufficient for quite some time to cover actual rents in most places and leave enough for food.

Low and shrinking AFDC benefit levels help to explain the conversion of many community food programs from "emergency" provision to chronic household supplementation, but low grants are only part of the story. Variously called "churning," "procedural denials," or "bureaucratic disentitlement," AFDC has been subject to administrative procedures at the local level that routinely deprive clients of support for periods of several months at a time. Cases were closed erroneously, or for failure to comply with procedural requirements that had nothing to do with need or eligibility, and the burden of proof was on the client when he or she reapplied. Deterrent practices in local welfare offices have been common for a long time. Such practices reflected a national disenchantment with welfare that began long before the recent round of welfare politics. Throughout the 1970s, programs for poor people were repeatedly accused of budget busting, creating dependency, fraud, abuse, waste, and throwing money at problems.

As disenchantment with welfare was articulated with increasing vigor in the 1980s, procedural or bureaucratic denials escalated at the local level, and Congress began trying to reform welfare at the federal level. The result was the Family Support Act of 1988, which, although it looks overwhelmingly benign in comparison to the PRWORA of 1996, allowed the states to implement a variety of strategies for reducing the rolls. Under this law, states could obtain "waivers" from the national eligibility standards and regulations that allowed them to experiment with time limits, work requirements, family caps, and a host of other devices. Training and employment programs, including transitional child care and health insurance, helped some families leave the rolls, but leaving the rolls seldom meant leaving poverty, and even these success stories continued to need the help of emergency food programs to make ends meet. Many other households were unable to comply with the new demands and saw their benefits reduced or terminated, increasing their dependence on emergency food providers. Part of the apprehension with which many soup kitchens and food pantries are facing the uncertain future ushered in by the PRWORA grows out of their experience with the previous round of welfare reform under the Family Support Act.

As the purchasing power of cash grant levels eroded during the eighties, and both national policies and local administrative practice became more restrictive, food stamps increased in importance. Food stamps are "indexed" to inflation, with both benefit levels and eligibility thresholds rising automatically with food prices, so as cash benefits fell behind, food stamps became more central, both within the household budgets of poor families and in the local economies of poor neighborhoods. But the Food Stamp Program (FSP) is also subject to bureaucratic disentitlement and a host of other shortcomings, and these constitute the final category of explanations for the growing use of emergency food.

Food Stamps

Food stamps and the other federal food assistance programs were created to fill the gaps between income, whatever the source, and household food needs. Why, then, don't food stamps prevent household food emergencies? When requests for emergency food first began to escalate in the early eighties, when they pierced the threshold of public consciousness, many people assumed that people seeking emergency food had not availed themselves of the Food Stamp Program. They were too proud, or they didn't know about the program or didn't realize they were eligible, or they were deterred from applying by the onerous application process. All of these reasons were true for some people, but together they explained only a minority of emergency food requests. Three other groups account for a much greater share of the use of emergency food by people with incomes low enough to qualify them for food stamps: people wrongly denied stamps, people who are in need but not technically eligible, and people who are receiving stamps but cannot make ends meet.

First, there is an unknown number of people who have been erroneously denied stamps to which they were entitled. FSP regulations change frequently and are notoriously complex and difficult to apply. Food stamp manuals often run hundreds of pages. Even when FSP personnel are well intentioned, well trained, and provided with ample time in which to fill out the requisite forms and enter the necessary data into computers, there are countless opportunities for error. When food stamp workers are overworked and underpaid, poorly trained and infected with a hostile attitude toward applicants, as is far too often the case, errors are common. Applicants who feel they have been wronged can apply for a "fair hearing," and the very high rate at which food stamp workers' decisions are overturned at such hearings suggests that many applicants are indeed wrongfully denied access to the nation's most basic defense against hunger.

What about people whose income is low enough but who are not technically eligible? Most of them are ineligible because they fail the "assets test." The law provides for an assets screen, designed to keep well-off people who are only temporarily without income from using the program. It excludes any household with liquid assets in excess of

$2,000 ($3,000 for households containing at least one elderly person). Stanis Laycock, founder of Project Hope, an emergency food and self-help program in Searsport, Maine, told me about her own experience with the assets screen after her husband was diagnosed with a degenerative brain disease and could no longer work. They applied for Social Security disability, but it took months to get the diagnosis and more months to establish his eligibility. They knew that they would eventually be getting disability insurance, so they weren't too worried at first.

> We had saved our six months of living expenses and all that kind of thing in the bank, so . . . I wasn't real concerned. But then we got to about November. He left work in March. In November, there was no work, no money left, and I was starting to get really scared. We were behind in our mortgage payments. . . . I figured that sooner or later the bank would cut me some slack—what were they going to do, throw me out in the road, when they knew money would eventually come in? But the supermarket wasn't real enthusiastic about extending credit for three or four months. . . . I went to the state because I thought, "Well, maybe we can get some food stamps." But at that time I had $2,500 in an IRA that my husband had given to me. And when the man at the State Food Stamp Office got to that place on my application, he took his pencil and made great big XXXs on the application and said, "I wouldn't go any further with this thing. Look what you've got!" and he threw it across the table. I broke into tears and I left. I cried all the way home.

Ironically, she used the IRA shortly thereafter to pay her taxes, but she wouldn't return to the Food Stamp Office, even when she no longer had her asset, because of the way she was treated there.

A more common barrier in the assets screen is the limit on the book value of a vehicle ($4,600), and the limitation to one vehicle. The vehicle limitations have been a particular problem in rural areas in which a car or truck is a necessity if a family ever hopes to be self-supporting again. Congress has been very slow to adjust upward the maximum value of an allowable vehicle. It is currently $4,600, but it remained stuck at $2,000 for nearly a decade before it was adjusted in the early 1990s. As a result, many studies of emergency food clients have found people in real need but ineligible because of a car they couldn't sell if they wanted to. Congress responded to these reports by "indexing" the vehicle value limit, but the index was only in effect for a year before the PRWORA "de-indexed" it, a move that will gradually return us to the situation that brought so many rural families to food pantries. The assets screen may make sense as a means of rationing a scarce form of assistance, but the opportunities for individual anomalies are enormous.

Even when assets are not an issue, the process of applying for the stamps is fraught with numerous opportunities for delay; Elaine Owens, a food provider in Benson, Arizona, gave me an example:

> If they don't have a birth certificate, it will take them another six weeks to two months, sometimes three months, to get a birth certificate for every child. I mean, these take months and months. It isn't something you think ahead, "Well, I'm going to go on food subsidy, so I'm going to make sure I have a birth certificate, I'm going to make sure I have something that proves that I pay utilities."

A significant proportion of emergency food recipients in virtually any pantry is composed of people who are waiting for a food stamp application to be processed.

Even when people finally qualify for food stamps, however, they frequently cannot make ends meet. This third category, people who are receiving the stamps but still need emergency food, is by far the largest. Almost all food pantries report that demand goes up at the end of the month, when stamps run out. Two and a half to three weeks is the typical period for which clients report making the stamps last. The fundamental reason why the FSP doesn't do away with the need for emergency food lies in the assumptions upon which it is based, the same set of assumptions that underlie the official federal definition of poverty. Basically, food stamps were never designed to provide enough food purchasing power to last the month, except for households with no income at all. They were designed to fill the gap between one-third of the household's food stamp relevant income, that is, its income after certain deductions, and the cost of the Thrifty Food Plan, the Department of Agriculture food plan upon which eligibility and benefit levels are based. If you can purchase the equivalent of the Thrifty Food Plan (TFP) with a third of your income, then, by definition, you are not poor and do not need help from the government. If, however, a third of your income is not sufficient to allow you to spend at the TFP level, then you are officially poor, and the FSP will give you enough stamps to make up the difference between a third of your income—30 percent to be precise—and the cost of the TFP. In practice, the stamp allotment is set at the cost of the TFP, discounted by 30 percent of household income after certain deductions. For the last several years, in recognition of the general inadequacy of the TFP, Congress has directed the secretary of agriculture to use a figure of 103 percent of the TFP as the basis for allotments, but the PRWORA has removed that tiny cushion, also, forcing the standard back down to the TFP and thus cutting benefits to nearly all food stamp households.

When the contemporary FSP was created in the mid 1960s, the 30 percent assumption may have made sense, but it is obsolete now for the same reasons that the poverty line is obsolete: other necessities, especially housing and medical care, cost more (in real or inflation-adjusted terms) than they did in 1964, and there are more goods and services competing for the household dollar. Households that are paying 60 percent or more of their income for rent, as are well over half of poor renters, cannot afford to allocate 30 percent of their income for food. An "excess shelter costs deduction" allows families spending more than half their income for rent to deduct the excess from their income for the purpose of calculating eligibility and benefits, but a cap on this excess shelter cost (currently $231 per month) and an overcall cap on gross income eligibility set at 130 percent of the poverty level limit the effectiveness of this deduction. Legislation enacted in 1995 would have eliminated the cap on excess shelter deductions, but the 1996 PRWORA restores them and further reduces future food stamp benefits by "de-indexing" the standard deduction that all households take as well. Although these cuts may sound minor, they add up. Exclusive of the immigration-related provisions, the PRWORA will cut an estimated $24 billion from the food stamp program over the next five years. Analysts estimate that about two-thirds of the benefit reductions will be borne by families with children, many of them the working poor.

Finally, there is the nature of the Thrifty Food Plan. It was designed as an emergency diet for temporary use. Technically, it is probably nutritionally sound, but the TFP is used to determine a level of expenditure; it is not an eating plan, but a dollar figure, and most households spending at the level of the TFP do not obtain an adequate diet for their investment. The TFP presumes nearly optimal circumstance for the purchase, transportation, storage, and preparation of food. It assumes that recipients are skilled comparison shoppers and that they have the knowledge, skills, equipment, time, and utensils to prepare many dishes from "scratch"—from raw ingredients. But even a food stamp client who has the requisite skills and knowledge to get the biggest nutritional bang for her buck and the desire to do so, may be at a disadvantage compared to the Thrifty Food Plan. The familiar saying that "the poor pay more" has been documented again and again when it comes to food. The TFP is calculated on the assumption that participants have access to a supermarket—or to stores with supermarket price scales; many food stamp customers cannot obtain food at the competitive prices assumed in the calculation of the TFP, or must pay for transportation out of their neighborhoods in order to do so. For these clients, the stamps would run out, even if they did allocate 30 percent of their cash income to food purchase, simply because the prices they must pay are higher than those used to calculate the TFP.

These factors explain why so many needy people are not getting food stamps, and why those who are receiving them often cannot make them last through the month. There are less attractive explanations, as well, of course. It is not really hard to convert food stamps to cash if you have other, more pressing needs. Just offer to shop for a non-food-stamp neighbor, pay for her purchases with your stamps and collect from her in cash. Unscrupulous street dealers will give you a percentage of the face value in cash, or accept them at a discounted rate toward drugs or other illicit goods. A soup kitchen volunteer introduced me to another approach to conversion: "I worked in a grocery store for many years. I was a meat cutter after I got out of the Marine Corps. I hate to say this, but I've seen people come in—and we had a 100 percent guarantee on our meats. They would buy a nice roast for $8 or $10, walk with the roast up to the cash register, pay for it with stamps, walk out the front door, bring the roast back and get cash for it, and then head for the wine counter."

Wine counter, shoe store, doctor, landlord. People convert their food stamps to cash because they have other, more urgent needs, and possibly because it is easier to get help with food than with most other necessities. Most emergency providers I talked with were philosophical about this. "I look at it this way," Elaine Owens told me. "If somebody's hungry, I feed them. And I don't care what their other situation is. I don't care if they've got their food stamps and went drinking or if they're sober, whatever; if they're hungry, I'm going to feed them. That's been my philosophy for fifty years and I continue to stick with it." Attitudes toward the Food Stamp Program ranged from sharp criticism to enthusiastic support, but even providers who felt that some clients abused their stamps were quick to point out that the children were the first to suffer, and they were not to blame. As Hawley Botchford, director of the Harry Chapin Food Bank of Southwest Florida, put it:

> Listen to a child. Say "Are you looking forward to Christmas?" and they get this funny look. Okay, no they're not going to get presents because the mothers can't afford it—it's the end of month. All holidays come at the end of the month! What do we have at the end of the month? No food stamps! There's no school lunches. . . . These kids, they didn't ask to be in this position. Whether or not their father skipped out or whether or not their mother's on drugs, or whether or not their mother is selling their food stamps or whatever, that's not that child's fault! Now, that child still has a potential. And we're denying that child the ability to achieve his or her potential by lack of nutrition while we are throwing it away in the dumpsters daily! To me, this is a sin.

But Are They Really Hungry?

Diversion of food stamps raises the question of the intensity of need. If people were really hungry, would they use their food stamps for shoes or rent? For cigarettes? Are the people who come to kitchens and pantries really *hungry*? For some frontline providers, this is simply not an issue. They welcome all comers, without any requirement that diners be destitute. Volunteer Betty Pilkey in the soup kitchen in Bath, Maine, engaged in active outreach to people she felt could use a hot meal, cheerfully served, and an opportunity for social interaction.

> I get a big kick out of talking the people into coming here to eat. There are a lot of men without wives and then there's little old ladies that are alone. "You're alone, and this'll give you a place to come, sit down, and talk to someone. If you don't like the food, we can always find something"—and they feel like they're not taking charity because we serve them on china dishes, it's not a paper plate thing, and it's not a food line thing. We wait on them. The food bank is very much the same way. You don't make them feel as though they're taking charity. You tell them you have this stuff and you have to give it away.

At the Preble Street Resource Center in Portland, Maine, the staff sees breakfast as a sort of bait to get people into the Center where they can connect with other services, and with each other. They keep the coffee pot running all day, but breakfast is the primary hook. Staff member Elizabeth Optkowski said,

> It's also used by the consumers as a place to socialize. Our agency kind of becomes their dining room and their living room, and a lot of clients come who have apartments, who have food stamps, who could make their own breakfast—they could afford it—but they come because they want to socialize with the workers, they want to socialize with the other clients. At the end of the month, a lot of times, families come in and take food home with them, so that's the time we can do outreach to families.

Not all kitchens, of course, define themselves as places for social interaction. At the soup kitchen in Immokalee, I asked Sister Judy if the diners came partly because they had nothing better to do, since the numbers rose so dramatically on days when there was little work in the fields. "I think they are hungry for the day they come in," she commented, "because . . . there's no socialization. Very little . . . even if they sit with their friends, there is only a little bit of talking. We put music on because the sound of the spoons hitting the bowls is so loud. So I say to people, 'They're not here because they want to socialize, they're here because they're hungry.' " In Immokalee, the need for a meal is aggravated by the housing situation, and most of the diners are so poor, and so hardworking, that the Center would not begrudge them a meal even if they could buy one at the convenience store instead, but what about more typical soup kitchens in more diverse areas?

In general, urban kitchens have little need to fear inundation by the comfortable for a simple but troubling reason. Soup kitchens still carry a deterrent stigma. It might become an issue if any substantial number of non-needy people started to drop in for a free meal, but few will do so. Long lines, uncomfortable waiting conditions, institutional food, lack of choice, all of these factors deter diners who have other alternatives. So does the company. In New York City, the Community Food Resource Center tried to create a community kitchen that would serve a whole range of Harlem residents, paying customers—or rather donating diners—as well as people who needed a free meal. "Our idea was to create a space that would make it comfortable for people to come together from all different walks of life in that neighborhood, for an inexpensive, nutritious meal," explained CFRC's director. The kitchen requested but did not demand a contribution, and at first, most diners did pay, though donations typically did not cover the full cost of the meal, which was subsidized by the Bureau of Nutrition of the State Health Department. Very quickly, however, the program attracted "very downtrodden men;" the paying customers dropped off, and the neediest and most disreputable took over. The community kitchen became a soup kitchen, despite its intentions.

Most people who choose to eat at a soup kitchen probably have very good reasons for doing so. Most often, the very good reason is hunger, and the hunger is obvious. Kathy Goldman told me why CFRC had started doing portion control in the community kitchen of West Harlem, the soup kitchen that evolved from the original neighborhood dining room approach:

We do portion control not just because it is easier and cheaper but because if you are sitting next to somebody and they got breast of chicken and a leg and you only got a leg, we have a fight on our hands. And they get mad at us. It can be a very volatile situation. Nobody is coming there for fun. It is the end of the road. Toward the end of the month, after the first two weeks of the month, when the numbers start going up, people really don't have food. There is a kind of under-the-surface desperation, as nice as people are, they are at the edge. Anybody who is coming here.

In the food pantries, there is less stigma, and the food is more than a meal at a time, so providers have had to work harder to deter the not-so-needy. While many pantries started out providing food to all comers, and some still do, most quickly adopted some sort of requirements for evidence of need. Pantries, after all, obtain food from stores and through food banks from wholesalers and manufacturers, on the grounds that it is going free of charge to people who could not otherwise buy it. Even pantries that have not needed to require proof of need in order to conserve their limited supplies for the truly needy have had to do so in order to satisfy donors that the food would not undermine their own markets. With or without such proof, however, most pantry staff and volunteers seem to be convinced of the need. A member of the board of directors of the pantry in Deer Isle, Maine, told me about an experience she had early in the pantry's life. She stopped by the pantry one day when she was all dressed up because she was on her way to pick up the pantry's check from a statewide fund-raising drive, and her own appearance heightened her sensitivity to the people she saw there. "And I thought, here I am with my little gold earrings and my new this and that, and the place was full of young fishermen . . . the expression on their faces was just heartrending. They hated being there. Absolutely hated it . . . and that's what the people who have never volunteered or don't really know anything about the pantry couldn't know." She went on to tell me that one of the island's oldest and most respected citizens had been very skeptical of the pantry at first—unconvinced of the need for it. "But she went down and sat in her car," and watched the pantry's clients come and go, "and after that she went down and took food every winter, and when you get someone like that on your side, a long-time native, it makes a big difference."

Although there are many areas of the country in which need actually intensifies in the summer, when children are no longer receiving school lunches, Deer Isle feels the heaviest demand in the winter, and this is another factor that convinces pantry volunteers that the need is real. As one volunteer put it,

> I'm sure there's a few that abuse it. There's a bunch in every crowd. But, on the whole, I don't think it's being taken advantage of very much, because we have very few people that come back month after month after month. A lot of people just come in the winter when they have lost their jobs—like, in the summer around here you can go clamming, you can go rake blueberries, you know, you can do a lot in the summertime, more than in the wintertime. And we usually pick up a lot more people in the winter, and then they don't come back when they're on their feet again.

Even the most generous and trusting express skepticism toward some pantry users. "Well, we have delivered food to young girls with two or three children, or more, who come to the door well dressed and in a fairly nice place to live, and that's when I think 'Hmmmmm,' " Deer Isle's former board chairperson told me. "But for every one like that you get ten who are in need. You have to think of it that way." Anyone who has ever taken a statistics course will recognize the choice implied here: a Type One or Type Two Error for food providers. Is it worse to accept as true claims of need that are actually false, or to reject as false claims that are actually true? Should the standard of evidence and proof required be so high that some truly needy will be excluded, or low enough to admit most of the truly needy, inevitably admitting some with false or marginal claims as well? Most emergency food providers have given up any hope of perfection, and faced with the choice, prefer to feed a few freeloaders rather than take the risk of excluding people in real need.

There is more involved here, however, than assessing the truth or falsity of claims of need. At the heart of the question, "Are they really *hungry?*" is a persistent confusion over the definition of *hunger.* As Stanis Laycock explained to me, "People think hunger means you don't have any food and there's nothing and you go for days and days without food.... There are different levels of hunger ... hunger means that people are skipping meals because there's not enough food to go the whole month." Researchers at Cornell undertook an in-depth exploration with women who reported that they had gone hungry or had problems obtaining food in an attempt to understand the meaning of the term from the point of view of those who have experienced it. They found just what Laycock suggested, that their subjects generally had two concepts—a narrower and a broader definition of hunger. As one woman in their original sample summarized:

> Going *hungry*, hungry is when there is absolutely nothing in the house. But going hungry is when you have to eat the same thing all week long and you have no variation from it and you know sooner or later you're gonna run out of that, too, because it's only gonna go so far. So each day you cut the portions down a little bit smaller and a little bit smaller. . . . And you have a tendency to send your kid off to play with somebody else so that they're there at mealtime so that they do eat.

How hungry do people have to be, and for how long, or how often, before we feel that it is appropriate to assist them? Most emergency food providers do not feel that people have to be "*hungry*, hungry" to warrant help; just plain hungry will do.

Toward the end of the 1980s, convinced that our conceptual understanding of hunger was inadequate to the realities of life in a postindustrial society, anti-hunger advocates and scholars began to use the concept of "food security" borrowed from the international development field, and to substitute the term "food insecurity" for hunger. They defined food security as "access by all people at all times to enough food for an active, healthy life. Food security includes, at a minimum (*a*) the ready availability of nutritionally adequate and safe foods, and (*b*) an assured ability to acquire acceptable foods in socially acceptable ways." Defining the problem as "food insecurity" rather than hunger gets us beyond the issue of sensations, and allows us to focus on the social situation and the psychological distress of people who do not have a reliable and secure source of food for themselves and their children. Advocates of the food security approach specifically exclude soup kitchens and food pantries from the roster of socially acceptable sources, along with begging, theft,

and scavenging. In fact, Barbara Cohen and Martha Burt, two leading proponents of the food security concept, define hunger as "the
process of being unable to obtain a nutritionally adequate diet from
non-emergency channels." People who have just finished a hearty
meal at a soup kitchen may not be "hungry" in the everyday sense of
the word, but they may still suffer from "food insecurity" if they do
not know where their next meal is coming from. People who know
their food stamps will run out in the third week of the month may not
be hungry for the first two weeks, but as the month wears on and the
effort to stretch the stamps becomes more arduous, they suffer from
food insecurity.

This is not just a semantic argument. In the mid 1980s, efforts to
measure hunger and count the hungry turned decidedly political, and
at the crux of the issue was the question of whether seeking food
at an emergency food provider was behavioral evidence of hunger.
The next chapter describes the rise of emergency food in the early
1980s, and explores the role of competing definitions of hunger in the
growth of the emergency food phenomenon.

CHAPTER THREE

The Rise of Emergency Food

Cleveland was a big steel town, and was dependent upon the auto industry and the steel industry and suddenly you had a city and surrounding counties that went from 4 and 5 percent unemployment rates to 21 percent unemployment rates, overnight. . . . There was a dramatic increase in what was being termed at that time the "New Poor." These were people who had historically not been poor, they had been employed people, they were primarily homeowners who had no money for food because they were struggling to meet their mortgage payments. Suddenly they—entire communities—were being thrown into crisis overnight, and emergency food providers started to spring up there very quickly in direct response. . . . Churches were the first ones to move into the fray; the church would be the first place a family would go to say "I have a problem; can you help me?" At the same time, you had a change in government philosophy toward benefits so that at the very moment that suddenly you had this whole new population in crisis, you had a government cutting back on exactly the programs that in theory they should be expanding. So individual church and community groups were starting to respond, simply, to what they saw in their neighborhoods as a need for help.

—Liz Krueger
Community Food Resource Center

IN THE EARLY 1980s, all of the factors that send people to soup kitchens and food pantries—unemployment and underemployment, excessive shelter costs, inadequate public assistance, and reduced food assistance—were suddenly intensified and made visible by a dramatic combination of escalating need and reduced social provision. On the one hand there was a recession, widely regarded as the worst since the Great Depression, which threw hundreds of thousands of people out of work and made near ghost towns out of some of the nation's once thriving industrial centers. Terms like "empty smoke stack," "Rust Belt" and "New Poor" entered our vocabulary. The poverty rate, which had hovered between 11 and 12 percent throughout the 1970s, rose steadily in the early 1980s, reaching a peak of 15.2 percent in 1983. On the other hand, the long, slow erosion of public assistance benefits that had characterized the seventies was suddenly overshadowed by a major assault on domestic social spending. Ronald Reagan sought and obtained from Congress a series of reductions in programs for poor people: cuts in income supports, Medicaid, housing assistance, energy assistance, unemployment compensation, and food assistance were finalized in the Omnibus Budget Reconciliation Act of 1981, commonly referred to as OBRA. Additional cuts followed in the next budget.

The Reagan administration claimed that these were not "cuts" but rather reductions in the rate of growth. Technically, that was true of most of the cuts; they did not reduce spending over previous years, but rather reduced it over what it would have been if the law had remained the same. The Congressional Budget Office estimated in 1983 that such reductions in human services spending would total $110 billion over the period encompassed by fiscal years 1982–1985. In the context of the rapid rise of need associated with the recession, as well as normal population growth and the impact of inflation, however, the overall impact of the OBRA changes was to reduce both the numbers of people eligible for various programs and the benefits they received. For example, changes in the Aid to Families with Dependent Children Program, then the nation's primary income transfer for poor children and their families, left about half a million former recipient families totally ineligible and reduced benefits to another 300,000. According to economist Martha Burt, "When the General Accounting Office assessed the effects of the 1981 OBRA, it found that many AFDC families who lost eligibility (1) suffered a substantial loss of income that they could not make up; (2) had fallen below the poverty level; (3) had not replaced health coverage formerly provided by Medicaid; and (4) faced more emergency situations such as refusal of medical care because of lack of funds, or running out of food."

"Running out of food," of course, was not confined to families who lost eligibility for AFDC. The New Poor of the recession were turning to food pantries in increasing numbers, and the homeless were showing up for meals at soup kitchens. Existing kitchens and pantries began reporting dramatically increased numbers. A 1983 survey by the Center for Budget and Policy Priorities, for example, found that more than half of the agencies included in its survey of sixteen areas of the country reported that the number of food baskets or free meals that they provided had increased 50 percent or more during the year between February 1982 and February 1983; nearly a third of the agencies reported a doubling of their services. In addition, areas with food banks reported a sharp increase in the number of programs providing such food assistance. Labor Union locals set up pantries in many of the Rust Belt communities, and suburban churches began to find themselves facing pleas for food from their own parishioners and from people passing through in search of work.

In traditionally poor neighborhoods, where food distribution had been occurring on an informal basis for a long time, the numbers increased and the clientele changed: "It used to be just two or three people a day coming for food," Brother Giles Needler of the San Damiano Friary told a New York Times reporter late in 1981. "Now it seems that the doorbell is always ringing. And before it was the knights of the road. Now it's mothers with five kids, families." Soup kitchens noticed a change in the clientele, as well. According to a Wall Street Journal report early in 1983, "As the nation's recession lingers, more families are swallowing their pride and taking handouts. They are crowding into public feeding halls to the point where they often outnumber the bums and shopping-bag ladies who for years have had charity soup kitchens mostly to themselves." The Journal, reporting from the midwest, quoted the Salvation Army commander in Tulsa, Oklahoma: "Most people we fed a year ago were derelicts and alcoholics, but today it's mothers and small children. We aren't shocked to see children anymore."

In the atmosphere of crisis that pervaded the anti-poverty community in the early 1980s, it was easy to focus upon the recession and the OBRA cuts as the prime suspects in the rise of destitution. Both the recession and the "Reagan Revolution," however, were only the visible tips of the icebergs of economic decline and a weakening commitment to the welfare state that had been developing for a long time. As Michael Harrington argued in 1984, the new American poverty "is not . . . the creation of Ronald Reagan . . . the structures of misery today are not simply the work of the ideological rigidity of a President . . . They are the results of massive economic and social transformations. . . ." The United States, according to Harrington, "joined the global economy for the first time" around 1970, "and the American poor began to suffer from the international division of labor in unprecedented ways." As economic security declined, so did willingness to pay for assistance to the poor. Both the assault on the welfare safety net and the rising need for assistance that characterized the early 1980s were rooted in large-scale global changes that were poorly understood at best.

Defining the Problem as Hunger

Certainly such massive changes were not likely to be effectively addressed by dishing out soup and handing out grocery baskets. In order to understand how soup kitchens and food pantries became the response of choice to the escalating needs unleashed by the recession of the early 1980s, we need to understand just how that need came to be defined as "hunger," and that requires a brief excursion into the sociology of social problems. Sociologists have argued for quite some time that social problems don't exist "out there," as objective realities, but rather in a socially negotiated process of selection and labeling. That does not mean that there is no harmful social condition objectively present. To the contrary, it means that among the enormous number and wide range of harmful social conditions, only a few are recognized and accorded the attention of society at any given point in time. As Herbert Blumer wrote in the classic statement on the subject in the early 1970s, "the recognition by a society of its social problems is a highly selective process, with many harmful social conditions and arrangements not even making a bid for attention, and with others falling by the wayside in what is frequently a fierce competitive struggle. Many push for societal recognition but only a few come out the end of the funnel." Of course, it is not really the problems themselves that are competing for societal recognition, but the people and organizations who have adopted such problems and want to promote them.

The "social constructionists" who have espoused this view of social problems have designated such people and groups "claims-makers." They talk about successful and unsuccessful claims and about the claims-making process, and analyze the roles of the media, powerful individuals, celebrities, triggering events, and well-financed or poorly resourced organizations in a successful claims-making process. Further, they argue that the essential nature of a social problem is not necessarily obvious from the outset. It, too, is socially constructed in a process they call "typification." As Joel Best has written, "Claims-makers inevitably characterize problems in particular ways. They emphasize some aspects and not others; they promote specific orientations; and they focus on particular causes and advocate particular solutions." Despite its sometimes inelegant vocabulary, the social constructionist perspective is a particularly useful one in studying harmful social conditions because it allows us to distinguish between the underlying condition and the labels that society applies to it, and it calls our attention to the interplay of politics, ideology, and luck in the process by which a condition gets recognition and acquires its name. How did the massive global economic dislocations that led to, but did not end with, the recession of the early 1980s come to be called "hunger," to be typified in such a way that food programs seemed an appropriate response?

First, there was the language of those who were experiencing the problem. They had other needs besides food, of course, but the need for food arises sooner and with greater urgency than most others. It takes a while to lose your home, but you get hungry right away, and when you do, it is hard to think about anything else. But there is another reason why people ask for food more readily than for other forms of help: they can see that there is plenty, and they can sense that food assistance is the easiest kind of help to get. When was the last time a panhandler on the street asked you for a contribution toward a night's lodgings? Even in the coldest weather, most beggars will ask for money for *food*; they know what works.

The panhandlers were another important factor in the rise of at least the soup kitchen side of the emergency food phenomenon. Although not all panhandlers are homeless, and most homeless people do not engage in begging, the public tends to equate the two, and an increase in street begging was one of the factors that called attention to the growth of homelessness in the early eighties. The same factors that caused the reported increase in household poverty—unemployment, low wages, inadequate public assistance benefits—contributed to the increase in homelessness, as did deinstitutionalization of the mentally ill, cutbacks in supportive social services, increases in drug addiction, and reductions in funding for addiction treatment programs. For homeless people who take refuge in shelters, whether individuals or families, prepared meal programs become an essential lifeline. And for those hardy souls who spurn the shelters and make their lives in rail and bus terminals, heating grates, abandoned buildings, or assorted habitats of their own construction, soup kitchens and sandwich distribution programs are sometimes the margin of survival. An increase in homelessness almost automatically leads to an increase in the demand for the prepared meal part of emergency food.

This does not fully explain, however, why so many churches and other organizations decided to start such food programs in the early eighties. After all, if the problem is homelessness, why not offer some form of shelter? Some groups did respond by creating temporary shelter, and some by creating permanent housing. In New York City, for example, churches and synagogues responded to Mayor Koch's 1981 call for assistance. By 1988, 132 churches and synagogues were part of the Partnership for the Homeless, which meant that they offered beds at night, usually bracketed by an evening meal and a breakfast. But many groups and organizations that wanted to "do something to help the homeless" were not prepared to provide shelter—too costly, too intrusive, too risky, too close for comfort, too much work—or could offer shelter to only a tiny fraction of the people seeking help. A hot meal, however, a chance to come in from the cold, a nourishing respite, were within their means, especially within the means of the large, downtown churches and synagogues that had well-equipped kitchens that often went unused for most of the week. By defining the problem as "hunger," these organizations brought it within the range of their resources.

The definition of the problem of poverty as "hunger," or even "hunger and homelessness," however, was not simply a grassroots attempt to respond to visible needs with available resources. It occurred at the societal level as well, in the realm of politics. The Reagan administration did two things in 1981 that, taken together, almost guaranteed that poverty and unemployment and to a lesser extent, homelessness, would be portrayed as hunger. The first was to include the federal nutrition programs on the hit list of domestic social programs cut back by OBRA. The nutrition cuts, especially food stamps and child nutrition, were substantial. The Congressional Budget Office estimated that over the combined fiscal years of 1982 through 1985, $12.2 billion less was available for food assistance than would have been true if the law had not been changed. But it was not just the size of the cuts that led to the hunger definition; it was the size, skill, and power of the network of individuals and organizations that were committed to protecting these programs, the same anti-hunger network or "hunger lobby" that had worked so successfully in the seventies for the expansion and improvement of food assistance. By targeting food assistance, the Reagan administration activated a cadre of particularly skilled and effective claims-makers.

The battle lines were drawn as soon as the cuts were proposed. The anti-hunger advocates argued that nearly all of those receiving food assistance benefits needed every penny's worth, every calorie, they were getting, and that expansions of the programs were needed to counter the effects of the recession. The Reagan administration argued that the food programs were bloated and full of cheating and abuse. They could be cut, the president argued, without harming the "truly needy." No, the advocates answered, cutting federal nutrition programs would inevitably produce hunger. The hunger lobby did not prove powerful enough to prevent the cuts, but it was powerful enough to set the terms of much of the debate. Still, the hunger label might not have stuck had it not been for the Reagan administration's response to the nation's dairy surplus.

The Politics of Cheese

In the autumn of 1981, with winter just around the corner and millions of Americans feeling the pinch of hard times, the press discovered that tons of publicly owned dairy products were in danger of rotting in government storage facilities. "From California to Georgia," the *New York Times* reported in October, "the Government stores 777 million pounds of nonfat dry milk, 544 million pounds of cheese and 274 million pounds of butter." It was the facility in Kansas City, however, that drew the lion's share of the attention; it was the largest, and perhaps the most picturesque of the facilities. The *Times* described it this way:

> America's biggest dairy case is deep inside the cold, dark, limestone tunnels under Kansas City. There, in the refrigerator-freezer that is the Agriculture Department's Inland Storage and Distribution Center, are 200 million pounds of surplus products, barrels of cheese and boxes of butter, stacked like frozen pillars and stretching over acres of gray stone floor.
>
> Dairy products bought under the Government's price support programs constantly roll in by truck and rail; 20 million pounds are added to the national inventory each week.

In fact, the dairy surplus had attracted the attention of Second Harvest at least a year before the press accounts of the fall of 1981. The food banking organization had enlisted the support of Arizona senator Dennis DeConcini who succeeded in attaching an amendment to agricultural legislation directing the Department of Agriculture to distribute surplus farm products to eligible food banks. Then Reagan was elected, and, as *The Progressive* explained, "when the new USDA administrators came aboard, this new program did not get ranked as a priority."

Eventually, however, the costs of not distributing the food were made public. What *The Progressive* described as "USDA's bovine pace" in implementing the legislation combined with the rapid accumulation of surplus dairy products acquired under price-support mechanisms to make the Reagan administration look particularly bad. "So far the Administration, acting in concert with the conservative Congress, has excluded one million people from the Food Stamp Program. Other substantial cuts are planned, all in the interests of a balanced budget. But in the case of this program, the bureaucrats at USDA are turning their backs on an effort that would not only mitigate any harm done by cuts in the food stamp program but also save money. The USDA now spends more than $36 million a year to store the surplus dairy products."

The combination of food waste at public expense in the midst of growing need proved irresistible. Three days before Christmas, President Ronald Reagan signed a measure releasing 30 million pounds of government surplus cheese for distribution to needy people. "At a time when American families are under increasing financial pressure," Mr. Reagan declared, "their government cannot sit by and watch millions of pounds of food turn to waste." In keeping with the president's emphasis on voluntarism, the distribution was to be accomplished through nonprofit organizations in states that chose to take advantage of the offer.

The dairy surplus was a magnet for media attention. Nearly everywhere it was distributed the cheese resulted in the creation of long, photogenic lines. Since its release was not authorized until late in December, there was almost a guarantee that some of these lines would keep people waiting in freezing weather. The following excerpt from the *New York Times* about the distribution in Washington, D.C., is typical:

> Stomping their feet and looking doubtful, poor people in the capital's northwest quarter lined up for more than three hours in the cold yesterday, waiting for the Government to finally yield some of its vast storehouse of cheese that has accumulated over the years as the result of Washington's subsidy of dairy farmers.
>
> For hundreds of these people, the subsidy program that is such a crucial issue year after year to the lawmakers downtown and to the

farmers out West came across on Sixth Street as just another Government runaround. For the supply of five-pound bricks of cheese ran out before the hungry crowd that wrapped for two blocks around the First Rising Mt. Zion Baptist Church could be served.

Some of the cheese turned out to have overstayed its welcome in the government's warehouses: it was already moldy. *Time* described it this way:

> As a present to the poor, the free cheese has its drawbacks. Needy recipients will have to scrape mold off some of the cheese, which has been stored in 150 warehouses or limestone caves in 35 states for as long as 18 months. But, insists Merritt Sprague, a commodity supervisor for the Department of Agriculture, "mold does not produce toxin that is harmful."

Even bad press is press. The cheese distribution, with its memorable details, called attention to the need, and helped to define it as hunger. It was embarrassing for an administration that was trying to convince Congress and the public that the Food Stamp Program and other federal nutrition programs were serving people who did not need their help. The long lines sent a message to many observers: If people were willing to wait that long, in those conditions, for a five-pound brick of possibly moldy processed American cheese, they *must* be hungry. Clearly the Special Dairy Distribution Program (SDDP), as the cheese giveaway was formally known, helped to put hunger on the American social agenda, and helped to mobilize the concern that was expressed by the creation of more and more soup kitchens and food pantries.

The cheese distribution had practical consequences for the expansion of the emergency food system, as well. State and county governments, United Way organizations, and other designated Emergency Distribution Organizations recruited thousands of volunteers to handle the actual distribution, and some of these, impressed by the need that they saw, went back to their churches and community organizations and initiated the establishment of food pantries. In some cases, churches and community centers that served as distribution points concluded that, since they had set up a space and a system to distribute the cheese, and since people were clearly in need of food, they might as well begin handing out other supplies too. Some food banks were authorized to handle the surplus dairy products; thus their inventories were reinforced by the infusion of cheese and, eventually, butter.

With hunger a recurrent topic on the nightly news, and dairy surpluses calling attention to the abundance of food available, a sort of snowball process occurred in many communities. As more kitchens and pantries sprang up, more food drives and appeals for financial support were organized, more people became involved with hunger-related activities, and more hunger stories appeared in the press. Each new kitchen or pantry, and each hunger walkathon or other hunger-related event helped to reinforce the definition of the problem as *hunger* in the public mind, and each new round of publicity for hunger elicited more anti-hunger activity.

In some localities, a hunger task force or commission or committee was organized to provide technical assistance to groups that wanted to create such programs. The process in Los Angeles was probably indicative. Diane Wright was hired in 1982 by the Los Angeles Interfaith Hunger Coalition; her job included compiling a directory of food programs, producing a manual on how to start a pantry or kitchen, and consulting with groups that wanted to start them—or expand an existing service. "I was busy all the time," she recalls. "I was the most popular woman in town . . . there was an explosion of food pantries . . . I got the same phone call five hundred times: 'You don't know what's going on out here—we've got people hanging out on the doorstep of our church, living in the parking lot, . . . we're getting more homeless people, . . . we want to start a food program.' " From organizations that already had programs, she got calls asking for help in identifying new sources of food, help in starting a food bank, or help in coping with a fundamental change in the nature of the requests they were receiving. "We're seeing the same people over and over again."

The Ideology of Voluntarism

Ronald Reagan may have fostered the pantry population explosion with his stirring calls for a return to the American voluntary tradition. Reagan made the call for increased voluntary action a centerpiece of his first term, commissioning a study of strategies for promoting voluntarism by the American Enterprise Institute, appointing a Presidential Task Force on Private Sector Initiatives, establishing the President's Volunteer Action Awards, and creating a President's Advisory Council on Private Initiatives. The president linked the call for voluntary action directly to his other great crusade, reduction of social spending. In his September 1981 address to the nation on proposed spending cuts, for example, after asserting that "We can be compassionate about human needs without being complacent about budget extravagance," he went on to say that his plan for reductions in a wide range of social programs

> doesn't mean we should discontinue trying to help where help is needed. Government must continue to do its share, but I ask all of you as private citizens to join this effort, too. . . .
>
> The truth is we've let Government take away many things we once considered were really ours to do voluntarily out of the goodness of our hearts and a sense of community pride and neighborliness.
>
> I believe many of you want to do those things again, want to be involved if only someone will ask you or will offer the opportunity. Well, we intend to make that offer.
>
> We are launching a nationwide effort to encourage our citizens to join with us in finding where need exists and then to organize volunteer programs to meet that need.

The extraordinary breadth of the political spectrum involved in emergency food programs undoubtedly reflects Ronald Reagan's encouragement. His invitation was probably welcome among some conservatives. The hunger politics of the seventies had left them in an awkward position. If they were against further expansion of tax-funded public programs, they could be painted as "for" hunger. Reagan's call to "organize volunteer programs to meet that need" gave them an opportunity to reclaim a piece of the moral high ground and prove that liberals do not have a monopoly on compassion.

Conservatives don't have a monopoly on compassion, either, however, and liberals found themselves in a bind. On the one hand, many were skeptical of the emergency food approach, and worried that cheese handouts would be substituted for food stamps or school meals. On the other hand, many politically liberal pastors and social service workers were confronted with the day-to-day reality of requests for food. Concerned about the increasingly harsh social environment, some worried that if they didn't feed hungry people, no one would. The organization that Diane Wright worked for had a strong progressive bent, and she attributed much of the hunger she encountered directly to the cuts in federal programs. She recalls the resulting dilemma:

> So it was really a weird job for me, personally, because I was helping people who couldn't stand to see hungry people in their neighborhoods and their church community or temple community. So they were providing a direct service, which they felt they had to do and I felt they had to do. And at the same time, we were all thinking. "Here we are handing out bags of food while those people in Washington are constantly cutting the programs, and they're causing poverty and making things worse." As far as I was concerned, the people in Washington had blood on their hands . . . but I wasn't going to stand by and watch people suffer just to make a political point.

Some liberals saw the creation of soup kitchens and food pantries as a way to promote contact between their more conservative friends, colleagues, or parishioners and hungry poor people and thus combat the stereotypes that were being so widely and effectively broadcast. And among those with experience in dealing with government, some were drawn in through their alliances with churches and community organizations in poor neighborhoods. That is, many local anti-hunger groups had worked for years to build coalitions with "indigenous" groups in poor areas in an effort to build a popular movement to sustain and lend credibility to their advocacy efforts. As these neighborhood groups began distributing emergency food, they turned to their advocate friends for help in dealing with government regulations and other problems, and before long, the advocates found themselves knee-deep in food pantries.

Evidence of Hunger

Probably the single most important factor in drawing uncomfortable progressives into the emergency food project, however, was its surprising utility as a measure of hunger. The rising numbers at soup kitchens and food pantries appeared to confirm the hunger lobby's arguments that the proposed cutbacks in food assistance would leave people hungry. Thus they provided a powerful counter to the Reagan administration's claims that the "truly needy" were protected from the budget cutter's axe. It is not an accident that several of the earliest and most widely publicized studies to document the rise of pantries and kitchens were conducted not by food bankers or emergency food providers, and not by the promotors of the new voluntarism, but by the beleaguered anti-hunger organizations that had been working for more than a decade to make such programs unnecessary. Frustrated in their attempts to prevent the budget reductions from falling heavily upon poor people, anti-hunger groups turned their attention to documenting the consequences of the cuts.

Many local or state advocacy groups produced hunger reports covering their own areas. The Food Research and Action Center maintains a collections of such reports, and the numbers tell us something about the level of interest in hunger. According to Marion Nestle and Sally Guttmacher, who surveyed state hunger studies in the early 1990s, the index "lists three studies completed in 1981, 19 in 1982, 31 in 1983, 40 in 1984 and an additional 30 or so for each of the three subsequent years." By 1991, there were almost 250 hunger reports in the collection. Other studies were national in scope. The United Church of Christ released a study in January of 1983. The Center for Budget and Policy Priorities published "Soup Lines and Food Baskets," in the spring of that year, and during the summer, both the Salvation Army and the U.S. General Accounting Office released reports on hunger and food assistance. In August, the National Council of Churches joined the list. Virtually all of these studies relied upon increased demand at soup kitchens and food pantries as a major indicator of mounting hunger.

The social constructionist perspective is useful again, in understanding what happened next. In order to gain public attention and attract societal resources, they argue, a social problem needs not only publicity, but also *legitimacy*. "It may seem strange," wrote Herbert Blumer, "to speak of social problems having to become legitimated. Yet after gaining initial recognition, a social problem must acquire social endorsement if it is to be taken seriously and move forward in its career. It must acquire a necessary degree of respectability which entitles it to consideration in the recognized arenas of public discussion." The advocates' claims of widespread hunger might have been dismissed as self-serving had they not found powerful allies among the nation's mayors, state and local officials involved in the distribution of the dairy surplus, and the very voluntary sector groups that had heeded Ronald Reagan's call for a rebirth of voluntarism. The mayors responded first.

Politically, mayors are the miners' canaries of recession. Because recession tends to be concentrated in particular industries, it is also concentrated in specific localities, and the local tax base is frequently hard hit. At the same time, mayors of large cities are often the people who have to cope with the real life fallout of federal budget cuts. In the early 1980s, many of America's big-city mayors were caught between declining revenues and escalating needs, due in part to OBRA cuts. In 1982, the United States Conference of Mayors, an organization that was formed in 1933 to coordinate the relationships between mayors and the federal government in the depths of the Depression, surveyed its membership to assess the impact of OBRA at the local level. The survey found that demand for emergency food and shelter had increased dramatically; in the fifty-five cities that participated in the study, the report estimated that less than half of the need for emergency services—shelter, food, fuel, income, and medical assistance—was being met. Several mayors, notably Ernest Morial of New Orleans and Coleman Young of Detroit, declared "hunger emergencies" in their cities, pointing to lengthening lines at soup kitchens and food pantries, and called for immediate federal emergency assistance on a par with disaster relief. In the summer of 1983, the Conference put out a second study, *Hunger in American Cities*, and then began issuing annual updates on hunger and homelessness. The mayors' demands became media pegs for increased coverage of hunger and food distribution, and lent the credibility of their offices to the advocates' claims.

The Uses of Emergency

In this process a very significant change occurred in the "emergency" component of emergency food. The label *emergency food* had been applied to food distribution programs, especially pantries, for some time, because they provided food to households experiencing "food emergencies," that is, to households that were running out of food and lacked the money to purchase more. The mayors' declaration of a "hunger emergency," however, changed the connotation from a household emergency to a societal emergency, and the new meaning quickly took hold. It is easy to see why the mayors resonated with the broader meaning: they were seeking emergency assistance for their communities. Likewise, it is easy to see why traditional anti-hunger advocates were attracted by the sense of urgency that the term "emergency" implies. The connotation would hardly have stuck, however, if it had not been useful to many actors in the emergency food drama. The idea that the growth of need was an emergency—a time-limited, unusual, urgent phenomenon—was functional or convenient for almost all of those involved: for the people who sought help at food pantries and soup kitchens, for emergency food providers themselves, for the media, for the Reagan administration and its allies, and perhaps for onlookers in the larger society.

For the people who turned to soup kitchens and food pantries for help, the term "emergency food" was perversely comforting. It implied that they hadn't lost their jobs forever, although it turned out that many of them had. An emergency is inherently temporary; things will get better; the emergency will be over. For those given to self-blame, the notion of emergency can be a relief of a different sort. We associate the term with things we can do nothing to prevent and little to avoid: floods, fires, hurricanes. If this is an emergency, it can't be my fault. More pervasively, perhaps, an emergency justifies, indeed dictates, adjusting one's expectations. We can do things in an emergency that do not live up to the demands we usually make on ourselves, without totally surrendering our standards. As one unemployed autoworker put it to a journalist who interviewed him in a Cleveland, Ohio, soup kitchen in the spring of 1983, "This is the first time I've been in a soup kitchen, and I'm not too proud of it, but I didn't eat yesterday." A mother of four, interviewed in Salt Lake City, Utah, for the same article, focused on the temporality of the situation as she declined to give her name or be photographed: "I don't want anybody to see me; I want to be back on my feet before anybody sees me."

Among providers, very much the same set of characteristics of an emergency is relevant. Anticipated brief duration was especially important. "If I had really known the extent of the hunger problem, I don't know if I would have gotten involved. I guess I thought maybe we could feed people for a little while and then it would clear up," Emma Williams told a reporter for New York City's *Daily News*, describing a food pantry she helped to set up in 1983. Madeline Lund helped to start a food pantry in her own church in Chicago's Irving Park neighborhood in the early eighties and now serves as the liaison between Chicago's food bank, the Greater Chicago Food Depository, and kitchens and pantries throughout the city. As she explained, "The people that are working in this kind of work thought that they were doing something temporarily, thought that this was an emergency need that would be met and then would disappear, like the breadlines in the Depression." The issue of standards also affects providers. You meet an emergency with whatever is at hand; you don't worry about the niceties of nutrition and balanced diets. You make do with the old stove and the freezer in the basement; you use paper plates and cups. You don't invest in new equipment because this is a short-term project, and you do not impose the same standards, on yourselves or your clients, that you might if you thought you were signing on for the duration of a long war.

For the Reagan administration, the functions of the emergency label were at once more subtle and more consequential. Like the clients and the providers, the issue of temporality was important. Any assistance it offered, as in the great cheese giveaway, could be temporary and time-limited, and this was consistent not only with its budgetary concerns but also with its ideology. If the supply-side economic theories and the behavioral critique of the poor underlying the OBRA cuts were accurate, the pain induced by the cuts would be short-lived, i.e., temporary. It was important, if for no other reason than ideological consistency, to profess a belief that any suffering that might be occurring would soon be eliminated by an economic recovery to be induced by the medicine of Reaganomics. The emergency would be over when the affluent began investing the money returned to them by tax cuts in new productive endeavors, and the poor availed themselves of the resulting job opportunities. If the situation was an emergency, then strong medicine was in order, and temporary suffering could be tolerated on the way to a greater good. The lack of standards associated with emergency behavior was also extraordinarily useful to the Reagan administration, which handed out cheese to the states with almost no specification of the circumstances under which it was to be given away. In an emergency, "anything goes."

Pressure for Congressional Action

Ironically, it was the Reagan administration's ideological commitment to smaller government and voluntarism that led to congressional action to expand and institutionalize the commodity distribution system. Both the U.S. Department of Agriculture and the state agencies that contracted to receive the cheese and pass it along to nonprofits to distribute initially expected the December 1981 release of 30 million pounds of cheese to be a one-time offer. In keeping with its anti-government stance, the administration sent out the cheese with virtually no rules and regulations; the implicit message was to get the cheese out as quickly as possible. As the storage charges and the dairy inventories escalated, however, the administration offered additional allocations of both cheese and butter. Once the cheese had attracted the attention of the media and linked the dairy surplus directly to hunger in the public mind, the government no longer had the option of destroying the cheese or letting it rot in the privacy of underground storage facilities. High price supports brought new dairy products in faster than the USDA could ship them out. By the spring of 1983, the states had taken possession of more than 300 million pounds of cheese and 130 million pounds of butter, and Congress began hearing from disgruntled administrators back home. The original SDDP did not provide any funds for states or local distribution organizations, and the Reagan administration opposed introducing such funds, eliciting sharp criticism from program administrators, who were incurring costs they could not continue to absorb.

Testimony by the director of the Greater Philadelphia Food Bank before a committee of the House of Representatives in March 1983 was typical:

> The cheese and dairy distribution program has been a success only because of the thousands of organizations who have participated, and in spite of the clumsiness of the design—and I use the word loosely—of this program. The costs to these organizations have been tremendous and many organizations in the future will not participate . . . because of no money being available for administration, transportation, and storage. . . . For the administration to suggest that no money need be available for distribution is ludicrous and self-serving. It always costs to give something away. For the administration to say that the past distributions are an example of what method can be followed in the future shows absolutely no understanding of the limits of the finances and the cooperative patience of charitable organizations. I think I can state with accuracy that no nonprofit organization will run its program into the red to assist the Government to distribute foods that are limited in variety, offer a limited amount of food to our needy citizens, and bails (sic) the Government out of an embarrassment that the Government itself has caused.

She asked not only for administrative funds, but also for delivery of commodities in family-sized units, "with all of the information about contents and nutrition currently required of the private food industry," with a minimum of required paperwork, on a regular and predictable schedule. Further, she warned against setting uniform eligibility criteria: "Individual charities must be able to establish their own criteria based on their program goals, as long as there is at least a self-declared eligibility on the part of individual recipients." She concluded by telling Congress that, as a taxpayer, she would rather see her tax dollars go to the needy through the basic federal nutrition programs such as food stamps and child nutrition "than go to an outdated price-support program for farmers and an accompanying commodities distribution program that really amounts to a trickle down to the poor. . . . it must be said that commodities distribution to the poor is neither a solution to the elimination of surpluses stored in Government warehouses nor to the problems of hunger in our Nation. It is simply a Band-Aid, a quick fix, and more concrete measures must eventually be taken."

State governments joined in telling Congress that they could not afford to continue the work unless some form of reimbursement for storage, transportation, and administrative costs were established. In fact, the commodity distribution projects had put the state governments in a bind. "There is no such thing as free cheese" might easily have become their motto. They could not do the work of intrastate distribution without hiring additional staff or diverting staff time from other tasks, and they often had to contract for warehouses and transportation. But as far as the public was concerned, the cheese was *free;* the taxpayers had already paid for it. A state that refused to take part on the grounds that participation was too costly risked appearing penny wise but pound foolish. No one really wanted to be left out of the bargain.

Most states and localities had been able to make temporary arrangements, often relying heavily upon volunteers, for the first few distributions of the "emergency" phase. When the distributions became larger and more frequent, however, totally voluntary operations became unrealistic. As the secretary of agriculture of the state of Wisconsin told a congressional committee, "You can only go to the well so often." His volunteer distribution system was beginning to unravel, and warehouses that had been storing the cheese for free when they thought it was a one-time event had begun to send bills, bills which the state agency could not pay, since it had no money allocated in its budget for such purposes.

Meanwhile, to complicate matters further, the commercial cheese industry was growing restive. Government handouts, the National Cheese Institute claimed, were reducing cheese sales and cutting into profits. USDA studies confirmed a decrease in sales, and the secretary of agriculture ordered a cutback in the rate of distribution, angering state and local agencies that had been gearing up to handle more, and subjecting the administration to another round of accusations of heartless indifference to the poor, and another round of bad press. Further, once attention was drawn to the federal stockpiles, local program administrators began asking for the other surpluses—cornmeal, for example, and flour and honey—that the Commodity Credit Corporation of the Department of Agriculture was holding in large quantities. The USDA offered to distribute some of the other CCC stocks in lieu of the cheese, but neither Congress nor the public was impressed with the administration's offer.

Too great a focus on the practical objections and concerns of state and local administrators obscures the sense of outrage that was also communicated to Congress. The comptroller of the City of New York, Harrison J. Goldin, labeled the situation a "national scandal," pointing out that the $2.2 billion the government would spend to purchase and store dairy products that year was roughly equal to the cuts in food stamps, Medicaid, and AFDC. He undertook to "mobilize all those who are repelled by the image of surplus food rotting in storehouses while Americans starve." Many who testified at the spate of hunger hearings that took place in Washington and around the country in the spring of 1983 told Congress that the situation was embarrassing, that it was reminiscent of the Great Depression, and that food handouts were too inadequate and too demeaning to be a serious response to deep economic problems. "There is a stigma associated with accepting any kind of a handout," Euclid, Ohio, social worker Walter Hoag told a subcommittee of the House Agriculture Committee when it held hearings in Cleveland. "Breadlines and soup kitchens, whether called pantries, caring and sharing, or cupboards connote a depression, and in another definition connote depression, being depressed." The director of the Greater Cleveland Community Foodbank, after stressing that any expanded distribution of commodities "must not be done at the expense of the entitlement programs," went on to argue that "any distribution of commodities should be temporary, and not handled in such a way that Government dumps its embarrassment on the backs of the poor. Frankly, that is the only reason we are discussing commodities. There is this embarrassment, the embarrassment of a price-support program gone wrong."

By the spring of 1983, Congress was ready to act. Its first move was limited in both scope and duration. In March, Congress added provisions for an expanded commodity distribution program to legislation (PL 98-8) called the Emergency Jobs Bill. Title II of the bill, introduced originally by Senator Bob Dole as S.17, created the Temporary Emergency Food Assistance Program (TEFAP). It provided for the distribution of additional surplus commodities held by the Department of Agriculture, adding rice, cornmeal, and honey to the dairy products of the SDDP, and it allocated funds to the states and to local and private agencies to reimburse them for administrative costs, but it specified that all of the money had to be spent by September 30, less than six months away. It was clearly intended to be a short-term measure. As Senator Dole said in a hearing shortly after its passage, "We would hope we are not trying to create a new entitlement program. S.17 was designed to be an emergency measure. At least that is how I view it." He added, however, a bit plaintively and with considerable prescience, "I assume others will want to continue it forever once it starts."

He was right. Before the ink was even dry on PL 98-8, no fewer than six bills proposing more permanent commodity distribution programs were under consideration. Three different congressional subcommittees held hearings on these bills, not only in Washington, but in field investigations around the country. One result was to keep the hunger issue in front of both the Congress and the public. Another was to lay federal foundations for an expanded emergency food system. A bill sponsored by Representative Leon Panetta passed in September, authorizing TEFAP for two additional years, requiring states to tighten eligibility requirements, and continuing funding, although at a reduced rate, for administrative, storage, and transportation expenses. With the prospect of large quantities of federal commodities and the promise of continued financial help, more community organizations were drawn into the food distribution process, and communities without food banks were given a new incentive to develop them. In the long run, TEFAP administrative funds would prove as important, or more important, to the stability of the emergency food system as TEFAP commodities, but in the early 1980s the quantities of commodities were very large. One study of food banks in the early eighties estimated that the Emergency Jobs Bill provisions alone would "increase the amount of USDA commodities in stock at some foodbanks from 10 percent to 50 percent of total stock."

The Jobs Bill also provided financial help, and thus financial incentives, to the emergency food system under another title, which created the Emergency Food and Shelter Program. This was also designed to be a one-time distribution of funds, to be administered by the Federal Emergency Management Agency (FEMA), but like TEFAP, it was quickly and repeatedly reauthorized. The Emergency Food and Shelter Program created a National Board composed of six national charitable organizations (the United Way of America, the American Red Cross, the Salvation Army, Catholic Charities USA, the Council of Jewish Federations and the National Council of Churches) which oversees the distribution of funds. The National Board funnels federal contributions to local boards, composed of local representatives of the same organizations, in areas with sufficiently high poverty rates to qualify. The local boards determine how the local share is to be divided between shelter costs and emergency food, and allocate the money among frontline providers. Some funds are reserved in a set-aside for programs serving needy people in areas not encompassed by local boards. Thus the FEMA program, as it is generally called, not only infused federal dollars into the emergency food system but also fostered the creation of local organizational structures that coordinated and promoted expansion of emergency food programs.

The Hunger Wars

The Reagan administration initially opposed the creation of TEFAP, and its subsequent extension, but as reports of hunger from advocates were reinforced by those from more mainstream sources—

mayors, churches, and even the GAO—the president had a change of heart. He withdrew his opposition to the extension of TEFAP and, declaring himself "perplexed" by reports of hunger, he ordered a "no-holds-barred" investigation, to be conducted by a President's Task Force on Food Assistance. He asked his friend and advisor Edwin Meese to direct the process. A commission of prominent citizens, including several vocal critics of public food assistance programs, was hastily convened in September 1983 and asked to report at the end of December. Meanwhile, two major Washington-based lobbying groups, Bread for the World Institute and the Food Research and Action Center (FRAC), each released a hunger report during the fall. The battle over the extent and credibility of hunger had escalated to a new level.

Although anti-hunger advocates like those at FRAC and Bread for the World claimed from the outset that the president's group was stacked with people predisposed to minimize hunger, the Task Force might have succeeded in achieving the classic functions of such a body—expressing official concern and compassion without obligating funds—had not its convener, presidential advisor Ed Meese, quite thoroughly discredited himself and thus his commission by some remarks to wire service reporters in December. "I don't know of any authoritative figures that there are hungry children," Meese told the reporters. "I've heard a lot of anecdotal stuff, but I haven't heard any authoritative figures." He suggested that allegations of widespread hunger were "purely political." A reporter mentioned what *The New Republic*'s account of the interview called "the most obvious physical manifestation of hunger—long soup lines" and Meese responded, "We've had considerable evidence that people go to soup kitchens because the food is free and that that's easier than paying for it."

To anyone who had volunteered in a soup kitchen, or even walked past a waiting line of miserable, ragged would-be diners, Meese's comment seemed not only uninformed and politically motivated, but profoundly insensitive. His remarks fueled a spate of Christmas editorials critical of the Reagan administration. The Task Force report, issued early in January 1984, further escalated the hunger wars. It alarmed and angered advocates by recommending the block granting of food stamps and other major federal food assistance programs, an approach that would effectively end their entitlement status and re-move the final floor under consumption, but it did little to resolve the dispute over hunger. The group concluded that there was no evidence of widespread clinical undernutrition, and that hunger in the ordinary, non-clinical sense of the term had not been, and probably could not be, quantified. "There is no official 'hunger count' to estimate the number of hungry people, and so there are no hard data available to estimate the extend of hunger directly," the report declared. "How many people go hungry in the United States because their income is too low or because they are experiencing temporary financial setbacks? No one who has sincerely sought a true and responsible answer to this question has been able to provide one."

Inconclusive as it was, the President's Task Force Report occasioned another round of publicity for the hunger issue. Advocates, food assistance providers, and members of Congress called the study politically motivated and again offered accounts of rising demand at soup kitchens and food pantries as evidence of hunger, and thus of a need for restoration of the funds cut from the Food Stamp Program and other public programs in 1981 and 1982. To the Task Force's preoccupation with methodology, they responded with outrage or derision.. Senator Kennedy, for example, put it this way: "Its call for an unattainable scientific precision in quantifying hunger is part of a familiar Administration strategy to ignore evidence of unfairness and injustice in America. . . . Hunger is not just a scientific question. It is a moral issue."

The controversy over the President's Task Force on Food Assistance, like the congressional hearings on TEFAP and the Conference of Mayors' annual surveys, served to keep the needs of poor people on the public agenda, and continually to define and redefine the problem as *hunger*. Furthermore, discussions in Congress heightened the growing legitimacy of the hunger issue. Anything that contributed to the visibility and legitimacy of hunger at the national level helped local groups to attract donors and volunteers and thus to expand and achieve stability. Conversely, each new local food program reinforced the definition of the situation as *hunger*, and, by calling attention to growing lines of would-be recipients, provided new evidence of a national hunger emergency.

How did emergency food grow from a handful of programs in the late 1970s, through its hasty proliferation and expansion on an emergency basis in the early 1980s to its current extensive, elaborate, and relatively well capitalized state? Sociologists call the process by which an arrangement, a program, an activity becomes a relatively stable, predictable part of a society *institutionalization*. The next chapter explores the institutionalization process in emergency food, both in the creation of a national system and at the local level, in the lives of individual organizations.

CHAPTER FOUR

Institutionalization:
From Shoestring to Stability

JILL STATON BULLARD, the director of the Interfaith Food Shuttle in Raleigh, North Carolina, is a dynamic, engaging woman with a ready smile and an infectious optimism. She got involved with food rescue by accident.

> My story is very simple. I was a North Raleigh housewife. I taught in an elite little preschool situation so I could be at home with my kids. We were soccer moms. . . . We were at the local soccer complex, a whole group that had been together since our kids were small, and we went to a fast-food restaurant and literally bought a sandwich and then they threw all the rest of the sandwiches away. We got there at 10:29 and at 10:30 the sandwiches went into the trash.

When Bullard and her fellow soccer moms saw the restaurant staff discarding the food, they asked what was wrong with the sandwiches. They were told there was nothing wrong with them; it was just time to throw them away. "You have got to be kidding," she remembers thinking, and explains: "We were raised with Depression-era parents; you ate everything on your plate because there were children starving in Africa. . . . You didn't take more than you could eat and you didn't throw good food away."

> So I said, "Could I speak to your manager, could we talk to someone about this, because, obviously, there is someplace that needs this

food." And he said that he couldn't afford to take it down there and they couldn't come up for it. So we started researching the feeding facilities. I knew nothing about them. I didn't know what a soup kitchen was. I had a general, vague idea, but I had never seen a soup kitchen. Never seen a homeless shelter. But we started talking to the directors of those places and they did need food. They needed good food. They needed it on a regular basis. There was no way to access what was there. So we just promised them that we would do the accessing. That we would find the food and transport the food.

Once the commitment was made, however, she realized she had a lot of questions. "How do you do it safely? How do you do it efficiently? Are we allowed, by law, to do this?" Of course, there were obstacles. One was the state's Good Samaritan law, which Bullard describes as "horrendous. It said, essentially, that if a donor had insurance, then he was liable." A majority of the potential donors that the Interfaith Food Shuttle approached, Bullard recalls, "said, 'I want to do this personally, but corporately it would mean my job. But if the law were changed, we could do this.' So we got the law changed." Bullard recruited law students and a law professor to research "Good Sam" laws, and enlisted help from the state health department and a caterer, Classic Food Systems, to learn about moving food safely. Once she had mastered the basics, things moved swiftly.

We bought these six Cambro units. We stuck them in the back of my station wagon and we started moving food. They are insulated, maintaining temperature controls, hot or cold, whatever. So we started with Cambro, and we outgrew my station wagon in six weeks. . . . It was kind of hysterical. I would pick up food up here, drive it down there, stick those containers in cars of priests who were going downtown, . . . they delivered them to the soup kitchens, picked them up, brought them back to me by 12:00 and I took them home and we did the whole thing again.

Very soon, Interfaith grew too big for this approach.

But as donors grew, as people became interested, . . . it just became so much bigger. It took over my garage. Then it took over our garage and our den. When it got to the bedroom, my husband said, "This is it. How much money do you need to get an office?"

The project needed not only more space, but more attention: "All of a sudden there was a time when I had to make a decision whether I would stay with the school or start doing this full-time." Bullard did leave teaching and went to work on the Food Shuttle full-time, without a salary at first. Eventually, the United Parcel Service (UPS) Foundation provided a grant to pay her salary. "They said, 'Jill, you are too big. Somebody has got to be in charge.' " With help from UPS and Bullard's full-time involvement, the Food Shuttle has continued to grow:

> We have seventy-five volunteers who moved 40,000 pounds a week. We have six trucks, three of them refrigerated. We move bread and desserts from grocery stores, we move restaurant food, hotel, hospital food. We do probably a million pounds of produce a year, out of the North Carolina State Farmers' Market. So we are getting really great food to people who need it. . . . We have set pickups; we pick up from every donor, every day. . . . Right now I am working at the maximum we can work.

She would have to add another truck and two more drivers to add any additional donors, or any more receivers, in the three-county distribution area.

Bullard's connection to UPS came through the early stages of what would become Foodchain. "We started without knowledge of anybody else; we didn't know anybody else was doing it." In the course of researching the Good Samaritan laws, however, the University of North Carolina law students heard about a meeting in Washington, D.C., of people doing similar work. At that point Bullard was still teaching, and she couldn't get to the meeting: "I was pretty much moving the food by myself with the priest. . . . The food would have stopped, which we couldn't do." Instead, she began making calls.

"I called these people and asked 'Are you really doing this? How are you doing it? What are you doing it with? Tell me how much it is costing? Do you have an office? Do you have trucks?' And it was 'Yes! Somebody else is doing this. I am not alone!' So I made Dallas the following year. Didn't make D.C., but made Dallas and it was like coming to a tent revival for me." She has attended every subsequent Foodchain meeting and has served on the organization's board. "I love it. I love the exchange, the enthusiasm, the diversity. It is empowering to learn from different people how they are going about it. . . . There has never been a time when I have been at this meeting when I haven't carried something home."

One of the things she has carried home is the idea for a reprocessing kitchen that can convert perishable donations into cooked and frozen dishes that can be kept for a longer time. Like the D.C. Central Kitchen in Washington, D.C., which has served as both inspiration and model, Interfaith's kitchen will train poor and homeless people to work in the area's booming food service industry. The county has donated a facility in a former community college, and has agreed to pay the utilities. A major medical center contributed two tractor trailer loads of kitchen equipment when it redid its own kitchen. The new project has already lined up its first jobs. It will be providing meals for an alternative school located at the same site, and for meals on wheels, as well as for its regular clientele of soup kitchens and shelters. "One of the wonderful things about this whole movement is that it is very hard to knock it. Everybody wants to help feed needy people. They don't want good food thrown away. They just want the mechanism to get it done."

From a chance encounter with sandwich disposal to an organization that moves 40,000 pounds a week, from the back of a station wagon to a small fleet of trucks, from the Bullards' garage to a central kitchen, the Interfaith Food Shuttle illustrates the process of institutionalization at the level of the individual organization. Providing emergency food could never have become the large, ubiquitous institution that it is today if thousands of organizations had not made journeys like the one Jill Bullard has described. But the institutionalization of emergency food is not just the aggregate of the transformation of individual organizations. It is also the outcome of the development of local systems, interactive groups of organizations that have their own dynamics, and of national networks that connect such local systems. Further, it reflects aspects of the national environment in which all of this organization building occurred, especially the continued visibility and legitimation of hunger as a social issue.

Accidental Programs

Like the Interfaith Shuttle, emergency food programs have tended to be accidental in origin, supply-driven, pragmatic, innovative, and heroic—heroic in the sense that extraordinary effort and dedication have been required for their development. No one planned the emergency food network. No one even seems to have envisioned or hoped for its current extensive, well-capitalized state. To a remarkable extent, it reflects a series of accidents. If Jill Bullard's team of soccer moms had arrived at the fast-food restaurant an hour earlier, or five minutes later, there might be no prepared and perishable food rescue program in Raleigh. PPFRPs are especially likely to be initiated by a chance encounter with a supply of food, or an unplanned run-in with need by someone already in touch with food supplies. The Potato Project of the Society of Saint Andrew was born when a minister conducting a workshop on world hunger made a chance remark about food waste that aroused the ire and incredulity of a potato farmer on Virginia's Eastern Shore. In the debate that followed, the farmer offered to give them a truckload of "culls," and the operation that now coordinates donation and delivery of millions of pounds of produce annually was born. The idea for the D.C. Central Kitchen, which served as a model for Jill Bullard's new reprocessing facility, was hatched when Robert Egger, who had been working in the nightclub industry for years, volunteered to cook for the "grate patrol," a mobile soup kitchen in which his church particpated along with the Salvation Army and seven other congregations. When the committee gave him money and told him to go to the grocery store to buy the food to cook, a lightbulb flashed in his head.

> I thought, Now wait, wait wait. This is just crazy. You all are buying food when I know for a fact—I mean all the men and women that I worked with in the seventies had gone to work for caterers in Washington in the early eighties and were dumbfounded by how much

food was being thrown away—I've got friends who are talking about throwing away all this food. You all need food. Why don't we get the two together.

Food banking, too, grew out of a series of accidental encounters, and it was also supply driven. In the late 1960s John Van Hengel, a Wisconsin businessman who had relocated to Arizona on the advice of his physician, began gleaning fruits and vegetables for a mission dining hall in Phoenix where he volunteered. Before the major building boom of the seventies pushed the borders of Phoenix out into the desert, many homes were built in old orchards, and he recalls that homeowners, distressed by the visible waste, were glad to let him pick for the mission. Finding more free food than he could gather by himself, he invited some of the mission's clients to join him, and soon they were harvesting much more than their kitchen needed. Van Hengel offered the food to other agencies but found the task of sorting and delivering it taxing, so he asked the pastor of St. Mary's Church for help. "Really, what I wanted to do was to get somebody else to do it. I was tired and I wanted to get out, but he was too smart for me," Van Hengel recalls. Instead of taking over the project, Father Ronald Colloty, a Franciscan priest, offered to help find what Van Hengel needed most, a space in which food could be stored and from which it could be distributed. Three days later, he called back with an offer of a vacant bakery building, about 5,000 square feet, which had been donated to the Franciscans. The pastor convinced his parish council to provide a small loan for operating expenses and to pick up the tab on phone and electricity for a year, and in November 1967, the first food bank in the United States, or in the world for that matter, opened its doors.

"From the fruit we went to the fields, from the fields we went to the packing sheds ... when a door opened, we walked in. If it worked, fine. If it didn't work, we backed out and went another way. It was trial and error," Van Hengel recalls of the early days. The trial-and-error approach, which has proven to be characteristic of the development of many components of the emergency food system, soon led Van Hengel to another major source of food. A community worker who was aware of the produce distribution project introduced him to a woman who was feeding her ten children from what she found in the dumpster behind a local supermarket. At her urging, Van Hengel visited the dumpster himself and was amazed by what he found: frozen food, loose vegetables, stale bread in large quantities, and in the market's back room, less perishable food awaiting transportation to the dump: leaking bags of rice and sugar, dented and unlabeled cans, and cases of jars and bottles consigned to the trash because one glass container had broken and sullied the others. Recognizing the potential, Van Hengel began meeting with grocery store managers, first in Phoenix and then in other Arizona cities, arranging to divert some of the rejected food to his distribution center in Phoenix. The woman who had led him to the dumpster depicted the process in a hand-drawn cartoon as a bank in which food could be deposited by those with excess and from which it could be withdrawn by people in need, and the term food bank entered the language. Van Hengel named his project the St. Mary's Food Bank to express his appreciation for the support of the St. Mary's parish.

Heroic Efforts

Of course, many people encounter such resources and never act on them, or begin a project but do not follow through. Almost every successful organizational development story I heard included extraordinary commitment and dedication by at least one individual. Jill Bullard's pattern of working without a salary for a period is not unusual; in fact, it is typical of pantries and kitchens and true of a surprising number of food rescue programs and food banks. Nuns with the support of their orders, a Sufi assisted by the other members of a communal living arrangment, a collective of pastors and their wives living "in community" and growing most of their own food, people on pensions, people with high-income spouses, people living on an inheritance—I ran into all of these among the food bankers and food rescuers I talked with, all of whom had worked for nothing, or next to nothing, in the early years of their organization's development.

They often began with very limited accommodations, like Bullard's garage and station wagon. Bill Bolling, the Atlanta Community Food Bank director, began in a space he calls "the cave—it was a basement, 4,000 square feet with no loading dock." FOOD Share in Oxnard, California, a thriving food bank with an extensive senior gleaners program, began in a garage; so did a food bank in Pasadena that eventually grew into the Los Angeles Regional Foodbank, now the largest in the nation. So did the Food Bank of Alaska. The Good Shepherd Food-Bank in Lewiston, Maine, started in an apartment with food scavenged from a dumpster. The Potato Project of the Society of Saint Andrew began work in a converted sleep shed with no electricity: "When we first started we started with one telephone that sat on a TV snack table, and a solar calculator, so if it was a dark, dreary day, you couldn't add on it," Marian Buchanan, one of the founders, recalls.

Many of the emergency food providers I interviewed remember their organization's infancy with a kind of nostalgia. Fran Ficorelli started the Heart and Soul Food Pantry in Niagara Falls, New York, along with other members of her prayer group, in 1982, just after her job at Occidental Chemical was eliminated. She remembers the early days as "wonderful."

> I received no paycheck all this time. . . . I decided that I had to truly trust in God. And I did. It was a very sad time but a wonderful time. A wonderful time! Because we were doing such needed work. And everyone pitched in. There were volunteers. No one was paid. And donations came in. But after a while, the glamour of it started to wear off.

When the glamour begins to wear off, as it inevitably does, some organizations go out of business, but among those that continue, there is an inherent drive toward stability. People tire of the herculean mode, of living at the edge, of exhausting themselves. Heroics are all right for an emergency, but they are not sustainable for the long haul. Part of the institutionalization of emergency food can be explained by simple fatigue; people take the steps necessary to get their workload to a manageable level or to achieve a reasonable balance between effort and reward. Robert Egger told me with considerable glee that the D.C. Central Kitchen had finally stopped being "on call" for pickups at night.

When we first started, we did on-call at night. . . . we were in Washington. There were parties every single night. And I got pickups you would not believe at night. I mean, oftentimes I'd get calls at one in the morning, and I'd be crawling out of bed saying, you know, "Geez, there's got to be a better way to make a living than this," but you'd get there and there would be three steamship rounds of beef, pans and pans and pans of the freshest, most beautiful asparagus you had ever seen in your life, strawberries, chocolate mousse, you know, beautiful food that would have been wrong to throw away and things that we could use the next day. . . . Honestly, in the four years that George Bush was president, I probably went to every party he attended, after he had left. It was . . . almost our motto: "You're eating the same food the president ate last night."

Eventually, however, the presidential party circuit became too difficult to sustain, and with a new administration and a tighter economic climate, less worth the trouble. "Catering's dropped off. . . . we saw that and just replaced it with other sources of food . . . large-scale processing kitchens like hotels, hospitals, colleges and universities, corporate cafeterias, the places that are always going to have leftover food." Egger misses the strawberries and steamship round, but the switch to more regular suppliers has finally enabled the D.C. Central Kitchen to end its on-call pickup service:

I can tell you I've never been happier in my entire life. I sent those letters out saying, you know, after six years, don't call me at home ever again. . . . If you know you're going to have something you can call us and we'll make arrangements, but for the most part we're just not available to call at random. It just got to the point where it was exhausting because there's still just a tiny staff here, and to run this place six days, seven days a week, and be on call at night, was just too much.

Strategies for achieving sustainability vary. Jill Bullard got a grant from UPS. Fran Ficorelli turned to public funds, obtaining a contract from the New York State Department of Health to open a soup kitchen; the funds allowed her to pay salaries for the first time, although they are extraordinarily low (she pays a staff of five from a grant of $55,000). Robert Egger replaced unpredictable catering with steady if uninspiring fare from cafeterias. Some organizations enlisted the Boy Scouts or declared November to be Food Bank Month. Regardless of whether the strategy is purchasing the services of a fund-raising consultant or seeking regular support from government or the more generous but fickle support of foundations, or finding a more reliable source of food, eventually almost all groups tire of the crisis mode and the emergency style.

To some extent, institutionalization is a by-product of growth. "They said 'Jill, you are too big. Somebody has got to be in charge. The buck has to start and stop someplace,' " Bullard recalled of the UPS Foundation's insistence that their grant be used to give her a salary. "They wanted the culpability factor. They definitely wanted that." As an organization grows, as more and more resources are invested, the need for financial accountability increases. This is true of almost any type of organization, but it is especially true of agencies like food banks and food rescue programs that invest in equipment and specialized space. Some emergency food organizations, like the Interfaith Food Shuttle or the D.C. Central Kitchen, had the good fortune to have founders who had, or could develop, the requisite management skills, but others have outgrown the managerial capacities of their creators, a situation which often provokes a crisis. When Hawley Botchford was recruited to take over the ailing Food Bank of Southwest Florida, for example, he found a situation that he summarized as "no money, big hearts, no business sense." Many of the emergency food organizations that have successfully made the transition from impassioned shoestring operations to fairly stable community institutions passed through a crisis phase along the way, and quite a number resolved this crisis by bringing in someone with a business or management background.

Local Systems

One of the reasons that the Interfaith Food Shuttle is starting a reprocessing kitchen is because such a facility allows a food rescue program to regularize its output, to become a predictable and dependable source of food for its client agencies. A simple food rescue operation that picks up from restaurants and caterers and institutional dining halls is in no position to guarantee a regular supply; it all depends upon what is left over on a given day. Once a reprocessing facility is created, however, prepared foods can be frozen until they are needed. Reprocessing kitchens, like food banks, serve as core organizations for entire local systems, contributing to both the stability and the growth of the overall local networks. Variously called emergency food networks, community food security systems, or just "member agencies" of a food bank or food rescue program, such local systems have dynamics all their own, and it is impossible to understand either the growth or the institutionalization of emergency food without looking at these dynamics.

"We couldn't have done it without the food bank," declared the director of a large New York City soup kitchen at a brief ceremony honoring the program's staff on the occasion of the project's millionth meal. It is a sentiment I heard expressed in numerous kitchens and pantries, and it is not mere hyperbole. Food banks are far and away the largest single source of food for member agencies. The Second Harvest study, for example, found that on average, food banks provided about half of all food used by member agencies; just over a quarter was purchased, and just under a quarter donated by other sources including churches, governments, merchants and farmers, and others. For pantries, the figures were even more extreme, with the food bank supplying, on average, more than 60 percent of the food distributed by participating pantries. Since so many frontline providers are small volunteer projects operating on the proverbial shoestring, the food bank is important as an anchor or stabilizing force in a local emergency food system.

Food banks contribute to the stability and longevity of member agencies in other ways besides supplying them with food at the low shared-maintenance rate: training and technical assistance in food handling and storage, for example, and nutritional consultation, even recipes. As intermediaries between large-scale food donors and recipient agencies, food banks have assumed the role of certifying the reputability and reliability of frontline agencies. It is the food bank that assures donors that food will be kept off the floor and at appropriate temperatures, and that it will go to "the needy, not the greedy";

and food banks monitor member agencies to back up these claims. As Madeline Lund, the agency relations director for the Greater Chicago Food Depository explained to me, "It is good for the donor; they don't have to figure out who is legitimate; they just know the food bank is legit and that is all that counts." Membership in a food bank may require frontline agencies to improve their equipment and storage capacity so as to comply with food bank rules, thus hastening the process of capital investment at the grassroots level. Where food rescue programs operate independently of food banks, they serve many of the same functions, teaching agencies how to store prepared food properly as well as providing foods for immediate consumption.

There is an intimate relationship at the local system level between institutionalization in the sense of stability, and overall growth. It is obvious that growth promotes a drive toward stability, just as it does in the individual organization. A food bank or food rescue program is unlikely to be established until there is a sufficient threshold of frontline agencies. But the opposite is also true—that stability promotes growth; the introduction of a food bank or food rescue program into a local system will almost always result in the growth of the capacity of existing organizations and the creation of new ones. Once a food bank or food rescue program is established, creation of new frontline programs is easier, both because there is an obvious source of supply, and because technical help is easily available. A church group or community agency that wants to start a food pantry can generally get clear guidelines from the nearest food bank; the specifications for membership are, in essence, a blueprint for creating a program.

In some cases, the food bank can provide more tangible help as well. "That's another area of food banking that people do not know," Food Bank of New Hampshire director Al Tremblay told me. "We try to help people get items that they wouldn't normally know how to get themselves. I've set up a soup kitchen in a community south of Manchester . . . with stainless-steel equipment. All commercial equipment. Didn't cost the guy a dime. And I even transported it for him." I asked Tremblay, who was once in the trucking business, how he had managed this.

Contacts, through contacts I had in my before life. I used to do a lot of rigging and a lot of storage for people like veterans hospitals, AT&T, New England Telephone, NYNEX, and treated them well, never burned them, never burned the bridges, and now they call me, "Al, we understand you're in this type of business—can anybody use this stuff?" . . . Because of past networking. Everybody gives me a wish list and I try to fulfill it.

The food bank's need for adequately equipped outlets can provide the impetus for capital investment. Bill Bolling recalls how the Atlanta Community Food Bank got into the freezer business:

In food banking, your best, your most nutritional food . . . comes in frozen. That's where you get your meat products and your dinners, frozen dinners and so forth. We couldn't understand why people wouldn't take our best food, . . . but as we surveyed them, because we were having to turn down a lot of food, we realized that most of these programs had donated equipment, somebody's donated refrigerator, and all they had was a little ice box to put the food in. And that's when we realized that, if we were going to move frozen food, we had to help build that capacity. So we bought three or four hundred twenty-three-cubic-foot Sears chest-type freezers. And we gave them to the agencies. They pay a dollar a month maintenance . . . And the frozen food just started pouring out.

Clearly, the relationship between food banks and their member agencies is not a one-way street. The kitchens and pantries sustain the food bank, and contribute to its growth and institutionalization just as the food bank sustains the kitchens and pantries. In the first place, there is shared maintenance—the fee that almost all Second Harvest food banks and some independent banks charge member agencies for food handling. It is generally around fourteen cents a pound, although some very large banks have been able to get it down as low as ten cents a pound. This is not the only source of income for food banks; in fact, for many it represents less than half of the income side of the ledger, but it is an important base. In effect, it distributes the fund-raising chore among the member agencies which, in many cases, are closer to potential donors, geographically and organizationally. It also takes agencies out of the hat-in-hand role and transforms them into customers, and it helps to ensure that they do not take more of a given food item than they can readily pass along to their clients. Although shared maintenance has caused problems for some food banks that have been accused by competing organizations of "selling" food to member agencies, on the whole the shared-maintenance system appears to work extraordinarily well.

Food banks need member agencies for reasons other than their shared-maintenance payments, however. In general, a bank has a stake in developing as many reputable member agencies as possible, at least until it reaches the maximum number that can be served from its current space and faces a choice between establishing a waiting list, reducing services to existing members, or moving to new quarters. Most of the food bankers I interviewed had moved several times already, and a substantial number had chosen their current location in part for its potential for additions. It is not just that such growth impresses potential donors, although it probably does. Food banks need members for the most practical of reasons, to get the food out as quickly as possible. Many food donations from wholesalers or processors are available only in large quantities—by the truckload, not by the pallet. A food bank can accept large donations of perishable food or food near its expiration date only if it can assure donors that the food will be redistributed promptly and reach its end users while it is still edible. In order to make such assurances, the bank needs a sufficient number of outlets, outlets that can be counted upon to pick up such foods at the bank or accept delivery where transportation is available. And at times, a food bank must be able to persuade member agencies to accept some foods that they might prefer to do without—frozen bread dough was an example that cropped up in several locations—in order to accommodate a donor who also provides other, more desirable foods. Like the development of individual emergency food organizations, local systems are, in part at least, supply driven. Symbiosis is visible throughout the system, and it is a symbiosis that fosters growth.

Government, the Silent Partner

Government is another important participant in the local emergency food ecology. Emergency food has successfully cultivated an image of reliance upon private sector donations and voluntarism, but government at all levels has been far more involved than such an image suggests, providing both food and money as well as crucial policy supports. Government commodities, as we have seen, were important in calling attention to hunger, and crucial in drawing many providers into the work in the first place. In the mid 1980s, the federal government was distributing more than a billion pounds of commodities a year through the TEFAP program. By comparison, in 1984, the year that TEFAP first topped a billion, the Second Harvest network handled less than 200 million pounds; the private network has yet to reach a billion pounds in a single year. The administrative funds associated with these large distributions helped to stabilize many programs created during the emergency phase, allowing the development of capacity—cold storage and transportation, for example— that would enable food banks to solicit and handle donations from other sources. "Early Money Is Like Yeast" is a favorite saying among political fund-raisers; it "grows" the campaign to which it is contributed. The same might be said of money or other resources that are provided early in the life of an organization, when it is especially vulnerable and has not yet developed its own resource-gathering capacity. The TEFAP commodities and funds, and the first few years of FEMA funding were the yeast of the emergency food phenomenon.

Many people remember the cheese giveaway of the early eighties, but fail to realize either the continuing nature or the considerable variety of public sector contributions. Cheese was not the only commodity distributed, and TEFAP was not the only federal program that donated commodities to local organizations, and the federal government was not the only level of government involved in the commodity purchase and donation business, and commodities were not the only type of support provided, and so on, creating a picture of enormous variation and complexity. The Second Harvest study in 1993 found that federal, state, and local governments together provided 30 percent of the average income received by participating kitchens, and about a quarter of the average received by pantries. Such averages, however, mask the significant differences among states and localities, many of which provide no financial support at all. A study by the U.S. Conference of Mayors at the end of the eighties found that just over half of the twenty-seven cities surveyed used local funds for emergency food, and about a quarter received state grants.

To the local provider, this can all be a bit overwhelming. A resource guide for emergency food providers in New York City, prepared by the City's Human Resources Administration in 1994, lists fourteen different programs providing food, funds, or equipment, of which seven are federal programs, three are programs of the state of New York, one is a local program (called Emergency Food Assistance Program, EFAP, of course, just to add to confusion) and three are private sector initiatives. Each of these programs has its own application process, distribution or funding cycle, eligibility requirements, and rules for participation. No other city or major metropolitan area would have precisely the same list, but many might have lists of comparable length and variety. The recent consolidation of federal commodity donation programs into EFAP (federal EFAP, not local EFAP) will shorten the list somewhat, but government will remain an important resource for local food providers. Clearly, the public sector has played a crucial role in the institutionalization of emergency food.

Government commodities and dollars have not been the only stabilizing forces. The local board system set up to distribute FEMA funds at the local level has helped to organize and stabilize emergency food systems in the two hundred or so communities that have such boards, including most of the nation's larger cities. Where small local organizations must deal with large governments, they often find that banding together helps, so in communities without FEMA boards, and in some that have them, coalitions of emergency food providers have added further stability, and sometimes an additional source of technical assistance, to local systems. Foundations, fundraising organizations, civic groups, schools, and agencies serving youths have all contributed to the institutionalization of local systems. Local systems, however, do not function in a vacuum.

The Growth of Food Banking

Like Jill Bullard's first encounter with Foodchain, connection to a national or regional organization can be a lifeline, and both Foodchain and Second Harvest are crucial rungs in the ladder of institutionalization. Food banking came first, preceding, as we have seen, the "emergency" period of the early eighties. While St. Mary's Food Bank in Phoenix was, by almost all accounts, the first food bank, John Van Hengel was not the only person to come up with the idea of soliciting donations of unsalable food from the grocery trade. Several similar operations were created quite independently. It is not really surprising when you think about it. The sixties and early seventies were characterized by a pervasive national concern about poverty, and, as we have seen, a dramatic focus on hunger. Many churches initiated social action programs and in the course of their outreach in poor neighborhoods discovered people without food. The federal government played a role by creating an Emergency Food and Medical Program as part of the War on Poverty, a program which encouraged the creation of pantries as well as helping people to gain access to the growing federal food assistance safety net. At the same time, an emerging environmental movement raised the nation's consciousness about waste, and a growing consumer movement raised standards in the grocery industry, the institution of "pull dates," for example. Add to the equation the increasing use of "dumpsters," to hold grocery store trash in such public locations as the edges of parking lots, and you have the ingredients of food banking.

While some of the early food bankers visited St. Mary's before starting their own operations, others, such as the Atlanta Community Food Bank, came up with the idea on their own. Bill Bolling, the founder and director of the Atlanta bank, recalls his surprise at learning that other food banks existed:

> I had never heard of food banks. And that's an interesting story. The first time I learned about food banks we were already incorporated

and up and running. I had spent the good part of a year trying to think out how it would work, and primarily working out the logistics with the donors—what were their main concerns? And I still remember getting a magazine called *Food Monitor*. It's still around [now *WHY* magazine]. And it had "All You Want to Know about Food Banks" or some such title on the front of the magazine. I got the magazine at home on a Saturday and I just couldn't believe it. My first impression was: what a blow to my ego! I thought I had thought it up, and there were half a dozen of them around the country at that point. . . . And then the second thought was, "I've got to write these people and find out how they do it."

Bolling attended the first meeting of what became Second Harvest in Phoenix and his reaction was a bit like Jill Bullard's discovery of Foodchain: "It was a real affirmation, after all, that the conceptual part of it was right."

It would be easy to imagine that Second Harvest grew out of a simple federation of banks like Bolling's, but the reality is more complex. The story of the birth of Second Harvest contradicts the prevailing notion of food banking as a wholly private sector initiative. The St. Mary's Food Bank, under Van Hengel's leadership, was quite successful, enough so to catch the eye of a staff member of the federal government's Community Services Administration (CSA), the Nixon era successor to the Office of Economic Opportunity, which had administered the war on poverty. In 1975, CSA offered St. Mary's an unsolicited grant to teach people from other communities how to set up food banks. St. Mary's turned it down; Van Hengel recalls that his board did not want to be involved with the federal government. As one former Second Harvest staffer explained:

> The federal government, CSA, gets no credit in the established history of Second Harvest, for its role. . . . It was people at the Community Services Administration, now nameless, faceless, bureaucrats . . . who were the ones who persisted. They came back another year. They said, "If you don't do it, we're going to find somebody who will." And that's how Second Harvest was born.

When CSA offered another grant the next year, the board voted to accept it. St. Mary's decided to create a separate project, called Second Harvest, to spread the food banking gospel. Van Hengel contacted the few food banks he knew about, and invited them to join.

The federal government funded Second Harvest for five years, to the tune of more than a million and a half dollars, including a large final grant from the Community Services Administration, awarded an hour before the agency was disbanded in 1982, which provided the organization with a $400,000 cushion to permit it to make the transition to private funding. "I've always said that Second Harvest is the greatest example in the United States of a wonderful idea that was nurtured and then really developed by federal dollars, that took it through those critical years, up through '82," declared John Driggs, the first chair of the Second Harvest board, at the organization's fifteenth birthday celebration. He went on to express his pride that the organization had weaned itself from public dollars and "became fully dependent upon private sector efforts."

Second Harvest obtained its own nonprofit organization charter (501-C3) in 1979, the same year it solicited its first national donor, and in 1980, it began distributing food from national-level donations to its member banks. In 1984 it completed the separation from St. Mary's by moving to Chicago, in part to be better situated to solicit donations from the big national food processors. National donations grew steadily, both in absolute terms and in comparison with locally donated product, until the end of the 1980s. From fifteen million pounds in 1981, donations directed through the national office grew to 285.7 million pounds in 1995, a little over a third of the total of 811.3 million pounds distributed by the network as a whole in that year. As Second Harvest became more and more reliant upon corporate headquarters donations, it developed an increasingly corporate style that alienated some of its more grassroots-oriented participants. At the same time, it gave more and more attention to specifying and monitoring the standards that would make the food industry comfortable with large-scale donations.

Once Second Harvest was established, food banking began to spread more rapidly. There were 13 member banks in 1979. By 1982, there were 44. There were 78 by mid decade, and the next year the organization began counting "affiliates" as well as fully certified food banks, and the total jumped to 203. The network lost a few members over the next few years, but has maintained a steady membership between 180 and 185 since 1990. In 1989, its executive director told a reporter that "We are very close to maturity in terms of the number of food banks that the country can support," and indeed, few new banks have been organized since the new decade began. Most major metropolitan areas have food banks, and several remarkable organizations serve large rural areas.

As a critical mass of functioning food banks developed, it became easier for new banks to organize and learn the ropes. "There's no school on food banking; you learn by your own mistakes," New Hampshire's Al Tremblay told me, but once there were established banks, newcomers could learn from those ahead of them on the learning curve. JoAnn Pike, director of the Good Shepherd Food-Bank in Lewiston, Maine, recalls floundering around for the first several years, scavenging food from the dumpsters behind local supermarkets, until she read an article in the paper about the Harvesters Food Bank in Kansas City. "Now I was raised in Kansas City. We called them and said, 'How do you do this?' " Pike recalls, and Harvesters replied "You don't pick the dumpsters, you go to the top of the company and say 'Would you donate products that are unmarketable and we will distribute them to the needy.' " The Kansas City bank was instrumental in helping the Maine operation move from dumpsters to donations: "They educated us on all the IRS regulations and led us through that over the phone and by mail," and provided moral support as well. "It was really, really difficult at first—to pick up the phone and say, 'I'm starting this thing that nobody's ever heard of. Would you donate your products?' Not only did we not have any money, at that time we didn't have any credibility. . . ."

Good Shepherd was one of the earlier food banks, and as the phenomenon spread, both the credibility and the technical assistance became easier to come by. Within the grocery industry, the Grocery Manufacturers Association became involved, encouraging its members to donate to Second Harvest–affiliated banks, as did the Food Marketing Institute. The nuts and bolts of food banking tend to be acquired through informal transfers of information, but once the Second Harvest Network was established, a newcomer could learn a lot from attending meetings. "They hired me and everyone stepped back, so the first thing I had to do was learn what food banking was," Hawley Botchford told me. "I called the other food banks in the state and they said, 'We're starting this organization, the Florida Association of Food Banks, and would you be interested in coming?' and I said 'Absolutely!' . . . Even though we're a little guy down here in the corner of the state of Florida, we went to every meeting we could scrape up the dollars to attend, because that's where we learn. The networking, the sitting there and saying, 'How do you do this,' and 'How do you do that?' That's where I get a lot of my ideas." All Second Harvest banks participate in regional organizations and many have organized state food bank associations as well. In the nineties, Second Harvest has turned its attention increasingly to obtaining larger and better donations at the national level, to an increasingly visible advocacy stance on issues of public policy, and to the development of innovations such as value-added processing, salvage sorting centers, and prepared and perishable food rescue programs.

Food Rescue

Although food rescue programs have their own national organization in Foodchain, the spread of food rescue programs and the development of Foodchain are intimately interwoven with the history of Second Harvest. The nation's first prepared and perishable food rescue program (PPFRP), City Harvest, was established in New York City by Helen Palit in 1982. It attracted considerable media attention, and as it garnered additional resources, it began to use full-page ads in the *New York Times* as part of its strategy for recruiting both food donors and financial supporters. In St. Paul, Minnesota, the CEO of Control Data Corporation read about City Harvest and went to the director of the local Second Harvest food bank looking for a partner to help replicate the program in St. Paul. The food bank, under the leadership of Dick Goebel, set up a program called Twelve Baskets (a reference to the biblical story of the feeding of the five thousand in which there were twelve baskets of food left over).

Once Twelve Baskets was up and running, Goebel, who was a member of the board of directors of Second Harvest, tried to interest Second Harvest in the food rescue approach, but Second Harvest was focused on its grocery industry mission and concerned about the liability and safety issues involved in moving perishables. Goebel decided to spread the word to other Second Harvest food banks on his own, so, with support from Control Data, he set up a workshop and invited other banks to visit. Atlanta and Tucson came and looked at the St. Paul project and went home and started their own. Oklahoma City and Kansas City caught the idea from them. Thus a newspaper was the vector for transmission from New York to Minnesota, while an organizational network, albeit a reluctant one, provided the transmission route for the next generation.

The process didn't stop there, however. Shortly after visiting Twelve Baskets, Bill Bolling read a letter in the "Dear Abby" newspaper column bemoaning the waste of restaurant food, and, with Goebel's blessing, he sent back a letter describing the Twelve Baskets program. Goebel recalls what happened next:

> It was a long letter and I said to myself, "Abby is never going to look at this thing." Well, lo and behold, six weeks later I get a phone call from Abby's staff assistant saying we got this letter and we really think it is a great letter, can we include your name of Twelve Baskets and your address, so that if people want to find out more about it they can. She said, "You need to know that Abby has 80 million readers, so you may get some response and you better be prepared to answer this." And I said, "Sure." What do I know? Anyway, the letter was printed and we did get a lot of responses. In fact, we got chapel offerings from Guam. It was just unreal.

The Dear Abby letter inspired a whole new generation of potential food rescuers, and it also caught the eye of the wife of a staff member at APCO, a Washington-based consulting firm, which was doing some work for the UPS Foundation. The Foundation, looking for a way to make an impact on the hunger problem, had retained APCO to identify promising strategies and opportunities. An APCO representative, at a Second Harvest board meeting to explore the possibility of a joint project with UPS, talked with Goebel about the letter his wife had shown him. "I was under the understanding that his wife was going to contact me to talk more about Twelve Baskets. Lo and behold, I got a call from APCO, who said 'We would like to have you come and be part of a focus group for a client of ours around perishable and prepared food programs. Can you suggest some other people?' " The client turned out to be the UPS Foundation, and thus was born a relationship that led to UPS funding for a prepared and perishable food rescue manual, a sizable number of grants to local projects (including the Interfaith Food Shuttle), and the creation of Foodchain. Both the growth rate and the learning curve in food rescue have undoubtedly been accelerated by the financial support and technical assistance provided by the UPS Foundation, which adopted food rescue as a national funding priority in 1988.

Food rescue was a natural for the UPS Foundation, according to APCO consultant Jane Humpstone who nurtured the relationship, because of the role of transportation. UPS was able to offer technical input as well as financial assistance. Recalling the beginning of the project, when APCO was first presenting its findings about food rescue to the UPS Foundation, she reported that it had been "exciting because it looked to be so obvious and so immediately appealing on a human level. The clincher was that it made such perfect sense for a company that specializes in getting something from point A to point B in the least amount of time to lend its professional and financial support to organizations that are doing the same thing, but not with packages. That was what sold UPS, aside from all the facts of the great projections on how much good work and how much impact and how much food was out there, which was all very exciting in and of itself. They really could grab that idea: 'We are helping people move stuff.' "

With assistance from the UPS Foundation, food rescue grew quickly. Some PPFRPs developed in cities where there were no food banks, or independently of food banks that already existed. Others were created by existing food banks, some before, and some after Second Harvest undertook its Prepared and Perishable Foods Initiative, and in at least one case, a food rescue program has been instrumental in starting a food bank where none previously existed. Both independent and food bank–based PPFRPs are eligible for membership in Foodchain, which currently has more than 120 members. Understandably, there has been some confusion, and some tension, between the two national organizations, but gradually they seem to be reaching an accommodation and a division of labor that allows them to work cooperatively on joint projects. Recently, they joined together to support national "Good Sam" legislation, signed by President Clinton in October 1996, which will provide nationwide standards of protection for food donors. Foodchain has had considerable success in soliciting national donors, like restaurant franchises or convenience store chains, that work through their local affiliates in communities that have food rescue programs.

As food rescue has grown, Foodchain has become more stable, better funded, more corporate. "If you had been at this conference six years ago, you wouldn't believe the difference," one regular participant in the organization's activities told me. That conference "was a one-room event. When you had breakout sessions, people just moved their chairs into the corners and talked. There was no program, there were no speakers, there were no meals. People went out and bought a sandwich and came back and talked. You can see it in the gatherings. It is already fancier hotels." In contrast, the 1995 conference where this interview occurred had all the trappings of an established annual meeting: awards luncheons, dinner galas, speakers, panels, workshops, breakout rooms, audiovisuals, bus tours, a printed program to help those in attendance choose among the simultaneous sessions and workshops, and the souvenirs—a Foodchain bandanna and a mug—that have become a hallmark of the emergency food phenomenon.

Legitimacy and Voluntarism

Neither the UPS Foundation's decision to look for a way to have an impact on hunger, nor the rapid growth of corporate involvement with Second Harvest, would have occurred had not hunger achieved a substantial level of what Herbert Blumer called legitimacy. Conversely, the involvement of major corporations and corporate foundations helped to raise the issue's legitimacy quotient, as well as its visibility, a process with substantial implications for the success of emergency food organizations at the local level. The ability of actors at the local level to elicit resources for their good works is profoundly influenced by several elements in what might be called the national environment: public perception of the extent and urgency of hunger and the level of public support for voluntarism and giving—the culture of charity. Like the programs themselves, these intangibles became "institutionalized" in the 1980s, thus contributing to the growth and permanence of emergency food. Let us look first at the progress of hunger in its journey toward respectability as a social issue.

By the time Jill Bullard began looking for donors in 1989, the contest over the existence of hunger had been won, and belief in the problem was widespread. Bullard says she had never been in a soup kitchen, but when she saw the sandwiches go in the trash, her first thought was that there were hungry people who needed the food, and organizations that could serve it to them. Both the hunger problem, and the emergency food response, had sufficiently penetrated public awareness that hunger was presumed. Potential donors raised questions about liability under the state's Good Samaritan laws, but not questions about the need for the food. "Everybody wants to help feed the hungry. . . . they just want the mechanism to get it done."

This is a considerable change from the contested turf of the emergency period portrayed in the previous chapter, with anti-hunger advocates claiming widespread deprivation, and advocates of the Reagan cutbacks claiming that the truly need had been spared. What had happened in the interim? Three factors seem to me to explain the change: first, a peculiarity of hunger measurement inherent in the emergency food; second, studies of hunger; and third, celebrity involvement with the issue.

Supply and Demand

The measurement anomaly has been present all along. In essence, in emergency food, supply releases demand; demand itself is supply driven. The more food a food pantry has to give out, the more people will find it worthwhile to line up to collect it. The demand for emergency food is profoundly elastic. I sat in a food pantry on a recent morning, when a half-dozen clients who had been sitting for some time on benches in the makeshift waiting area suddenly got up and left. It turned out that they had overheard a staff member, on the phone, telling a caller that the pantry would be closed the next day in order to receive and unpack a delivery from the food bank. The clients left because they are only permitted to come once a month and they did not want to use up their opportunity while the shelves were relatively bare, when they could return in two days and find them full. This is not "cheating." This is rational behavior; in fact, it is precisely the kind of ability to "delay gratification" in which the culture of poverty theorists used to tell us the poor were deficient. They were waiting to "spend" their food pantry shopping opportunity until it would yield the maximum utility.

In some situations, the quantity and quality available influence the decision of *whether* to use the pantry, not just when. If supplies are limited to a few low-value items, it is not worth the wait; if they are abundant, it is. It is the same logic that lengthens the lines at the soup kitchen on "chicken days." One pantry director told me that his numbers increased sharply over October. "Cold weather?" I queried, thinking of my own propensity to eat more when the air turns chilly. No, he answered. Neighborhood families were planning ahead; they were trying to make sure that they would be on the list for the pantry's special Thanksgiving and Christmas distributions.

Such rational calculations at the level of the single household or organization aggregate into large numbers across local systems and across the nation. The number of people seeking emergency food generally rises when the supply rises. When a major source of supply decreases, however, local providers will often scramble to fill the gap in order to avoid turning people away or reducing rations. As the system institutionalized, the programs and resources expanded, the number of people willing publicly to define themselves as hungry by seeking food from emergency food providers rose, and as the numbers rose, the problem became more visible, and more resources were solicited to address it, and so forth. As long as we use the number of people seeking emergency food as a primary indicator of the level of need—of hunger—then the size of the problem will increase as the solution grows larger, especially since the underlying causes of hunger—low wages, underemployment, high rents, inadequate public assistance—have continued unabated since the early 1980s. In emergency food, demand and supply are inextricably linked in a sort of measurement double helix.

Studies of Hunger

This limitation on the utility of measures based on behavior alone lends particular weight to studies employing alternative approaches. Hunger studies are important, however, not only for the information that they produce, but also for their contribution to keeping the issue in front of the public. Writing in the *Columbia Journalism Review* in 1987, journalist Michael Moss analyzed the coverage of poverty in the United States in the 1980s. About hunger, he wrote, "The sharpest spurs in the media's side to do stories on hunger—apart from the occasional utterance by Edwin Meese that hunger is a liberal myth—have been the periodic commissions, field investigations, and assorted studies issued by experts." Several major studies grew directly out of the standoff portrayed at the end of the last chapter, occasioned by the report of the President's Task Force on Food Assistance in January 1984. Conservatives argued that liberals were exaggerating the hunger problem and offering, in Ed Meese's memorable words, only "anecdotal stuff." Liberals charged that conservatives could not see the misery that was in plain view, and that, in Senator Edward Kennedy's words, they were demanding an "unattainable scientific precision in quantifying hunger." Meanwhile, however, several groups of anti-hunger advocates and their allies in the academic world set about designing studies that would yield more convincing evidence.

The first to report was the Physician Task Force on Hunger in America, based at the Harvard University School of Public Health. This was a re-creation of a group that the Field Foundation had sent to Mississippi in 1967, where it had found severe poverty-related malnutrition. It was also the group that had returned a decade later and reported with cautious satisfaction that the nation's nutrition programs were succeeding. Now the group undertook to retrace the steps of its earlier investigations in Mississippi and elsewhere. In addition, it calculated an overall national number, based on a combination of poverty figures and estimates of food assistance participation. To do so, the doctors used an inferential approach derived from the nature of the poverty line. Since poverty is defined as the inability to afford a minimum diet, they reasoned that families living below the poverty level and not receiving food stamps were very likely to be hungry. Furthermore, since studies repeatedly showed that most households with food expenditures at the level of the Thrifty Food Plan, upon which food stamp allocations are based, do not obtain nutritionally adequate diets, the physicians reasoned that some proportion of food stamp recipients were probably hungry as well, an assumption supported by reports from all over the country that requests for help at soup kitchens and food pantries went up at the end of the month after food stamps ran out. Based on these and other calculations, the Physician Task Force came up with an overall estimate of 20 million Americans hungry at some point each month.

A group of medical doctors affiliated with Harvard, the nation's oldest and most prestigious university, has a large bank account of respectability, credibility, and expertise to invest in its work, and a Task Force that has mobilized itself at two previous crucial junctures has a special bonus to offer to the press. The Harvard doctors received a great deal of press coverage—more than a thousand print news reports and a great many editorials and Op-Ed pieces—in the seven weeks after the release of their report in February 1985. The electronic media responded with thirty-one network and ninety-three local TV news programs, including a thirty-minute documentary on CNN, a five-minute segment leading the NBC *Nightly News*, and two minutes on ABC's *World News Tonight*. Six weeks later, CBS did a follow-up report. Although the defenders of Reaganomics continued to object to the methodology of the study, the 20 million hungry Americans figure caught on. It became a useful tool, both for advocates trying to undo the cutbacks of the early Reagan budgets and for emergency food providers trying to raise funds and other resources for their projects. The Physician Task Force report was undoubtedly a crucial step in the legitimation of hunger.

Meanwhile, a group of advocates and researchers based at the Food Research and Action Center in Washington, D.C., was working on an even more intensive approach to the study of hunger. Developed under the auspices of the Connecticut Association for Human Services and called the Community Childhood Hunger Identification Project or C-CHIP, this survey was designed to measure the incidence of hunger in low-income communities. C-CHIP is a point prevalence survey of families with children and incomes under 185 percent of the federal poverty threshold. It asks a whole battery of questions described by its creators as "designed to detect food insufficiency that occurs because of limited household resources." For example, "Thinking about the past thirty days, how many days was your household out of money to buy food to make a meal?" Households are designated as "hungry" if their answers on five of eight key dimensions indicate inadequate food resources. C-CHIP is designed to be administered locally, and to yield local hunger data, but by carefully selecting locations across the nations, FRAC was able to create national projections as well.

Celebrities: Giving Hunger a Good Name

Although the investigations conducted by experts provided the major "media pegs" for attention to hunger, they were not the only ones. Celebrities, as any good social constructionist can tell you, are another powerful magnet for attention, and hunger has had its share. Perhaps the major demonstration of celebrity power, media power, and the utility of the entertainment connection came in 1986 with Hands Across America, a plan for a Coast-to-Coast human chain to dramatize hunger and homelessness in America and raise funds to combat them. Participants were asked to sign up for a particular segment of the line, and to pay for the privilege by making a contribution to USA for Africa, the star-studded group that had produced the phenomenally successful *We Are the World* album to raise funds for famine relief in Africa. The funds were to be disbursed through a cooperative process involving both anti-hunger advocacy organizations and emergency food providers. "Hands" as its creators called it, reflected the philosophy of singer-songwriter Harry Chapin, an anti-hunger activist and founder of the anti-hunger organization World Hunger Year, who was killed in a car crash in 1981. Chapin had influenced many in the entertainment industry with his activism and deep social concern. "Harry always believed that ultimately governments would have to cure these problems," recalled Hands creator and USA for Africa president Ken Kragen. "But people move governments, and the media moves the people, so you start by encouraging the media to cover these issues." Hands Across America was designed, consciously, from the outset, to be a media-driven event, one that would raise consciousness as well as money. The date was set for the Saturday of Memorial Day Weekend, May 25, 1986.

Hands Across America's broad appeal, its success in enlisting corporate sponsors, including Coca-Cola and Citibank as its two earliest and largest underwriters, its ability to turn out hundreds of entertainment industry celebrities, along with at least 5.4 million other Americans, and its utility as a ready-made photo-op for politicians made it a crucial event in the process of giving hunger a good name. Perhaps the ultimate proof that it was respectable to be concerned about hunger and homelessness in America came when President Reagan made a down-to-the-wire decision to join the Hands Across America line which wound past the White House. An account of Reagan's decision by journalist Joe Morgenstern is revealing:

> One last-minute stroke of good luck that no one could have predicted came from the White House. During most of the week before Memorial Day weekend, President Reagan had said no, he wouldn't stand on the Hands line, even though he approved of the project and wished it well. Then, in a widely publicized conversation with some high-school students, he said he thought the problem of hunger was mostly a matter of lack of knowledge; it wasn't that people were going hungry because there was no food, the President maintained, but rather because they didn't know where to go for the proper assistance.
>
> This may well have been a true statement, although an incomplete one, since the Reagan administration, in the budget cutting fervor of its early years, had eliminated an outreach program designed precisely to tell the poor how to avail themselves of food stamps. But true or not, the President took a terrible drubbing in the press as a result of what he'd said, and two days later the White House announced that he would, after all, stand on the Hands Across America line. A spokesman denied any connection between the bad press and Mr. Reagan's change of heart, while Maureen Reagan explained that her father simply hadn't realized he was invited.

Hands eventually raised about $15 million to fight hunger and home-lessness in America, and USA for Africa added additional money to bring the total to $20 million, considerably less than they had ex-pected. It is more difficult to measure the consciousness-raising as-pects of the event. There were certainly communities that took a closer look at their own hungry and homeless as a result of Hands. And there was plenty of coverage. As Morgenstern summarized, "Hands certainly succeeded in calling its cause to the attention of the public—not just by raising some vague level of consciousness, but by playing on the media's habit of riding piggyback on big running sto-ries. The result was several months of news about Hands itself, accompanied by hundreds of reporting pieces about hunger and homelessness on TV, in the newspapers, and the news magazines—pieces that would never have been commissioned, let alone seen the light of day, had it not been for Hands' stimulus."

The real significance of Hands, however, was probably the halo effect from the hundreds of celebrities who did promotional adver-tisements and stood on the line. If basketball stars and rock musi-cians, the president of the United States and the CEO of American Express, the Boy Scouts of America, and the United Steelworkers could publicly declare themselves to be against hunger, then hunger must be a real problem, and it must be okay to be against it. Hands was probably the crucial event in what might be called the taming of hunger, and thus a major contributor, apart from its funds, to the in-stitutionalization of emergency food programs at the local level.

There were other consciousness-raising, and legitimacy-conferring, media events after Hands—two made-for-TV movies aired in March of 1988, "God Bless the Child" on ABC and "A Place at the Table" on NBC. The ABC showing was accompanied by an extended version of the public affairs program *Nightline,* devoted to discussion of the film and the problem of poverty in America. In 1991, the release of the first national projections derived from the C-CHIP studies was made into a media event by an appearance on the Capitol steps by the CEOs of several major corporations, explaining that allowing the per-sistence of childhood hunger was imprudent from a workforce devel-opment point of view and thus bad for business. And, of course, the annual appearances by politicians to help serve Thanksgiving or

Christmas dinner at soup kitchens kept the flow of pictures and sound bites alive. By the end of the eighties, hunger was nearly as American as apple pie. And as hunger grew more respectable—and bipartisan—it became easier for business to put additional resources into the hunger relief industry, largely through the food banking mechanism, and easier for conservatives to recognize anti-hunger activity as a legitimate expression of voluntarism.

Voluntarism as Ideology

The promotion of volunteering is the remaining element in the cultural context that has fostered the institutionalization of emergency food. Both individual volunteering and the formation of voluntary associations are long-standing and highly regarded parts of American culture. In the Reagan administration, the promotion of voluntary responses to the nation's pressing social problems reached the level of a major public education campaign. Sociologist David Adams has argued that Reagan made a virtual "civil religion" of voluntary action, complete with a mythic past in which Americans had solved their problems by getting together with their neighbors, a fall from grace period in which they had come to rely on big government, and a hope of salvation through a renewal of voluntary action. Reagan repeated these ideas every chance he got—in fact, he defined a rebirth of voluntarism as one of the central missions of his administration, "just about as important as anything that I could be called upon to do." Toward this end, he commissioned studies, established awards, and created commissions, and sent them out to "rediscover America . . . , the America whose initiative, ingenuity, and industry made this country the envy of the world, the America whose rich tradition of generosity began with simple acts of neighbor caring for neighbor." It is not clear that Reagan actually succeeded in fostering volunteer activity. As sociologist Susan Chambre has shown, not only did federally sponsored volunteer programs not expand under his leadership, but the proportion of American adults engaged in volunteer activity actually declined, significantly, during the Reagan years. There was, however, a shift of volunteer effort into social service and welfare organizations, and a steep rise in the number and proportion of volunteers who engaged in fund-raising.

President Bush emphasized the volunteer theme even more strongly with his memorable image of the "thousand points of light." A Points of Light Initiative Foundation was created, and the president began designating daily points of light, that is, one citizen or voluntary organization or project each day. Helen Palit, the founder of City Harvest, was among the first dozen points, and numerous other emergency food providers were accorded the honor. The point is not that people undertook emergency food projects in hopes of joining the presidential firmament. (In fact, I have known anti-hunger activists who have worried that they might be selected, and would have to choose between denying their organizations much deserved recognition by turning down the accolade, or, by accepting, being used to prop up an ideology with which they were fundamentally at odds.) The point is that by constant reiteration of the doctrine of voluntarism and perpetual news stories on the topic, the administration reinforced the notion that individual generosity and voluntary action were the answer to the nation's pressing problems in general, and hunger in particular. The presidential celebration of the American voluntary spirit did not begin with Reagan, and it certainly did not end with Bush, as we have seen with the new Clinton administration campaign headed by Colin Powell, but it reached an intensity during the Bush years that undoubtedly left a mark on the culture.

At one point in our interview, Jill Bullard told me about her four children. One was out of college, two were in college, and, she said, "I have a nine-year-old daughter who does not know when Mom didn't do this." Children who were in first grade when Ronald Reagan entered office were graduating from high school when George Bush left. Children who were born the year Ronald Reagan was elected are filling out their college applications now. We have a whole generation of young people who have grown up with food drives and soup kitchen lines, who think that destitution is a normal part of American life, and that handouts are the normal, and perhaps the only imaginable, response to it. This is institutionalization in another sense, in our consciousness, in the fabric of our expectations.

No amount of recognition from presidents or celebrity identification with the hunger problem could have brought about the enormous growth and institutionalization of emergency food had food programs not proven useful to powerful sectors of our society. *Institutionalization* is a good word, because it implies not only that an organization or a cluster of activities becomes an "institution," but also that is does so in interaction with the other, preexisting institutions of society, and that is certainly true in the case of emergency food. This phenomenon became institutionalized because it fit so well into the agendas of other powerful institutions, particularly government and business. This is true especially, although not exclusively, in the context of the massive waste or potential waste generated by those institutions. The next chapter explores the uses of emergency food to major institutions in our society.

CHAPTER FIVE

The Uses of Emergency Food

IN 1990, eight years and five reauthorizations after it had created its emergency commodity distribution measure, Congress finally changed the program's name from the Temporary Emergency Food Assistance Program (TEFAP) to The Emergency Food Assistance Program (TEFAP), preserving the acronym by which the program was universally known, but removing the increasingly obsolete and embarrassing *Temporary*. The hope that emergency food assistance on a large scale would be a phenomenon of short duration, articulated by nearly all the protagonists of the hunger wars of the early eighties, had clearly proven to be ill founded. Perhaps Bob Dole was right when he complained about his original TEFAP proposal that others would "want to continue it forever once it starts."

The name change seemed slightly comical to me. Was it the emergency or the program that was no longer to be regarded as temporary? Congress did nothing at the time to make the program permanent, adhering to its previous pattern of time-limited extensions, so maybe the intent was to acknowledge that hunger had become a permanent feature of our national life. The notion of a permanent emergency is certainly unattractive, but a close look at the life-styles available to many poor people reveals what might be termed a state of chronic emergency—medical care from the emergency room because they are uninsured, a bed in the emergency shelter because they are without permanent residence, food from the emergency food provider on a regular basis. Maybe Congress had fallen into the spirit of the original motto of food banking: "The poor you have always with you, but why the hungry?" Whatever the logic of the legislators, the name change signaled the extent to which government had become attached to the emergency food project.

When food piles up in government hands, as did Ronald Reagan's cheese, it makes government look bad, and government officials feel uncomfortable. Furthermore, it costs money to store and insure. Given the quantities of surplus commodities that the federal government was obligated to purchase under price-support agreements in the early and mid 1980s, when more than a billion pounds a year were distributed through the emergency food system, it is not surprising that Congress repeatedly reauthorized TEFAP. The cheese, however, was not a one-time aberration. We have faced this situation before, and we will probably encounter it again, because an agricultural surplus is a predictable outcome of the structure of our economy—and one that is certainly far preferable to a shortage of farm products. But a surplus always threatens profitability, and government will always be under pressure to intervene to protect the nation's food-producing capacity by protecting the profitability of farming, one way or another. An episode from the Great Depression of the 1930s reveals these structural dynamics with great clarity and puts our recent—and probable future—engagements with government surplus disposal in context.

A Parallel from the Past

The year is 1933. The nation, in the depths of the worst economic depression in its history, has rejected Herbert Hoover's "No one has starved" approach to the issue of federal assistance to the unemployed, and now it is Franklin Roosevelt's turn. His fledgling New Deal administration is simultaneously grappling with unprecedented poverty and destitution, and an overwhelming surplus of unmarketable farm products—the paradox of want amid plenty, they call it. A Federal Emergency Relief Administration (FERA) has been established by Congress to dispense federal grants in aid to the states for unemployment relief, and under the dynamic leadership of "relief czar" Harry Hopkins, cash has begun to trickle into the empty pockets of the unemployed. Relief grants are low, however: nothing for rent, except to prevent immediate eviction, almost nothing for clothing, nothing for hospitalization, a pittance for medication when deemed absolutely necessary, and a minimal food allowance. Families that have done without for years are grateful for the help but hungry, still hungry. Imagine the reaction, therefore, when the federal government begins buying up baby pigs and turning them into fertilizer.

Confronted with the prospect of another ruinous bumper crop, the Agricultural Adjustment Administration (AAA), the new agency charged with restoring "balance" to agriculture by cutting down on the nation's farm surpluses, tries to forestall an impending glut on the hog market by offering a bonus for the early slaughter of unripe pigs and piggy (pregnant) sows. From the very beginning, the pig slaughter generates outrage! How could the government be sponsoring the destruction of wholesome food when people are going hungry? Letters pour into the White House and the AAA, offering to relieve the administration of any surplus pigs it doesn't need: "I'll take a whole pig, dead or alive or made up into pork," writes an unemployed man from Chicago. "Why, oh why destroy what is so good to eat?" inquires an Ohio couple who have "not had a pork chop or any part of a hog in 2½ years." Others threaten dire consequences, political or even supernatural, for any politician so careless with the earth's bounty: "Willful waste brings woeful want," warns letter after letter.

The pig slaughter itself is a public relations nightmare. Midwestern farmers, faced with a drought-induced shortage of corn, send far more baby pigs to market for the account of the secretary of agriculture than have been anticipated, and the pigs pile up at the stockyards, where pens and equipment were built to handle fully finished hogs, not little pigs. The piglets escape and run squealing down the streets of Chicago and Omaha, eliciting a certain fuzzy public sympathy. But the real problems arise at the point of processing. The hog-butchering equipment cannot be made to process pigs lighter than eighty pounds, and so these, the great majority of the pigs, are to be ground up for "tankage," a sort of liquified pig sometimes used for fertilizer. The drying and storage facilities for tankage are soon over-filled, and the processors, glad for the government contract and anxious to get on with the work, begin looking for other ways to dispose of the tanked pigs. Rumor has it that they are dumping the stuff into nearby rivers. They bury some of it on farms. And they deposit some of it into gravel pits on the edge of Chicago. The weather turns warm. The stench is unbearable. Clouds of blue flies descend on the neighborhoods nearest the pits. The press has a field day.

At the height of the criticism triggered by the gravel pit episode, the Roosevelt administration announces a new program to purchase edible farm surpluses, beginning with the pigs, and distribute them to the unemployed. "Swift Roosevelt Blows Deal with Discontent; Grumbling Silenced by Order applying Food and Clothing Surplus to Relief . . ." headlines a feature story in the next Sunday's *New York Times*. The *Times* editorial welcoming this initiative is even more revealing. It will not only relieve the farmer and the unemployed, the *Times* avers, but it will "relieve our minds of the distressing 'economic paradox' of unprofitable surpluses existing side by side with extreme want." Two weeks later, Roosevelt and Hopkins announce the formation of a new agency to carry out the work of procurement and distribution, the Federal Surplus Relief Corporation (FSRC).

Taking the Curse Off the Pig Slaughter

The activities of the FSRC proved to be quite successful in appeasing the outraged public, and they quickly became the centerpiece of the replies that AAA officials sent to the many citizens who wrote in to complain about production control in general or the pig slaughter in particular. The pig slaughter created discomfort within the administration as well as an angry public reaction, and the FSRC helped to solve the resulting morale problem as well: "To many of us, the only thing that made the hog slaughter acceptable," wrote Secretary of Agriculture Henry Wallace a year later, "was the realization that the meat and lard salvaged would go to the unemployed." Wallace could have been speaking for public consumption, as a politician, of course, but the memoirs of AAA officials suggest that the distaste for the pig slaughter was widespread among employees, and the FSRC was a welcome solution.

Relief officials were not enthusiastic about commodity distribution; most of the leaders of the relief establishment were publicly committed to the principle of relief in cash as essential to the preservation of the dignity of recipients, and the commodities presented a whole series of logistical nightmares, but with relief allotments at the near starvation level, they could hardly refuse free food. The Roosevelt administration viewed its commodity project as a temporary means to resolve the political pressures generated by the so-called paradox of want amid plenty, a dramatic gesture to, as one contemporary journalist put it, "take the curse off" the pig slaughter, and a way of stretching meager relief budgets during a short-term federal emergency relief effort.

Once the program of government procurement and distribution was started, of course, it developed constituencies of its own that argued for its continuation and expansion. Very quickly, its utility was discovered by agriculture: individual growers, producers' cooperatives, agricultural extension agents, processors, distributors, chambers of commerce, state governors, members of Congress, all notified the corporation of the availability of their own particular favorite product and its eminent suitability for relief. As one writer put it, apparently hoping to make an FSRC purchase an annual event, "Last year and the year before, the Government purchased apples in this state and in the state of Oregon loose in cars. From the standpoint of the growers, this was a mighty fine thing."

When the federal government tried to get out of the direct relief business in 1935, shifting to a combination of social security for the aged, work relief for employables through the WPA, and "return" of the "unemployables" to state and local care, the "mighty fine thing" from the standpoint of the growers became a bone of contention. The relief establishment was determined to be rid of commodity distribution, both because it did not want to continue the practice of relief in kind so despised by Depression era social workers, and because federal surplus commodity distribution would contradict the ideological basis of the new relief set up. Roosevelt and Hopkins were insisting that the "unemployables" were the responsibility of the states and municipalities, and that the employables would be given what they wanted most, work. By continuing to distribute commodities, the federal government would be undermining both major planks of the new relief platform.

Keeping the Relief Outlet Open

The Agricultural Adjustment Administration (AAA), on the other hand, was committed to "keeping the relief outlet open." "The Corporation has become an accepted outlet for the unmarketable portions of agricultural crops," wrote a triple A staff member to Secretary Wallace; "Destruction may be as defensible as factory shutdowns," he continued, "but it is more offensive to the general public." Writing early in 1935, as the deadline for the relief overhaul approached, the Agriculture Department's Food Survey Committee declared: "It would seem highly undesirable that the AAA program involve the physical destruction of any surplus next year, even if these surpluses should be due to favorable weather. Food costs will probably be high through much of the year and it would be politically as well as humanistically undesirable to destroy food supplies at the same time many millions of persons were on low relief or work-relief incomes." Recognizing that surpluses were not a reliable basis for provision, "with dribbles at some times and gluts at other times," the Food Survey Committee proposed a larger and more regular commodity distribution program that would "provide a sufficient flow of commodities to justify setting up and keeping in continuous operation local machinery for its distribution to those on relief."

The impasse was resolved by a tactic that might sound familiar to the architects of the TEFAP name change. The organization's name was changed from the Federal Surplus *Relief* Corporation to the Federal Surplus *Commodities* Corporation, in conformity with Harry Hopkins's request that the name be changed "to something which includes the word 'commodities' so that it is identified in the public mind with our farm program rather than our relief program, although the commodities themselves . . . will be distributed through local and state relief agencies." The governance of the renamed organization was transferred to the Department of Agriculture, where it was promptly and thoroughly adapted to its new role as a tool for farm income maintenance.

Gluts and Dribbles

A food assistance program dependent upon surpluses might have been a continuing boon to the poor, despite the priority placed on farm incomes, if surpluses had been a steady source of supply. When surpluses mounted to record levels in the late 1930s, the Department of Agriculture tackled the problem it labeled "underconsumption" by expanding its commodity distribution program and creating an innovative food stamp program to channel surpluses to the poor through the normal channels of trade. By their very nature, however, surpluses are extras, amounts above what the market will bear; they are subject to the "gluts and dribbles" phenomenon identified by the Food Survey Committee. In the years following the FSRC change of name and address, food assistance dependent upon surplus proved to be a very weak crutch. When drought reduced production, as it did in the "dust bowl" years of the Depression, or war provided alternative markets as happened in the forties, families and programs dependent upon surplus commodities were left with meager fare indeed. In fact, surpluses dwindled so low in the early years of World War II that the food stamp program was terminated altogether, and counties were permitted to withdraw from the commodity program if they did not want to share in the costs of distribution. Many of the nation's poorest counties did just that, setting up the situation, discovered by anti-poverty investigators in the late 1960s, in which some of the nation's neediest citizens lived in counties which operated no federal family food assistance program.

History Repeated

It is easy to identify three distinct stages in this story which repeat themselves quite clearly in the 1980s. First there is a public relations emergency created by the pigs, or in the early eighties, the cheese, and a (temporary) emergency response. The Special Dairy Distribution Program may have been a bit less successful than the FSRC in taking the curse off surplus accumulation, but the cheese is fondly remembered by many who received it, and it was certainly a big improvement, from a public relations standpoint, over letting the dairy surplus turn to mold or dumping it in the sea. The cheese distribution allowed Ronald Reagan to restate his concern for the poor and deflect attention from his administration's compromise with farm interests in a bill that actually raised dairy price supports over the next four years, thereby almost guaranteeing an ongoing problem. The signing of the bill, according to the *Times*, "was overshadowed by the President's action on the stockpile of 560 million pounds of cheese," which occurred in the same Oval Office ceremony.

The second stage consisted of pressure for routinization, for conversion to a more permanent basis, as the utility of the program is discovered by various constituencies. The New Deal created the FSCC; the eighties gave us TEFAP. In the latter case, the pleas of farmers and processors were augmented by those of food banks and their member agencies. Price supports were fairly secure, and the Commodity Credit Corporation was committed to purchasing farm products, whether or not the relief outlet remained open; this time it was Catholic Charities USA and Second Harvest and the Salvation Army and the Red Cross as well as kitchen, pantry, and food bank directors and the mayors of large cities and state commodity distribution directors and representatives of warehouses and trucking firms who journeyed or wrote to Washington to tell Congress why funds for administration, transportation, storage and handling of federal commodities must be added, and then maintained. As the institutionalization process described in chapter 4 proceeded in organization after organization and community after community, it was not so much a matter of keeping the relief outlet open—it was open and expanding—as keeping the current of federal support flowing through it.

Finally, in the third stage of the story, there are reductions in the surplus, and the poor are left with less, and this bit of history, too, repeated itself in the modern version. Despite its special relationship with government, dairy farming is a business, and so is the dairy processing industry. Businesses need profits, and surpluses threaten profits, either by undermining prices or, if government is purchasing and distributing large quantities, by undermining markets. When nature fails to reduce the surplus to manageable levels, the industry will try to enlist the aid of government to do so, and that is exactly what happened with the dairy surplus of the early eighties. When the protests of the National Cheese Institute revealed that the industry's tolerance for free cheese distribution to the poor had reached its limits, the Department of Agriculture looked for another way to avoid the burdensome purchase and storage charges to which it had become obligated. It came up with the Dairy Termination Program, commonly known as the Dairy Herd Buyout, which paid farmers to "eliminate their herds," that is, send their cows to the slaughterhouse. Many dairy farmers took advantage of USDA's offer to buy their whole herds, and, for a while, at least, dairy surpluses decreased. CCC cheese inventories went from a peak of 933 million pounds in July 1983 to 98 million pounds at the beginning of fiscal 1988, and in February 1988, the assistant secretary for Food and Consumer Services of the U.S. Department of Agriculture testified with pride that shipments of cheese and nonfat dry milk through the TEFAP program would end in April.

By the time they did so, however, the nation had created a very large number of emergency food programs that depended upon such commodities as a major element in their supply. The loss of the dairy products might not have been such a blow to these programs had not capricious nature intervened. A severe drought in 1988 sharply reduced the supply of many other TEFAP commodities, from a glut to a dribble in the space of a few months. Emergency food providers proved a remarkably astute constituency, able to marshal immense moral force as well as pragmatic arguments, to lobby for some replacement for the disappearing surpluses. Unwilling to leave them in the lurch, Congress directed the secretary of agriculture to purchase commodities specifically for the program.

In doing so, it fundamentally changed the nature of TEFAP from a surplus disposal program to a food procurement program, a switch that changed the politics of the appropriations process. As long as the items distributed were surpluses already purchased as part of the government's price-support operations, proponents of the program could argue that the money had already been spent and the question was what to do with the product. The administrative funds that were so crucial to many emergency food providers were small potatoes by congressional standards. It was easy to argue that the nation should spend $50 million to get a billion dollars' worth of wholesome American agricultural products into the hands of hungry Americans. Once it became necessary to appropriate funds for commodity purchase as well, however, the program was set on a collision course with fiscal austerity. The commodities purchased specifically for the program were especially welcome at the front lines because they included canned fruits and vegetables and, particularly valuable, canned meat, but the bounty proved to be short lived.

As soon as the switch had occurred, the process of weaning began. Congress appropriated less money for commodities, and then less money again. In fiscal year 1995, the Clinton administration budget proposed $0 for commodities purchase, although it was willing to appropriate $40 million for "administrative costs" in order to sustain the distribution network, that is, to maintain the infrastructure of food banks, pantries, and kitchens as well as state agencies, that had become partially dependent upon TEFAP administrative funds. The symbolism of paying for bureaucrats and program administrators but not for food was too powerful, and eventually Congress came up with $25 million for commodities purchase, but this was a far cry from the billion dollars' worth of products that were poured into the system annually during the surplus heyday of the mid-eighties. The 1996 "welfare reform" legislation introduces some stability, directing $100 million annually in mandatory commodity purchases for the next five years, less than a tenth of the program's peak contribution, but predictable, at least.

The Halo Effect

In the modern version of this story, as in its New Deal incarnation, it is almost impossible to separate the waste management functions of emergency food from its general halo effect. That is, "feeding the hungry" is an activity that is so widely thought of as "good" that it has the power to take the curse off unpopular activities, whether or not they involve food waste. Perhaps this is why gangster Al Capone opened a breadline—coffee and doughnuts, actually—during the Great Depression, or why the brochure for the Virginia chapter of an organization called Hunters for the Hungry urges hunters to donate part or all of their kill to food providers, pointing out that donation will "get good publicity for deer hunters and for the sport of hunting." Even where there is not a negative association to be counteracted, feeding the hungry offers the possibility of "virtue by association." I cannot remember a Thanksgiving in recent memory on which the news has not shown governors, mayors, and even the president of the United States, often accompanied by teenaged children or beaming spouses, serving food in a soup kitchen or shelter. Emergency food has become the accepted icon for caring about hungry people—for the businesswoman who sponsors a food drive in her office, for the Little League team that walks in a walkathon, and for the politician who dons an apron and carves turkey in the church basement or the VFW post on Thanksgiving. Thus the halo effect exists regardless of whether or not waste prevention is involved. But when political damage is incurred by the specter of large-scale waste of government-held food, and when the very product that was about to be wasted can be used to feed the hungry, there is a double benefit, a magnification, in which the whole is clearly greater than the sum of the parts. We like avoiding the waste, we like feeding the hungry, and we like the two-for-the-price-of-one character of the resulting project. No wonder the halo effect of emergency food is particularly visible in the context of waste.

Nevertheless, the halo effect of feeding the hungry, and the creation of what the triple A staff called a "politically and humanistically" acceptable outlet for government-owned surpluses are not the only bonuses that government has come to expect from the emergency food system. There are more tangible benefits, as well, beginning with the savings in storage and insurance costs. Annual storage and handling costs to the Department of Agriculture for the dairy surplus had reached $43 million by the end of 1981. By the fall of 1983, columnist George Will calculated that taxpayers "are currently paying $275,000 an hour to buy more surpluses, and are paying $5 million a month to store the stuff." During the first two years of the distribution program, the federal government was able to shift some of these costs to the states by shipping out dairy products for which the states then became responsible, and the states, in turn, were able to limit costs by enlisting large numbers of volunteers to pick up and distribute the cheese. Even when Congress required the Department of

Agriculture to begin reimbursing states and voluntary EDOs (Emergency Distribution Organizations) for administrative, storage, and transportation costs, the heavy reliance on volunteer labor kept costs well below what they would have been in a system reliant upon public employees. No one, to my knowledge, has calculated what actually dumping the cheese and butter would have cost, but this expenditure, too, was prevented by the national effort to feed the dairy surplus to the poor. For as long as there were actual surpluses, the storage costs not incurred were a net gain to the government. Once the system switched to purchased commodities, of course, that equation changed.

Assisting the Criminal Justice System

Emergency food assists government (and reduces expenditures) in other ways as well. I was struggling with the giant institutional can opener one morning at a soup kitchen in which I volunteered, when a tall black man of about thirty-five came in the door and asked for the Sister in charge. She talked with him briefly, gave him a form to sign, and immediately set him to work cleaning the bathroom. I was taken aback at her somewhat peremptory tone and her failure to introduce him to the rest of us; I imagined that he had done something to displease her, and I hoped it would not be my turn next as I was certainly not mastering the balky can opener. I even worried about racism, since the other volunteers were all white or Hispanic; did the Sister think we wouldn't welcome an African American? Later on one of the more experienced volunteers explained to me that he was "from the court," and doing his "community service" at our kitchen. When I got over my discomfort with the language—"community service" is what I have spent much of my adult life encouraging students to undertake—I realized that along with the complexities of ordering food and coordinating volunteers and managing hundreds of hungry and sometimes difficult clients, the diminutive nun was now also serving as an extension to the probation system, free of charge.

Such community service has become the penalty of choice, in many jurisdictions, for people arrested for driving while intoxicated. They scrub pots in soup kitchens or sort salvage in food banks or help gleaners bring in the harvest. Perhaps association with such caring and socially conscious volunteers will rub off on them, instilling a greater respect for the rights of others. In any case, it is far cheaper than incarcerating them. Project Glean in Concord, California, claims with pride that more than half of the court-ordered participants "work off their speeding tickets and then return as true volunteers."

Community service in lieu of fines or incarceration is not the only way in which emergency food has made itself useful to the penal system and vice versa. In many areas of the country, prisoners maintain gardens, even farms, that supply fresh produce for food banks. In some areas, relationships between government agencies and food banks or other emergency food providers have become quite extensive and elaborate. Arizona had a head start, since Arizona is where food banking began, and it has developed a remarkable system of cooperation among the Arizona State Department of Agriculture, the Department of Corrections, and the Association of Arizona Foodbanks that yields hundreds of tons of produce very year. Clark Skeans, a retired businessman who now works full-time at the Association of Arizona Foodbanks as the Arizona Statewide Gleaning Distribution Coordinator, explained the system to me. The State Department of Agriculture's inspectors serve as the contact point. "They will learn of a grower that isn't going to harvest what is left in the field. He is going to disk it under. . . . They approach the grower and say 'Give us a window of a couple of days so that the food banks can come in and glean your product.' " If the grower agrees, the inspector calls Skeans. "What I do then is arrange to meet the inspector and somebody from the Department of Corrections and somebody from the food bank . . . in the field, and we will just walk the field—look at the quality of product and the volume of product. Determine the kind of resources we need to support the gleaning activity. The prison will be able to see the location logistically from a security standpoint. And during the examination of the field, set a time when we are going to start the process . . . it is usually the next day."

Prison labor is ideal for this system for two reasons—it is free (to the gleaning network) and it can be mobilized and deployed on short notice; that window of opportunity is often literally only a day or two in duration. On the other hand, the Corrections Department retains a portion of the produce gleaned, and thus reduces its own food expenditures. It is another case of the halo effect, when you think about it. How many farmers would let the Department of Corrections bring inmates into their fields to harvest crops if the prison system were the sole beneficiary? But by including the food banks, and thus harvesting for "the hungry," the project has been able to enlist enormous good will. The State of Arizona seems to appreciate the benefits; after several years of patchwork funding pieced together from federal grants and local donations, the gleaning network has now secured a commitment for almost all of its budget from the State. As Skeans reported, "The State was able to see how beneficial it has been and how much we have accomplished. We are spending $85,000 this year for 10 million pounds of produce. That's less than a penny a pound. And what can you buy for that? It is a good return on investment."

Gleaning is not the end of the cooperation between the emergency food system and the corrections system. The county Sheriff's Department provides a great deal of the trucking needed to get the produce in, keeping some of the produce to offset its costs. The county jails also provide trustees as regular labor for the food banks. In the town of Willcox in the southeast corner of the state, a team of prisoners from the nearby Arizona State Penitentiary at Fort Grant comes every weekday to do the heavy work at the Southeast Arizona Food Bank Warehouse. Their tasks include unloading trucks, sorting inventory, shelving, and carrying boxes of food out to the cars, vans, and trucks sent by food pantries in the region for pickups. Since the area is a haven for retirees, and the pantries seem to be run, to a considerable extent, by senior citizens, the car and van loading function is important and the sheer muscle power is welcome. The woman in charge of the detail, Officer Webb, told me that the food bank was the most desirable work detail in the prison, one that the inmates compete to get. The working conditions are probably better than those in some of the alternative assignments, but both she and the food bank director Rey Martinez, who pioneered the system, felt that the real attraction was the usefulness of the work: the men felt needed, valuable, and respected. They appreciated the courtesy with which they were treated by food bank staff and pantry volunteers, and Rey Martinez explained, "many of them have families that are benefiting from the food."

Like the exchange in my soup kitchen, where free labor to clean the bathrooms and mop the floors was exchanged for free supervision and record keeping, the Southeast Arizona Food Bank Warehouse is engaged in an exchange with the penitentiary. The prison provides an armed corrections officer, but Martinez provides much of the day-to-day direction of the team's work, and tries to help inmates find jobs when they are paroled or complete their sentences. Both the food bank and the prison system probably save money; both can certainly claim substantial contributions in kind on their bottom lines.

Reducing the Demand for Public Assistance

The major way that the emergency food phenomenon saves government money, however, is through reduced expenditures in public assistance programs. This contention is difficult to quantify, but important to explore, nevertheless. Conceptually, there are at least three avenues through which the expansion of emergency food may be saving public sector dollars. First, there are the preferences of clients themselves. Many emergency food programs go to great lengths, as we shall see in chapter 8, to treat clients with kindness and to create a welcoming atmosphere, a clear contrast to the treatment routinely accorded welfare recipients in many public assistance offices. Instead of demanding that they be treated fairly and respectfully at food stamp certification interviews, some clients have simply found it easier to make the rounds of pantries. Clearly, application and certification procedures at kitchens and pantries are far less burdensome than those in public bureaucracies. One study that compared TEFAP with food stamps in the early 1990s reported that "evidence collected from focus groups indicates that the elderly perceive the FSP application and issuance procedures to be significant barriers to participation," and suggested that this might help to account for the much greater representation of the elderly among TEFAP recipients than among food stamp users. In a study of soup kitchen and food pantry users in New York in which I participated in the late 1980s, we found substantial numbers of people whose income data suggested that they were eligible for food stamps but who had concluded that the stamps were not worth the misery of the treatment they received, or who had simply given up after repeated efforts to establish their eligibility.

By making the pantries and kitchens kinder, gentler help, are emergency food staff and volunteers deterring people from obtaining benefits to which they are entitled as a matter of right? This is not an outcome that would be universally rejected by emergency food providers. Some got involved with food pantries in a conscious effort to help people stay off public assistance, and others prefer assistance in kind specifically because they have little faith that their clients will spend food stamps well and wisely. But most of the kitchen and pantry directors, food bankers and advocates I've spoken with want people to obtain all of their available public benefits before turning to emergency food, if for no other reason than to conserve their programs' limited supplies of food for people who cannot access public supports or people for whom such aid is not sufficient. From the point of view of government bookkeeping, however, each person eligible for a major public benefit like food stamps who fails to apply for it because she can rely upon private assistance instead, even publicly aided private assistance, represents a short-term saving.

Such choices freely made by informed clients may not be troubling from a social policy perspective, but the stories of harassment and abuse that clients report from their encounters with public bureaucracies make the characterization of the choice as "freely made" inaccurate, even where clients are well informed about their rights. Of course, many clients are not well informed about their rights. One of the most significant cuts that the Reagan administration made in the Food Stamp Program was the termination of federal funds for outreach efforts, a cut that has never been fully restored. Soup kitchens, and especially food pantries, have taken on this role as best they can, and more and more pantries and kitchens have developed the capacity to help clients establish their eligibility for public benefits, but this activity creates yet another drain on inherently limited staff or volunteer time.

Facilitating Bureaucratic Disentitlement

It is not only the choices of clients, of course, but also the choices of public officials, that help to shift the costs of providing food for the hungry to the voluntary sector. In the climate of fiscal austerity created by efforts to simultaneously reduce taxes, expand military spending, and cut benefits and services for poor people, bureaucratic performance as well as legislation can effectively reduce de facto benefits. In such a climate, a message travels down the line, from politician to agency administrator and from administrator to frontline worker, that errors which reduce benefits or fail to provide them will be tolerated, but errors of overcalculation or wrongful issuance will be penalized. The federal error rate standards in the Food Stamp Program institutionalized this preference years ago. That is, error rates, for many years, included only errors of overissuance. Advocates complained, and finally the federal government's auditors began to count errors in which benefits were found to be too low as well as those in which they were too high. Mistakes that lead to failure to approve benefits to which people are actually entitled still do not count, however, since the government auditors sample only open cases. The existence of a visible private food safety net makes such a policy easier to carry out, for the frontline worker and the agency administrator alike. The frequency with which income maintenance clerks and other public assistance personnel refer unsuccessful applicants to food pantries suggests that emergency food programs provide a sort of moral reassurance for agency workers—they are not consigning applicants to out-and-out starvation.

In New York City, for example, the city's Human Resources Administration was the primary source of referrals to food pantries in the late 1980s, and advocates charged that the city was referring people to private food pantries instead of issuing Expedited Food Stamps and Immediate Needs Grants to which applicants without resources were entitled. A local Interfaith Hunger Policy Task Force reported that the federal error rate standards were fueling this process by making the city more willing to risk a wrongful denial of benefits than a wrongful approval. At one point the city proposed to open its own emergency food pantries to supply immediate needs instead of increasing use of the Expedited Food Stamps option. Advocates were able to show that the city's proposed emergency food centers, which were to be supplied by private vendors, would be more expensive than issuing the Expedited Food Stamps, even if the federal government subsequently found every one of the issuances to be in error and penalized the city accordingly for an excess error rate, and the plan was abandoned, but the fact that it was ever seriously considered shows something of the chilling effects of the error rate sanctions.

Reassuring the Decisionmakers

Finally, at a more speculative but more consequential level, it appears entirely plausible that legislators enacting cutbacks have also been figuring private food assistance into their mental and moral calculus. There are no instances that I have found of public entitlements eliminated with the availability of emergency food as a public and official rationale. When General Assistance was terminated in Michigan or Illinois, or sharply reduced in California or New York or any of the other states that enacted cutbacks over the past half-dozen years, no one said publicly that public assistance was not needed because private assistance was available. Emergency food providers, however, clearly saw the cutbacks as an attempt to shift more of the responsibility for feeding the poor to the voluntary sector. When Los Angeles cut its general relief in increments from $334 to $212 a month, 109,000 people in L.A. County lost benefits. The director of the FEMA local board, Gene Boutillier, described the reaction of emergency providers: "That creates enormous resentments on the part of the food pantries because it feels to them, very accurately I think, as if government and the citizenry are dumping these 109,000 people on them. It feels that way because it is that way."

On the prescriptive side of the ledger, a greater role for churches and private charities had been urged, publicly and explicitly, by conservatives in general and by two of the primary architects of reductions in public assistance, Ronald Reagan and Newt Gingrich. The sections of the 1996 PRWORA Act that bar legal immigrant non-citizens from receiving a whole host of public assistance benefits specifically exclude "emergency" programs from this provision. It is difficult to imagine that the architects of the new welfare law were *not* counting on the nation's well-publicized network of kitchens and pantries to pick up the slack. Certainly the leaders of the emergency food movement interpreted Gingrich's comments and the Contract with America in that manner. I think of this as the "Herbert Hoover Doctrine": private charity is the American way; it can do the job; no one will starve.

The emergency food system, therefore, has helped government "save money" by giving potential clients an alternative to collecting their rights under existing law and policy, by reassuring administrators engaged in creating a harsher, more deterrent climate, and by enabling legislators to choose with impunity reductions in already inadequate programs. Taken together with the halo effects described above, and the capacity of the system to absorb embarrassing surpluses when they reach problematic levels, it is not surprising that government, regardless of party, has consistently taken steps to assist, protect, and preserve the emergency food system. Some functions of the system, of course, have not been "regardless of party"; that is, they have been closely allied with the conservative social agenda. We shall consider these in the final chapter of this book, but it is important to realize that much of what emergency food does for government, it does regardless of which ideology is ascendant or which party is in power. Government has developed an interest in maintaining the emergency food system.

Corporate Welfare: It's Always a Business Decision

In this endeavor, government's efforts have been complemented by those of another powerful institution, business, because soup kitchens and food pantries, and especially food banks and food rescue programs, have proven extraordinarily useful to business as well. Sometimes the business involvement falls under the general rubric of "cause-related marketing," the use of association with a good cause as a marketing strategy, or a combination of marketing strategy and good deed. What better good cause for a package-moving company than helping food rescue operations move food safely. What better good cause for any food company than fighting hunger. Recently, I received in my mailbox a postcard alerting me to the Stamp Out Hunger Food Drive, sponsored by the National Association of Letter Carriers, in conjunction with the United States Postal Service. A bright red box on the card indicated that the colorful postcard had been "printed with the generous support of Campbell's Soups, Feeding America for Over 100 Years!" The Campbell's Soups part of this acknowledgment was a replica of the cursive lettering of the familiar label, a motif that was reproduced on the brimming bags held by the letter carriers pictured on the card. Because these bags appeared to be filled primarily with cans of Campbell's soups and related products, the company gets a bit of subliminal advertising. Who knows? Perhaps millions of Americans will include at least one can of Campbell's soup in their donations, although soup is *not* the ideal item, because the typical can of soup provides too few calories and too few nutrients to make a major contribution to the well being of a hungry person. Even if the subliminal advertising does not work, however, Campbell's will earn Brownie points for contributing to an all-American cause.

When overproduction or unmarketable products are involved, the functions that emergency food serves for business are remarkably similar to those it fulfills for government—the halo effect, the preservation of employee morale, an acceptable outlet for unsalable products, and tangible financial savings—although the order of priority is probably different. That is, government is inextricably involved in politics and constantly in the public eye, so looking bad by destroying or wasting edible commodities, for example, is probably a more urgent problem than incurring financial costs for storage or disposal. For business and industry, the situation is reversed. Many firms make efforts to be "good corporate citizens," and to maintain an image of such corporate good citizenship, but nearly everyone involved in large-scale donations agrees that the bottom line comes first. As one corporate executive put it, "It is always a business decision."

"When I came to Second Harvest," Deb Keegan, the organization's director of marketing, explained, "we were about packaged goods, and we were about selling Second Harvest as a charity. I decided that we needed to be about the entire grocery industry, from grower to retailer, and we needed to market ourselves not as a charity but as a business, because I assumed companies gave, not because they care—they do care—but they give because of economics. It saves them money." After exploratory interviews with ten of its major donors, Second Harvest reported that "All companies agreed that their disposition decision was based first on economics. Each company placed Second Harvest right before the dump in their product disposition decision tree.... Their first option is to sell, for any price." Among the components of the business decision, "the tax benefits for donating, reduction of disposal costs, and ease of the system were cited by 9 of the 10 donors as primary factors for their decision to donate.... Public relations and employee morale were less important factors."

Financial Savings

The avoidance of dump fees is a straightforward calculation for most firms; they know what dumping will cost, and donating the products is usually cheaper. Sometimes this creates an anomaly for food banks; if they are unable to pass the product along to member agencies, they may end up incurring the dump fees themselves. They try to avoid such situations, of course, but sometimes, as one food banker explained to me, "we are pressured to accept donations of things that we don't want and don't have any use for, or we want to appease a donor, because you have to be there for them.... Some people, you are fortunate to get in there and you don't want to alienate them." Her food bank has developed a relationship with local pig farmers, who will accept edible products for pig feed, and a composting project for vegetables, so the food bank seldom pays dump fees. In any case, a donor avoids such fees.

The tax benefits of corporate donations in kind are somewhat more ambiguous. Amendments to the federal tax law passed in 1976 provide that non-subchapter S corporations, that is, corporations that sell stock to the public and have more than fifteen stockholders, may deduct from their taxable income the cost of acquiring any property subsequently donated plus half the unrealized markup—that is, half the difference between their cost and the fair market value of the product, with the total deduction capped at twice the cost. The intent is to provide an incentive for donation while eliminating a situation that existed prior to 1970 in which firms could actually be better off by donating than by selling. The confusion has come over determining the fair market value, which is clear for some products, but not for others. "There have been some companies that have been audited and not gotten through," Keegan explained, "because what they determined to be the fair market value is not what the IRS determined to be the fair market value.... There are some major donors that don't take the tax benefit because they don't want to go through all of that, trying to determine what's fair market value." A Sara Lee executive told me that Sara Lee allows local subsidiary and plant managers to make charitable donations of product without clearing them with the central office so long as they are *not* claiming a tax deduction; otherwise, they must obtain the approval of the parent company: "It is simply a matter of control, so that our tax department is able to monitor what's being given away as a tax deduction, to avoid future problems with the Internal Revenue Service." Further tax law changes in 1986, involving inventory and the basis for calculating value, are reported to have made donation less attractive.

Despite these complexities, however, nine of the ten companies surveyed by Second Harvest in its exploratory study reported that they regularly take the tax benefit, and rated it as an important factor in their decision to donate rather than dump. Several states offer tax deductions or tax credits, as well. Virginia, for example, has a program that gives corporations a tax credit, right off the bottom line of their tax bill, of 50 percent of the value of any food donated. Food bankers continue to lobby, both for a clarification of the federal law and for additional state-level tax provisions.

The Role of Leadership

In a situation in which tax savings or the avoidance of dumping costs are clear and compelling, leadership from the top of a corporation may not be of great importance, but I was impressed in my interviews with the extent to which individual corporate executives had become caught up in the underlying mission of "feeding the hungry." Bob Lauer was the president of the Sara Lee Foundation and was serving his third term on the Second Harvest board when I interviewed him in 1994. He attributed Sara Lee's fairly extensive commitment to corporate citizenship to the company's CEO, John Bryan: "John was very active in the civil rights movement in Mississippi, as a young man, in the community. And he just has that sense of commitment. And a sense of fairness, and of justice. And when you have a person at the top with that kind of character, it's contagious in a sense, and he has always encouraged the Sara Lee Foundation." When I discussed with Lauer his own history of involvement, however, it is clear that his commitment to helping hungry people predated his involvement with Sara Lee, or his service as a Second Harvest board member. I asked him if feeding the hungry was something he had given thought to before he was invited to join the Second Harvest board, and his reply was immediate. "I wouldn't have gone on the board if I hadn't had a real interest in that. . . . I saw the fact that I was with this big and well-recognized food company as a good reason for me to get involved in something that I felt strongly about, and that was trying to help hungry people. I grew up in a community where people, including myself, I have to be honest, didn't have food. Once you do that, as you may know, you never forget it. So the idea that I could help was important." Lauer's parents were itinerant farmworkers who followed the tomato, cucumber, and sugar beet crops. I asked him if he had grown up with strong feelings about waste of food, and his answer brought me up short. "Well, you know, I didn't see food wasted. Because the people that I associated with ate everything. . . . My mother never threw anything out. She just kept warming it up and serving it until it was consumed, and so I didn't see waste as I was growing up . . . we didn't have pets, because that meant they would get some of the food. The people in the community I lived in, we didn't have dogs or pets, because we ate what people normally would give to their dogs."

Employee Morale

While it may be rare to find corporate executives who are motivated in part by memories of deprivation, it is certainly not so unusual among frontline employees. Employee morale, another factor frequently cited as a motivation for corporate donation, is difficult to quantify, but a real factor, nevertheless. It seems something of an add-on when we are talking about large-scale corporate donations, from company headquarters to Second Harvest, for example. Donors were sure that it would be bad for morale if employees knew that the end product of their work ended up in the dump; they were less sure how employees would know, or what steps were taken to communicate to them the decision to donate to a food bank. In a random survey of 2,012 households designed to measure public attitudes toward hunger and hunger relief activities, Second Harvest encountered 107 people who were employed in the food industry. Asked if their companies ever contributed food to any hunger relief organization, a quarter said they did not know, and a fifth believed that their employers did not make such contributions. Fully 85 percent, however, said that they would favor company donations to Second Harvest.

In smaller-scale settings, the morale factor can be quite significant. Employees like to know that their company provides snacks for the Scouts or hot dogs for the Little League, and that the leftovers from company picnics go to help the homeless. In the restaurant industry, in specific, and the prepared and perishable food rescue movement in general, preservation of employee morale is a very big factor. As Jill Bullard put it, "they were part of their food and they didn't want to see it treated as trash." Employees in cafeterias and restaurants resent the practice of throwing food out at the end of the day, whether because of pride in their efforts, or because they and their neighbors could make good use of it at home. "When I was in college I worked at a food service operation in a large hospital," food banker Joanne Grisanti told me, "and it was really, really striking to me that there would be a lot of leftover food. The people who worked in the kitchen got paid very low wages and they weren't allowed to eat any of the food that was left, or take it home. So you had people on really limited incomes, personally throwing pans and pans of meat down the garbage disposal every night."

Food service managers, however, have very specific reasons for not allowing employees to take the food home with them: "We couldn't let them take it home because there is always the risk of someone overpreparing just so there will be extra to take home. There are also strict policies about taking company property out of the building, so we had to maintain the corporate rules as well as just what makes sense in terms of food," the corporate services manager of a large midwestern company explained to me. For her, the discovery of a safe, reliable food rescue program came as a big relief: "For many years our employees had been asking us why we throw away all this food every day." In that environment, the food rescue movement provides more than a halo or a convenient disposal option for the corporation; it removes a nagging, daily source of employee dissatisfaction and disrespect.

Many people think of food rescue as the occasional bucket of soup or the last pan of lasagna that doesn't sell in a cafeteria, but the rules that prohibit reuse and prevent employees from taking home food apply to enormous quantities of food left over from major events, as well. "Right now, the growth in the program is in special events," Rose Anne Healy told me about Miami's Extra Helpings program. "We are seeing an explosion of community events . . . Last month we picked up from the Miami Grand Prix, Honda Classic, the Doral Open, the Lipton Tennis Tournament, we had the Super Bowl." Pat Thibideau, now the executive director of the Chef and the Child Foundation, was drawn into food rescue by one specific event at Sea World, a convention of weight-conscious cheerleaders, where she worked as a sous chef. "We had cheerleaders and they didn't want to eat their lunch. Their lunch was cold fried chicken. They wanted an apple or an orange, so there were forty-five hundred pieces of cold fried chicken, which placed me between the chicken and the dumpster. I wouldn't let them throw it away. I put myself in the way and said, 'No, we are not going to do this.' And we actually saved that and we took it down and we served it for lunch" to the homeless people who congregate in Orlando's parks and sleep under its bridges.

The Halo Effect Revisited

At the local level, general public relations are a greater factor than at the national level. "It is cause-related marketing for them because they are associated with us," a food bank staffer told me of local donors. "They can tell anyone that they do their part to help fight hunger in the community and they support the food bank." There is also a convenience factor: "There are a lot of small sites. Everybody is coming and asking for food. So if they say 'Sorry, I donate to the food bank' they don't have to deal with all these little guys. It is kind of like the old argument saying 'No, I give to the United Way.' " Even at the local level, however, dollars and cents are probably the decisive factor. As Madeline Lund explained:

> Most food donors donate for business reasons. That is not to say that we should not continue to tell our story . . . about who it is that they are serving and why we are doing this, because maybe, eventually, at some point in the future, it will be to our benefit that they are also committed in their hearts and their souls. But we should not assume that it is the heart and soul that is going to save us. It is going to be an inventory control problem. It is going to be a packaging error. It is going to be the business solution that is going to really be the spur that encourages them to donate to the food bank.

The business solution, however, like the surplus commodity disposal solution for the Agriculture Department, has a built-in self-limiting process.

Gluts and Dribbles in the Private Sector

Susan Cramer has worked in the anti-hunger field for a long time. Currently, she is the grants director for Mazon, A Jewish Response to Hunger, but she worked for Second Harvest as its communications director and in other capacities during much of its formative period. As she explained: "One thing Second Harvest has done is help food companies realize where the waste is in their production pipeline. . . . One of the trends we talked about a long time ago as a possible future trend was that the success of Second Harvest would be a signal to any thinking food industry executive. If their company got inducted into what we, at the time, called the Million Pound Club, those companies that were honored at our conference every year for giving more than a million pounds, wouldn't they wonder where this food came from?" This prediction proved accurate. Donations to food banks have served to alert businesses to the points in their systems at which waste was occurring. The infamous razor knife is a prime example. After the quantity of slashed cereal boxes came to the attention of cereal processors, they switched to shipping in cartons with pull tapes, and an important source of breakfast goods for pantry bags dried up. Food banks, kitchens, and pantries got less, and local providers had to look harder than ever to make up the difference. According to the *Washington Post*:

> What these groups are experiencing is the unintended effect of a nationwide cost-saving effort embarked upon three years ago by grocery manufacturers and retailers. The businesses are trying to recover an estimated $30 billion in sales lost each year to damaged goods.
>
> Gradually, they redesigned every step of the food distribution process. In packaging, cans were reinforced with stronger metals to reduce crushing. In delivery, pallets were changed so that fewer crates fell from trucks . . . and increasingly, fewer sets of hands are touching each product. . . . Grocery scanners also have trimmed waste by allowing retailers to know exactly when a particular product is running low, and only then to order more. That way, items don't reach their expiration dates sitting on the shelf.
>
> Even the environmental movement lent an inadvertent hand: Efforts to reduce the amount of packaging on products eliminated many of the little cardboard boxes that encased such items as deodorant—boxes that often got crushed in shipping and rendered products unfit for retail customers.

I sat in on a session at the Second Harvest National Conference in the summer of 1994, in which representatives of the food industry discussed these trends with the food bankers who made up the audience. After a series of highly informative, fairly technical presentations on industry trends in grocery manufacturing, and the Efficient Consumer Response (ECR) movement in marketing, a long-time friend of Second Harvest who headed an independent marketing agency reminded the audience that he had been on the "gloom and doom" panel two years earlier, and that the challenges he had predicted then had become more and more real. "It's happening," declared Augie Fernandez. "It's happening, and it's not about giving and receiving. It's about business in America. And it's about something that's really unusual; its about *defects*. Isn't it amazing after looking at the food industry, [you're] saying 'Don't get rid of your defects. Keep them!' Why don't you say that about the airlines?"

He pointed to the auto industry in Michigan as an example of a business that had not taken care of its defects. "And what did it do? It put a lot of people on the street, and it put a big burden on the food banks. . . . So it really isn't about giving and so forth; it is about defects. You should not build your future of success based on someone else's defects. You can't do that because when that person corrects his defects, you're going to be in trouble."

In fact, food banking did find itself in trouble, or at least under stress, as ECR made strides in the food industry: "I feel like I'm on a treadmill going backwards," the director of the Capital Area Community Food Bank reported. "The demand just seems to keep going up while the supply shrinks." Her plight was replicated around the nation. Food bankers and kitchen and pantry directors have been remarkably resourceful at spotting new supplies, identifying new forms of waste, but it seems only reasonable to expect that these, too, will be corrected. And where they are not correctable, a secondary market will doubtless develop.

"Secondary market" is a term used to designate brokers who buy salvaged goods and manufacturers' rejects and resell them, at flea markets, discount stores, roadside stands, and increasingly in Eastern Europe. Although some manufacturers and some retail chains designate Second Harvest or a local food bank to receive their reclaimed product as a matter of policy, many do not, and the secondary market has become a significant competitor with food banking as a destination for these goods. "Because of the emphasis on the bottom line," Susan Cramer pointed out, "the secondary salvage market is a much greater competitor for Second Harvest than it ever used to be." The choice between donation or sale to a secondary market is driven by the corporate bottom line, and as the secondary markets have become more organized and more extensive, they can afford to pay more for their products, thus becoming an ever more attractive alternative to food banking.

The Local Hustle and the Soft Money Shuffle

Unfortunately for local food banks and frontline providers, the sharpest reductions in food industry donations very nearly coincided with the cutbacks in federal commodities brought on by the drought and the Dairy Termination Program. The decline in national-level donations sent local organizations scrambling for new sources of food. A 1989 reduction of more than one-fifth to the Second Harvest food bank of St. Paul, Minnesota, necessitated doing "a lot more running around," according to its director, Dick Goebel. "We have to get into the marketplace and be more aggressive," Goebel told the *Chronicle of Philanthropy*. "We have to find where the food is and get at it. It is a good kick in the pants for us." The director of the Greater Chicago Food Depository took a similar, upbeat approach: "We do a lot of local hustle. . . . What we try to do is stay one step ahead of where we feel the next product surplus is going to be." Many food bankers, however, have found the local hustle exhausting, and are less optimistic about their ability to stay a step ahead. They are hopeful that some sort of change at the national level, an enhanced tax deduction, or one that is easier to file, may make donation to food banks once again more attractive in comparison with selling to the secondary market.

The ups and downs of corporate and governmental donations, and the resulting "local hustle" are part of what has driven the emergency food system into the pursuit of foundation funds and another tiring exercise that might be called the "soft money shuffle." "I am seeing a lot more fatigue in the field than I used to," Madeline Lund, of the Greater Chicago Food Depository, told me at an advocacy conference in Washington, D.C. Some of it she attributed to overload, referring to the advocacy agenda: "This is just one more thing that somebody wants us to think about or to do." A great deal of the fatigue, however, she felt was due to the constant need for fund-raising, and the tendency of food banks to take on more tasks than they could handle in hopes of securing new funds: "Advocacy, farm projects, gardening, food purchase programs and delivery programs . . . some of that is an unfortunate result of the nonprofit's need to continuously have new programming in order to receive funding. . . . It is like trying to figure out a different kind of celebration every year and hiding a can of tuna fish in each balloon. 'We haven't done anything with farming yet, so let's do a farm project, or let's do a pilot or a study about a farm project, because that will infuse more money into the food bank.' "

She referred me to back issues of the foundation directories for confirmation of the shifting focus: "Homelessness will be popular for a while and then they will go to battered women and children and then they will go to something else, substance abuse or education or early childhood development or whatever. It is not the foundations' fault, because they see their role as R&D. So, to accommodate R&D you have to be able to follow the trends or try to stay ahead of the trend, even, if you can." She hastened to add that food banking, like any other business, needs to be able to experiment, "so the foundations provide a very valuable service by doing that," but still, the tendency toward faddism in foundation giving creates a constant need to repackage or re-present one's work. The combination of the local hustle and the soft money shuffle leaves many in the emergency food community on the edge of exhaustion. "We are tired," she told me simply, "we are tired."

The fickleness of funders, however comprehensible it may be, raises the issue of the uses of emergency food once again. It was useful to government to dispose of surpluses, and when there were no more surpluses, it had to fight for a trickle of continued government support. Emergency food is useful to industry when there are unmarketable items, but industry has made very clear that it will try to correct its flaws to produce fewer such items: "You should not build your future . . . on someone else's defects." And it has been useful to foundations and donors who want to "do something about hunger," or "help the homeless," but foundations operate under a normal constraint to innovate and to fund innovations. So what is the future of emergency food? When I asked Contra Costa food banker Larry Sly about the change in his organization's sources of support, he identified two major growth areas. "Canned food drives are one of our main sources. Looking at where we stand, Second Harvest is leveling off, TEFAP is leveling off, our growth areas have been a prepared food program that we instituted and canned food drives." Will food drives and food rescue programs prove to be the ever expanding source that emergency food providers need to balance the ups and downs of industry, government, and foundation contributions?

Certainly, the system has shown an increasing reliance on food drives. It was a very fortunate thing for providers that the Boy Scouts began Scouting for Food in 1988, just as government and corporate donations both began to fall off. When it had served its purpose for the national organization as a national Good Turn, however, it became a local option. The National Association of Letter Carriers have recently made their annual springtime drive a nationwide event, but it seems reasonable to imagine that this, too, may wear thin after a while. Food drives are reported by some communities to be a good source of high-protein foods, but, no matter how successful a canned goods drive, it is usually seasonal in its impact; the supplies run out after a couple of months. Unless a community is prepared to sponsor four to six drives a year, canned goods donated at the household level cannot be the central ingredient in a stability strategy. John Momper, the director of the Alameda County Food Bank in California, told me that his organization was now conducting drives year-round. When I asked whether he thought public interest could be sustained for year-round drives on an ongoing basis, he was thoughtful: "Unless there's something, a new twist to it, it may lose its effectiveness."

Food rescue is still on the rise. The supply of wasted restaurant and institutional food appears nearly inexhaustible, and the Department of Agriculture now estimates total food waste, from point of production to the household garbage pail, at 96 billion pounds a year, a quarter of the nation's food supply. A 1997 "national summit on gleaning and food recovery," cochaired by Vice President Al Gore and Secretary of Agriculture Dan Glickman, was designed to mobilize people at all points in the food system to save "enough food to feed 450,000 hungry people," much of it through prepared and perishable food rescue programs. If the past pattern holds true, however, someone will soon find a profitable use for prepared food surpluses, outbidding food rescue programs in the same way that the secondary market sometimes outbids food banks for excess corporate product. Alternatively, the quantities of food being donated to food rescue programs may alert food service managers and food service industry executives that too much food is being prepared, and the number of choices in the employee dining room or the college cafeteria will be downsized. The one thing that emergency food providers can probably count on is change, change and the fact that the other institutions involved in emergency food will pursue their own institutional priorities.

No Guarantees

The New Deal story recounted earlier contains a caveat: There is no guarantee of a happy ending. The federal government procured and distributed commodities when this activity was useful to powerful constituencies, and it let the program fall into disrepair when those constituencies lost interest. In the long run the most significant function that the Federal Surplus Relief Corporation and its successor, the Federal Surplus Commodities Corporation, played was the one predicted by the *New York Times* the day after the surplus purchase arrangement was announced: it would "relieve our minds of the distressing 'economic paradox' of unprofitable surpluses existing side by side with extreme want." The FSRC and the FSCC transferred a portion of the surplus to some of the hungry, and that was enough—enough to relieve the sense of outrage, the widespread discomfort about want amid plenty crystallized by the pig slaughter. They provided moral relief, independently of any assessment of the extent to which they actually relieved hunger or reduced the surplus. Precisely because the paradox made New Deal Americans so uncomfortable, they were ready to accept a token solution of matching complementary symptoms. I don't believe that we have changed so much in sixty years; we are still vulnerable to token solutions to the problem of hunger.

The same strong feelings about hunger and waste that make emergency food attractive to government, corporations, foundations, youth organizations, and civic groups make involvement with emergency food projects desirable for individuals, and the efforts of individuals are also an essential ingredient in the emergency food recipe. The next chapter explores the uses of emergency food from the standpoint of the individual donor or volunteer.

CHAPTER SIX

The Seductions of Charity

THE OUTGOING MESSAGE on the gleaners' phone line at FOOD (Food On Our Doorstep) Share in Oxnard, California, tells callers that the crop of the day is carrots and the meeting point is map location #12. It is a little after 8:00 A.M. when I pull my rental car off the road at a dusty vacant lot near the intersection of Pancho Street and Pleasant Valley Road in Camarillo, a small Ventura County farming community about 12 miles from Oxnard. An assortment of gleaners is already gathered at the rendezvous point, sorting through a cardboard box of bakery goods and fruit sent over by the food bank, and chatting about the results of a recent election. Most gleaners take something from the "goody box," a package of muffins or a few kiwis, but there is still plenty left for the field foreman—"a little *mordita*" (the Mexican slang for a bribe) the FOOD Share farm and field coordinator tells me. How appropriate: *mordita* means "little bite." At 8:30 sharp, the gleaners return to their cars. We pull out in a convoy, heading for a nearby farm where we will be picking up unharvested carrots to feed the hungry of Ventura County.

The cooperation of the field foreman is important to the success of the project, because FOOD Share's gleaners will follow along just behind the foreman's crew of Chicano farmworkers. First comes a tractor pulling a farm implement that digs the carrots up from the rich soil and tosses them aside. Then come the farmworkers who deftly select and bundle the carrots that are the right size and shape for the market. Then come the gleaners who pick up the carrots that are misshapen, or simply too long, short, fat or thin for market standards, remove their greenery on the spot, and deposit them in special five-gallon buckets. A pail is issued to each gleaner, along with a hat and a cutting tool, upon payment of a fifteen-dollar annual membership fee. In addition to this minimal equipment, the fee covers insurance, protection for gleaners who may damage an irrigation pipe or break an ankle, and for the farmowners who permit untrained lay people to enter their fields. Carrots are popular with the gleaners because they are easy to pick and the fields in which they grow are relatively free of mud; they require neither special expertise nor protective clothing, though most of the gleaners have remembered to wear hats to ward off the sun's powerful rays.

The gleaners work briskly, filling the buckets, then dumping them into huge molded plastic bins on the back of the food bank's truck. There is an air of casual camaraderie, and there are bits and pieces of conversation, but on the whole, they concentrate on the task at hand. The carrot fields stretch as far as the eye can see, and it is clear that our work will rescue only a fraction of the discarded carrots that might be had. As one eighty-year-old gleaner told me, explaining his sense of urgency about the work, "It's kind of corny, but if I don't save that carrot for God's purposes, it's gone." After approximately an hour and a half, the project leader shouts "Time. Pick for yourselves." Most gleaners empty their current buckets into the collection bin and pick one last pailful for home use. They are gone from the field before the midmorning sun begins to wilt the carrots and makes outdoor work dangerous for the elderly among them.

Once the pick is complete, the project leader drives the bins back to the food bank warehouse located on the outskirts of Oxnard. As our bins of carrots arrive, they are piled onto a loading dock and transported by pallet and forklift to a pallet scale, a rectangular flatbed of metal large enough to hold two pallets, just inside the back door. Once the weight of the pallet and bins is subtracted from the total, I learn that we have picked 1,461 pounds of carrots for the soup kitchens, food pantries, brown bag programs, and other feeding projects of Ventura County, carrots that otherwise would have shriveled in the field and been plowed under. The weight is recorded on a receipt, one copy to be sent to the grower for tax purposes, the other retained in the food bank's files. The carrots are washed with a hose and placed in cold storage or boxed and bagged for pickup by the 250 agencies providing food, either as prepared meals or as groceries for home preparation, to people in need.

The FOOD Share warehouse, which begins operations each morning at about 5:00 A.M., is a bustling and stupendously noisy place. A substantial portion of the ambient noise is contributed by "Bugsy," a propane-powered machine that pours a stream of forced air down across the open doorway, a loud but fairly effective device for keeping bugs out while allowing humans, trucks, and air unobstructed access. Phones ring, forklifts rumble around, people shout, and wood and metal clang together as trucks are loaded and unloaded. It is not a tranquil environment nor a place for the fainthearted. Physically, the warehouse looks much like any food wholesaler's warehouse, a dimly lit, cool, cavernous space, filled with rows of floor-to-ceiling metal shelves loaded with boxes of "product," and flanked by walk-in refrigerators, freezers, and desk cubicles. At the opposite end from the loading dock, two heavy soundproof doors connect the warehouse to "up front," a modest suite of well-lighted, modern, carpeted offices where the rest of FOOD Share's business is conducted.

As far as possible from the noise of Bugsy and the loading docks, but still inside the warehouse proper, an eat-in kitchen provides a locus for sociability among the volunteers and staff. A rack holds dozens of mugs bearing names and the logo "Volunteers Are the [heart written as a symbol] of FOOD Share," and one entire wall is devoted to a huge "birthday calendar" with a birthday poster for each volunteer who has a birthday in the current month. When I visit in November, almost every day of the month has at least one poster, and some days have two or three. Each poster has the volunteer's name, the date, and some sort of computer graphic. Coffee and pastries are available in the kitchen in the morning, and a cheerful, energetic woman named Celia prepares and serves a one-dollar lunch to about twenty people each day.

Although advanced age is not a prerequisite for volunteering at FOOD Share, the organization has traditionally been largely a project of retired people; as one annual report put it, "Without senior volunteerism, the food bank would not exist." The gleaners are informally referred to as "senior gleaners." Ventura County is home to several retirement communities, and a fifth of its households contain at least one resident aged sixty-five or over, so there is an ample supply of seniors to keep the food bank running. The gleaners I met at the carrot field were almost all retired and ranged in age from the mid fifties to the late eighties; several of them had learned about the project from neighbors in Leisure Village, a retirement community close to the rendezvous point. The project leader, Dr. Fred Clark, a missionary educator retired after forty-two years service in Africa, was eighty-seven years old at the time of my visit, and soon to be eighty-eight.

The gleaners were generally enthusiastic about the project, and very articulate about the benefits they derive from it. One gleaner at the carrot field summed it up neatly: "After I retired, I started looking for something to be active at and volunteer at. . . . I've been doing this about three years, since I retired. I do it at least three days a week. I come out every morning. It's like physical exercise and besides, it's helping other people. I kind of enjoy it . . . seeing the people and talking and that kind of thing." A retired retail manager elaborated on the enjoyment factor. "What we're doing is fun. I'm in it for the fun, the companionship; I get to visit with people from all over the country. Well, see, I'm retired, and it's real nice to get a whole bunch of people to visit and talk with, and to joke with, so it's fun, and the fresh air and exercise, I know that's good for me. And I think it's great that we can take food in so that anybody who really needs some can get it. It's a good feeling."

Almost every one of the gleaners I interviewed stressed the health benefits of exercise and fresh air. Dr. Fred Clark, the project leader for the carrot pick, has been gleaning with FOOD Share almost since the beginning, and he comes nearly every day. When he goes on holiday and stops gleaning, he explained with a laugh, he gets "all lamed up from lack of use." Comparing gleaning to the physical activities available at the Leisure Village where he lived, one volunteer stressed the extra benefits of the FOOD Share approach: "For an outlet, though, where all around us are unemployment, starvation, and people in need, it is something that is very personally satisfying to be able to help both ways—you help with the fact that you get some exercise out of it, and you help more so because you can feed unlimited numbers of people through the FOOD Share program. . . . I don't know why more people haven't learned about FOOD Share or haven't learned about physical well-being through being physically active. It's a two-way street, and it works beautifully." Another gleaner equated his harvesting work to jogging; he jogs on Tuesdays and Thursdays and gleans on Mondays, Wednesdays, and Fridays. I asked one warehouse volunteer, retired after many years' work as a skilled electronics technician, if he had ever done electronics work for the food bank, and his reply was quick and decisive: "Absolutely not. This is all physical, which I really enjoy because I need physical work to do. It's a lot of my exercise." The outdoor setting, the contact with the earth is also important: "I'm a peasant at heart, I love to work in the dirt. I don't have much space for gardening. This kind of satisfies it," one gleaner confided, but she went on to connect her satisfactions directly to the uses of the harvest: "I just think there's so many hungry and homeless people and it's so unnecessary in a country that is supposedly as wealthy as ours. So many people are so unfeeling about the homeless, and I'm glad that I'm able to contribute something."

The social side of the activity was important to some volunteers: "I enjoy it," Fred Clark told me. "I like the group. It's a nice group of people. You find one or two who only come out for what they can take home but most of them are here to help other folks." A woman who volunteers at the warehouse agreed: "What's meaningful for me about FOOD Share are the people that are here. They're all down-to-earth. I mean I really feel like it's a family. They're warm and friendly and the men and the women are really special." After I concluded my interview with Lyle Gunderson, a volunteer who, among other activities, trains and certifies other volunteers and staff in forklift operation, he tapped me on the shoulder to add a parting comment: "I want to tell you that the people here are so great, it's just like going back fifty years in my youth."

For the many FOOD Share volunteers who have retired, the organization's greatest contribution may be a sense of purpose. FOOD Share recognizes their contributions, not only with mugs and birthday greetings but also with meaningful, sometimes crucial roles in the operation of the organization. Some work five days a week and are virtually indistinguishable from employees. All have "real work" which needs to be done. The staff member in charge of resource development commented that the volunteers are "the heroes and heroines," and then went on: "But to the older people, it gives them a goal, a purpose . . . They want to be in there doing something. They want to be wanted and needed. It's very good for them, very therapeutic." This might have sounded condescending to me if I had not heard precisely the same sentiment from many of the senior volunteers themselves. As one put it, after commenting that many of the older people he knew were bored, "The retired person who has no reason to be active in any type of thing—imagine what a wonderful thing it would be to have some direction for action, a reason to get up in the morning, a reason to live. And it's basic—it feeds people."

Who Volunteers?

In 1988, the *New York Times* Business section ran a full page advertisement for *Cosmopolitan* magazine, aimed at potential advertisers, that portrayed a glamorous young woman, accompanied by the following text:

> I was never a volunteer anything. Who had the time? If you want a career you have to put in the hours. If you happen to be husband-hunting you have to slosh around in the social jungle. How much can one person do? Find the time, my favorite magazine said. You're needed, you won't be so self-involved and your life will be enriched. So here I am every Tuesday night in the soup kitchen, making sandwiches. I think I am a better person. I know I am a happier one. I love that magazine. I guess you could say I'm That COSMOPOLITAN GIRL.

When I first began taking a closer look at emergency food, the image of volunteers that I had absorbed from the media was one of yuppie stockbrokers helping out on their lunch hours, or the Cosmo Girl expanding her horizons. The reality, however, is much more diverse, and, on average, much older. As the agency relations director of the Greater Chicago Food Depository put it, "The typical agency is five seventy-five-year-old black churchwomen."

Retired people are not the only volunteers in the emergency food system, of course, but they are an indispensable element. All in all, senior volunteers constituted the backbone of most of the programs I visited, and the increasing longevity and vigor of retirees is part of what has made the emergency food phenomenon possible. FOOD Share is a remarkable organization, and the senior gleaners are an extraordinary group, but in many ways, they are typical, and the satisfactions they expressed—companionship, the pleasures of shared work, and a sense of meaning and purpose—were the satisfactions identified by volunteers of all ages, everywhere I went.

The "Good People"

An opportunity to socialize was clearly significant for many of the volunteers I talked to, especially those who lived alone. "Well, I come in a little bit early so I can sit here and yap with the crew," Helaine Whiteley told me in the cheerful kitchen of the Good Shepherd Food-Bank in Lewiston, Maine. "I don't know about the rest of the volunteers, but I live by myself and I consider it a wasted day if I don't come in here. . . . There's a lot of kidding going on here. And this is a good, friendly place. All the volunteers are good, friendly people, as you have probably noticed."

The idea that the others are "good people" was a nearly ubiquitous sentiment. I heard it from volunteers in tiny pantries and from food bankers. "I'll get out of my office at times when I'm getting a vicious headache because of the amount of paperwork that's being created, and I'll just take the time off and go downstairs and I'll get with the volunteers and sort salvage with them. I find my best volunteers are the elderly," declared Al Tremblay. "I have a crew from the Methodist church in Salem . . . from sixty-five right up to ninety-two. . . . If you're feeling low and downright lousy on one given day, when those people walk through the door, your whole attitude in life changes. They are a delight to work with. They're unbelievable people, and it makes the job easier."

It is not surprising, of course, that a program director should feel partial toward the people who contribute free labor, but food bankers expressed a similar appreciation for the rest of the network. "I really felt very much at home with most of the people," Hawley Botchford said about his experiences at Second Harvest conferences; "Harry Chapin told a story that Pete Seeger had told him about being involved with the good people. You may not always win, but you're involved with the good people, the people that do things, the people that get involved." There is a pervasive feeling that these are the people who care, who stop quibbling over political or philosophical differences and get on with the job, who light candles rather than curse darkness. There is also a welcome sense of shared values: "I did some consulting, fund-raising consulting for other nonprofits," June Tanoue told me, and "I just found food banking and the people who are involved with it to be my cup of tea. I enjoy them. Just having the same kind of values of wanting to prevent waste, of wanting to help people, is really important." Al Tremblay reports a similar sense of shared values with his staff: "My staff is probably the most dedicated staff I've ever seen in my entire life. If private enterprise would have a staff like that to work for them, they'd be millionaires. They're dedicated people and they all feel the same way I do."

The Pleasures of Diversity

The fact that there are shared values, however, does not necessarily mean that there is sameness. In some emergency food settings I visited, it appeared to me that part of the satisfaction that people experienced was precisely the pleasure of working shoulder to shoulder with people who are different from themselves. I packed pantry bags one morning at the Yorkville Common Pantry, with a group composed of two members of the pantry's decidedly Upper East Side, upper-crust board, two community volunteers from the surrounding East Harlem community, both women of color, and two Mennonite volunteers, one from Georgia and one from Pennsylvania, who were part of a mission to New York City and work regularly at the pantry, several days a week—and, of course, one "participant observer." Together this group of women—the men were otherwise engaged—represented the essence of demographic diversity, differing in age, race, education, first language, religious belief, and social class. There was a lot of chatting and laughing; perhaps I was projecting, but I sensed that all of those present were enjoying the opportunity to interact with people whose lives are very different from their own, and quite specifically enjoying being part of such a diverse team.

There is another kind of diversity which people in several locations mentioned to me as one of the central pleasures of their work in emergency food, and that is political diversity. Bernice Belton is a longtime progressive activist who is on the board of directors of the Food Bank of the Central Coast in Watsonville, California. She talked about the experience of working with some of the area's largest growers:

> We had numbers of representatives from agribusiness on the board of the food bank. Now, to radicals and progressives, the word agribusiness is anathema, and it is to me, too. I think they have done some very destructive things to our economy and to our society. On the other hand, I remember coming out of a meeting with them and saying, "My God, I have been upstaged." I thought *I* had the most commitment to feeding the people and it turns out I didn't. That some of those agribusiness people are as committed to feeding the poor. We may come from different places philosophically, but their commitment is as great or greater than mine.

Working with people from agribusiness did not change Ms. Belton's fundamental commitments, nor deter her from joining the picket line when Green Giant workers went on strike. "I think the urgent thing is that I have never given up my philosophy, in terms of working with people who I would consider on the other side," but she treasures the board's diversity and feels it has enriched her life. "The people I am working with, all of us are so different from each other; it is such a new experience for me that I found it irresistible. I was working with an ex-nun and a working nun and a cabinetmaker and agribusiness and somebody who comes out of the business community and somebody who comes out of a chemical abuse program that she works for." The diverse composition of this board of directors is not an accident; it reflects the philosophy of food bank director Willie Elliot McCrae.

> I'm a guy who likes to bring diverse people together . . . because you have to adjust to new realities and new frameworks . . . just the process of growth and change is difficult, but you have got to stir the pot regularly. One of the ways to stir the pot intellectually is to not

always talk to people who think the same way as you do. That is why, if you don't get a diverse group of people sitting around the table talking to each other, none of us can maintain that intellectual youthfulness.

The common experience here, between the Yorkville Common Pantry volunteers enjoying their social and ethnic diversity and the Watsonville food bank board enjoying its political diversity is the discovery that people who one thought were very different are in fact very much the same, the recognition of a shared core of humanity. Even where food banks' boards are not so politically and socially ecumenical, and even in situations in which kitchen and pantry volunteers are remarkably similar, there is one other sort of "diversity" in which this recognition takes place, the discovery by volunteers and staff of the humanity of the clients. Bill Rae is the director of Manna Ministries in Bangor, Maine, and he gave me a graphic account of this discovery process:

> I think the people that come in here, the first-nighters, the people that come in here for the first time, are scared shitless. Because they don't know what they're going to meet. And by the time they leave at the end of the night, they realize that the people are just like everybody else. And they are changed. I know they are changed. I can see it in their faces. Every group that I see coming in here, that has never worked with this clientele before. They come in here on what I call a moral obligation—God says for me to do this—so they come in here to do it. They want to all stand behind the counter. They want to dish out food; they don't want to go out and serve the poor people. And I encourage them to go out and talk. All of a sudden they'll see somebody they know from school, or from the grocery store line or from the unemployment line. The change is that they are not all rapists, or thieves, or alcoholics. There is a metamorphical change that happens in these guys, in the people who come in here, not the guests, I mean the volunteers.

Some volunteers, of course, did not have such fears of stereotypes to begin with, or had lost them somewhere else. Barbara Brown is one of the regular helpers at Manna Ministries soup kitchen. She had made her transition from fear to recognition in a church-sponsored mission to New York City a year or so earlier, but she struggled to describe for me the change. "I think perhaps your frame of mind, to work in this type of work, has to be different. I know before, I can say a year, two years ago, I would go across the street instead of walk past a street person. I didn't even want to be near them." Now, however, she looks forward to her work at Manna. "I just enjoy seeing them, seeing the homeless get a meal."

Meaning and Purpose

The pleasures of diversity, sharing a task or a meal with people who are different from oneself, taking small steps toward healing the divisions that characterize our society, these are, in a sense, "process" satisfactions—like sociability or getting fresh air and exercise—aspects of the work that make it enjoyable. But in most of my interviews, it was clear that these satisfactions were not as important as the goal itself, not as important as having a goal. It is difficult to overestimate, I think, the importance of being needed, of having a sense of purpose and a meaningful role. One of the things that impressed me most in the Scouting for Food sorting and packing marathon that I visited in New Jersey was the intensity of the younger children, and the obvious pride they took in completing each task. Our society offers children few opportunities for real work; chores at home are probably less prevalent than they were when there was typically a parent at home to see that they got done, and household chores have a different meaning, in any case, than work done outside the home, in the world of adults. Ellen Teller is an attorney who works primarily as a lobbyist on the staff of the Food Research and Action Center. Like many members of the FRAC staff, she also volunteers in a direct service capacity—in her case in a women's shelter near her home. Her daughter, Eliza, started going with her to the shelter before she reached school age: "She loves baking the brownies and she loves serving them. She loves serving them, knowing that she made them. There's a real kind of personal fulfillment there." Creating opportunities for children to experience the fulfillment of a job well done and share in an activity with a larger goal may be one of the most positive functions of emergency food.

For people who are retired, especially those who have had busy and demanding careers, the absence of purposive activity can come as a shock. Catherine Walker got involved with the soup kitchen at Guadalupe Center in Immokalee, Florida, seven years ago, shortly after she retired from thirty-seven years with the telephone company in New York City and relocated to southwest Florida. She saw a notice in the church bulletin about the need for volunteers at the lunch program that serves migrant agricultural laborers and other impoverished people in the desperately poor farmworker community of Immokalee.

> We were new and we were recently retired, both my sister and I, and we decided we needed to do something and felt that this would be something worthwhile . . . so we've been coming ever since. . . . I always remembered a friend of ours, when she retired, said she had to get involved in things because otherwise she would not be organized and she would spend all day in bed or lolling around the house in her pajamas. So we decided we weren't going to do that either, and, after working all those years, you felt you had to do something. You had to keep yourself busy.

She might have volunteered at the hospital or the library, she said, but she felt that there were plenty of people to do that sort of volunteer work and that she wouldn't really be needed, while at the soup kitchen, "You are helping people, I think, maybe just a little bit more than some of the other things . . . It's good and it makes us feel good which is why I think a lot of people do the work."

Next door at the Guadalupe Social Services offices, I met Bill and Rosemary O'Connell, who had been coming to southwest Florida for years before they decided to retire. They had known that they would volunteer at Guadalupe before they left Hartford, Connecticut. "Actually, I don't think I would have retired if we didn't have this. I have to do something," Bill told me, and his wife agreed: "I think that was one of the final convincing things for Bill to retire, that we had this." Clearly, however, working at Guadalupe Social Services is not just "something to do." Bill and Rosemary, who had worked as volunteers with soup kitchens in Hartford and with the food bank there, communicated intense feeling about the depth of poverty in Immokalee:

"We were driving down one day from Orlando to Naples and we drove through Immokalee. And just by looking at the landscape we just decided that when we finally moved down here we were going to start working here," Bill recalled. "There's just something about the need of these people, who are often forgotten people here," Rosemary said, and Bill agreed: "I just see this disparity in terms of the desperation of most of these people. . . . You end up with the desperate of the desperate. . . . So I think if you can somehow help them from day to day, and . . . that you've got the skills that may be helpful to them . . . it's sort of neat." Bill is a lawyer, and Rosemary has office management experience, so the skills they have brought to Immokalee are more than welcome.

Satisfactions for Staff, Too

A sense of satisfaction in using skills for a good cause is not reserved for volunteers, however, nor for people in any particular age group. Paid staff also feel good about doing good. "It's just a great-feeling job. When I go to work in the morning, I am happy. I am never disappointed with it. Sometimes you need to stay focused on who you are helping and not on how many people you are not helping that you could help. You have to say 'Look how many people I am helping,' " Rose Anne Healy told me. Healy is the director of Extra Helpings, a prepared and perishable food rescue program associated with the Daily Bread Food Bank in Miami, Florida. She came to Extra Helpings from a business background.

> For a business person, it is such a great opportunity because it is a win-win for everybody and it makes so much sense. It is such a simple idea but yet it can really grow. It was exciting for me because I knew I could use all my business skills, because I do everything. I do the marketing, the finance, I take care of the trucks, I take care of employees, I do everything. It was a great opportunity and I love the idea, so I went for it.

I asked her if there was anything she missed from her years in business, and she laughed and said "getting money," but then she went on to indicate that the other rewards compensated for the comparatively low salary scale. "The rewards are great. When I ride on the truck and pick up food and drop it off. That feeling is great. I get thank-yous throughout. Those are the rewards. . . . You fall in love with it. That is a general theme of a lot of people I have talked to that were in the business world and stumbled on this. You fall in love with it and then you are in it forever."

The strong sense of commitment that many paid staff members have demonstrated by working at very low salaries is often rooted in religious belief or political commitment, or in the reinforcement provided by the job itself, but opportunities to put skills developed elsewhere to socially constructive use were clearly part of the satisfaction. "I'm kind of hooked on food banking," Joanne Grisanti told me. Grisanti is the operations director of the Food Bank of Central New York. "One of the things I love about it is that it is suited to the skills that I have; all this mixture of skills I have picked up along the way kind of fit in this."

Second Harvest's director of marketing, Deb Keegan, who came to the food bank network after completing her undergraduate work and an MBA while working as a stock broker, captured the sense of having found a home for her skills that I got from many of the staff members I interviewed:

> It's perfect. I mean it scares me, because I can't think of where I could go that could be better, or like where would I go next. Nothing could be better suited for me than this, because I get to use everything I learned in school, I get to use all my MBA stuff, I get to use stuff I learned as a stock broker, I get to use my sales skills, I get to work in a really nice office on Michigan Avenue, I get to work with corporate America, I get to work with wonderful people, and I get to do something *good* for the world.

It's not just the use of existing skills, but the opportunity to develop new ones that appeals to some of the staff. "I like to wear a lot of different hats, try a lot of different things," Alameda County Food Bank director John Momper said, although he hastened to add that "there's too much work for one person." "It has been very exciting working in food banking because things are always changing and our organization has grown a tremendous amount in the past few years,"

Joanne Grisanti reported. "We've put on many programs. Every year we start one or two new things. . . . One of the things that is so exciting about food banks is you are limited only by your imagination. . . . I like to be creative in my job." Creative, and successful. For many in the food banking and food rescue parts of the emergency food system, success, measured by growth, expansion, and responsiveness, is a reinforcement in itself. "I have been here four and a half years," Grisanti reported, and "we have gone from moving 2 million pounds of food to moving 10 million pounds. Our staff has gone from five people to twenty-seven. We have gone from having one small straight truck to having five trucks, six by the end of the summer, including a tractor trailer." Jean Beatty, the founder and director of Channels, a food rescue program in Harrisburg, Pennsylvania, said that she had always liked a challenge. "I get satisfaction about addressing any problem, I don't care what the problem is. I know I am skilled at certain things, like coordinating people, and it is a great satisfaction to have the end result serve 100,000—according to our agencies, we are feeding 100,000 unduplicated people through this program. That is a lot of people."

Frontline providers find it more awkward to express pride in their growth; who can rejoice in increased numbers of people in need? "If we were a business, I guess you would consider it a very successful business, because now, this past summer, we hit over 750 people a day, which is remarkable if you think about it because the cooking area is eight by ten," Kathy Goldman said, describing the limited cooking facilities that have provided more than a million meals from the Community Kitchen of West Harlem. They can and do take pride in their ability to rise to that occasion, to respond to the growing demand. In the final analysis, however, for staff as for volunteers, it is the purpose of the activity, not the process, that provides the most enduring satisfactions. Al Tremblay explained to me why he still carries in his wallet the ad that connected him with his job as director of the Food Bank of New Hampshire:

> I think probably all my life working in transportation, marketing, there were days when I'd say "yuck—I have to get up and go to work." Like all of us do, right? Since I've been in food banking,

there has not been one day that I haven't been anxious to get back to work. I love it. I love my job. It's a satisfying job. You can go to bed at night tired but knowing that you've accomplished something, and if I can look at a small child's face, smiling, getting something to eat, and know that I was responsible, partly responsible, for getting it there, I've got to tell you, its a feeling that's just—I cannot even tell you what it feels like. It's just good.

For some of the people most heavily involved in emergency food, it is the prevention of waste, as much or more than the provision of food for the hungry, that generates that good feeling. When I asked JoAnn Pike, the founder and director of the Good Shepherd Food-Bank in Lewiston, Maine, what kept her going, emotionally, during the years that Good Shepherd struggled from month to month financially, she said it was the waste prevention factor. "It was so deeply ingrained in me when I was a child that you didn't waste food—and knowing that the food was out there. I really didn't have a lot of experience with people that were hungry. But it was the principle—you know, there was food that was being wasted, and I was sure that somebody needed it."

"The food waste issue is what gets me," declared Jane Humpstone, one of the APCO consultants who nurtured the relationship between the UPS Foundation and Foodchain. "I will never claim to be a hunger advocate. I don't have a problem with advocating for things that help hungry people, but I think it is more the waste that I can't stand to see. To see stuff that is so valuable as food, on a social level, on a nutritional level, on an economic level just get tossed out because nobody can figure out what to do with it."

More Blessed to Give

Whether the primary goal is feeding the hungry or preventing the waste of good food, many of the people most heavily involved in charitable food programs are moved to action by their religious beliefs and derive particular satisfactions that are rooted in those beliefs. The emergency food system is permeated with religion. More than 70 percent of the pantries and kitchens affiliated with the Second Harvest Network are sponsored by churches or other religious organizations. And even that high number probably understates the prevalence of religious orientation since the category that Second Harvest used, "church affiliate," seems to have excluded many religiously motivated activities that are not based in a particular church. FOOD Share in Oxnard, for example, grew out of a Bible study group, but it was a Bible study group composed of members of a whole variety of congregations. Jewel Pedi, the founding director, who recently retired, identified the organization as nonsectarian, but pervaded by "a Christian attitude straight on through." While most food banks are incorporated as independent, secular nonprofits, many were initiated by churches or by people responding to the demands of their faith.

Herneatha Barbour, the president of the Dorcas Missionary Society at the Childs Memorial Baptist Church in Philadelphia, explained to me a bit about the biblical basis for the group's Wednesday soup kitchen.

> Well, you have to go back to the Word of God . . . First Corinthians, chapter 13 [the famous passage about the importance of love, or in some translations, charity] and First Corinthians, chapter 10, verse 33 [a passage that instructs the Corinthians to imitate Paul as he imitated Christ], and you look at that, and that's our daily goal. And then we based it on the principle of Jesus, who said "Inasmuch as you fed these and you did that, . . . you did it for me." We based it on that, and I always said, "If you're going to help people, you have to get them indoctrinated or revitalized with the love of Christ in them because a meal is not going to do it."

Ms. Barbour persuaded the weekly prayer service that normally met in the sanctuary upstairs to move down to the basement where the meal was served, and that provided her with the ongoing ministry she wanted to make sure was a part of her meal: "The only thing I ask is that if anybody's on that floor for fifteen minutes, I want to hear the Gospel coming across, plain and simple. So that people can understand that there's somebody who loves them just like they are."

Ms. Barbour's efforts to make sure that her meal program was one that expressed her core beliefs have been more successful than she hoped, and she has found, in this work, more satisfactions than she expected: "I think one important thing about this ministry . . . is how much good it's done in us. For us. And bringing us together. And nurturing us. And teaching us so much about concern and compassion and how to share our love with one another—it has just done marvelous things." Her work with the Wednesday soup kitchen has become the most important thing in her church life:

> If I had to choose one thing to do in my church, if they told me you can only be allowed to do but one thing in this church now, for the rest of your life, everybody knows without a shadow of a doubt what that thing would be for me. And that would be that Wednesday program. I'd let go the Sunday school class, and I love being in that classroom with those little ladies. I love everything I do, but my greatest love is here where I see what God says in his Word the church, the born-again believer, should be about. I see it taking place on Wednesdays in that couple of hours we're together. We give the Gospel. We feed the hungry. We get clothes for them . . . and we counsel. We try to nurture them. And we do everything, a little bit of everything the Word of God says we as Christians ought to be about.

For some Christians in the emergency food endeavor, the salient scriptures come from the Old Testament. Bill Blodgett is a minister who is assistant director of the Good Shepherd Food-Bank in Lewiston, Maine. He explained for me the theological base of his commitment to food banking:

> In fact, that is the whole philosophy behind food banking, not just us, but any food bank. . . . The Lord tells the Israelites, "When you harvest your fields, don't go back and pick up what you've left over. When you pick grapes from your vineyards, don't go back over and grab what you've missed. Leave it for the poor, the fatherless, the widow." The gleaners. It was gleaning, and all that has been done in food banking is to take the concept of gleaning from a rural, agricultural society and transplant it to an urban, industrialized society. The principle is the same thing, it's just that what we glean comes in cans and boxes instead of directly off the trees or the ground.

Jewish anti-hunger activism draws on the same Biblical passages. "I can quote the exact part of the Talmud for you that talks about feeding the hungry and clothing the naked, and the blessings of doing so," Irv Cramer told me, referring me to Isaiah 58:10. My knowledge of the Old Testament is a bit rusty, so I looked it up: "If you pour yourself out for the hungry and satisfy the desire of the afflicted, then shall your light rise in the darkness and your gloom be as the noonday." The next verse promises even richer rewards: "And the Lord will guide you continually, and satisfy your desire with good things, and make your bones strong; and you shall be like a watered garden, like a spring of water, whose waters fail not." Leviticus is the other major text, according to Cramer, the passage about leaving unharvested the corners of your fields, the same passage that inspired both Bill Blodgett and the formation of the Senior Gleaners in Oxnard.

Cramer is the director of Mazon, A Jewish Response to Hunger, an organization that raises funds in the Jewish community by asking Jews to contribute amounts equal to 3 percent of the cost of their "life cycle celebrations": weddings, Bar and Bat Mitzvahs, birthdays and anniversaries; Mazon then distributes this money to anti-hunger activities and programs. Although Mazon raises its funds exclusively in the Jewish community, drawing upon Jewish traditions, it funds groups of all religious persuasions and secular groups as well. The Torah and the prophets are not the only source of Mazon's tradition. Its connection to celebrations, especially, has more modern roots:

> More recently, in Eastern Europe, where my grandparents came from—there are many in this country whose forefathers and mothers came from Eastern European backgrounds. Mine are from Russia and Poland. In those communities, which are fabled communities—the "Fiddler on the Roof" communities. . . . there was not only a tradition, but the tradition became a law, in a sense, that you could not begin such a celebration—a wedding, for example—the rabbi would not allow the celebration to begin until the poor of the community were sitting at the table as honored guests and sharing in whatever there was, along with everyone else. So the tradition is very old and very rich and very clear.

Cramer is particularly clear about the benefits of Mazon to the givers themselves: it not only helps "the people who ultimately receive the benefits of the dollars we raise . . . , it also embellishes the

Jewish community in doing it." He has "a rather large piece of evidence" for this contention, "and that is that we get thousands of checks accompanied by letters thanking us—people are sending us money and thanking us. They are saying things like, 'The wedding was beautiful in its physical manifestations of the flowers and the food and the music and all of those kinds of things. But there was a piece missing, a piece of human decency, and by inviting Mazon to the table, that is to say, the poor at the table, we were very proud and we felt that the circle was completed; our children learned, our guests appreciated because they understood, it felt good.' "

Liturgy

Mazon's emphasis on feasts and celebrations is consistent with a broader religious reliance upon liturgy as well as scripture, ritual as well as content, to transmit values and norms. Table graces are a common means of acknowledging the sacredness of food as well as expressing gratitude, and a fair number of them remind diners of others who are hungry: "Give food to the hungry, O Lord, and hunger for You to those who have food." Both the Christian Eucharist, or Communion, service and the Jewish Passover Seder frequently contain the words "Let all who are hungry come and eat." It would be hard to grow up in a practicing Christian or Jewish household in the United States without absorbing some notion of the sacredness of food and the concomitant obligation to feed the hungry.

The liturgical connection is not a one-way street. It not only reminds believers of their duty to the poor, it infuses much emergency food activity, especially the preparation and serving of meals, with a liturgical or sacramental character. Jean Beatty, of Channels in Harrisburg, told me that her idea for a series of community dinners in poor neighborhoods with food supplied by Channels, came from the "spiritual aspect" of food,

> the spirituality of food being the source of life. The giver of food providing for us first so that we must provide for others. That is all part of a shared meal. And of course that is where your liturgies come from in all religions, that it is a shared meal. You are, in fact,

all one. We have to know we are all one before we start helping other people.

The ritual power of food, and the compelling sense of complying with the dictates of one's faith may have a lot to do with the remarkable staying power of emergency food. While both religiously motivated and secular people involved in emergency food programs express frustration with their failure to make a dent in the underlying problems of hunger and poverty, many religious people can fall back on the consolations of faith, on the conviction that they are doing what their religion requires of them. Jim Kirk is a pastor at the Moorings Presbyterian Church, in Naples, Florida; a great part of his ministry is involved with the Collier County Coalition to Feed the Hungry, the Fill-a-Belly Foundation, and St. Matthew's House, a combination soup kitchen, food pantry, and residential recovery program located in Naples. He explained to me the importance of simply doing what one's faith demands, regardless of the immediate outcome:

> If people are involved in homelessness or hunger, or any social service, and they're doing it to be successful, it's going to be very frustrating. Because even Jesus said, "the poor are with you always." But I think if people do it, not to be successful, but to be *faithful*, then I think you find the energy and the strength and the hope to continue. I'd love to think that we could eradicate homelessness, but I don't know if that's going to happen in my lifetime. My motivation is to do it because I feel I've been called, as a religious person, to feed the hungry and clothe the naked and provide shelter for those with no shelter.

The Hand of God

If it is unreasonable to expect success, what keeps people motivated and engaged? Can the feeling of being faithful, of being obedient to the instructions of a higher power, keep people energized through the low periods and uncertainties inherent in this work? For some believers, of course, the answer is yes. For others, however, faith provides other reinforcements in the form of evidence that God looks with favor on their efforts. Religious people in the emergency food system often find confirmation for the rightness of their involvement in what they perceive as small miracles. JoAnn Pike, of the Good Shepherd Food-Bank, told me a whole string of stories about just-in-time donations. "In the spring of 1982," she recalled, "we had a second walkathon that didn't produce like we expected it to, and we'd made a lot of promises, and just financially it looked as though we weren't going to make it—that was a day I was particularly depressed and was ready to cash it all in—that day we received an anonymous check for thirty thousand dollars.... Financial miracles seem to come easy.... I think everybody who gets into this kind of work knows that those kinds of things happen. It's like God really does care about the poor." Financing isn't the only arena for miracles, either. Pike wrote an article for the November 1994 edition of *More Than Food*, Good Shepherd's monthly newsletter, entitled "Lest We Wonder If God's Hand Is Upon This Work" in which she described the nick-of-time location of a compressor for the freezer to replace one that had broken, saving eighty-seven pallets of frozen food. That she located the compressor through a woman attending a prayer meeting at the home of a board member, that "the exact compressor we needed" was stored close enough to the food bank to get there in time to save the frozen food, and that the grocery chain that owned the compressor was willing to donate it to Good Shepherd, were, Pike declared, "God's Hand upon this work of feeding hungry people throughout Maine."

Roger Davis, the farm and field coordinator at FOOD Share in Oxnard, sees the same hand in the workings of his complex and unpredictable system of identifying fields for his gleaners: "Sometimes I feel it's God providing because a couple of times I haven't known what I was going to have the next day and all of a sudden, somebody calls in and says 'I have some oranges, can you come and pick them?' Or I'll call on one of the foremen on one of the ranches and I'll say, 'How about this broccoli over here?' and he'll say, 'Oh, yeah, you can come tomorrow and get it.'"

The point is not to debate whether these examples reveal the hand of God or effective networking; the point is that many people involved in the emergency food system experience such rescues as evidence of God's favor. This, in turn, reinforces the conviction that they are carrying out the will of God, that they are being faithful, a powerful satisfaction for anyone steeped in faith.

"Teach Your Children Well"

As with almost all such powerful satisfactions, parents want to share them with their children. When a child was presented for baptism in the church in which I grew up, the minister asked the parents if they intended to "rear this child in the nurture and admonition of the Lord." It is a quaint phrase, but one that captures the sense of responsibility that many parents feel to pass along their religious faith to their children. So if their religious beliefs direct them to feed the hungry, it is not surprising that they take particular pains to involve their children in this activity, nor that they experience particular satisfactions when their children respond. Jill Staton Bullard, the director of the Interfaith Food Shuttle in Raleigh, articulated this conviction with great clarity when I asked her if she was glad that she had stumbled across food rescue. "Absolutely. It has truly changed my life, the lives of my family. My kids have grown up doing this. My friends' children; it has become a way of life. It has infiltrated their schools, their churches and everything else." She went on to talk a bit about her youngest daughter "who does not know when Mom didn't do this."

> I can remember when she was little and she used to go with me. She said "Mom, I want to see a hungry person." We would go into the soup kitchens and we would go into the shelters and she would play with the kids. But she said, "But, Mom, I want to see a hungry person." And then one day, she was in kindergarten, and she stood up in front of her class and she said, "Did you know that hungry people look just like us?" . . . This has been such a blessing to all of us. My children are blessed. I am blessed. I am the most blessed person I know.

A desire to teach compassion to young children, however, is not limited to people with strong religious convictions or overtly religious discourse. Laura Aziz, a mother who had brought several of her children to a pre-Thanksgiving bag-packing marathon at the Yorkville Common Pantry, explained to me that she had to make a special effort to find ways in which her four children could safely help the hungry, because she did not want them to give to panhandlers on the street, but she didn't want them to become hard-hearted and mean-spirited, either. Her children, she said, "can't avoid encountering" homeless people on their way to school, "because there's somebody on almost every block, especially in the colder weather." The younger children, she continued,

> want to talk back to the people who talk to us . . . and I discourage that, but I don't want them to interpret that as these people aren't worthy of our attention. They wonder when they're younger, why don't we give money to them . . . and so I've made a point of telling them that there are ways to help people, but I'd rather give money to an organization that has the resources and the professional back-ground to help people get themselves on their feet, and that giving a quarter or fifty cents or five dollars to a guy may buy him a meal at McDonald's, it may buy him something a lot less healthy than that like drugs or liquor, but in twelve hours he's right back where he started. And now the oldest, they're kind of used to it. And that bothers me. That's why we're here, because I don't want them to ei-ther ignore or to get hardened to or to blame the people who are on the street.

While Laura Aziz's children in New York City can't help running into homeless people on the way to school, other parents bring their children to help out in emergency food settings precisely because they don't ever see destitute people, except on television. Asked about involvement of children in the food bank of primarily affluent Contra Costa, California, director Larry Sly replied, "We try to get as many in there as we can. . . . it's really an education piece that I think is very important, for kids who probably have never seen a poor per-son in their life. . . . And I think the people who do have social con-cerns look at this as a way, a safe way of having their children—you're not going to have your kid go down and deliver meals to the per-son under the overpass—but at least they're doing something. It highlights the issue for them; they can see that they're making a difference."

Parents are not the only ones who have found the emergency food phenomenon a useful arena in which to teach compassion and related values to children. The Boy Scouts of America, as we have seen, have made effective use of it. So have other youth-serving organizations, church youth groups, and innumerable schools, both public and private. The same characteristics that make volunteering in a soup kitchen or food pantry appealing to such a broad spectrum of people in our society make emergency food particularly useful to school service learning programs. As the director of Community Service at the Fieldston School in New York City explained about the school's involvement with the Yorkville Common Pantry's Thanksgiving canned goods drive, it works for students at a wide range of levels of sophistication. "They felt so accomplished because they had organized all the cans," she said of two of the younger students in the Thanksgiving drive; "it taps into . . . the need for immediate gratification. There is a product at the end of it. You see it. You are fed emotionally. It is a balancing act, because at that age, in high school, developmentally you have the philosopher and the concrete thinker in one group. So the project has to address both the concrete thinker, who gets tremendous pride out of the cans, and the student who is out there, ready to change the system. All of them are fed in different ways."

The Relief of Guilt

"For Thanksgiving I'll be in my country house on Long Island," one of the student bag packers said to me, "and I'll have a good time. I think I will feel a little better because I'll know that I have done something to make somebody else's Thanksgiving a little happier." Unconsciously, perhaps, this student was comparing his own privileged life-style to that of the people who would consume the Thanksgiving bags, and anticipating feeling, in essence, less guilt because of his efforts at the pantry. I was surprised at how infrequently the subject of guilt surfaced in this study. Almost no one talked about guilt as a motivation for their own or others' participation. There were a few exceptions. Bill Rae at Manna Ministries in Bangor, Maine, talked about appealing to guilt as a way to solicit donations. "Christmas and Thanksgiving, I can appeal right to your guilt . . . You go out and you spend money, and you feel guilty about spending three dollars, so you give one and say, 'My conscience is clear.' " And Larry Sly described some of his canned goods drives as "almost unabashed guilt tripping." APCO consultant Jane Humpstone mentioned "white, professional person's guilt" as one of the factors that motivated staff members at her firm to work extra hard on the UPS/Foodchain project. Bill Bolling identified guilt as one of the generic factors that draw people into emergency food work: "People start either with a sense of calling for the work or a sense of guilt that they have so much. Well, guilt doesn't carry you forever. It's a great motivator in the beginning but it won't carry you through the hard times." The only people I ran into who spoke specifically in terms of atoning for injuries were people in twelve-step programs like Alcoholics Anonymous who were quite consciously trying to "make restitution" for past harms. Emergency food programs are particularly well suited to this function because there is a fair amount of physically demanding and sometimes distasteful work—scrubbing pots, for example—which can certainly provide a sense of penance, and because the outcome of all this effort—food for the hungry—is easily identified and widely recognized as "good."

A more diffuse and pervasive feeling, however, is closely related to guilt. An extraordinarily large number of people articulated some version of "There but for the grace of God go I" in explaining their decision to volunteer in a soup kitchen or food pantry. The prevalence of that sentiment was startling; it is one of the phrases that appears with the greatest frequency in my transcripts. At first I was perplexed by some of these assertions; among the subset of volunteers who had themselves experienced life in the soup kitchen line, especially those who had in some way been rescued from addiction or alcoholism, the phrase made sense to me. But what about the well-heeled volunteers who were in no way in danger of becoming pantry or kitchen clients? What did they mean by saying "There but for the grace of God go I"? Were they being disingenuous? Perhaps they only meant to express a sense of gratitude for their own relative prosperity, but over time, I came to feel that they were expressing something deeper: a nagging suspicion that there might be some connection between their own privileges and the misfortunes of the dinner guests, a sort of survivor guilt for the affluent.

Something Unambiguously Good

Even for those with little or no guilt to assuage, the immense moral force of emergency food is attractive. "There is this sense that this is good work, and that there is a real strong tie between feeding people and a lot of different religious beliefs; people think that feeding people is a good deed and almost a religious act," Ellen Teller summarized. It provides a sense of being on the side of the angels, something that is morally unambiguous in an age of uncertainties. An opportunity to do the right thing and to feel part of something larger than one's individual efforts.

It is clear that emergency food has found a niche, many niches, in our society. It provides meaning and purpose, a reason to get up in the morning, to senior citizens whose efforts are no longer welcome in the labor force, and to children whom we have largely deprived of meaningful productive roles. It offers opportunities for companionship to the isolated, and an arena for use of skills for the dedicated. It offers a chance to cooperate with those who are different—demographically and politically—and a means to build bridges across the widening gulf that separates the have-nots from the haves. It provides the faithful with a chance to carry out the dictates of scripture and conscience, and parents and schools with a means to teach compassion to the young. It assuages bruised consciences and affords participants a sense of doing the right thing. And it gets food to hungry people. There are many other worthwhile endeavors that might afford the same satisfactions that people report from their participation in emergency food, but I am convinced that emergency food provides a particularly intense dose of these satisfactions for two reasons. One is the moral relief bargain discussed in the Introduction, the multiplication of satisfactions because most participants are able to "be good" or "do good" on both the hunger relief front and the waste prevention front, simultaneously: a sort of moral two-for-one. The other is simply food itself, the way in which it mobilizes all sorts of less than conscious feelings and forces, its ritual significance and emotional power, and the intensity of our feelings about hunger.

The sources of satisfaction that people reported—achievement, positive use of their skills, a sense of purpose and efficacy, good companionship, teamwork, healthful exercise, and making a positive difference in the lives of others—all of these are the generic benefits of good works, whether performed by volunteers or staff. The fact that so many people have turned to the emergency food system to find these gratifications prompts some reflection. Have we created a society that does not routinely provide these basic human satisfactions to people in the course of their daily living? The impression created by my interviews, especially with senior citizens and other marginalized groups among the volunteers, is that, indeed, ordinary life provides precious few of these gratifications for an extraordinary number of people. Hillary Rodham Clinton diagnosed this problem quite correctly, I believe, in a speech in April 1994, when she said that "we lack, at some core level, meaning in our individual lives and meaning collectively—that sense that our lives are part of some greater effort, that we are connected to one another." There are far too many people in our society for whom we have, in essence, no useful work to do; from whom we expect little or nothing. Some of them are eating lunch at the soup kitchen; some of them are serving the soup.

I admire the seniors and other volunteers who have found this crucial work to do, instead of, as one volunteer put it, "sitting around grousing." I am a perennial volunteer myself, and expect that I shall continue to be during my retirement. Still, it troubles me that it requires an "emergency" program to provide opportunities for meaningful engagement and teamwork, and that so many people—Second Harvest products reached slightly over a tenth of the population in its most recent survey—should have to rely upon the efforts of people whose obligation is purely voluntary in nature. If emergency food programs were doing a great job of delivering food to the hungry—if they *could* do a great job—perhaps we would not need to be troubled by our attachments to these other functions. But what if emergency food does not do a great job of feeding the hungry? What if the aid it offers is uneven, unreliable, of unpredictable quantity and erratic quality? Would the benefits to providers justify perpetuating a system that does not really do a good job of getting food to those in need? The next two chapters explore the shortcomings of emergency food.

CHAPTER SEVEN

What's Wrong with Emergency Food?
The Seven Deadly "Ins"

THE SUN RISES behind the roller coaster, a giant orange ball in an otherwise gray July sky. Even the intense heat and humidity, however, do not dampen the almost palpable enthusiasm of the volunteers gathered to help launch Operation Blessing's Hunger Strike Force Convoy '94. Beginning at Steeplechase Park in Coney Island, New York, the convoy of huge red tractor-trailers will crisscross the country, engaging in "hunger strikes" that will distribute 3.4 million pounds of food, an estimated 2.2 million meals, in New York and sixteen other cities. With the boardwalk and the old parachute jump as background, volunteers, including evangelist Pat Robertson and celebrities Ossie Davis and Carole Lawrence, will be passing out prepacked bags of groceries to holders of the 2,000 vouchers that have been distributed in Coney Island. The activities will be broadcast, live, on Robertson's daily *700 Club* television show.

According to a glossy red, white, and blue press kit distributed at the event, Operation Blessing International Relief and Development Corporation, now an independent humanitarian nonprofit organization, was founded by Robertson and his Christian Broadcasting Network (CBN) in the late 1970s to distribute items donated by *700 Club* viewers to people in need. The Hunger Strike Force, established in 1992 as a "benevolence and relief outreach of Operation Blessing," consists of seven tractor-trailers that collect "donated and reduced-cost items from farms, food processing companies, and manufacturers" and distribute them throughout the United States.

Whether it is the desire to feed the hungry, the opportunity to witness for their faith, or the lure of the cameras and celebrities, an appeal for volunteers to help with the Coney Island launch has been oversubscribed. Operation Blessing wanted about a hundred volunteers; it started turning them away when the list reached 230. Many of the volunteers I talk to have taken a day off from work to be present. Most have been recruited through the mailing lists of the 700 Club, although some have come through local churches affiliated with the Christian Hope Network or through the Salt and Sea Mission, the local Coney Island sponsor. Both the Salt and Sea contingent and a group from the New Hope Fellowship Church who are handling refreshments were asked to show up at 5:00 A.M., so participation means a long day, as well as a hot one, for many of the volunteers.

Setting up for the event has been no small task. Steeplechase Park is essentially an enclosed grassy field with a circular roadway connecting its three gates. There is no running water; there is no electricity. There are no rest rooms. A large white tent has been set up to shelter the refreshments for volunteers and the TV crew: coffee, bagels, snacks, soft drinks, and gallons and gallons of bottled water to combat the heat. A portable generator supplies electricity; two "Location Services" trailers are available for changes of clothing and makeup for major participants. Portable toilets have been ordered but do not arrive until the event is nearly over. An enormous web of wires covers part of the field, supplying lights and sound for the broadcast. Another part is left free and open so that a helicopter can come and go. Operation Blessing's red, white, and blue color scheme prevails; the white tent, red tractor trailers, blue denim outfits for the Operation Blessing staff, including Robertson and his wife, DeeDee.

Remarkably, all of this has been planned and carried out in a few weeks: "About two or three weeks ago we got this call that the Hunger Strike Force was coming to New York and they needed our help and an office in order to coordinate the whole thing, because it involved getting permits, it involved looking at sites, and . . . it was like a whirlwind," the woman who has coordinated the refreshments tells me. I am amazed at her cheerfulness and equanimity as she reports that it is hard to keep her glasses on because they keep fogging up in the steam bath atmosphere of the refreshment tent.

Volunteers are not the only ones who arrive early and feel the heat. There has been some confusion about the starting time; the Operation Blessing staff expects to begin distribution at about 11:30; many of the would-be recipients have been told that it will begin at 10:15. In any case, voucher holders start lining up outside the gates at around 8:00. Many have the sort of two-wheeled shopping carts commonly used in urban areas to bring groceries home from the market; a few veterans of the waiting game have folding chairs. Mothers with small children try to keep their offspring under control, but there is the normal amount of fussing and crying. When 10:15 arrives, several of the waiting clients shout the time in the general direction of the gatekeepers. As Robertson starts filming, he tells his audience that "right now thousands of people are lined up right where we are."

As the line on the outside lengthens, the sense of excitement inside mounts. I interview the woman who is checking the preregistered volunteers in at the gate; she turns out to be the director of development for public relations for the Christian Broadcasting Network. I ask her why so many people have volunteered and she replies:

> I think people really want to help. I think they care about other people. . . . It's hard as an individual to find a way that you can be a hands-on person in assisting someone else, and this is an opportunity to have hands on and to help change another person's life.

I pursue my question with the volunteers themselves, and there is a remarkable unanimity to their answers; they are there to serve the Lord by feeding the hungry, to show that they care. They believe that it does not make sense to preach to hungry people, you must feed them first. "I know that before we could feed anyone something spiritual, we got to give them something so that their stomachs wouldn't grumble; then they could listen to what we're saying," declares Philip, a cab driver from Trinidad. When I ask him about the appropriateness of using food as a lure, he replies simply: "Jesus used it; there must be something to it."

Just before 11:00, the volunteers are rounded up and formed

into two lines, and exhorted to "love 'em real good as they go by." Stretched out shoulder to shoulder on both sides of the roadway, the volunteers form a sort of human fence that directs the flow of recipients from the entering gate to the distribution truck with a stop under a tree to pick up a free copy of the New Testament. As the weary voucher holders pass between the lines, the cameras roll and the volunteers shout messages of love and encouragement. After spending some time in the midst of the line of volunteers, I listen in on Pat Robertson's broadcast and press conference: "There's my wife, DeeDee, helping give out food to these people; they're getting bags of very nutritious food," he tells his viewers. "These are poor people who don't have any money and don't have enough to eat." When I watched a rerun of the program later that day, I discovered that Robertson's live segments from Coney Island were interspersed with information on the hunger problem around the country, background material on Operation Blessing in general and the Hunger Strike Force Convoy in particular, opportunities to become a member of the 700 Club by sending $25 a month to "ensure that things like this continue to happen," and with testimonials from satisfied 700 Club members who feel good about the work carried out with their contributions.

I move on to the exit to observe the departure of the beneficiaries. The parcels they have been handed are quite small, and I expect to hear some grumbling, but the people departing appear gracious and appreciative. A volunteer named Ed comments that he is a little disappointed in the size of the package: "I guess I expected them to be maybe three to four times the size . . . most of them have shopping carts and I guess I expected to see them filled to the top, instead of just one small parcel, but I assume they have a lot packed in there."

In his lilting Caribbean accent, sprinkled with the "you know"s typical of much Caribbean English, Philip, with whom I have talked earlier, comes to terms with the small size of the packet:

Well, I think it depends upon what's inside the package, you know, but, well, I'm not sure what's in the package, but I would have expected something more substantial . . . a little bigger package, maybe, you know. That's what I was thinking, you know, it might be a little bigger package, because it's not like a hot-cooked meal, that you give a person a meal, you know. But even so, praise God, you know. At least the people seem to be grateful, because they're smiling, they seem to be happy and they're receiving it well and it seems that there's a high level of appreciation on behalf of the people who're receiving the package, so it must be good.

Well, Praise God, you know. God uses whatever; even though the packages are small, remember the five loaves and two fishes, how God blessed and multiplied, so this might be a blessing like that for the people, you know. And then again, God uses the small things in life to bring a bigger blessing, most times so, Praise God; thank God for the small packages, you know. Amen.

Feeling as if I have just witnessed some verbal or theological sleight of hand, I turn to another volunteer who has overheard my conversation with Philip. Betsy works full-time for a Christian ministry, and she articulates her perspective with great conviction:

I've been very closely watching the faces of the people that have been coming through. And I know for me there have been moments when I've caught somebody's eye, and if eyes could speak . . . there is just such a sense of people feeling loved and feeling cared for. And certainly needs are great and needs are complex, and yet I feel like this is one way that God's love can be expressed in a tangible way. To say, yes, that there really are people who care and that you're not alone. And, you know, although it's a small bag of food, but yet it's a tangible expression to say that God cares and he's there for each person.

You wish you could give everybody three bags of food, but resources are limited, so you respond with what you have. I've been very impressed with the gratitude that people have had, and I'm reminded of one woman, an elderly woman who came walking through and she looked up and she caught my eye and she said, "I just know the presence of the Lord is in this place." And you can see the faces beaming, because people are really feeling cared for, so I think that this is a way of demonstrating that God really loves each one of us.

I ask Betsy if she knows what is in the packages, and she says no. In fact, none of the volunteers I talk to knows what is in the packages or expresses much interest in their contents.

When everyone who has lined up is served, the other four trucks roll out. These contain produce—white potatoes, yams, apples, and so forth, and they are headed for four distribution points in New York and environs where volunteers are waiting to unload them. The Steeplechase Park phase of Hunger Strike Force Convoy '94 is over.

"So Too Much for the Too Little"

If Betsy and Ed and Philip could have returned to Coney Island with me the next morning, they might have come away from the Hunger Strike Force experience with less glowing memories of love expressed and gratitude returned. I went to collect community reaction to the giveaway, and after I found the group of women gathered on the steps of the Fellowship Baptist Church, I got quite an earful. Located in a row of old ramshackle houses between the towering housing projects and Coney Island's seedy downtown, Fellowship Baptist operates both a soup kitchen and a food pantry, and it had acquired some of the leftover bags from the giveaway. We opened three, to confirm my impression that each bag contained exactly the same items: a 3-pound bag of white rice, a 3-pound bag of dried kidney beans, a 24-ounce can of beef stew, a 12-ounce can of sliced chicken in gravy, an 8-ounce can of beef taco filling, two 8-ounce bottles of salad dressing, both Santa Fe ranch, and four individual-sized bottles of egg cream, two vanilla and two strawberry.

In the first place, as the ladies let me know, it wasn't enough. "It's not enough for a family of four, and most people do have at least four in their family; I got seven," one woman declared. Mother Bradley, a community leader who serves as the president of the tenants' association in her building and is the founder of a thriving children's garden, was even more critical of the quantity: "They called it Operation Blessing but I do not see any blessing from that; they took away from the blessing because, how in the world are you gonna feed, I'm not even counting the people with four or five in a family. I'm counting two people. Two people. How in the world are you going to feed two people with one small can of chicken? And they gave that little stew. If a single person have two kids, okay, what are you going to do, mix in water? It doesn't even feed—one bag—a family of three kids, not counting the grown-up. And you call this a blessing?" As one of the women put it, "It was so too much for the too little."

Quantity was not the only gripe. One of the women gathered on the steps critiqued the menu: "It's not really consisting of what we eat anyway. I mean in the summertime, I don't cook beans. I don't eat white rice; I eat brown rice, and I never buy white rice, so actually this rice will be given away to somebody who eats it." Aware, perhaps, that she would eat white rice if she were very hungry, she suggested: "Actually I think this food should be going to Rwanda where those people are starving." The egg creams came in for special notice: "Egg cream, that's no food!" An egg cream is a traditional New York City soda fountain drink made of milk, flavored syrup, and seltzer. It does not contain an egg, and it is not usually made with cream. Freshly concocted at the corner store, they are popular; bottled and shipped in from a warehouse in Virginia Beach, they invited derision. Who would send bottled "New York Egg Creams" to Brooklyn? Some of the senior citizens sitting in the garden in front of the Bernard Haber Houses described them as a "pretty sparkling beverage," and seemed happy to have them. The seniors, who can eat several meals a day in the dining room of their housing complex, clearly viewed the Operation Blessing giveaway as a treat, a little something extra. Among those who had expected real food to tide them over for a few days or a week, the egg creams were a joke.

The major complaint about the menu, however, was the absence of the fresh produce that had filled the other four tractor trailers, the ones dispersed to Manhattan, the Bronx, Long Island, and New Jersey. "I waited around there until they finished, and they opened those trailer trucks, and there were bags of onions, apples, carrots, yams, and all of the other stuff. I asked the question why. I was told they were gonna take it to the Bronx and Manhattan. Why weren't it given out here?" When I noted that the Fellowship Baptist Church seemed to have obtained some of the fresh vegetables, Mother Bradley explained that she had taken the phone number off the truck and given it to the pastor of the church who called and arranged to acquire some of the produce to distribute. Despite her success in getting the more desirable fresh food, Mother Bradley remained critical: "I think it's a shame that they're getting this food here in the community and they give out this small amount to the families that need it and just do a promotion. People can't live off of a promotion. . . . 'Go over there and shake Ossie Davis hand,' they tell me. What am I going to shake Ossie Davis hand when Ossie Davis is giving out this little food? . . . I was very upset with Ossie; they saw this small package . . . it seem like they would ask, they would open it. I took my Operation Blessing shirt off . . . I really refuse to wear that shirt again."

The other set of complaints I encountered had to do with the voucher system. Nearly everyone I talked to thought that the vouchers could have been better distributed by working through the community organizations that are close to the people in need. Some of the criticism may have been a matter of noses out of joint. A voucher for free food is a source of power in a poor community, and understandably the people who see themselves as local leaders wanted a piece of the action. But some of the criticism seems to have hit the mark quite accurately; the vouchers were not given to many of the agencies and organizations that work with poor families on a daily basis. The pastor of the Catholic church was given thirty vouchers, but he was misinformed about, or misunderstood, the date, so his thirty were not distributed in time. Mother Bradley says that vouchers were handed out to passersby on Surf Avenue, the street that people walk down to get to the famous Coney Island Amusement Park, so they went to people who were neither needy nor local. Further, the vouchers were not adjusted to family size or other family needs. "When you do something like this," one of the Fellowship Baptist folks told me, "when you give somebody a voucher to get food, you ask them how many in the family, how many in your family that you have to feed? Then you go according to that, if you want to give somebody something. Why give us this little bit?" The Operation Blessing vouchers were strictly one to a household, until the end of the actual distribution, when the staff realized that they would have a lot left over. Then, according to the word on the street, they gladly gave two or three bags to a customer.

Whether it was because the vouchers were given to people who didn't really need the food, or whether the word got around the neighborhood about what was in the bags, or whether the heat and humidity deterred people, the thousands of people that Pat Robertson described to his TV audience collected only a bit over 800 of the 2,000 grocery bags prepared for them. I found this out the hard way, after I left the women on the steps of Fellowship Baptist and went by the Salt and Sea Mission to check out its reaction to the giveaway. The Mission looked closed up from the outside, but inside I found the Salt and Sea crew hard at work, disaggregating the 1,152 bags that had been delivered to them after the show at Steeplechase closed down.

I pitched in, emptying bags and sorting them into piles of salad dressing, beef stew, taco filling, rice, beans, sliced chicken with gravy, and, of course, egg creams. The egg creams were the most difficult because they had been taped together in sets of four, two vanilla, two strawberry, and we were trying to free them. I kept thinking of those volunteers down in Virginia Beach, lovingly, I assume, wrapping those bottles in tape, the heavy-duty kind used for mailing. I'm sure that the egg creams were eventually consumed; they have a high sugar content and the alcoholics and addicts that frequent Salt and Sea certainly crave sugar. Meanwhile, the unpacking party remains engraved on my memory as the most depressing episode in my research. Maybe it was just the unrelenting heat and humidity; Salt and Sea is barely ventilated, certainly not air-conditioned. Maybe it was the wry humor of the staff and the monumental patience of the Mexicans who, stranded in New York without green card or relatives, have become regulars at the Mission. Maybe it was the pathos of undoing work carefully done, like untrimming the Christmas tree. Packing such bags, as I have experienced it in a variety of settings, is an upbeat, hopeful, convivial experience, but unpacking them is a letdown. The unpacking marathon, for me, symbolizes the rampant inefficiencies of emergency food.

The Seven Deadly "Ins" of Emergency Food

The Operation Blessing Hunger Strike Force Convoy '94 food giveaway in Coney Island in the summer of 1994 was certainly not typical of emergency food. I have chosen it as a place to begin a discussion of the shortcomings of the emergency food system precisely because it displayed almost all of them. Most of the projects and programs I have visited are troubled by one problem or another, or are constrained by fundamental limitations of the emergency food approach, but none rivals the Coney Island giveaway as a catalogue of grievances and problems. Further, because the Hunger Strike Force giveaway was televised, something that I have hardly ever encountered in another emergency food program, some of its faults were exaggerated. But that is precisely what allows us to see more clearly the problems inherent in the whole phenomenon. The point is not what was wrong with the Hunger Strike Force launch, but rather that the giveaway is a metaphor for the whole emergency food system. Or perhaps the better term is caricature; like a snapshot or a cartoon, the giveaway captured a momentary reality in an ongoing, complex phenomenon; it simplified some features and exaggerated others. Like a caricature, it reveals essential features, and these features tell us what's wrong with emergency food. This chapter will consider six of what might be called the seven deadly "ins" of emergency food: Insufficiency, Inappropriateness, Nutritional Inadequacy, Instability, Inaccessibility, and Ineffiency; the seventh, Indignity, is so important that it warrants a chapter of its own.

Insufficiency

We might as well begin with the criticisms articulated by disgruntled recipients of the giveaway: the quantity, quality, and appropriateness of the food. Quantity poses an immediate problem. Who is to say how much is enough? If a community is hit by a flood or a hurricane and its food resources are destroyed, disaster relief programs will try to bring in enough food to meet the need, enough food to feed everyone who is without private food resources until some semblance of normalcy is restored, until the supermarkets are restocked and most people have money to use them. Soup kitchens and food pantries, however, do not have resources sufficient to permit an unlimited distribution for this seemingly permanent disaster. Kitchens generally feed anyone who shows up until the food is gone; if they run out frequently they may institute a ticket system so that clients will not be inconvenienced by a long wait for nothing. Almost anyone who has had the job of announcing that the food is gone, or even that the tickets are gone, will tell you that it is the most disagreeable part of the work. In a New York City study, more than a third of kitchens reported turning away food seekers, and close to half reported having to thin or stretch meals.

Some kitchens try to cope with shortfalls by limiting portion size or the number of refills; no seconds until everyone has had a first is not an uncommmon rule in relatively small kitchens, where people who want seconds can reasonably wait until everyone has had a chance. In a kitchen serving hundreds of guests with rapid turnover of seating, however, such a policy won't work. Clients desiring seconds could be sent to the back of the line; more commonly, such kitchens permit refills as long as they are consumed on the premises—all you can eat, but not all you can carry away. I remember a noontime meal at CHIPS, a soup kitchen in my neighborhood, in which we thought we had prepared too much and encouraged diners to return for seconds and thirds, only to be hit with a last-minute influx of hungry people for whom we did not have enough. It was not a matter of bad planning on our part; it is inherent in the phenomenon that you cannot plan with any confidence. Even when there is replacement food available, a substitute that can be heated up if the day's entree gives out, the situation is less than ideal. I watched the anxiety mount at the back end of the line at the soup kitchen at Our Lady Star of the Sea in Key West, Florida, as word spread along the queue that the pasta and sauce were running low and we were reheating the remainder of the previous night's clam chowder. When people are getting their only solid meal of the day, they want it to be big and hot and just like the meal of the guy in front of them. "People get pissed off if the person next to them is eating chicken and they are eating hot dogs," the director of an agency that sponsors a large soup kitchen told me. "You don't need anything that causes a ruckus." The quickest way to evoke rage in the human infant, I've been told, is to frustrate the gratification of her oral needs. Sometimes the same applies to adults.

Pantries use a variety of approaches to try to match available resources to apparent need. Almost all limit the frequency with which a client can obtain food from the pantry, although these limitations vary greatly from pantry to pantry. Some, still clinging to the notion that they are designed for the occasional unusual event—fire, eviction, sudden job loss—limit clients to once every three months. In Milford, Pennsylvania, where the Ecumenical Food Pantry is almost the only emergency resource, a given family may pick up three Friday nights a month, but not four; the Pantry does not want to become a regular part of the family's life, but it has nowhere else to send a family in real need. Where limiting the frequency of visits does not sufficiently stretch the available food, pantries may maintain a waiting list. At the time of my last visit to the Yorkville Common Pantry, there were a thousand families on its rolls. Of these, some were permitted to visit weekly; some twice a month, and some only once a month, depending upon need as determined by the staff. Another several hundred households were on the waiting list. It seems almost a contradiction in terms, a waiting list for *emergency* food.

The alternative, of course, is for pantries to give less food per household than they would like. But this gets us back to the question of how much is enough? Should the amount be determined by some sort of in-depth assessment of need, some calculation of how long the family is likely to be without resources? Very few pantries have the staff to conduct such an assessment. One reason that food pantries can operate relatively cheaply, in fact, is that many do not do case management or assessments requiring trained staff. A given amount for a given family size is the norm, and the amount is determined by some mysterious alchemy of the total amount of food available to the pantry, the ideas of adequate quantity held by its founder, director, or board, and the amount that can reasonably be carried home by most clients, depending upon proximity and the means of transportation available. Most of the recommended packing lists I've seen work out to about 20 pounds of ready-to-eat foods in cans and jars, plus several pounds of rice and/or beans, and enough nonfat dried milk and/or powdered juice concentrate to make about eight quarts of beverage for a family of four. The most rational explanation I heard for a given quantity was in Delaware, where many food pantries were originally started to tide families over while applications for Expedited Food Stamps were being processed. Since state law required the applications to be processed within three days, the pantries tried to provide a three-day supply of food for each household. When the law was changed to allow the state food stamp agency five days instead of three, however, the pantries did not raise their allocations.

If there are no real norms for quantity, how could the ladies at Fellowship Baptist be so sure that the amount distributed in Steeplechase Park was too little? First, there was the disappointment factor; they had expected more. Second, there was the uniformity factor; the amounts at the park were not adjusted for family size, and nearly everyone felt that this was "unfair." Third, there was a sort of ratio of inconvenience-to-reward at work. If the weather had been cooler, if people had not lined up so early, if distribution had begun when they expected it, they might have been satisfied with less. For poor people, as for the rest of us, there is an opportunity cost factor; what else might one have done with the time spent waiting in line. The longer the wait, the higher the opportunity cost, the greater the benefit needs to be to justify the inconvenience or the sacrifice of other activities. Most poor people in the United States are not literally starving, and they don't have all day. As a man in one of the cheese lines of the early eighties put it when he turned out to be the first person after the cutoff, the one who would have been next if they had not run out, "I'm out of work with four kids and I could have been looking somewhere else for food or a job, 'stead of standing here for some cheese." In fact, it turned out that the Operation Blessing crew could have given twice as many bags to each customer, since more than half of the prepared bags were delivered to Salt and Sea to be unpacked. But like the soup kitchen that overprepares or underprepares, this does not so much reflect bad planning as the impossibility of planning. No one knows how many people will show up for a mass distribution; distributions of federal surplus commodities under the TEFAP program have been subject to similar uncertainties.

Inappropriateness

If the quantity needed is difficult to estimate, the choice of food pantry items—or soup kitchen menus, for that matter—is virtually impossible to get right. There is simply no accounting for taste, and in this consumer culture, we are encouraged to develop tastes and preferences to a science. The point of including the comment of the woman who said she did not eat white rice was not that Operation Blessing should have packed brown rice; I suspect that even more people would have been unhappy with that choice. It is that almost no predetermined list of foods is going to suit the dietary needs and preferences of any large group of people. And when the consumer has no say as to the composition of the bag, mistakes are bound to happen.

Packing bags one morning at the Yorkville Common Pantry, the menu called for two 15-ounce cans of vegetables. I assiduously avoided canned peas, since I hate them, and I put in lots of canned corn because it is my favorite canned vegetable. What if the recipient likes canned peas and hates canned corn? More troubling, the manager came down and told the volunteer packers that we could put in either peanut butter or jelly, but not both, since there was not enough. In a culture in which consumer choice has been elevated to an art, in which one must, to be a fully participating and mentally healthy adult, choose on a daily basis not between peanut butter and jelly but between smooth or chunky peanut butter, between peanut butter made from peanuts produced on industrial farms or organic peanut butter, between peanut butter containing salt, and sugar, and emulsifiers, and peanut butter composed wholly of peanuts, in a culture in which advertising urges us to look for a product with a name like Smucker's or touts the benefits of all-fruit spreads, why am I choosing *for* people whose tastes and preferences I may not share? This is exactly why food stamps were invented in the late 1930s: to channel the subsidized consumption of surpluses into the "normal channels of trade," so that recipients could choose what they could best use. If food stamps were more generous, or rent payments were scaled to income, or wages were more adequate, people would be choosing their own spreads and my aversion to canned peas would not be imposed on anyone else. The emergency food system almost ensures that such errors and mismatches will occur. I was surprised the first time a pantry client told me that she passed along to others, or donated to another pantry, items from her pantry bag that her family did not like. "If you were really hungry," I thought to myself, "you'd find a way to use whatever you receive." Then I visited a pantry that was giving out canned liver in broth, and I reconsidered.

Canned goods drives are particularly likely to produce anomalies in the pantry bag or the soup kitchen menu. As such drives have become more and more important as a source of food, pantry staff have learned how to manage them to elicit the products they need most, but inevitably some households contribute inappropriate items. Among the foods donated to the Yorkville Common Pantry's Thanksgiving drive one year were: chestnut puree, unsweetened baking chocolate, kasha, hair-styling mousse, a container of green tomato piccalilli, and a package of bubbling green denture cleaner. Ethnic diversity can sometimes interact with social distance to make food donations appear strange to recipients. Sister Judy, the nun who directs the Guadalupe Center, explained, "Because it's Immokalee and because we have so many cultures here, I have a real hard time with food drives. Because people clean out what they don't want in their food closet, and chances are the Mexicans and Guatemalans and Haitians don't want it either . . . I would like to see a pantry where they could come in and shop and take what they need instead of going to a door and receiving a bag and taking it home."

Nutritional Inadequacy

Beyond people's preferences, there lies the issue of what's good for them: nutrition. One critic of the Operation Blessing bag pointed out that the stew, the chicken, the taco filling, and the salad dressing were all high in sodium and relatively high in fat—not suitable for senior citizens, she concluded. Pantry bags are difficult to assess, because one would need to know about the people to be fed and the other food resources with which the pantry food is to be combined. Soup kitchen meals are an easier target, and they generally fail the test. A 1986 study of soup kitchen meals in the state of New York found that over half of the kitchens did not provide at least one-third of the Recommended Dietary Allowances for an adult male or female for calories and a whole host of specific nutrients, especially protein, thiamine, niacin, vitamin C, and vitamin A. A national study released in 1988 found soup kitchen meals frequently deficient in fruits, vegetables, and dairy products. Meanwhile, studies of homeless diners in New York City soup kitchens found that more than two-fifths reported that their soup kitchen meal was their only meal of the day.

Food banks have particularly been the targets of nutritional critiques, but the large quantities of snacks and sweets that they handle do not reflect the poor eating habits or misguided food preferences of food bank directors; they reflect what is being produced in the United States, and particularly, what is being produced in the areas of greatest competition where test marketing failures and strategic over-production to corner the market are most likely to lead to donations. And they reflect what is being sold. What the supermarket sells is what ends up at the food bank through the salvage process. The director of the Food Bank of New Hampshire estimated that about 80 percent of the goods that come in from his reclamation centers are usable, but that less than a quarter of those will be nutritionally desirable.

> The rest of it is junk food, but it's still usable; when you're hungry, a box of crackers will taste mighty good. A candy bar . . . If you look at a major supermarket, you see . . . aisle after aisle after aisle of junk food. So that's what we get. That's what America eats. We're a bunch of junk food junkies.

To the considerable extent that the emergency food system is supply driven, rather than need driven, it will continue to distribute more sweets and snacks and less canned fish and fresh vegetables than nutritionists recommend. "Sometimes we cringe at what we give out, but it's food, and so we give it out," Hawaii food banker June Tanoue told me.

Instability

The government commodities are generally not unfamiliar, and with the exception of the high fat and high sodium content of the butter and cheese, they are nutritionally sound. The mothers and grandmothers on the steps of Fellowship Baptist told me that a lot of people thought the Operation Blessing giveaway would be like the mass distributions of commodities: "Actually, we're used to the peanut butter and the flour and the butter. That we like, because we can bake our Christmas cakes with the flour, we can cook corn bread with the cornmeal . . . nobody's ashamed of that. Like giving out the cheese. They don't give the cheese anymore." But the disappearance of the cheese points to another troublesome aspect of dependence upon donations, surpluses, leftovers. Commodities accumulate in government hands when production and market conditions interact to produce a large surplus, or to make it more profitable for farmers to sell to the government at supported prices than to sell on the open market. When this happens, the government eventually takes steps to correct the situation; otherwise, it is obligated to incur mounting purchase and storage costs, and mounting public disapproval. Thus the great cheese giveaway of the early eighties was followed by the federal Dairy Herd Buyout, in which the government paid dairy farmers to go out of the dairy business altogether. As a result, most of the dairy surplus disappeared; there hasn't been cheese among the TEFAP commodities for a long time.

For the Agriculture Department, this may be economic planning; for soup kitchens and food pantries, it has meant the loss of a major source of a valuable high-protein food. Surpluses are inherently temporary; they are not a reliable resource for a permanent or long-term program, as poor people learned during the Great Depression. When the emergency to which emergency food was addressed was regarded as temporary and expected to be of brief duration, surplus agricultural products appeared a handy and economical means to feed the hungry, and the hungry appeared a socially acceptable way to get rid of a surplus. But when a program goes on, year after year, and a need persists, the temporary nature of surpluses becomes a curse. Impermanence is a built-in characteristic of the surplus commodity component of the emergency food supply, making it perennially unreliable, and causing staff to work ever harder to solicit new sources to replace those that have disappeared.

A very similar process, as we have seen, has occurred among the private donors from the manufacturing and grocery trades. As they corrected the problems that led to the overproduction or cosmetic irregularities that led to the donations in the first place, the donations stopped. No company is going to keep putting the labels on upside down so that there will be peanut butter at the food bank. Although we can predict in a general sense that many food resources will disappear, we cannot usually predict when a particular one will exit the scene, adding a precariousness to the whole endeavor that leads me to characterize it as fragile, despite rising investments in capital equipment, space, and sophisticated technology. Money resources are also scarce and undependable, contributing to the fragility of the system. Contributions from individuals often decrease just as need grows, because they are derived from the paychecks of people who feel threatened or are experiencing reduced income. Foundation grants have proven increasingly difficult to get as the novelty of emergency food, or the novelty of each innovation within it, has worn off. Funding sources like Mazon increasingly fund only food relief projects that include advocacy or at least a full range of social services, and some funders that once promoted emergency food have simply moved on to other interests.

Even public money, which some emergency food providers saw as more reliable, has proven unsteady, and when it is available, the purposes for which it can be used are often severely limited. As the Food and Hunger Hotline, a New York City organization that connects callers in need with emergency food services, pointed out in a recent report,

> Only a small fraction of the moneys allocated by federal, state, and local governments for soup kitchens and food pantries can be spent on administrative expenses (including staff). At the federal level, FEMA sets aside 2 percent for administration, SNAP allows 5 percent of state funds, and EFAP an average of 9.5 percent of city money.
>
> The lack of funding for overhead, supplies, equipment, and staff obliges neighborhood-based food programs to rely on volunteers to do everything from write funding proposals to prepare food baskets.

The Hotline found that 68 percent of the hours worked at soup kitchens and food pantries in the city were contributed by volunteers. An earlier study of New York State pantries and kitchens outside New York City found that "only 23 percent of the pantries had a paid staff person whose primary responsibility was to the food pantry and its clients," and nearly half of the pantries were operated entirely by volunteers. Among soup kitchens, "on an average day, only 14 percent had a paid staff person on duty."

Dependence upon volunteers adds to the fragility of the system, since volunteers, by definition, can not be controlled. Many emergency food volunteers are extraordinarily dedicated, but others come for a brief stay and move on. As the director of Manna Ministries in Bangor, Maine, put it, "A lot of volunteers are what I call 'short steamers.' They'll come in real hard, real heavy, to gratify something inside themselves, and then they get burned out and they stop, so that's a continuous turnover. You have to understand that. You can't knock them. You can't look negative. Just realize they've met that need in their life. That's good. Now they can go on to whatever they have to go on to." It may be good for the individual volunteer, but it's not so good for the hard-pressed program. As the Hotline pointed out, "Reliance on volunteer labor creates unpredictable labor shortages, obliging programs to shut their doors, especially in the summer and fall months."

The unpredictability of the food supply, and the unreliability of financial support take their toll on volunteers as well. A long-time staff member at a large midwestern food bank talks about the stresses that contribute to volunteer attrition. The typical agency, she says, is in a small church, and "even if it isn't currently being run by all elderly women, that is the way it started." They set out to do something informal and temporary, and

> here we are, fifteen years later and it is not going away and it is becoming more institutionalized and you have to learn how to run a business if you want to stay alive. The clients are . . . well, let's not even talk about grateful, the clients are barely manageable. Substance abuse is a bigger problem among your clients, no matter where you are. Food resources are hard to come by because the food banks have them all sewed up and legitimately so. . . . So they are worn out and they are elderly.

The unreliability of resources is reflected in both actual closings and cutbacks in emergency food services and in a constant anxiety among pantry and kitchen directors. A study of New York State kitchens and pantries conducted in the mid 1980s found that approximately half of the pantries in the state encountered problems in obtaining enough food, money, volunteers, or transportation in any given quarter of the year from July 1985 to June 1986. Kitchens experienced even more problems than pantries; on average, more than four-fifths reported trouble obtaining sufficient food, money, volunteers, equipment, and/or transportation in each quarter of the same year, with the percentage climbing above 90 percent in the summer and fall quarters. "It is misleading and dangerous," concluded a study prepared by Cornell University, "to consider private food assistance as an integral part of the nation's food assistance safety net. Private food assistance may adequately meet short-term emergency food needs, but it is a fragile, highly variable, at times inaccessible, and limited approach to meeting the chronic food shortages experienced by many clients."

These problems had not been solved five years later. According to the 1992 Census of Emergency Food Relief Organizations in New York State, 30.3 percent of the state's 1,697 food pantries, and 40.2 percent of its 496 soup kitchens were jeopardized by lack of funds, 21.5 percent of pantries and 9.3 percent of kitchens by lack of food, and 14.6 percent of pantries and 16.0 percent of kitchens by lack of volunteers. Because of its highly elaborated "Nutrition Surveillance Program," the state of New York probably has more extensive data on the condition of soup kitchens and food pantries than do most other states, but the Second Harvest study suggests that the sense of jeopardy is widespread in the emergency food system. Just over a fifth of the pantries and just over a quarter of the kitchens in the Second Harvest study reported that their programs were "threatened." Lack of funding, unpredictable funding, and increasing demand were the most frequently cited reasons, mentioned by at least two-fifths of those who felt that their programs were unstable, with lack of volunteers, lack of specific foods, a general lack of food, and lack of space mentioned by at least a fifth of those that reported feeling "threatened." Such bean counting is useful in providing an assessment of the overall health of the system, but it tends to obscure the day-to-day reality at the kitchen or pantry door. During a lull in the Operation

Blessing preparations in Steeplechase Park, I asked Debbie Santiago, the director of the Salt and Sea Mission, about a sign I had seen on the Mission door that said "Food Pantry, Wed. and Fridays, when available. "We feed people meals seventeen times a week, and we have food pantry, when available," she told me. "I always put 'when available.'" I asked how often it was available, and she replied: "It's never available for everyone who needs it, ever. We do bread distribution and bagels and doughnuts every day. But as far as actual food pantry bags, we do it every week, twice a week, but we never can give to as many families as need it . . . I hate turning people away; I know what it is like to be hungry."

Inaccessibility

All of this uncertainty is aggravated by another troublesome characteristic of the system, the lack of convergence between need and supply. As a system, emergency food is essentially unplanned; it grows like Topsy. Kitchens and pantries spring up wherever someone is moved to create them. The overall effect is a little like the voucher distribution that angered the residents of Coney Island. Although individual pantries may work very hard to tailor their bags to household size and need, overall the system is haphazard and erratic, fragmented and in some cases duplicative. There are gaps in coverage, and areas that are comparatively overserved, feast or famine. While this characteristic of the emergency food phenomenon is widely recognized, only a few communities have undertaken studies that document the pattern. Why study the situation, after all, if no one has the authority, resources, or responsibility to remedy any discernible imbalances?

In Cleveland, a careful study that compared the number of meals served or meal equivalents provided with the number of persons in poverty in the city's thirty-six statistical planning areas found "a wide disparity in the availability of emergency food services to the poor." A ratio was calculated for each area, and the poor in the six best-served areas were fifteen times more amply accommodated than those in the six least served areas. To some extent, such disparities reflect the resource-driven nature of emergency food. In Manhattan, for example, the borough's two wealthiest city council districts have more soup kitchens than the two poorest; the wealthy districts simply have churches and synagogues with the resources to sustain such programs. A very elaborate study conducted by the School of Public Policy and Management at Carnegie-Mellon University in Pittsburgh found that "there are large differences in access to pantry services among neighborhoods and communities in Allegheny County." The study found no differences by either race or age: "Poor whites and poor blacks did not differ; poor elderly and poor young did not differ. The only characteristic that is systematically related to the proportion of needy who are served is distance of the community from the Food Bank." The report went on to speculate that this might reflect both an awareness factor—the farther from the food bank, the less aware of it communities were likely to be—and logistical factors such as transportation and other perceived barriers.

Issues of distance and transport, of course, are particularly significant in rural areas, both transportation of food to a food pantry, and transportation of food from a pantry to the homes of clients. As a Second Harvest spokesperson, Chris Rebstock, explained to a congressional committee at a hearing on Hunger in Rural America, "the client who ultimately receives this product from the soup kitchen or from the pantry is often faced with transportation difficulties. By definition, rural areas require the travel of significant distances, most often with little or no public transportation. Logically, some of those who are most in need are least likely to have access to the transportation which would allow them to avail themselves of the services." Some rural pantries have taken concrete steps to address such transportation problems. The pantry in Deer Isle, Maine, has made a point of involving pantry recipients with cars in the delivery of groceries to elderly, disabled, or sick clients who have difficulty getting to the pantry; Allegheny County (Pittsburgh), Pennsylvania, has experimented with a pantry on wheels to reach the more rural parts of the county. Nevertheless, access remains an issue for pantries serving rural populations.

Getting food from the food bank or other sources to the pantry is a continuing challenge. Old men with pickup trucks may be an engaging image, but it is not always a predictable resource. The Food

Bank of Alaska has dealt with transportation challenges of staggering proportions. Alaska is 656,424 square miles, and a single food bank based in Anchorage tries to serve the entire state. Director Jack Doyle explained the nuts and bolts of transporting federal surplus butter around his enormous domain:

> Here come these van loads of butter; for us to move butter around the state of Alaska means that we pay the highest price for transporting it on airplanes so that it will still be kind of frozen when it gets to the next spot so it can be stored. We have found that the least expensive way for us to move product off the road system is the U.S. Post Office, what's called "bypass mail," and it's a complicated way of doing it. It's labor intensive, but the products can be moved for about 32 percent of what it would cost for air ordinarily. But we have to wrap every package. They set exterior limits on the size. We have to weigh each one of those, we have to put postage on it, we have to put it on a pallet, we have to identify every box, we have to wrap the pallet with cellophane, and then we have to call the post office and find out which airplane, air freight, do they want us to have that load to. Then we have to have our driver there to meet the guy at the post office so it can be loaded on the airplane. But that's all part of moving freight around Alaska.

Fortunately, most of the products that the food bank ships around the state can be carried by truck, at least to those areas served by roads: "Within the road system, we have trucking firms and wholesale grocers that are moving our product at no cost to us or to the agency at the other end. They're simply doing it on a space-available basis at no cost. It's a big saving."

Transportation is not the only way in which rural food banks are disadvantaged. In the first place, they tend to have far fewer local sources of "product": processed and manufactured foods to be distributed. "Whereas, in Chicago, being a transportation hub and a manufacturing hub and a food processing hub, we're in food bank heaven," Madeline Lund pointed out; "food banks in the middle of Iowa and North Dakota and in parts of Kansas, obviously they are not going to have some of the same advantages that we have." The lack of local sources for products to distribute is aggravated by other characteristics of rural social life such as a limited financial donor and volunteer base. Even where food resources are locally available, these other limits may inhibit the creation of a food bank. Rich Ryan is a professor of public administration and political science at the Imperial Valley Campus of San Diego State University. He worked for years trying to start a food bank to serve the poor of Imperial Valley, one of the nation's most productive agricultural areas, and one of California's greatest concentrations of poverty. He points out the anomalies of trying to organize on a volunteer basis in such a rural area:

> Ironically, in those areas most in need of a food bank, it may be difficult to find the volunteers and organizational skills necessary to create a community distribution center. Imperial County, California, has the lowest median income in the state, and local agencies cite escalating demand for food assistance. At the same time the county has a $1 billion agricultural economy which creates an abundant supply of edible but economically nonmarketable food. Without a fully functional food bank, surplus food cannot be distributed among poverty income families in the county, nor can gleaning programs be organized. . . . The inability of low income, poorly educated populations to assist themselves is a weakness of decentralized approaches to alleviating hunger.

Ryan goes on to point out that such difficulties at the local level interact with national political and social trends to create even greater inequality:

> Nationally, however, political leaders may misperceive the ability of voluntary organizations (the "thousand points of light") to take up the slack of government program cuts, or policy makers may seek to mask the impact of budget cuts by pointing to the effective work performed by food banks. Those areas without a strong voluntary effort, then are forced to depend on trimmed government programs. Communities with a greater success rate with voluntary organizations will be able to establish community safety nets while those which are not able to create a food bank or similar operation will live with an increased number of hungry people.

Ryan's story has a happy ending. Eventually, a grant application was successful, and the Imperial Valley has just celebrated the opening of a food bank of its own, but the persistence and dedication required to wait out years of frustration are scarce commodities in urban or rural areas.

Like the voucher system at the Operation Blessing food giveaway, the fundamental structure of the emergency food endeavor fails to ensure that those in greatest need have the greatest access to food, or indeed, any access at all. Some poor people just don't live where a program is available; others may live in an area with multiple kitchens and pantries and still not have meaningful access. Some programs are only open once or twice a week, some only during the daytime hours, or only in the evening. "There's no need to go hungry in New York," a homeless man told me as we waited in line for the midnight sandwich distribution across the street from Grand Central Terminal. "The only time I was hungry was the first two days I was homeless; then I got hold of the *Street Sheet*, and I've been okay since." The *Street Sheet* is a directory of all the food and shelter resources available to homeless people, with their days and hours of operation; it is laminated to protect it from the weather and updated regularly. Or, in a pinch, call the Food and Hunger Hotline; if you tell them where you are, they'll tell you the addresses of the nearest open soup kitchen or pantry. Many communities have invested in information and referral systems designed to connect people in need with available food—telephone-based services like the Hotline, or printed guides like the *Street Sheet*. But just keeping such information systems up to date as to days and hours is a complex task, and most such systems are perennially out of date.

Inefficiency

The effort and expenditure required just to connect hungry people with available resources raises the question of efficiency. Individually, many food banks are spectacularly efficient operations; they have set new standards in the nonprofit world by bringing the norms and techniques of business, just-in-time delivery, total quality management, and efficient consumer response, to social service delivery. But overall, the system is rife with inefficiencies. If volunteers in Virginia

Beach spend hours taping together bottles of New York City egg cream that volunteers in Coney Island must spend hot, frustrating hours untaping, that is inefficient. But we do not need to go to such an extreme case to find the inefficiencies of the emergency food system. The Boy Scouts drive portrayed in chapter 1 may be among the most elaborate, but nearly any food drive involves purchasing food at retail, carrying it home or to a collection bin, transferring it to a central collection point, redistributing it to a local pantry, and then handing it out to a family or individual in need.

Centuries ago, the human species invented cash, small, light-weight units of purchasing power that rapidly came into wide use because they were so much more efficient, flexible, and exact than barter. In the field of poor relief, the debate about relief in cash versus relief in kind has been lively at least since the late 1800s, with cash preferred precisely because it permits households in need to obtain what they need most, and provision in kind advocated either because goods were cheaply available or because relief givers feared that recipients would misuse cash. In the late 1930s, a pair of economists in the U.S. Department of Agriculture found a solution that combined the flexibility and choice of cash with the limitation to necessities of relief in kind: a food-specific money called food stamps. Every time I contemplate the enormous labor that goes into a canned goods drive, only to deliver to families in need bags of groceries that may offend their tastes or fail to meet their needs, I am reminded of the underlying logic of food stamps.

The elaborate systems developed to procure and deliver canned goods are not the only inefficiencies in the emergency food system, but they serve to illustrate the point. At a fundamental level, we have set up a duplicate food system, in which food pantries substitute for supermarkets and corner stores, and soup kitchens serve in lieu of cafeterias and coffee shops. This nation has a food distribution system that is famous all over the world for its ability to deliver variety and economy to even the most remote places in the country. Ironically, the period in which soup kitchens and food pantries have proliferated is also a period that has seen the reduction of supermarket availability in many inner-city neighborhoods. I am not suggesting that the emergency food system undermines or competes with the for-profit food system. I am suggesting that the same underlying inability of the economy to generate adequate jobs and income has brought about both phenomena. With adequate income, or adequate food stamps, many of the families now lined up at food pantries could go to the store of their choice at their own convenience and select the foods they want most, and stores would have sufficient markets to remain profitably in business, and volunteers would not have to collect and sort and pack, and so forth.

Effort is not the only factor to be considered in determining efficiency. If we conceptualize efficiency as a ratio of output to input, then the monetary costs must also be assessed, and some value must be assigned to the output. Pat Robertson's Operation Blessing giveaway must have incurred substantial financial costs. There were the tent and the refreshments and the T-shirts and the hats. There was the helicopter. There were all the technicians and the generator and the lights and the location trailers, and the portable toilets, even if they were late. There were the trucks themselves, and the costs associated with the food, even if it was donated, and there were the staff members to coordinate the whole thing.

Meanwhile, I priced the bag of groceries that was distributed. Even at the inflated prices of a Brooklyn corner store, and even with no attempt made to secure bargain prices—looking at small bags of rice, for example, instead of dividing up a large bag—I calculated that a casual shopper could have obtained the contents of one bag with a cash outlay of $13.50. Since 2,000 bags were prepared, we might calculate that the Coney Island giveaway was supposed to give away a maximum of $27,000 worth of food. How much more than that did Operation Blessing spend to do the giving? Operation Blessing, of course, had other agendas, other outputs, besides the distribution of 2,000 grocery bags. New members may have been recruited to the 700 Club, and certainly the volunteers I interviewed left the experience convinced that they had expressed God's love in a meaningful way. Like a pep rally, the excitement and good cheer of the giveaway built identity and left a residue of positive feeling. The volunteers did not hear the complaints the next day, and they didn't have to unpack the uncollected bags. From an organizational standpoint, the expenses associated with the launch of the Hunger Strike Force Convoy '94 may have been a good investment, but as a method of getting food to the hungry, the ratio of output to input was low.

Of course most emergency food programs do *not* incur most of the costs that Operation Blessing incurred, but there are costs, and they are not always obvious. Someone paid for the bags the Boy Scouts used, and paid to have them printed with a special Scouting for Food logo and recommended donation list. Someone paid for the gas in the station wagons and the drivers and mobile phones for the collection trucks and the heat at the Ciba-Geigy employee cafeteria and the hot dogs and the sodas, and snacks for volunteers. Just because something is donated does not mean that it has no value. The New York City Food and Hunger Hotline calculated that even at minimum wage, the hours contributed to the city's soup kitchens and food pantries in a recent year were worth $18,780,837. Emergency food programs achieve their reputation for efficiency by simply failing to count as a cost any resource or component that is donated.

Indignity

The people who lined up for hours in the broiling sun for the Coney Island distribution would not have omitted the inconvenience factor, nor the humiliation factor, from their answer to the question "What's wrong with emergency food?" In fact, the negative experiences of clients are so important to a diagnosis of the ills of the emergency food system that they deserve a chapter of their own. The next chapter explores these aspects in some detail.

Social policy analysts use adequacy, reliability, coverage, efficiency, equity, and contribution to social cohesion as basic measures for evaluating social programs. While individual programs may pass many of these tests, taken as a whole emergency food fails most of them. Coverage, adequacy, and equity are interdependent; that is, if you do not have access to a program, if you are excluded from its "coverage," then the adequacy of the benefit it offers is irrelevant to you, except as a measure of the inequity of excluding you if your needs are equal to those of others who are "covered." The goal, in theory at least, is to cover all of those with a definable need with a benefit adequate to meet that need, and to treat people who are in roughly the same circumstances approximately the same.

If you are designing an emergency food system, you may set out to make a food pantry bag sufficient for a certain number of days of meals available, and accessible, to any household without food resources or the money to purchase them. In the adequacy department, you might specify that the bags be sufficient in quantity to tide a household over until it could reasonably be expected to obtain food from other sources, or available on a regular basis. And, further, since the notion of adequacy embraces quality as well as quantity, you might specify that the meals provided be of sound nutritional quality, meet some specified percentage of the Recommended Dietary Allowances (RDAs), for example. Equity would dictate that households in similar circumstances have similar access to food pantry provisions of similar value. Predictability would mean that people in need could rely upon this safety net to be available and deliver a known quantity of help. Contribution to social cohesion would mean that the assistance would be offered in such a way that clients were integrated into the larger society, not excluded from it. We don't need to take this exercise any further to expose the absurdity of applying these standards to emergency food. Emergency food quantity, quality, coverage or accessibility, predictability, and social cohesiveness are not determined by some sort of societal plan to meet basic needs; in fact, they are driven as much by supply—by available food resources, volunteer time, space, and the like—as by need. Standards of equity seem irrelevant; these are standards that apply in situations in which recipients have rights. They cannot be applied to charity, precisely because the charitable giver has no responsibility to provide equitably. In ways that are both profound and pervasive, the shortcomings of emergency food are the limitations of charity. The next chapter explores the consequences for recipients of the charitable character of emergency food, and the efforts of emergency food providers to mitigate its inherent indignities.

CHAPTER EIGHT

Charity and Dignity

HE COULDN'T have been kinder, the tall pastor with the straight brown hair and the slight sag to his shoulders. I knocked on the door of his study in a classic white wood-frame Congregational church on the Maine seacoast late one Friday afternoon in August 1993. I was looking for the Tree of Life Food Pantry. I hesitated, embarrassed, because I hadn't followed my usual research routine of calling ahead to request an appointment. Casually dressed because I had thought my research completed for the week, I was heading for a campground to enjoy the weekend when I noticed the Tree of Life sign and decided, on the spur of the moment, to try to squeeze in one last interview. I stumbled in my attempt to explain my presence; he hurried to my rescue: "Do you need food?" His tone was respectful, his smile encouraging, his eyes caring. Yet I felt devastated, humiliated. It was a visceral reaction that stripped me of status, degrees, prestige, identity. I learned in that instant a major fault of emergency food: that it humiliates the people who ask for it. A more clever researcher would have prolonged the inadvertent fiction to find out just how a stranger in need is treated at the Tree of Life. I fumbled for my card and hastened to explain my purpose, and the interview that followed was one of the most rewarding in the process that produced this book. But even as I thanked him for taking so much time with me on so little notice, I knew that the pastor would never know how much he had taught me with his innocent question.

If I had played along with his misunderstanding, had asked for food and filled out a simple declaration, I would probably have continued to be treated kindly and I would have received a bag of whatever was on hand. In part because of the spirit of its founders and dedicated volunteers, in part because of the generosity of wealthy summer residents of Blue Hill and vicinity, the Tree of Life Food Pantry has possibly the least bureaucratic eligibility determination process of any that I encountered. "We can't ask people; we can't put any qualifications whatsoever on our recipients. If they ask for it, we give it to them; that's all," declared the pastor. In order to preserve this no-questions-asked procedure, the pantry has repeatedly turned down governmental funds and commodities, preferring to rely on the local donations that come without strings attached. Tree of Life has not had difficulty in raising funds: "There's a tremendous energy and tremendous generosity and the people around here support it, so the money comes in—we don't even ask. It just keeps coming in." Thus the pantry can afford to err on the side of generosity. But even in so hospitable and undemanding an atmosphere, where an assertion of need is the only requirement, the whole weight of our culture's attitude toward those who need help came crashing down upon me. I was being offered charity. Not an earned recompense for earlier contributions, not an entitlement based on our mutual interdependence, but a gift, given in response to my very deficit. For a brief moment, I was the hungry person dependent upon the kindness of strangers, and I felt, profoundly, my powerlessness, my inadequacy, and something verging on shame.

I have thought about it many times since. Why was it so distressing? *Charity* is one of those remarkable words that helps to identify the fault lines of a culture. For some people, its connotations are wholly positive. It signifies unselfishness, tolerance, altruism, even love. In fact, it was used in place of *love* in the King James Version of the Bible, so that many people now in adulthood grew up hearing the famous passage from First Corinthians rendered as "And now abideth faith, hope, charity, these three; but the greatest of these is charity." Charity is virtue.

For many other people, however, the word has a thoroughly negative connotation. It is the gift, offered with condescension and accepted in desperation, that is necessitated by incapacity and failure. It is the last resort, the end of the road. It carries a stigma, a badge of shame, that is almost too much to bear. Our literature is full of characters who would rather suffer severe privation than accept it. I especially remember Katie, Francie's mother in *A Tree Grows in Brooklyn*. When her husband dies, leaving her pregnant and destitute with two children to raise, her sister suggests turning to Catholic Charities. Her reply is immediate. " 'When the time comes,' said Katie quietly, 'that we have to take charity baskets, I'll plug up the doors and windows and wait until the children are sound asleep and then turn on every gas jet in the house.' " " 'Don't you want to live?' " her sister asks, and again Katie's reply is instructive: " 'Yes, but I want to live for *something*. I don't want to live to get charity food to give me enough strength to go back to get more charity food.' "

Charity Wounds

Part of the contrast in connotation arises from the bifurcation of roles between givers and receivers. Katie was looking at charity from the viewpoint of a potential recipient. Most of the exhortations to charitable behavior are aimed at potential donors. It certainly is "more blessed to give than to receive." "Though we laud charity as a Christian virtue," anthropologist Mary Douglas has written, "we know that it wounds." But why does it wound? One of the people who contributed most to my understanding of the wounds inflicted by charity is Ester Bradley-Delgado, a dynamic African-American woman in her mid-forties. Compact and energetic despite disabling health problems, she is a minister who runs the Daily Bread Food Pantry in Santa Cruz, California, a program that she helped to found in the aftermath of the 1989 Loma Prieta earthquake. She described for me her experiences as a food pantry client at an earlier stage of her life:

> I was a single parent; I have two boys and I raised them on my own. So being a single parent, you have to just sort of, you know, reach out for a little extra to carry you through, especially at holiday time. And overall, my experience had been real clinical. That's the word that I use: . . . clinical. No emotion. No connection with the people. Just . . . you're in there; you're a number. You fill out this application, sit in this line, you're a number, and that's the Salvation Army and we'll take care of you and you go into a file. And that's it. Make

sure that you have your proof of address, your medical card for your kids, proof that you even have the kids. It's almost like a person was made to feel like they're trying to steal something or they're trying to rip off.

Because of her experiences there, and at another pantry where she encountered a pervasive rudeness, she has clear rules for her volunteers about how clients are to be treated:

I said when we started a pantry that I would never have anyone suffer at this pantry the abuse that I suffered and the demoralization of emotions . . . I have a very firm, firm belief that if you cannot treat a person with dignity, then you don't belong here. Because sometimes people end up at that door, they've already gotten to their very lowest. To come to a food pantry, I mean it's demoralizing; they think, ". . . they're going to look down on me." And when they muster up all of their courage to call the food hotline and then show up at that door, the least thing that they can leave with is their self-respect.

Bradley-Delgado's critique—the suspicion that clients encounter and the bureaucratic procedures with which they must comply, the absence of warmth and human connection, and, especially, the sense of being looked down on, the demoralization—surfaced again and again in my interviews, both in conversations with clients and in discussions with volunteers and staff members. Sometimes even a very mild note of criticism can wound a client. Stanis Laycock turned to the food pantry at her church, where she had been active for years, when her husband became disabled and their money ran out while they were waiting for disability insurance:

So I went to them and they gave us some food, and then they gave us more food, and then I had to go back again and ask for even more food and something was said about "You need more food?" And I didn't know what to say, and then I realized that the way the food cupboard was run was an on-call food cupboard, but they didn't expect to give anybody food more than occasionally, that they had no concept about what it was like to be without food. The people that were running it didn't understand . . . So I didn't go back there anymore.

Dick Goebel, the director of the Second Harvest food bank of St. Paul, Minnesota, identified a problem that I ran into in several places: "Food shelf coordinators always become very possessive. 'It's my food. Are you worthy?' You have to get away from grilling people, making them run through unnecessary hoops." Asked how he helped them overcome this tendency, he replied, "I could preach at them. I am a Lutheran, I am good at guilty," but he had found it far more effective, he said, to bring in an articulate client or former client willing to tell the food shelf volunteers what it was like to be on the other side. "You have to be able to have people come who can articulate that from their own experience."

Sometimes, the harsh attitudes that result in what Bradley-Delgado calls demoralization reflect an underlying ideology. One soup kitchen in Austin, Texas, gave new kitchen users a handout that reads, in part, as follows:

> WELCOME TO ANGELS HOUSE! Angels House is a Christian ministry to persons who need a meal. . . . A person who comes to Angels House for help should realize that he or she has a serious life problem including bad habits, some of which are willful idleness, lack of self-discipline at the job site, alcoholism, drug abuse, including nicotine addiction, chronic faultfinding with others and general unruliness. ANGELS HOUSE DOES NOT EXIST TO SUPPORT PEOPLE WHO WILLFULLY AND CONSISTENTLY INDULGE ANY OF THESE BAD HABITS. Evidence of refusal to turn away from these bad habits . . . will be grounds for denying help at Angels House. YOU MAY BE ASKED TO LEAVE AND NOT RETURN TO ANGELS HOUSE UNTIL YOU WANT TO LEAD A NEW LIFE.

It is not surprising to find a soup kitchen with a harsh attitude toward its patrons; after all, for decades soup kitchens have been associated primarily with assistance to the denizens of the nation's skid row districts. Historically, such attitudes have been persistent attributes of the charitable endeavor in general. In the emergency food sector, however, I have been struck by the extraordinary efforts of providers to avoid, overcome, or at least minimize the negative, demeaning aspects of giving help. What is interesting, in light of the proliferation of such establishments in the last fifteen years, are the attempts to create soup kitchens and grocery distribution programs that preserve dignity and offer a warm, welcoming environment. Can this goal be achieved, or are these programs inherently demeaning? By exploring the steps taken by emergency food providers to minimize suspicion and bureaucracy, combat depersonalization, and promote dignity, we can clarify both the potential and the limits of charity.

Suspicion

Suspicion and bureaucracy are inextricably intertwined. Proofs of identity, of address, of household composition, and of eligibility for various other means-tested programs, the time-consuming paper-work that casts the pall of bureaucracy over programs that started out as friendly neighborhood resources, are required because providers operate in an atmosphere replete with suspicion. These are the suspicions that arise whenever you offer "something for nothing": the suspicion that those seeking help may not really need the assistance, the suspicion that they may be seeking more than their share, and the suspicion that they may plan to resell or otherwise misuse the benefit. Even providers who are not personally concerned with these fears must deal with them, because these providers are, in turn, dependent upon the generosity of donors who *are* concerned about them.

In general, these questions are far less difficult for soup kitchens than for food pantries. Soup kitchens benefits are consumed on site, they cannot be resold, and many kitchens consider the willingness to wait in line to be evidence enough of need. Suspicion persists in the larger society, as we have seen. This was the essence of the much publicized comment by presidential counselor Edwin Meese that the Reagan White House had received "considerable evidence that people go to soup kitchens because the food is free and that that's easier than paying for it." Meese's comment, however, was part of the ideological skirmish over whether growing lines at soup kitchens could be taken as evidence of a politically embarrassing rise in hunger in America. Frontline providers tend to share the perspective articulated by *Seeds* magazine in its guide for people considering starting a soup kitchen:

Will you serve everyone who comes in or screen for need and/or eligibility? A soup kitchen without screening is more efficient. Feeding an occasional freeloader is a small price to pay for a generous, welcoming atmosphere that eases the pain of being dependent on others.

Futhermore, as noted in chapter 2, some soup kitchens welcome and solicit participation by a broad range of guests. Financial need is not the sole criterion for receiving service.

Pantries, however, face a more difficult challenge. Pantry products are not consumed on-site, and some of them have considerable market value. As the value of the benefit rises, so does the potential for "abuse," but even here the standards are murky and the pantry operator may be caught between a genuine desire to help and a need to protect the integrity of the organization. Resale or barter for drugs, alcohol, or tobacco is occasionally suspected and universally condemned. Resale to obtain funds for some other necessity may be a bit more understandable, but creates immense public relations problems for the pantry. Pantry operators may comprehend a client's urgent need to convert a box of donated groceries into, say, a pair of school shoes, but the donors who provide the food, the grocers and food companies whose market is undermined if donated food is resold, are not so understanding, and the pantry is dependent upon such donors for the wherewithal to meet the needs of its clients. In Deer Isle, Maine, one enterprising client was found to be stockpiling the pantry's products in hopes of opening a coffee shop. While the scandal did not completely destroy the pantry, it made many hours of work for the organization's dedicated volunteer board members who visited donors all over the area to explain that this was not the norm and that steps were being taken to prevent a repetition.

Will people who could afford to purchase food show up at a pantry for a food box if it is made readily available? It is a real bind for those providers who are most sympathetic to clients and most concerned about protecting their dignity. If you place too many hurdles in the way of would-be clients, if you ask too many questions and require too many pieces of paper, you risk deterring those whom you most want to help. But if you offer food with no questions asked, if you make your pantry too attractive, it may be flooded with people whose need is marginal, alienating donors and displacing the truly needy. Few pantries have sufficient resources to permit them to adopt the if-they-ask-for-it-we-give-it-to-them policy in effect at Tree of Life. Most pantries screen applicants themselves or require a referral from some source better able to determine need.

The referral versus on-site screening debate further illustrates the bind in which pantry operators often find themselves. Screening on-site means that the whole apparatus of eligibility—the proof of address that shows that you are not homeless—that you have a place to prepare the types of food typically dispensed by food pantries—the birth certificates or Social Security cards that attest to the existence of the children whom you have claimed on your application, the Medicaid card or welfare ID, or even a pay stub and rent check that show your need, must be processed at the pantry itself. No wonder clients complain of suspicion and bureaucracy. And it means that the unpleasantness of turning away an unsuccessful applicant is the responsibility of the pantry—and frequently of a well-meaning but untrained volunteer. On the other hand, screening on-site allows a pantry to bend its rules to accommodate an unusual case, an applicant whose need is real and urgent but does not readily fit predetermined guidelines; such flexibility is of prime importance to many caring people who have been drawn into the emergency food endeavor.

Relying on referrals can remove both the unpleasantness and the paperwork from the premises and is common among smaller pantries that lack the resources to conduct their own assessments. When a new client shows up hungry, however, and must be sent to another organization, which may or may not be open and ready to assess the need, the requirement for a referral may appear to be just another hassle. As one pantry director put it, "If a referral letter is coming from a social agency or health center where they are seeing the person as a patient and they know they need food and they refer them, that's one thing. But if somebody has to walk over to a church and get a piece of paper that says they're referred to us, when there's really no relationship behind that, that is almost like harassment."

In some communities, the rationale behind requiring referrals from a central source like the Red Cross is an effort to prevent people from receiving aid from multiple providers. As the *Seeds* handbook puts it, "Many people . . . are concerned about those who make the rounds of churches, searching for handouts." Such "professional pantry shoppers" reflect a fundamental contradiction built into the system. On the one hand, most pantries will supply a maximum of three days' food. On the other, most forbid giving to an individual household more often than once per month or even once every three months. For clients who come in the aftermath of an actual emergency or an exceptional occurrence, such limitations may make sense. But increasingly, poor families use food pantries as a chronic supplement to low wages or public assistance that does not last the month. Food stamps typically run out after two and a half to three weeks. A three-day supply will not fill the gap, so of course those who have access to multiple pantries will seek help from several. While some operators fight a losing battle to maintain the emergency character of their cupboards, most have become philosophical about regular and multiple use. "We don't go into that," an elderly volunteer in Belfast, Maine, told me about an existing but ignored procedure for discouraging double dipping. "They do it anyway, see; you can't stop that. People that are hungry are hungry."

Depersonalization

The rules and regulations that appear to applicants as manifestations of suspicion also contribute to a second complaint: dehumanization or depersonalization ("no emotion, no connection . . . you're a number"). As with any form of social organization, this is an experience that varies with the size of the group as well as the attitude of the providers and is far more typical of large pantries and kitchens staffed by paid employees than of the small volunteer efforts. Nevertheless, emergency food providers work hard at overcoming this depersonalization, trying to welcome clients and treat them as individuals. Madeline Lund's role as the agency relations coordinator of the Greater Chicago Food Depository takes her into hundreds of pantries and kitchens. She summarized for me the various ways to make clients feel at home when they come in:

There's the physical set-up of the room. Is there a place for somebody to wait? Is the heat on? Are the lights on? Is the place cheerful, and do they have access to bathroom facilities? Some of the best food pantries serve coffee and donated doughnuts, and they talk to the clients using Mr. and Mrs. instead of "hey you."

Ester Bradley-Delgado trains her volunteers to greet clients with a smile and exchange pleasantries before moving to the paperwork, and she tries to make sure they don't leave the premises without "an encouraging word." Doreen Wohl, at the West Side Campaign Against Hunger food pantry in New York City, positions the computer so that its screen faces applicants and explains the reason for each question asked. Joyce Hoeschen, one of the founders of the Bath Area Food Bank Soup Kitchen at the Knights of Columbus Hall in Bath, Maine, keeps a reserve of cakes in the freezer and brings one out with candles anytime she discovers that it is a guest's birthday. And Madeline Lund stresses with her agencies the importance of keeping modest notes about each client's personal situation: "So that if you told me that 'my son is in the hospital,' the next time you came in I could ask you 'How's your son?' . . . It's not that everybody's going to be a social worker or anything like that," she continues, "but one thing I feel the clients have in common . . . is that virtually no one is listening to them, really.

> So many of them are alienated from their family ties. If they're fortunate enough to be working, they're not in a position where their boss is really going to have significant personal interaction with them, so their boss isn't listening to them. Their landlord isn't listening to them. Nobody's really listening to them, so the best thing the pantry operators can do—in addition to the food—is to provide that listening ear. . . . You're not going to be able to solve all their problems, but I think that that helps tremendously in terms of human dignity.

Indignity

Human dignity is, in the last analysis, the crux of the matter. People who turn to a soup kitchen or food pantry are asking for help in meeting one of their most basic needs. In our culture, with its stress on independence, it is tantamount to an admission of failure. Dependency is the natural state of the human infant, and as psychiatrist Willard Gaylin has pointed out, the experience of prolonged dependency in infancy and childhood shapes much of the feeling and behavior that we recognize as human. The progress of the human child toward maturity is laden with psychological and emotional as well as physiological challenges. It is not surprising, therefore, that dependency is associated in our culture with immaturity and independence with adulthood nor that the issue of dependency arouses strong emotions. "It is an indignity," Gaylin argues, "for an adult who has no intrinsic needs for care and maintenance to be reduced to the level of a child. . . ."

Promoting Dignity by Preserving Choice

One theme that runs through the efforts of emergency food providers to protect the dignity of their clients is in fact the attempt to preserve adult roles. This is difficult in a society that has basically discarded many if not most of the clients of emergency food—a society that has no valued roles for them to play. Some pantries, however, have made a major effort to preserve at least one significant role, that of shopper. In the most typical form of pantry, bags are packed for the client, the contents determined by the available supply, the size of the household, and the whims of the packer. If the client cannot use or does not like some of the foods included, well, too bad. Several clients told me that they donated such items to another pantry or passed them along to others in need. In a shopping pantry, however, the available foods are displayed on shelves or tables, and clients are provided with a shopping list indicating the quantity they may select from each category—grains, proteins, fruits and vegetables, desserts, etc. Although the avoidance of waste is one motivation for establishing this system, a more urgent concern is the effort to preserve dignity through the exercise of choice. Shopping is an adult activity; it implies competence and individuality, and it casts the client in an active rather than a passive role.

While most people who operate pantries on a shopping basis

seem enthusiastic about them, not everyone likes the idea. I asked Fran Ficorelli, who runs a prepacked pantry along with a soup kitchen and a food rescue program in Niagara Falls, what she thought of the shopping pantries she had seen. Her answer was blunt:

> Very bad. Very, very, very bad. What I don't like about it is mostly the people who run it. I have seen it in several places. . . . How do you monitor it? In other words, if you have tuna fish on your shelf, how do you see to it that they are not grabbing half a dozen cans and putting them in their pockets. You have to follow them around. The only way you can achieve this in a fair manner is to follow the person. What does that do to you? I don't want to be followed around. If I go into a store and somebody is following me around, I'll leave. I won't buy anything. I try to design . . . what we do by how I would feel if somebody did that to me.

Doreen Wohl, who converted the pantry sponsored by the West Side Campaign Against Hunger from a prepacked format to a shopping situation, solves the monitoring problem by simply having a volunteer "check out" each client—she doesn't follow them around, but an experienced volunteer at a checkout table makes sure that clients have gotten everything to which they are entitled, and nothing to which they are not.

Not all emergency food providers, of course, are so convinced of the importance or advisability of allowing clients to choose. For some the decision to offer pantry bags or soup kitchen meals is derived, in part at least, from a critique of the behavior of poor people that would have been right at home in the nineteenth century. I discovered this when I asked people if an increase in the food stamp allotments would help alleviate the need for kitchens and pantries. The most commonly articulated concerns had to do with shopping skill and nutritional knowledge, the perception that emergency food clients do not do a good job of spending cash—or using food stamps—an updated version of the nineteenth-century concern with thriftlessness. "People run out at the end of the month," a volunteer in Bath, Maine, told me about food stamps. "That's because they're not using them right. They're buying their potato chips and soda and ice cream and cookies and cakes—and their kids need that, but they don't need it every day." A nutritionist working with the pantry in Deer Isle expressed frustration with the food stamp concept: "I don't agree with the Food Stamp Program as far as they can buy anything they want to, including ice cubes—I found that out last year and I just about died! I called Augusta [the state capital], and yes, they can buy ice cubes."

Among the general population, however, she felt that the concern was not just nutrition, but also fairness: "I think the feeling is, 'I can't afford to buy lobster for my family, but a food stamp person can.'" An interview later the same week elicited precisely that feeling from a bank manager in Bath who volunteers regularly at the soup kitchen. Asked why she preferred the soup kitchen/food pantry approach to food stamps, she said plainly:

> I've seen them go and actually purchase some food, and then they'll get the change from the food stamps and then go ahead and purchase their drugs or beer. I've seen them eating better than I eat, actually, on food stamps. They can buy prime rib or lobsters. I don't see it fitting in. I think the food bank and soup kitchen are wonderful. They eat what we put out or peanut butter and jelly sandwiches if they don't like what we have.

Concern about diversion of benefits to what the nineteenth century would have termed "vice" was fairly frequent. In Oxnard, California, a regular volunteer at FOOD Share told me that he believed the food bank approach was far superior to government welfare programs because it ensured that food ended up on the table: "It's not like the Food Stamp Program; the people get the food stamps and I know that some of them misuse it; they trade their food stamps for cigarettes and trade their food stamps for alcohol, drugs. I know this because my wife's cousin has a store and she's seen it happen." Back in Maine, another volunteer recounted a similar story. Asked about expanding the stamp program to reduce the need for soup kitchens like the one he was working in, he was adamant:

> No! And I'll tell you the reason why. I worked in a grocery store for many years. . . . I've seen them going through food lines . . . and buy cigarettes, which is illegal—but yet, the stores will sell it to them as long as they don't get caught. And I say, No! I say, this program is

great. At least they're getting something in their stomachs that's worthwhile.

I don't want to distort the picture. There are many emergency food providers who are staunch supporters of food stamps, who are ambivalent about emergency food in part because it does not provide consumers a choice. Eric Kolbell, the social action minister at New York City's Riverside Church, which has run a five-day-a-week food pantry since the early 1980s, summarized this perspective succinctly when I asked him about expanding food stamps: "Anything that would give the clients more autonomy, more selection, more efficiency, and more dignity in allowing them to get their groceries has to be better than a food pantry." Or, as Guadalupe Center director Sister Judy Donher said, after comparing prepacked food pantry bags to children's Christmas toys selected by volunteers who don't know the children, "When I see somebody at Christmas time handing them a bag, I think, 'You don't have a clue what those kids want,' and I don't think we have a clue what people like to eat." What she would prefer, she said, "instead of having a pantry or instead of having it set up like a supermarket is to give them a voucher for a real supermarket . . . that way, they would choose what they want."

Soup Kitchen Stigma

While soup kitchens and other programs that serve prepared meals may have an easier time than pantries when it comes to issues of screening and eligibility, they may face a more difficult challenge in trying to preserve dignity within the program. Soup kitchens are regarded, by clients and volunteers alike, as even lower status than pantries. One client, interviewed for an extensive study of poor women's definitions of and feelings about hunger, is illustrative. She had received food "from WIC, commodity distributions, and food pantries, leftovers from her mother, and partial payment of bills to have some cash available for food." But when asked about using a soup kitchen, she said, 'I didn't get that far down.' "

The stigma attached to soup kitchens has deep roots in history. During the potato famine that disabled Ireland in the 1840s, when the meager work relief provisions proved wholly inadequate to avert starvation and the relief committees found the purchase of grain too expensive, soup kitchens were touted as the solution. Alexis Soyer, a famous French chef who normally presided at the kitchen of London's Reform Club, had caused a stir in his adopted city by composing recipes for very economical soups, which he prepared and distributed to several hundred of the London poor each day. He proposed a soup distribution plan for Ireland despite medical objection to the nutrient quality and quantity of his recipes, and as Cecil Woodham-Smith has written, his "claim that a meal of his soup, once a day, together with a biscuit, was sufficient to sustain the strength of a strong and healthy man, was too tempting for the British Government to ignore. After all, Soyer enjoyed immense prestige; he was perhaps the most famous chef in Europe, and at the request of the Lord-Lieutenant, he was invited to come to Dublin, install boilers, and superintend his scheme for the mass distribution of soup." Woodham-Smith's description of Soyer's effort warrants reproduction:

> Soyer's new model soup kitchen was constructed in front of the Royal Barracks in Dublin. . . . It was a wooden building about 40 feet long and 30 feet wide, with a door at each end; in the centre was a 300-gallon soup boiler, and a hundred bowls to which spoons were attached by chains, were let into long tables. The people assembled outside the building and were first admitted to a narrow passage, a hundred at a time; a bell rang, they were let in, drank their soup, received a portion of bread, and left by the other door. The bowls were rinsed, the bell rang again, and another hundred were admitted.

Once in operation, Soyer's kitchen dispensed some 8,750 rations daily, well over the 5,000 that had been anticipated. And despite powerful objections that "it was a mistake to feed the destitute like wild animals," the soup kitchen approach was implemented in many parts of Ireland. In some areas of the country, Protestant groups established schools and kitchens and offered food to families who would convert, or at least send their children for a Protestant education. Roman Catholic families that did so were accused of "taking the soup" by their neighbors, and were called "soupers," a term that sig-nified humiliation and betrayal, a selling out of one's birthright for a mess of pottage.

It is probably not a lively knowledge of Irish history, but rather a more recent set of associations that make some of today's soup kitchen guests uncomfortable with the option. Until very recently, Irene Glasser has written, soup kitchens had "the popular image of storefront dining rooms with steaming vats, serving an elderly, alco-holic population. . . ." These kitchens were largely the province of fundamentalist churches and urban missions, and like the Irish soup-ers, their guests were often required to participate in religious rituals as a prelude (and prerequisite) to the meal.

Many contemporary soup kitchens work hard to distinguish themselves from this tradition, but the soup kitchen label is hard to avoid. It is used by public programs that provide resources at the fed-eral, state, and local levels; most food banks use it to classify pro-grams and the public knows what it means. "Some of our volunteers here thought the term 'soup kitchen' had a stigma, and they thought we should change the name," Jerome Hoeschen told me, referring to the extraordinarily welcoming program in the Knights of Columbus Hall in Bath, Maine. "I told them, 'Look, before we opened, we prayed about this. What are we going to call it? Why not call it the Soup Kitchen because everybody knows what a soup kitchen is.' So that's what we did." After the volunteers raised the question, Hoeschen raised it himself with the board of the Bath Area Food Bank, which is the kitchen's parent organization, "and I got a startled look of astonishment from everybody. They said, 'What do you mean change the name! What's wrong with Soup Kitchen?' So they voted that this is the end of the discussion."

Dignified Soup Kitchens?

Despite history, stigma, and the inherent difficulties of doing so, many prepared meal programs try to create environments that en-hance dignity and self-respect. For some, as in the pantries, the crux of the matter is the client's ability to exercise choice. "I think we want to try to keep a lot of the 'choose what you want' philosophy that we have here," declared the manager of a breakfast program in Portland, Maine. The program was getting ready to move to much needed larger space, and she was concerned that the new cafeteria might cramp the program's style. "In the winter we offer oatmeal and we always have fruit and pastries—we try to allow people to choose for themselves what they want to eat and allow them to butter their own toast. We hope to still be able to do that." Pressed on the merits of the approach she had been using, in which clients simply milled around a large U-shaped table and helped themselves, she was clear that the issue was control:

> Control over how much you get and what you get. They have control and empowerment to choose—if they want to put two tablespoons of sugar or one tablespoon of sugar, that's their choice. I think that when it's served to them, the gravy gets where someone else puts it. It's nice to be able to do it yourself as you would at home, if you had a home.

Even where the facility does not permit this sort of choice, kitchens often take pride in serving an attractive meal that demonstrates respect for guests. "We serve no pork products," Kathy Goldman told me of the Community Kitchen of West Harlem:

> There are a lot of Muslims and this way it would welcome everybody. The meals are wonderful. . . . We serve fresh fruit at least three days a week. The other two days it is canned. We serve a protein item. Chicken. We do some neighborhood specialties like ox tails, which people love. People love liver and onions. I hate it but they love it. We try to do things that people really like.

Some soup kitchen operators find the essence of dignity in offering table service in which volunteers act as waiters and waitresses. "I think from the beginning, they prided themselves on serving a sit-down meal for the people, with real dishes, real silverware, and served respectfully," recalled Sister Judy Donher, describing the establishment of the soup kitchen at Guadalupe Center in Immokalee, Florida. The real dishes have been replaced by heavy-duty, dishwasher-safe, molded-plastic divided tray-plates, but the meal is still served respectfully. The program distributes tickets for each of its four seatings in order to avoid the formation of a long waiting line. "We don't have a line," Sister Judy told me, "and we're real proud of that." One of the long-term volunteers explained: ". . . the original theory was that people like this, who come here, have to stand in line for everything that they need. And so it's nice to be able to come in and have them sit down and feel that people are concerned about them."

Recently, the establishment of cafés for homeless people, restaurants in which people can choose from a menu and place orders, have carried the notion of table service and nice surroundings even further. No cash changes hands, but guests must have reservations and, in most, a reservation card supplied by a service agency. "The atmosphere is sedate and quite attractive, much like any small inexpensive but tasteful restaurant, with original art pieces on the walls," reads a description of the St. Joseph's Bread and Roses Cafe in Venice, California, which serves breakfasts and lunches to 120–140 homeless people each day. "A key tenet of the café is to treat the clients with respect and hospitality, thus providing them with a sense of dignity and self-worth." One guest at the Inspiration Cafe in Chicago, which features fresh flowers on the tables and volunteer waiters that include actors, firefighters, writers, and real estate agents, summarized his feelings about the restaurant this way:

> Everywhere you go, everyone you talk to, once they find out that you're homeless, all of a sudden you're not a human being, you're a thing to be discarded. What happens at the Inspiration Cafe is totally different. At least for a few minutes a day, here you're treated like a human being.

Although the café approach is currently on the rise, it is not without its critics. "It's kind of a white middle-class thing, you know. Let's put white tablecloths down because white tablecloths equal dignity," declared the director of a food reprocessing kitchen that trains dozens of homeless people each year for jobs in the food service industry and supplies meals for soup kitchens throughout a major metropolitan area. "And, no," he continued, "jobs equal dignity. Being able to buy your own food is dignity. I think what they do is very well intentioned; I just don't see the long-term logic to it." Some of the cafés,

including the St. Joseph's Bread and Roses Cafe, described above, do
provide jobs, or at least job training and apprenticeship, but they are
generally volunteer operations at heart.

The simplest and most obvious strategy for promoting dignity is
also probably the least employed: the common meal that blurs or
erases the distinctions between givers and receivers, providers and
clients. I participated in such a meal offered by Manna Ministries in
Bangor, Maine. A supper of chili dogs, corn bread, Kool-Aid, milk,
coffee, and cupcakes was prepared in the church kitchen and transported by van to a nearby park where it was shared by volunteers,
staff, families from the surrounding neighborhood and street people,
mostly homeless men. It was not a wholly idyllic evening—volunteers
were uncertain about when to offer seconds, and a brief conflict
erupted between a volunteer and a guest—but in general it was relaxed and festive, more like a church picnic than a traditional soup
kitchen. The numbers were small—perhaps forty-five people ate, including five or so volunteers and one visiting sociologist. Except for a
brief grace, there was no preaching or proselytizing. It certainly realized the goal, articulated by many emergency providers, of offering a
meal without shame or stigma. With the exception of some of the
most ragged and unkempt street people who huddled around a coffee pot set up on a picnic table under a shelter, a passerby would have
been hard pressed to distinguish the guests from the providers. Significantly, this is very much like the test of nonstigmatization applied
by federal law to school meal programs—that a casual visitor to the
cafeteria be unable to tell who is paying and who is receiving a free
meal.

This is not an approach that could be instituted by a kitchen that
serves hundreds of people in shifts, where there is steady pressure to
finish a meal and move on so that another tired, hungry patron can
have your seat. One student who studied three relatively large soup
kitchens in New York found that in a period of approximately two
hours, an average of six guests occupied each seat in one program,
thirteen in a second, and fifteen in the third; the director of the
largest of these programs characterizes the meal experience as: "Eat
it and beat it." In a given lunch period, seven or eight volunteers and
one paid director in a large soup kitchen in Brooklyn normally serve

1,100 guests, a ratio that certainly does not permit a common meal approach.

Acting Out Inequality

Logistics and efficiency, however, are not the only reasons for the rarity of a shared-meal format in soup kitchens. Call it social distance, call it inequality, call it what you will, many soup kitchens are pervaded by an us-and-them dichotomy. While it may not be intentional, it is generally quite obvious. The interactionist school of thought in sociology, and more specifically, the "dramaturgical" perspective pioneered by sociologist Erving Goffman, are useful in understanding this aspect of the social world of soup kitchens: if you look at a soup kitchen as a theatrical stage, guests and volunteers play predefined roles communicated and reinforced by costumes, props, and patterns of action and inaction. The guests are confined to a line, waiting, or seated at tables, while the volunteers are nearly always on their feet, active and moving freely about the room. The guests are waiting, as if they had all the time in the world, or eating, while the volunteers are bustling about, often so busy that they don't have time to eat at all. In cold weather the guests are generally wearing coats throughout the meal, and even in warm weather, they may have most of their wardrobe layered on their backs; many clutch bags of belongings. The staff and volunteers, on the other hand, are generally provided with a place to stow their coats and bags. It would be easy to identify them by their clothing, even if they were not wearing the ubiquitous aprons that signify their status.

In some kitchens, the differences in props, costume, and demeanor are made more visible by differences in race. I have been in soup kitchens in which all of the participants—both guests and volunteers—were white, and others in which all were people of color and a few in which both clientele and volunteers were heterogeneous, but kitchens in which most or all of the volunteers are white and most or all of the patrons are people of color are not unusual. The soup kitchen at the Guadalupe Center in Immokalee, which works as hard as any to create a dignified and welcoming atmosphere, is a case in point. When I visited, the volunteers, recruited by a church in wealthy Naples at the other end of Collier County, appeared to have a great deal in common with each other and precious little in common with the guests. All were white, most were women, most had gray or white hair and were wearing casual clothes in pastel colors, and all were wearing white Guadalupe Center aprons and white disposable surgical gloves; they posed a marked visual contrast to the diners, mostly young men with dark skin and dark hair in T-shirts and jeans. The enormous difference in life-styles and life prospects, the sense of two separate worlds, that is visible when the Naples volunteers wait tables at the Guadalupe lunch program reveals the social inequality that is the essential context of charity.

Of course the social distance is imported from outside the dining room; it is not created there, only re-created. It is already visible outside the door, and not just in Florida. When I showed up early one morning at a breakfast program in Maine and joined a line of waiting guests, they asked if I was a volunteer and politely directed me to another entrance. The nearly complete bifurcation of roles—active givers and passive receivers—may exaggerate the distance that already exists, however, and may, in a sense, rub it in. "Don't you feel great being Mr. Kind!" a guest at a Catholic Worker soup kitchen once shouted at a volunteer within the hearing of psychiatrist and social critic Robert Coles, provoking what he recalled as "a painful moment of recognition." All roles are not equally valued in this production, and if the role of Mr. Kind makes the player feel great, how does the role of Mr. Grateful Receiver—or Mr. Hostile or Ms. Depressed—make its occupant feel? And what happens to our perceptions—of ourselves and of the people playing opposite us—if we play these roles over and over on a daily or weekly basis.

Many emergency food providers shared with me their discomfort with the us-and-them character of these programs, the split between givers and receivers, and many try to acknowledge the contributions that clients make to their own well-being: "I'm convinced we got much more out of it than did the people who were eating," recalled Rabbi Ellen Lippman about the program she had organized at her seminary. In fact, such gracious acknowledgments were common, even routine among the volunteers I interviewed, but for other providers they are not enough. There is still an exclusion of clients from roles of authority, from full participation. A staff member at a foundation that funds kitchens and pantries expressed her frustration: "One of my current pet peeves is the overwhelming information that I get that shows that all the effort in helping to turn people's lives around didn't involve or include the people whose lives need to be turned around. It's all the people who have, helping the people who don't have but not bringing the people who don't have into the picture."

Reciprocity: Sharing the Work

One way to bring the people who don't have into the picture, of course, is to offer them opportunities to contribute. Reciprocity, social scientists tell us, is a fundamental organizing principle of human societies; both giving and repaying are demanded by social groups, and these obligations are maintained by sanctions including dishonor, guilt, and shame. Those supporting sanctions were what I was experiencing in that church basement in Maine, shame at being taken for someone who would accept food from strangers without an intention to repay. They are sanctions with which recipients of emergency food must cope on a daily basis. As anthropologist Mary Douglas has argued, charity "wounds" because it excuses the recipient from obligations to repay that are deeply embedded in both culture and psyche and fundamental to human social life.

With or without anthropological sophistication, a substantial number of providers have made concerted efforts to provide clients with structured opportunities to reciprocate by recruiting them as volunteers. The day-to-day work in soup kitchens and food pantries is composed primarily of simple tasks that require little education: opening cans, sorting vegetables, packing bags, stocking shelves. More frequently than in any other type of social service with which I am familiar, emergency food providers have welcomed clients into the volunteer role.

The use of clients as volunteers can have a significant impact on the overall functioning of the organization. Doreen Wohl, director of the pantry maintained by the West Side Campaign Against Hunger, described the experience that led her to convert her pantry from a prepacked bag model with minimal involvement of clients to a shopping pantry in which many clients double as volunteers:

> Bags were packed by church volunteers for people. . . . People were pampered. The guests, the participants in the program were pampered. Everything was done for them. They were not accepted as volunteers, and there was a limited contact. . . . Probably my biggest eye-opener came one day when the staff was late. And I believed that we needed to open up on time, and so I recruited from the pantry line. I asked for volunteers, and all of a sudden, people came alive and they had personalities, and they were eager to offer, and the functions were done very well. It was great! And I pinched myself: what are we doing here? We're doing *for* people rather than working *with* them. And so, after a lot of discussion and a great deal of doubt, we've changed the format of the program.

She went on to assess the new, more inclusive format and it is clear that the changes go well beyond logistics. In the first place, the pantry can now serve more people, and with the extra help, has established a separate time for senior citizens. Furthermore, the atmosphere has changed. Under the old system, with church members packing the bags, she noted, "the conversation in the pantry by the volunteers was usually about something totally unrelated to the pantry, what was going on at the church, the latest play, what was going on up at Columbia University. . . . There was really a very limited relationship with the participants in the program."

After the change to a shopping format and the inclusion of clients as volunteers, "People became people. We now know people as people, and relate to people as people. The conversation in the pantry is with people and about people, and about food, just like you might have in a normal supermarket."

Doreen Wohl was not the only one to report positive side-effects from recruiting volunteers from the pantry line. Ester Bradley-Delgado prefers volunteers selected from among her clients because she feels they know better how the clients feel and can be more easily trained to treat pantry applicants with respect and dignity. In fact, she feels that time in the line is the best training, and that volunteering at the pantry is, in turn, good training for the job market. Nevertheless, her fundamental point is that clients who volunteer increase their self esteem:

> I watch them in action and they feel very proud of themselves . . .
> When they're at the pantry, they're giving, and they're very proud of
> that . . . They make a big deal of going into the storeroom, and see-
> ing that we have enough to give out and everything is balanced out;
> it is a big deal to them, and sometimes when they go through and
> play out their little role, it gets to be a bit annoying to us, but we let
> them do it because it's a big deal.

The clients who regard their contributions as a big deal, and the staff members and volunteers who encourage them to contribute are right: it *is* a big deal, though not necessarily for the reasons they imagine. Giving, and repaying, as the anthropologists cited above have taught us, are fundamental to the maintenance of human social bonds. It is through contributing that we establish rights; the old adage popular in many poor communities says it all: "What goes round, comes round." Clients who help are establishing moral and social rights to draw upon the collective resources of the community. Unfortunately, the opposite is also true. Clients who do not help are unable to establish such rights, and most emergency food programs can use the help of only a small proportion of their clients. Most are left in the passive and dependent role that is so characteristic of charity, however kindly and gently it may be administered.

Neither the clients who volunteer nor those who do not, however, have any legally enforceable rights to the assistance offered by most kitchens and pantries. This is seldom a primary concern of hungry recipients; those to whom I talked were much more concerned with the civility with which they were treated than with the existence of rights in the abstract. They routinely told me that they preferred the welcome they received at a particular kitchen or pantry to the disrespect and abuse they perceived at the welfare department where many of them *did* have legally defined and enforceable rights. Even if it is not a top priority on the agendas of hungry people, however, the absence of rights in emergency food programs is, or should be, a matter of concern. We are creating a society in which substantial numbers of people are dependent for their very subsistence on the kindness of strangers and the whims of givers. Furthermore, we are doing so, in part at least, because we have allowed our public assistance programs to become so brutal and abusive that people prefer lining up for handouts—limited and unreliable handouts—instead. What has happened to the ideal of dignified, reliable, public provision, courteously administered? Is our concern for dignified treatment in private charitable programs an evasion of our responsibility to insist upon it in public affairs?

The volunteers and staff in kitchens and pantries who expressed so much concern for the protection of dignity were focused upon the experience of recipients, but the damage done by the indignities of charity is not confined to the clients. It affects givers as well. Very few of us can act out the role of Mr. Kind, day after day or week after week, without beginning to internalize it. And very few of us can interact with people who are playing the role of supplicants without beginning to see need as their defining characteristic. The daily interactions in a soup kitchen and food pantry emphasize the differences between the givers and the receivers instead of the things they have in common. The other side of Doreen Wohl's report that clients who volunteered in her food pantry "came alive and . . . had personalities" and "became people" is a process by which clients in more typical programs cease to be individual people with personalities and become—"them." The problem is not just the depersonalization that Ester Bradley-Delgado reported, but the perception of people as somehow inferior. Charity is simply not something we offer to people we see as our equals. The transactions in soup kitchens and food pantries undermine our cultural commitments to equality by daily defining people who use emergency food as appropriate objects of charity.

This definitional process does not stop at the soup kitchen or food pantry door. Through the remarkable web of donors and contributors described in chapter 1, it is carried outward into the culture. It is communicated by fund-raising literature and appeals from the pulpit. It is implicit in the food drives. It is reinforced by the annual Thanksgiving and Christmas newspaper and television photos of people lining up for holiday meals. It is passed along to the schoolchildren who collect canned goods. In a subtle but persistent manner, it infiltrates our culture with the idea that it is acceptable to have significant numbers of people in our society waiting for food handouts, that such handouts are an appropriate response to their needs, and that these are people for whom a handout at the discretion of the giver is good enough. No wonder that food stamp offices and welfare centers fail to recognize the rights of applicants and recipients. We become a society of givers and receivers, rather than a commonwealth of fellow citizens. Charity erodes the cultural prerequisites for a vigorous democracy.

Writing at the turn of the century, in a period in which charity was increasingly subjected to the critique of the progressive vision, Hull House founder Jane Addams said:

> Probably there is no relation in life which our democracy is changing more rapidly than the charitable relation—that relation which obtains between benefactor and beneficiary; at the same time there is no point of contact in our modern experience which reveals so clearly the lack of that equality which democracy implies. We have reached the moment when democracy has made such inroads upon this relationship, that the complacency of the old-fashioned charitable man is gone forever; while, at the same time, the very need and existence of charity, denies us the consolation and freedom which democracy will at last give.

Addams was arguing that the charitable relationship is inherently one of inequality, that democracy should eliminate such inequalities, and that the continuing need for and existence of charity were evidence that it had not yet succeeded.

Setting aside, for the moment, her optimism about the eventual triumph of democracy, Addams's comment has the ring of truth to anyone who has spent a lot of time in emergency food programs: the complacency that might once have made us comfortable with the bifurcation of roles into active givers and passive recipients is eroded, but the need is so urgent that many people feel compelled to respond, despite the imperfections of the response. The next chapter explores the ambivalence that emergency food providers feel about the system they have created.

CHAPTER NINE

The Ultimate Band-Aid

SEVERAL YEARS AGO, I received an invitation to the tenth anniversary celebration of New York City's Food for Survival Foodbank. The cleverly designed invitation depicted a truck, emblazoned with the food bank's logo and the anniversary slogan, "Ten Years On the Road to Ending Hunger." I decided to attend, and on the 28th of October, 1993, I found my way through a maze of autobody shops, salvage operations, and light industry to the food bank's warehouse adjacent to the Hunt's Point Terminal Market in the Bronx. As I entered the modern facility, I encountered a twenty-foot-long truck constructed entirely of cans of food, courtesy of the American Institute of Architects CAN-ART project, and I was given a program shaped like a truck. When I departed, two hours later, I was handed a miniature shopping bag containing the food bank's brochure-style annual report, a green-and-white CHECK-OUT HUNGER button, and a small wooden model flatbed truck bearing a thick phone note pad, printed on both sides with the motto of the celebration, now adjusted to read 10 YEARS OF PARTNERSHIP ON THE ROAD TO ENDING HUNGER.

It was entirely fitting that a truck be the icon for the food bank's birthday. By the time it turned ten, the food bank owned a fleet of nine trucks, five of them refrigerated. Fully "65% of all food distributed is delivered to our agencies" reads the side of a truck in a graphic displayed in the program. This is a service of major significance and consequence in New York City where parking, insurance, and repairs are so expensive that many food bank member agencies cannot afford to maintain vehicles of their own. By 1993, the food bank had reached a ten-year distribution total of 100,000,000 pounds. One thousand nonprofit programs were served by the warehouse, of which 735 were emergency providers: soup kitchens, food pantries, and shelters. They provided the equivalent of approximately 4 million meals each month. The official theme of the tenth anniversary was partnership, the partnership through which emergency food is delivered.

There was an alternate theme, however, to complement the partnership motif. Just inside the cover of the program, right above the Food For Survival Mission Statement, is a quote from the executive director, Lucy Cabrera: "I come to work every day, hoping my organization will be unnecessary . . . soon." A desire to be out of the emergency food business, to see the end of the need for a secondary, and second-class, food distribution system for poor people was the counter-theme of the gathering.

The partnership essential to the organization's success was reflected in the roster of speakers. The local provider agencies were represented through the chair of the food bank's board, Jewel Jones, pastor of the Manhattan Bible Church which is home to the Love Kitchen; he set the tone for the day by saying that he would prefer to be presiding over a "door closing ceremony." Jones was followed by Sister Christine Vladimiroff, president and CEO of Second Harvest, who announced that Food For Survival was the 1993 winner of the annual Excellence in Food Banking Award. Sister Christine committed the resources of the Second Harvest Network to continue to support Food For Survival "until we make those policy changes, until we make those programs available, so that food will be accessible through ordinary channels for all in our communities." A speaker from the mayor's office declared October 28 Food For Survival Day, and then the keynote speaker, Secretary of Agriculture Mike Espy, urged cooperation in an effort to eliminate hunger "so that no secretary of agriculture has to come here ten years from now and has to stand here to admit, ashamedly, that we continue to have a problem."

Where government is present, advocates are seldom far away, and both national and local anti-hunger advocates were represented at the birthday party. Rob Fersh, the director of the Food Research and Action Center, arguably the heart of the Washington-based national level anti-hunger advocacy network, spoke briefly; he congratulated the food bank for having a vision that goes beyond day-to-day feeding, and joined it in calling for public policies that "provide food as a matter of right to children and their families . . . so they don't have to go to soup kitchens and food pantries and proclaim their poverty." Local advocates were represented by Kathy Goldman, the director of the Community Food Resource Center, a local anti-hunger advocacy organization that was one of Food For Survival's parents. Goldman captured the underlying spirit of the day when she described the conflict that many who are closely associated with Food For Survival feel: pride in its achievements and efficient operation, something akin to awe at the amount of food it is able to redistribute, and shame and anger at the deprivation that necessitate the program's operation. "Sometimes you look at these boxes and cases and you think that what we have here is a representation of misery." She turned to Secretary Espy and asked him point-blank "to help put us out of business . . . we don't want to be here . . . This shouldn't be necessary."

Ambivalence

No one at the birthday party can have missed the irony, the sense of contradiction. On the one hand, the decor and the program and even the party favors stressed the achievements of Food For Survival in terms of more and better trucks, bigger, better warehouse space, more tons of food distributed and meals served. On the other hand, absolutely every speaker, indeed every welcomer, introducer, presenter, and speaker, echoed the board chair's desire to close the organization down, the executive director's hope to find herself out of a job.

This divided consciousness is not a peculiarity of Food For Survival nor an aberration of New York City. I found it almost everywhere I went. Asked for a summary statement, Ken Horne, a founder and director of the Society of Saint Andrew's hugely successful gleaning operations, captured the feelings of many of the providers I interviewed: "My frustration is that we've done so very well and we're not any closer to solving the problem than we were when we started." At one level, this pervasive ambivalence reflects a simple chagrin at the persistence of the need. There shouldn't *be* hunger in affluent America, the land of plenty. "Abolish my job! There shouldn't be a need for this," Fran Ficorelli, the director of Heart and Soul, a food pantry in Niagara Falls, New York, told me.

> We need to end the hunger, not keep finding ways to find more money so we can keep feeding people. That is not what our focus needs to be. We need to do that and continue to do it until it is solved, but we must be looking at ways to solve the problem, not continue it, because all it is doing is growing and growing and growing and we are saying we need more money. . . . The hunger issue is something we should hang our heads in shame, the entire country.

The ambivalence that many emergency food providers express, however, goes beyond the problem of hunger to the nature of the response, to the limitations on what emergency food can actually *do* for a person or family in need, and to the institutionalization of what had originally been perceived by many as a short-term response to an "emergency." Ellen Teller, a lobbyist for the Food Research and Action Center, whose work has brought her into frequent contact with emergency food providers since the mid 1980s, explained it this way:

> Whenever there's a crisis, there's an incredible outpouring of support. There are hurricanes and earthquakes and you see all this food and all this support coming in. . . , but what I think we're seeing now is a feeling that there's this sort of long, sustained level of crisis in the country and that you have some people saying "This is no longer a crisis. This is becoming a way of life." . . . It's a real fear, I think, with the emergency food providers; they didn't expect to be in this for the long run. They expected that the country was in some kind of a crisis for a short period of time and they were going to help out. They never thought they were the answer.

When providers say that emergency food is becoming a way of life, they may have their clients in mind, or they may be talking about themselves. "When we started we were serving an emergency situation," Fran Ficorelli explained. "It was true emergencies. It developed into serving chronic needs. There are still some emergencies . . . no doubt about it. And there always will be, which is why we will always need a certain amount of food pantries and soup kitchens, to address emergency needs. But we have come to use this as a solution to chronic problems and I find this handout method to be totally demeaning and destructive to the human spirit." She also worries that her programs have become "enablers" for some of her more impaired clients. "I don't have blinders on, I see that we are enabling some of the people who come to our soup kitchen, because there you deny no one. At the pantry we have the freedom to say 'I'm sorry I can't help you this time.' And we send them to the soup kitchen. 'Go get a meal.' We are not sending anyone away hungry. I am struggling with the fact that we are seeing drug users and alcoholics. We know that they are selling their food stamps and they are coming to us and getting a meal . . . but there are still a lot of people who really need it, and if it is a drug addict who is getting a meal, at least he is healthier."

She is concerned about emergency food becoming a way of life for herself and her staff, as well. "What I see happening is that now people like myself are doing things to protect our jobs. . . . And I am doing the same thing. I am doubling my grant request, because that is what I need and if this is the way the government wants to do it, I will do it, but it is not the best way to do it. So I find food providers are very well meaning people, but deep down inside, we need our jobs, too."

Other direct providers report that salaries are so low, fringe benefits so scarce, and the work so demanding that there is little danger that they will become wedded to their jobs, but as the process of institutionalization proceeds and organizations invest more and more in capital—in space, equipment, and the like—salaries will probably climb as well. Each milestone along the path toward permanence raises these issues. For Bill Bolling, director of the Atlanta Community Food Bank, the irony became distressingly clear when he once again ran out of space to rent in his current location and, like food bankers across the country, began to consider building a space of his own:

I had to rent twenty [thousand additional square feet] about a mile away because we have no more space here. So we are faced, as many food banks are around the country, with the fact that we're probably a permanent fixture in the community.... A good example is that many food banks now have bought their buildings. Many food banks have actually built their own facility that will work for them instead of just kind of taking what anybody gives you. Now that's a real change. When you do that, you're saying, "Hey, we're permanent." ... I think many of us didn't believe that until recently. Didn't want to believe it. I think my goal always was to work myself out of a job or to peak out and start getting smaller, or diversify our services.

A concern about the implications of permanent space is not limited to large-scale food banks. "We're at a fork in the road, now," the Reverend Rob McCall told me, because his church, in Blue Hill, Maine, had received a gift of land for the construction of a building to house the Tree of Life Food Pantry. This meant "finding somebody who's going to help us do the 501(c)(3) and the whole nine yards. So we've decided to leap in that direction. I have real reservations about it," he continued,

> because I'm afraid that the Holy Spirit will flee when we get too much caught up in our own operation. It's been five years or more ... we started in the basement of the parsonage and then we came to the church and then we went to a building downtown and then they tore that building down so we came back here, and it makes it kind of hard but it also keeps ... the spirits up and it keeps people's commitment up. Now we're going to have a place with carpets and flush toilets and warm in the winter and, you know, the whole nine yards. I don't know what's going to happen. We're going to turn into an institution.

Understandably, the ambivalence about institutionalization is more pronounced among those who originally got into the business as an anti-hunger activity or who thought that the problem would be short-lived than among those for whom prevention of waste and environmental concerns are prominent. "It [food banking] is so efficient, so sensible," Joanne Grisanti of the Food Bank of Central New York told me, "of course it should be here. And even if we eradicated hunger in our community, there would still be a place for food banks. There is always going to be waste. There are always going to be not-for-profits that need to cut costs to feed people, and this is a way to be an educational tool, a resource for the community, a way to recycle."

Nevertheless, Grisanti shares the underlying critique of emergency food as a response to acute symptoms rather than prevention or cure: "People need to change . . . their focus of how they run their programs. Don't just hand out food to people. Don't just keep putting Band-Aids on. . . . Are we just going to perpetuate the problem? Are we just going to be handing out food or are we going to be doing something to really change something? Are we going to add to people's security? I would like to see food banks do that."

"Band-Aid" is the phrase often used to signify the limitations of emergency food. "It's never enough," Ester Bradley-Delgado told me in her small pantry in Santa Cruz. "These food pantries are just Band-Aids. They're not the solution." But like Ester, many emergency food providers work hard to go beyond the Band-Aid, and the organizations that fund and otherwise support emergency food providers continually urge them to expand their horizons. Irv Cramer, director of Mazon, uses a vivid illustration to explain his rationale for pushing providers to do more:

> If you and I had $100 million sitting on this table and we decided this afternoon that we were going to use it to feed everybody who is hungry in America—not the world, by any means, but America—there's a clear calculation that says that we could give them ten meals—we could give them breakfast, lunch, and dinner for three days and breakfast on the fourth day, and by sundown of the fourth day every last one of them would be hungry again. What they would have had is a relatively brief respite from the agony and the pain of the hunger, but not a single one of them would have been lifted out of poverty because they wouldn't have had, perhaps, shelter that they need, and job training and job referral and day care and clothing . . . a great many people who are hungry today are capable of being lifted out of their circumstances of poverty, given the particu-

lar kinds of help that they need. . . . So we tend not to fund agencies that are just providing food and putting it across a counter or table, as we know how endless that is.

Beyond Band-Aids

Some frontline providers, of course, do a great deal more than just distribute food. I can share only a few examples, chosen because they illustrate both the possibilities and the problems associated with efforts to go beyond the Band-Aid. World Hunger Year (WHY) maintains a data base with more than 20,000 entries of groups working to eliminate hunger and poverty in this country; it contains thousands of examples of projects that work, many of them collected as part of WHY's Reinvesting in America program, and a substantial number of them are described in Robin Garr's recent book, *Reinvesting in America*. If you look, you will probably find some in your own community.

Comprehensive Services

Where the primary goal is providing additional services beyond emergency food, the examples are legion. Some are food pantries or kitchens that have grown into more comprehensive programs, others are broader programs that have added food, something that became more feasible, of course, once the infrastructure of food banking and food rescue was established. One organization that has done a particularly good job of integrating food with its other services is the Preble Street Resource Center in Portland, Maine. Preble Street serves homeless and other poor people, offering medical care, housing assistance, and a day shelter. It provides a relaxed, sociable, and ample breakfast every morning. As breakfast program manager Amy Donahoe explained to me, "The philosophy is that the breakfast is a hook." Once people come for breakfast, they can be introduced to the other services available, not only the other Preble Street services, but any service that wants to send an outreach worker. The relaxed atmosphere, Amy suggests, helps people connect with those who can help them:

People feel comfortable here. Our philosophy behind having outreach services here is that people are comfortable here, this is sort
of their place . . . their turf. They don't have to go to the big scary
office and say "I might need services." They meet the outreach
worker here and he says "Maybe you could use a caseworker." . . .
Once they're comfortable with him because they've had coffee with
him at breakfast and chatted with him, it goes from there.

She listed eight programs that regularly send outreach workers to
breakfast, but stressed that people are welcome to come just for
breakfast as well.

Some soup kitchens and food pantries have found that the most
useful way to broaden services is to help clients gain access to public
sector benefits for which they are eligible. The Community Kitchen
of West Harlem, which recently served its millionth meal, is a project
of the Community Food Resource Center, the advocacy organization
whose director asked Secretary of Agriculture Espy to help put the
food bank "out of business." After the kitchen settled into its current space and its daily numbers began rising, the downtown CFRC
staff found themselves bombarded with phone calls from the kitchen
about diners who could not get food stamps or general assistance or
SSI or needed help with housing. Finally, CFRC opened an "entitlements clinic" on the premises, in which a particularly skilled community worker helped people obtain the public benefits to which
they were entitled. It proved so successful that CFRC joined with
the New York City Coalition Against Hunger, a coalition of emergency food providers, to replicate the model on a citywide basis. A
peripatetic outreach team called Food Force travels from pantry to
pantry and kitchen to kitchen, with a portable printer and a laptop
computer equipped with software that permits very accurate preliminary determinations of eligibility for food stamps. The Food Force
field-workers can determine not only probable eligibility but also an
estimate of the dollar value of food stamps to which clients are entitled, and they can print out copies of the whole calculation and give
them to clients to take with them to the income maintenance center.
Because the project is publicly funded and has the cooperation of the
city's Human Resources Administration, Food Force has been able to

track its own results. Some 88 percent of the program participants it screened in its first operating year appeared eligible for food stamps; of these, about half subsequently appeared at income maintenance centers and completed applications, and a remarkable four-fifths of these were approved for the stamps.

While programs like Preble Street and Food Force that have the support of substantial networks of allied services and skills may have reduced the tension between immediate food needs and underlying issues, agencies with fewer resources struggle with this tension as well. "I could not be a director here and just do emergency services," Sister Judy Donher told me of the Guadalupe Center, which feeds several hundred people each day in its soup kitchen and provides clothing as needed to the migrant agricultural laborers and other desperately poor people of Immokalee, Florida, the home base of the East Coast migrant stream. The Guadalupe Center is particularly proud of its after-school program. "Our mission is twofold—it's to provide emergency services and promote quality of life. The board does not want to see the children of this generation being the soup kitchen line of the next. So we're working at both." It is a constant struggle to raise sufficient resources, and Sister Judy spends a sizable portion of her time trying to raise funds, and educate potential donors in the wealthy Gulf Coast communities at the other end of Collier County while she is at it. "My job is as much education as it is caring for the poor, because I need to educate those people in Marco Island and Naples that Immokalee exists and that Immokalee shouldn't exist. This kind of poverty shouldn't exist in the United States, and we need some help. People are pretty generous with us, but I think the donors have to see that we want to make a dent in the poverty situation. I think if I was just running a soup kitchen I would be having a real hard time raising money because people are getting tired of that."

Jobs

Providing jobs is another strategy by which emergency food providers try to move beyond the Band-Aid stage, at least in the lives of individuals. Sister Judy has hired both a part-time dining room manager and a cook from among Immokalee's poor migrant families, and her after-school program hires local teenagers as tutors for younger children. All over the country, food banks and food rescue programs are experimenting with job-related activities. The D.C. Central Kitchen trains several groups of homeless men and women each year for work in the restaurant and food service industry, an approach that is being replicated by Raleigh's Interfaith Food Shuttle. A similar project in Indianapolis, The Fisherman Plan, trains three groups of about a dozen each year with an outstanding record of placement and retention. The Community Kitchen of West Harlem is soon to move to a newly renovated facility that will include a training kitchen, and is hoping for training funds from the Harlem Empowerment Zone. Even in its old, tiny, inadequate space, the kitchen provided jobs with health benefits for nine people, including several teenagers who delivered "meals on heels." The Alameda County Food Bank in Oakland, California, considered a job training and placement program, but reduced its goal to job readiness after some research on what job training requires. The same characteristics that make emergency food appealing to unskilled volunteers, and allow it to serve as a sort of sheltered workshop for disabled people, mean that there is a considerable amount of entry-level work, suitable for people with limited work experience. In food banks, especially, because they are run essentially like any other warehouse, people can learn jobs that really do exist in the private sector. Providing jobs is one of the most promising approaches to moving beyond Band-Aids.

Empowerment

Next door to the Guadelupe Center, Guadelupe Social Services, an affiliate of Catholic Charities USA, operates a food pantry and provides emergency social services, including grants for utilities or rent. The director of Guadalupe Social Services, John Witchger, is a tall, pale man with a somewhat otherworldly aspect; I was not surprised to learn that he had studied for the priesthood before becoming an organizer and social worker. He defines the fundamental issue as empowerment, not so much the addition of more comprehensive services as organizing clients to work together. "Mine is what might be called a religious motivation or a spiritual motivation," Witchger told me. "I've always been attracted to jobs that are more working with people, but not so much charity as a broader vision of leadership development and actually empowering people, getting people active in solutions to their own problems.... Charity's a hell of a lot easier than trying to get people to get out on their own and that's why, I think, more people like to do it. You feel good after you've done it because you think you've helped them. But the question is, have you really helped them?... No one should be doing charity unless they're doing empowerment work, and they have to go hand in hand ... an operation that's just doing charity is probably causing more problems than they are helping and I can see that from what we're doing every day."

Witchger's efforts at empowerment have led to the development of several community organizations and projects, a soccer field and a food co-op, but such efforts are difficult to sustain among the constantly changing migrant population. Meanwhile, Witchger struggles with the task of balancing the time-consuming organizing efforts with the day-to-day responsibilities of securing resources for the food pantry.

> Well, it's a big challenge for me because I have a multiple role of doing fund-raising, ... management, and ... program development. So not only am I trying to look and envision new programs, which I love to do, I'm also trying to manage a program that we have and raise funds on top of it for the whole thing.... I get this real sense from our donors that the majority of them, and I surveyed it a couple of years ago, the majority of them would prefer just to do charity ... a lot of people mentally and financially haven't made a transition to empowerment.

Even if his donors were more willing, however, he concludes, he couldn't really cut back on the food pantry and emergency services: "Every day I'm faced with it. I do some interviewing, still, in the front, where you're talking to a woman face-to-face and understand her reality. Monday I had a client and the woman has seven children.... So, her youngest was born with some type of brain deformity and now the family is cut back to one income earner. She has to stay home with the baby. She's going back and forth to the hospital.

And the husband works in the fields. So he's getting thirty, forty, fifty dollars a day, depending on whether it's first picking, second picking, what crew leader he's with and all that. I mean it's tough enough to raise seven kids. So they're in a big bind. What do they do? I can't . . . say, 'you know, I'm going to let you starve to death until you begin to do something for yourself.' "

He worries, however, that the food pantry props up the farm labor system at the root of such problems:

> In the worst analysis, it is an awful thing—what we're doing is allowing an oppressive system to continue. We're enabling minimum wage jobs to continue at minimum wage . . . we're providing a safety net, and I know that because you can see from the numbers—when there's full employment here, we may see four or five clients, ten clients a day, a lot of them injuries, there's no medical insurance. When there's no work, our numbers are forty, forty-five a day.

When Witchger talks about empowerment, he is talking primarily about local organizing and cooperation, developing indigenous leadership and letting the community set its own agenda. Many of his clients, however, would benefit from a raise in the minimum wage, or greater protections for farmworkers, or from some easing up of immigration policies. Other emergency food clients in other parts of the country need other policy changes. Much of the discussion, in and around the emergency food community about addressing the underlying causes of poverty has to do with engaging issues of public policy: advocacy.

The Advocacy Challenge

Advocacy has been a bone of contention in the broader emergency food community almost since the proliferation of kitchens and pantries began in the early 1980s. A great deal of this discussion has focused on food banking, and specifically at the top, or the center, on Second Harvest, and the reasons are built right into the nature of food banking. On the one hand, food banking has, potentially, a great deal to contribute to anti-hunger advocacy, both the legitimacy that comes from the involvement of large, successful corporations, and the credibility that comes from day-to-day work of the member agencies with poor people. On the other hand, certain inherent features of food banking tend to limit its advocacy role. One of these is its need to maintain the cooperation of the food industry.

When the Second Harvest Network began devoting itself more and more to acquiring large-scale donations, in the mid 1980s, it also began to adopt a corporate style, which filtered down to many member banks. It was an orientation that some elements of the anti-hunger community found discomfiting. Some of the concern had simply to do with style—it seemed somehow inappropriate for organizations that were dedicated to feeding the hungry to sport fancy offices, glittering fund-raisers, and expensive annual conferences in resort settings, and some who had been involved at the beginning of food banking missed the grassroots spirit. Second Harvest defended the corporate demeanor as a necessity. "The fact that Second Harvest today is less grassroots and more corporate stems in part, according to some of its board members, from a genuine belief that a more businesslike approach to food banking is the best way to ensure a continuous and increasing flow of food. The food industry is always concerned about the proper handling of products and brand name protection," wrote journalist Lynda Crawford in a 1989 article entitled "Food Banking: Who Benefits?" that sparked considerable discussion in anti-hunger circles.

It wasn't only the style issue that bothered long-time advocates. It was also the limit on the organization's willingness to take positions that might offend potential donors. "After a decade of distributing increasing amounts of food while watching the numbers of hungry people rise," Crawford wrote, "many activists want food banking to do more. The development of an efficient warehousing and distribution system in food banking has been good for meeting the emergency needs, they say, but has come at the expense of political advocacy that calls for economic reforms and public education to end poverty." Basically, critics argued that in order to make themselves attractive to potential donors, food banks were refraining from taking positions that might be uncomfortable for corporate decision makers, and that they were "unwittingly sending a message that they are the solution to hunger." The tension between securing maximum food resources on the one hand, and advocacy aimed at the causes of hunger on the other persists, with food bankers taking positions all along a spectrum.

In the early 1990s, a change in leadership at Second Harvest signaled the beginning of a new hospitality to advocacy. Under the leadership of Sister Christine Vladimiroff, by the mid-nineties Second Harvest itself had become much more outspoken about the causes of hunger and poverty and, as we shall see, about the appropriate roles of business, charities, and government in addressing these causes. It had begun to urge its member banks to become more active in local, state, and national advocacy efforts.

Such urging, however, does not always fall on receptive ears. Many food bankers believe that they must concentrate on doing their job—which they define as securing and distributing food—to the best of their ability, and leave advocacy to the advocates. "We are the ultimate Band-Aid," Contra Costa food banker Larry Sly told me when I interviewed him at a Second Harvest board meeting in Chicago. "I mean, I never go out there and tell anybody that we're the answer to the hunger in this community. It's not true. We are the ultimate Band-Aid. But unless somebody (who is not us) comes in and takes action to deal with the issue of hunger, it's going to always be there, and our job is to really be that effective Band-Aid if we can."

Bread for the World is one of the voices that has most strongly urged food banks to devote increased time and effort to public policy advocacy and to encourage their member agencies to do the same, arguing that "agencies work daily with clients who are impoverished and can speak with particular authenticity about the depth and complexity of their situation." Bread's 1994 Fourth Annual Report on the State of World Hunger summarized the organization's plea:

> Food banks and other direct service agencies can draw upon a wealth of resources to turn toward advocacy. They have powerful community leaders on their boards, mailing lists of concerned people, and relatively large budgets. Even 5 percent of those budgets devoted to education and 5 percent to advocacy would make a ma-

jor difference. Charitable organizations have, by and large, earned the respect of the public. That respect forms a reservoir of good will that can be gently tapped to draw more people from service to citizenship.

When it surveyed seventy-one food banks, however, the Bread for the World Institute (BFWI) found that two-thirds of the banks had no budget at all for lobbying and only four of the seventy-one banks had allocated 2 percent or more of their overall budget to lobbying activities. A little over half of the banks surveyed had at least one staff member who does some lobbying work, and "an even greater number of food bank directors indicated that they would like to include advocacy as a program activity."

Board Objections

If they would like to, why don't they? The BFWI report is low-keyed but revealing; the problem it seems is with those very same "powerful community leaders" that constituted such a potential resource for advocacy: "Many do not have boards that currently support this type of activity." Since many people are invited to join food bank boards in order to connect the bank with potential donors or to provide expertise about trucking, warehousing, or food processing, food bank boards tend to include more individuals from business backgrounds than do many other nonprofit boards. I asked one midwestern food bank staffer if her board was an obstacle to advocacy, and she explained: "Some of our board people are very conservative business folk, very prominent Republicans in our state. They would find it uncomfortable if we were identified a little too closely with Democrats and Democratic thought." The same broad appeal that has contributed so much to the success of anti-hunger fund-raising means that food bank boards often include political conservatives. Hunger is "not a left/right issue anymore," Andy Cohen told me, and went on to describe the board that he chairs for the Food Bank of the Virginia Peninsula: "Among our board members, we have members whom nobody would classify as being liberals. We've got four retired army colonels, none of whom are right-wing reactionaries but none of whom are wide-eyed radicals."

Time Constraints

Even where a board is supportive, however, effective advocacy is time-consuming and many food bankers report that their calendars are already crowded. The food bankers I met were almost all extraordinarily energetic people; only type-A personalities need apply. But the job is potentially endless, and there is a fierce competition for the time of a food bank director. One described herself several times in our interview as stretched tight like a rubber band. It was difficult to imagine adding one more thing. Any advocacy undertaken by a director will come at the expense of something else, and few banks have sufficient resources to hire staff to concentrate specifically on advocacy. A food bank director at the Second Harvest National Conference in 1995 pictured for the group the choices she faced in very specific terms: should she spend the afternoon writing a letter to members of Congress about WIC expansion, or should she receive delivery of three tractor trailer loads of breakfast cereals.

The time crunch is particularly acute for banks that are expanding rapidly, moving to new space, or undergoing a capital campaign. Mary Glick, the director of the Food Bank of Delaware, indicated that both she and her board wanted to contribute more to advocacy. "Being more proactive has always been a hope of mine and the board's. Our barrier primarily was capacity building to do a primary mission, which was to get the food out, and that meant getting a building that was adequate, getting a staff," both of which had proven time-consuming and demanding. Now that she has adequate space for her administrative operations, she has hired someone whose job description will include both advocacy and organizing. Hawley Botchford made a similar point about the Harry Chapin Food Bank of Southwest Florida: "Our first purpose is to provide food security to southwest Florida," he asserted, "but our ultimate goal is to end the causes of hunger. And if we work just as hard to end the causes as we do to assure an adequate diet for people, then I think we're doing our job." But having stated the ideal, he grew more realistic: it would take time to achieve that balance. His first challenge had been the new building. "My next challenge is financial stability. When I get that, that I don't have to worry each month whether we're going to make payroll, I will put my energies toward the causes of hunger and working toward those things."

Courting Donors

Making payroll, however, means raising money and that is another reason why food bankers often tread softly on potentially divisive public policy issues. Too open an advocacy stance might alienate potential donors. As one food banker explained:

> We are very successful at raising money. More than two-thirds of our money comes from individual donors. Financial donors giving to the food bank is a no-brainer in my opinion. If you live in a large metropolitan area, you get off the expressway at some point and there is somebody panhandling there. You don't trust these people because you see *60 Minutes*. . . . And to make yourself feel better, it is so much easier for you to rip out your checkbook and send a check to the food bank because we are doing a lot of direct mail to you anyway. So we make it real easy for you. You get an envelope in the mail periodically. Write your check and send it back. . . .
>
> You don't have to have the same ideology as somebody at the food bank. You don't have to have the same political party as somebody at the food bank. You don't have to have the same work ethic or social service ethic or religious belief or any of that stuff as people at the food bank. All you have to do is want to make yourself feel just a little bit better for ignoring the people that you are ignoring all the time.

She paused and rephrased it to put a more positive spin on it: "Or, the food bank gives you the opportunity to make a worthwhile and significant contribution in a broad-based community effort to address a very serious social problem. So either way, we win. And we win without having to be in anybody's face. And we win without having to take sides. And we win without having to have a stated position on this, that, or the other thing."

Would an overt advocacy stance drive donors away, I inquired. "Yes, we would lose some of the donors because we have people in all parts of the political spectrum right now. And if we were a little too left, then the right would give us up and if we were a little too right, then the left would give us up." Of course, this is a situation faced by any nonprofit that considers advocacy. What makes the situation different for food banks is twofold. First, the issues around which they might undertake advocacy—legislation related to poverty and hunger, for example—are issues that traditionally divide Americans into liberal and conservative political camps. The American Cancer Society, in contrast, might advocate for more federal dollars for cancer research or a speedier approval of new drugs without alienating any substantial portion of its constituency. But, second, the food bank movement has attracted support from an especially wide political spectrum, certainly a far wider spectrum than the group that has traditionally supported efforts to increase government spending on programs for the poor or close tax loopholes that benefit the rich.

Even Mazon, which encourages advocacy among its grantees, has to pay attention to how it presents itself to its donors. Rabbi Ellen Lippman, who serves as the organization's New York City staff person, explained some of the challenges she confronts: "We still have a lot of people in our community who . . . think that if we just have enough soup kitchens and enough meals, that that sort of solves the problem. We do fund-raising, and . . . I have to be very careful about talking about the advocacy projects that we fund." If she can translate an advocacy project into human terms—"that it enabled thousands of kids to get lunch in the summer when they hadn't otherwise, if we can phrase it in a way that . . . there's sort of somebody eating at the other end of the work, then people seem to feel comfortable with that."

The Human Touch

Down at the front lines, where the meals and grocery bags are actually distributed, similar constraints apply, plus one additional one. The overwhelming majority of people serving meals or packing bags are volunteers, and volunteers are often less enthusiastic about advocacy than about direct service. Preparing a meal with a group of other people and serving it is fun; writing to your representative is work. Bread for the World has had some success in enlisting congregations to participate in "Offerings of Letters" in which time is spent during a church service writing letters in support of public policies like the

WIC program, but in general, it has been far easier to recruit volunteers for the food pantries and soup kitchens than for advocacy in the public arena. Rabbi Lippman told me that when people call her for information about how to start a soup kitchen, she often tries to steer them into advocacy instead, urging them to call their statewide coalition against hunger or similar organizations to see what needs to be done in the public policy arena. When I asked her how they reacted, she was frank: "They're not so excited. . . . You don't have the human relationship."

The Reverend Rob McCall feels that it's the manageability and immediacy of emergency feeding work that makes it more popular than advocacy: "I'd like to know ways that we could, without expending too much more energy, have more impact on the big picture. Although I think I'm living in a community where, for whatever reason, people are almost retreating from the big picture, and there's something that energizes them and makes them feel good when it's something that's manageable, when it's something that isn't all caught up in all of these whys and wherefores and how are we supposed to do this and how are we going to end hunger, and all this kind of stuff. I think there's an energy there that's released when there's a focus for this compassion."

Furthermore, frontline providers are apt to be even more concerned about making sure that there will be enough food. It is they, after all, who will actually have to turn people away empty-handed if there is not. I met Herneatha Barbour, the woman whose faith-based commitment to the Wednesday soup kitchen she manages at the Childs Memorial Baptist Church in Philadelphia is described in chapter 6, at a meeting sponsored by Bread for the World, the opening of its national campaign to "Transform Anti-Hunger Leadership" by forging alliances among frontline providers and anti-hunger advocates to work for more fundamental change. I asked her what she thought of that larger agenda, and she replied:

> Well, I'm kinda sorry you asked that one. I'm sure it's meant to be very good and I'm sure a lot of it is very good, [but] I think this is more of a long-range planning thing, whereas now, in our city, especially with all the taking people off of welfare and everything, you

need something for right now. I'm not sure how much of the right-now need we're meeting.

Nevertheless, Bread for the World and Mazon and FRAC and other advocacy-oriented groups continue to work hard to enlist the efforts of frontline providers, because they can speak with a special conviction and authority. Jeff Ambers is the executive director of the Yorkville Common Pantry; he explained why he felt emergency food providers could make a difference:

> I often see that food advocates, unlike welfare rights advocates, are well thought of by the society at large. They are ususally attached to churches and religious organizations and they feed the hungry. It's a very supportable activity that makes everyone associated feel good. I think that they can play an important role in educating the broader community on the needs of poor people beyond just giving them a meal. On the housing, welfare, employment needs of people . . . They have the legitimacy that other advocates for the poor don't have, but should have. . . . Advocates for the hungry are not viewed as change agents that should be feared. We are not engaged in class struggle, we are just feeding people, and that is something that should be supported, so that we have to help people bridge the gap.

Opportunity Costs

Some emergency food providers, of course, were already advocates before they were drawn into the emergency food project. They are advocates first, and emergency food providers second. For them, the issues surrounding the balance between direct service and advocacy are different. On the one hand, emergency food is a labor-intensive, unpredictable, crisis-ridden activity, often involving loading docks, pallet jacks, cold storage, and assorted rodents, to say nothing of difficult clients. Getting involved with emergency food incurs what planners call "opportunity costs"; it unavoidably means taking time away from the analysis of legislation or the preparation of testimony. For example, the Community Food Resource Center in New York City had already been in operation for five years, combining a primary focus on advocacy with a few excursions into economic development, when it was invited into a Harlem church to establish a community kitchen. The original idea was not a soup kitchen but a place where the community could gather and where people from all walks of life could enjoy a nutritious meal at little or no cost. Very quickly, however, the project was overtaken by the deterioration of the economy and all of the forces that led to increasing homelessness and deeper misery at the bottom. By 1987, when the pastor left the church and the meals program was promptly evicted by the vestry, it had become a full-fledged soup kitchen. A fight with the vestry, the search for new space, and the daily operations of the program became an increasing drain on the time of CFRC's executive director, Kathy Goldman.

A few months ago, as CFRC prepared to serve its millionth meal, I asked Goldman if she was glad that the organization had taken on the kitchen project. "I can't be sad that we served a million meals to people who needed food. You can't be sad about that," she said at first and quickly identified other concrete achievements: the entitlements clinic and the number of poor neighborhood residents who had gotten jobs at or through the kitchen. Then she grew more reflective. "I think there have been terrible costs to the organization," she said, thinking about the time she had spent fund-raising for the kitchen and writing reports to funders, including the State of New York, and "all of the baggage that goes with having a huge contract like that. All the politicking around when we are threatened. Writing letters to the forty-two people, all of that. I'm not saying it is not worth it, I am just saying that it was a big cost because it ate a certain amount of my time, I would say a day a week."

On the other hand, the community kitchen and several other direct service operations that were added later, have enriched and informed CFRC's advocacy. "As an organization, it gives us a lot of insight. We learn a lot from people there. We learn who's coming and why and when and what is going on . . . It is the kind of thing that leads you into the kind of advocacy that is going on here . . . the listening to the people that you hear from in direct service and determining your advocacy from that, rather than sitting in an office and saying 'Gee, I think it's a great idea to do this.' . . . It has become a really wonderful combination and I think it is great." She went on to

add that the direct service operations clearly added to the effectiveness of the advocacy. For example, CFRC has often been able to
make constructive suggestions for changes derived from the intimate
knowledge of the street-level situation obtained at the kitchen and
the entitlements clinic. The suggestions don't obviate the necessity
for "going and yelling," as she put it, at bureaucrats and legislators,
but "we prefer to yell and suggest." The fact that the organization is
"out there" on a daily basis, feeding people, has also added greatly to
its credibility, a treasured resource for advocates, and has undoubtedly helped with fund-raising as well. The point is not that all groups
should combine advocacy and direct service in one organization, but
rather that the two can be mutually reinforcing.

   In her role as a grant maker, Susan Cramer has tried to influence
the behavior of local groups to ensure just such synergy: "Mazon
doesn't fund food pantries or any emergency feeding projects unless
they have a strong, well-defined anti-hunger advocacy component
and/or referral component. They have to demonstrate to us that they
are doing more than just feeding people, that they are working with
other organizations that are addressing the causes of the clients' hunger or they themselves are trying to find out why these people are in
line. . . . When I get an application from a group that says 'We feed
people, no questions asked,' I call them up and I say 'We want you to
ask questions.' We try to link them with FRAC." She had seen the results of her efforts at the most recent FRAC policy conference: "A lot
of the groups that were there are Mazon grantees who didn't know
about FRAC until they got funding from us."

Beyond Advocacy

The work of engaging local groups in advocacy that FRAC and Bread
for the World try to accomplish with organizing and education and
Mazon tries to promote through its funding strategy is also pur-
sued, closer to the ground, by local coalitions like the San Francisco
Anti-Hunger Coalition, discussed in chapter 1, or the New York City
group mentioned above. Many thoughtful people and groups, however, believe that even an active participation in reforming public
policy will not be enough. Penny Braun, a staff member at the Asso-

ciation of Arizona Foodbanks, told me about her experience at a FRAC conference several years before our interview.

It was clear to me and some other people that although food stamps and other federal food programs were important, that when you are looking at long-term food security for this nation, that was not going to be it. At one end of the continuum you have the kind of emergency stop-gap measures that food banks and soup kitchens were about. In the mid-range we have a lot of the federal programs. But there is a real lack in the long-term view of things, of a lot of resource and creative energy being focused in that long-term way.

Susan Cramer expressed a similar idea:

We move beyond emergencies, but even the things we are funding, like efforts to expand access to federal food programs, don't begin to touch on the whole macroproblem, . . . the whole issue of access to food on the broadest possible scale. I think those are issues that, if we are to end hunger in this country and in the world, we need to take a more serious look at: sustainable agriculture, access to food in the inner cities.

Bill Bolling put this in a slightly different perspective:

We need to think, how can we get the food closer to the people, how can we help people get control of their lives, empowerment, it's kind of an overused word, but how can people get control of their own food and not just wait for the trucks to deliver? . . . so you think, community gardens, farmers' markets, co-ops, buying clubs, where people have a say, and investment in their own sourcing.

This broader perspective has, in fact, been receiving attention from a loose coalition called the community food security movement. It has grown out of the interactions of hunger activists—the ones described in chapter 2 who became disenchanted with the language of hunger and moved to "food insecurity" instead—and farming preservation activists and people concerned about the food systems of cities and of "bioregions." This is another group that has tried to move beyond the Band-Aid of emergency food to integrate poor people into systems in which they can help to produce their own food, and to approach food security from a community, rather than a household, standpoint. The community food security movement has continued to grow, and there have been some spectacular local projects developed, but in the last four years, its potential impact on hunger has been overshadowed by a shift in policy which has placed the protection of federal nutrition programs on center stage.

The Assault on Entitlements

At the time of the Food for Survival tenth anniversary celebration in 1993, advocates and frontline providers were still optimistic about building on the gains that had been won in the Mickey Leland Childhood Hunger Relief Act, which had been passed by Congress the previous August. The Mickey Leland Act reflected substantial cooperation between full-time advocates and emergency providers; many of its key provisions were influenced by the experience of frontline providers with the factors that prevented families in great need from using the food stamp program. In November 1994, however, just a year and a week after the birthday party, everything changed. The 1994 congressional elections gave Newt Gingrich and a very conservative wing of the Republican party control of the House of Representatives, and changed the entire national discourse on poverty, welfare, and food assistance. The publication of the Contract with America, which included not only the dismantling of the welfare system but also the block granting of federal nutrition programs, sent a chill through the anti-hunger community. Suddenly, the need for advocacy escalated.

The leaders of major emergency food–providing organizations mobilized quickly; in late December, they mounted a press conference in the Murrow Room of the National Press Club to denounce proposals to cut back on federal nutrition programs including food stamps, WIC, and school meals. The press conference bears a closer look, not only because of the wide political spectrum represented by the organizations that participated, but also because it articulates a set of beliefs about the proper relationship among the public, private, and voluntary sectors in addressing issues of hunger and poverty, that probably represent the public consensus of the major direct provider organizations.

The president and CEO of Second Harvest, Sister Christine Vladimiroff, addressed the issue of public-private cooperation:

> Part of the solution to hunger calls for partnerships between the business and charitable sectors and it counts on the generous giving and volunteering by individuals. But, crucial to the effort is the key role played by the public/government sector. . . . Yes, charities do a great job! We are efficient and effective. We are close to the people we serve. We are local, grassroots responses of neighbor feeding neighbor. It seems to us that the government can and should look to charities for leadership. . . . We can tell you what works well, what doesn't work and what might work better. We can show you how to cut out waste and how to have a flat, efficient administration with resources reaching people in need. We can provide you with models of success that can be duplicated. **What we will not do, what we cannot do, is concur with those who call for government to cut programs that provide hungry Americans with access to food.**

There were really two issues in the public/private debate that Sister Christine and the other speakers at the press conference were addressing: capacity and obligation. "Can charities do more?" asked Sister Christine. "Should we be expected to do more?" How much is it reasonable to expect of voluntary givers, and are there basic responsibilities of government that should not be passed off to the voluntary sector?

The Reverend Fred Kammer, S.J., president of Catholic Charities USA, "the nation's largest network of social service agencies," summarized the national organization's perspective on both capacity ("Clearly, private charity cannot feed all the nation's hungry families") and obligation. The division of labor, he argued, was all wrong. "Our agencies are constantly struggling to meet the basic needs of people. We *should* be providing more services that help people regain self-sufficiency. Instead, over the past dozen years we have been forced into the emergency food and shelter business . . . Instead of our resources helping people overcome the obstacles in their lives, we are faced with working families who come to us for food when their minimum-wage paychecks won't last the week. And we provide hot meals to too many hard-working people who cannot find jobs and cannot make ends meet with government benefits. We have less time to help them retrain for new jobs or overcome problems such as addiction or abuse.

"We believe that only government has the capacity—not to mention the political and moral responsibility—to promote the general welfare. That begins with the food needed to support life. . . . If federal food programs were adequately funded, we wouldn't need to operate soup kitchens and other emergency feeding programs." Calling for welfare reform that would strengthen families rather than force them into the streets, Father Kammer urged adequate funding for both food programs and income support and action to create decent jobs: "We are a national community that cares about those among us who are less fortunate. Let's start talking about ways to get children what they need: loving families, decent homes and neighborhoods, parents who have jobs, and especially, food on their own dining room tables."

There are dissenters, of course, within the ranks of emergency food providers. Some, like Amelia and Dick McKenny who helped to found the Deer Isle Pantry in Maine, acted specifically out of a desire to reduce the role of government. At one point they became involved in a dispute with other pantry board members about a grant of FEMA funds. The McKennys wanted to send it back. "We really don't need government money. . . . We don't need a FEMA grant; we don't need commodity foods . . . I really believe in less government."

The McKennys' position is unusual; all over the country, emergency food providers scramble for federal, state, and local funds when they are available, and principled refusals are rare. With the exception of committed conservatives like the McKennys, the specter of a reduction in federal food assistance brings anxiety and incredulity to the emergency food community. As David Beckmann, president of Bread for the World, told the press in the aftermath of the announcement of the Contract with America: "The math just doesn't work." Beckmann is an economist as well as a Lutheran minister and his calculations were convincing: "Newt Gingrich says churches can bear yet more of the cost of caring for people in need. But if you divide $60 billion among the 350,000 churches in this country, the math just doesn't work. Every church in the country would have to add $170,000 to its budget to meet the needs Newt Gingrich wants to walk away from. . . . We already have 150,000 private organizations in this country that are passing out food to growing numbers of hungry people. The government must also do its part."

There were other national leaders of the emergency food community at the press conference, someone from the Salvation Army, someone from the Council of Jewish Federations, the director of FRAC to help with the questions, but one local provider was also included, perhaps to add a down-home touch and diversify the roster of speakers. Marie Bledsoe of the Community Outreach program of the Mount Carmel Church of God in Christ in Kansas City, Kansas, described several success stories of her church's efforts to help poor families regain their independence. "Removing the safety net which many of the federal programs provide," she argued, "will hinder the Mount Carmel Church and many other charities from achieving our vision of promoting and fostering self-sufficiency in those who seek emergency food assistance from us. If the proposed cuts take place, we will be forced to spend our time looking for the most economical places to purchase more Band-Aids. . . ."

Welfare "Reform"

The passage and subsequent signing of the Personal Responsibility and Work Opportunity Reconciliation Act of 1996 (PRWORA), commonly known as "welfare reform"—and widely labeled "welfare deform" by anti-hunger advocates—confirmed some but not all of the fears articulated in the press conference, and added some new twists. This act was hundreds of pages long, but the main provisions of concern to emergency food providers are three.

First, the legislation tore a gaping hole in the food stamp safety net. Until the passage of the PRWORA, food stamps were the closest thing this country ever had to an income guarantee, a floor under consumption. As Peter Edelman, who resigned from the Clinton administration in protest over the new law, has written:

> Perhaps the most troubling cut is the one limiting food stamps to three months out of every three years for unemployed adults under age fifty who are not raising children. The Center on Budget and Policy Priorities describes this as "probably the single harshest provision written into a major safety net program in at least 30 years"—although it turns out that more states than the drafters anticipated can ask for an exception that was written to accommodate places with disproportionate unemployment. One of the great strengths of food stamps until now has been that it was the one major program for the poor in which help was based only on need, with no reference to family status or age. It was the safety net under the safety net. That principle of pure need-based eligibility has now been breached.

The philosophical implications of this piece of legislation remain staggering. There is no longer an implicit guarantee that no one need starve, no one will starve, in America. There is no longer a publicly funded unconditional right to food. Emergency food providers, however, are more concerned with the practical implications. All over the country, they are trying to figure out how to cope. In Michigan, where some 50,000 people will be affected, and hope for a waiver application by the governor is slim, a column in *Breadlines*, the newsletter of the Hunger Action Coalition, offered some advice to providers.

> First realize that there is no way you, as an EFP, can feed all of the people who will be dropped from food stamps. Determine how many you can feed with the resources you have. You may want to have a criteria ahead of time of who you will serve and what the qualifications are . . . find out what resources are available for people you will not be able to serve. . . . It will be easier to turn persons away if you have information to give them on where they can go to get some sort of service. . . . We recommend using the food bank to get food but do not run up food bank bills based on money you think you will get. Do not promise people food based on donations you think you will get. . . . Be aware that as you have to turn some

people away there may be some issues of anger you have to deal with. You may want to have some established safety guidelines in place. . . . Learn some crisis management skills if you are seeing more people in crisis. Remember you cannot be all things to all people.

It goes on, but I think the point is clear. Existing providers are fearful but trying to cope. As in the early eighties, new providers are gearing up as well: in several Michigan counties, groups of fifty-two churches are trying to organize "rotating soup kitchens" in which each church would provide meals for a week each year.

Unemployed people without dependents are not the only ones who are losing food stamps under the legislation. In fact, all food stamp recipients will face an erosion of the value of their benefits over time, because the act freezes the standard deduction and lowers the Thrifty Food Plan. Among those most affected, however, are non-citizen immigrants, who will lose food stamps along with a host of other federal benefits, unless they qualify for one of several individual exemptions. The 1996 act also deprived non-citizens of SSI benefits, but before this part of the law had a chance to be implemented, Congress and the president agreed on a restoration of such benefits to elderly and disabled non-citizens who were already in the country on August 22, 1996—about two-thirds of the people scheduled to lose SSI benefits under the law as originally passed. New arrivals will not be eligible for SSI benefits unless they become citizens, but the restoration of benefits to those aged and disabled immigrants who were already in the country will mitigate some of the harshest impacts predicted for communities with large concentrations of immigrant households.

Although the restoration agreement was welcome news to emergency food providers, it falls far short of undoing the damage to the safety net for non-citizens. There is a great deal of fear and confusion in immigrant neighborhoods, with even eligible immigrants reluctant to apply for programs, and agencies and caseworkers unsure who is eligible. In this context, the soup kitchens and pantries, with their relatively unbureaucratic procedures for establishing eligibility, began seeing sharply increased numbers before the law was even due to take effect, numbers that they attribute to the chilling effect of the anti-immigrant sentiment articulated in the national discourse over welfare reform, and a widespread fear among immigrants that inter- action with a public agency could result in deportation. The food stamp cuts to non-citizens remain in force, and states have taken a va- riety of steps to replace part or all of the missing food supplements, adding another layer of confusion and potential error to an already cumbersome and complex process. No one really knows how the wel- fare reform legislation will play out in the long run, but almost every credible scenario includes increased demand for emergency food.

Neither the immigrant provisions nor the food stamp cuts were part of President Clinton's plan when he let the genie of welfare re- form out of the bottle, but drastic changes in support to children and their adult caretakers were. Most emergency food providers I have spoken with cannot imagine the impact that the "fall off the cliff" provisions of TANF (Temporary Assistance to Needy Families) will have when they begin to take effect—in five years nationally, but sooner in those states that opt for shorter limits. Perhaps they hope, individually, to be out of the emergency food business before that happens. Perhaps they are too busy looking for food for immigrants and adults without dependents. Perhaps they are simply caught up in the immediacy that has always characterized emergency food.

Stretched to the Breaking Point

In any case the advocacy versus direct service dilemma has intensi- fied dramatically with the passage of the PRWORA and will continue to haunt emergency food providers even if additional provisions are modified. On the one hand, advocacy is more urgent than ever as states try to hammer out the new welfare laws that will have a profound impact upon the lives of poor people. Emergency food providers are urgently needed in the efforts to inform and educate state legislators, and will continue to be needed as state agencies be- gin drafting regulations to implement the new laws. Advocacy has be- come more demanding, however, because instead of one team of Washington lawyers and economists analyzing the impact of a pro- posed piece of legislation, there will now need to be fifty teams, one in each state. Advocacy resources are stretched thinner than ever. But emergency food providers are also stretched thinner than ever, coping with the already rising numbers, and looking for resources to gear up for more. Some of them may want a way out; I certainly would not continue to volunteer if most of my job was going to be turning people away hungry—or counting the number of people I had to turn away hungry in order to document the size of the problem, as providers are now being asked to do. And some may find themselves more convinced than before that emergency food is only a Band-Aid, and probably not a big enough Band-Aid at that.

Meanwhile, however, like the guests at the Food For Survival tenth anniversary celebration, most emergency food providers feel they must continue their work, or else. As Bernice Belton of the Food Bank of the Central Coast in Watsonville, California, put it, "The reality is that there are ever-increasing homeless and poor, including working poor, who need to be fed. . . . So the reality is that the need for food has increased and the resources for providing it haven't. And if there weren't food banks, I think a lot of people would starve."

Conclusion

IN THE COURSE of my travels, several people referred me to a parable of uncertain origin that captured for them the situation of compassionate people confronted with a steady stream of need. It depicts a village on the bank of a river. One day a resident of the community sees a baby floating down the river. She rushes out to save it, and, with the help of her neighbors, finds dry clothing, a crib, a blanket. The next day two babies are rescued, and the day after that, several more. Soon the babies are arriving in large numbers, and they become a regular feature of life in the village; very nearly the whole village becomes involved in rescuing them. Finally, one of the villagers suggests making an expedition upstream, to see how the babies are getting into the water in the first place. The villagers, however, are afraid to take time and energy away from the immediate rescue project, afraid that babies will drown if they are not there to save them.

Asked to weigh a known, compelling, and widely recognized good—rescuing the next baby—against an uncertain gain, finding out what's happening upstream, which may or may not be something they can do anything about, it does not surprise me that many people in our mythical community have decided to stick with the rescue project and leave explorations upstream to someone else. Nor does it surprise me that after a while, the townspeople begin to regard this as a way of life and stop talking about "after the babies stop coming," that groups of volunteers decide to pool their resources and hire someone to direct the work on a full-time basis, and that they begin to develop pension plans for baby rescue directors.

This story must have gotten around, because I have heard versions of it in several places. "I think this is very typical of what's happening nationwide with the feeding programs," one community organizer told me, after recounting her version of the tale. Does this story capture what is going on in emergency food? Are providers so busy rescuing people from hunger that they are unable to take the time to determine what, or who, is pushing them into the soup kitchen lines?

Eventually, of course, the metaphor breaks down in several important ways. First, while the baby story assumes a steady flow of newly endangered babies, frontline emergency food providers tell me that the most discouraging aspect of their work is seeing the same faces over and over again. The thing most likely to send them upstream seeking the source of their clientele is a frustration born of watching people's lives on hold, month after month and year after year. Talking about a soup kitchen she had helped to start at Hebrew Union Seminary in New York City while she was studying to become a rabbi, Ellen Lippman told me that at first "it seemed like a wonderful thing to do . . . but I've been back occasionally, and . . . there are some of the same people there as there were then, six years earlier." As a result she has gotten involved in "upstream" advocacy activities. "Now when people call me to ask how to start a soup kitchen, I actually tell them not to. . . . I encourage people to look into doing advocacy work." Like Rabbi Lippman, many other emergency food providers *have* looked upstream. Most have at least some idea about the underlying causes of hunger in America, and some have made very cogent and sophisticated analyses. They know quite well what is going on upstream, and they grumble to each other about it as they struggle to pull one more baby from the swiftly moving current or fit one more table into their already crowded dining halls.

Their analyses do not often reveal, however, clear instructions for doing anything about these underlying causes, at least not with the organizational tools that they have at hand. In fact, the more penetrating the analysis—the more deeply the causes of hunger appear to be embedded in the globalization of the economy, the transformation of family and community, and the nation's mounting appetite for inequality—the more daunting the task becomes, the more likely some are to retreat to a sphere in which they are confident that they can make a difference, like a soup kitchen or a food pantry.

During the movement against the war in Vietnam, we used to call this phenomenon the "paralysis of scale." When many of us first got involved in anti-war activity, we thought the war was a big mistake; our leaders had misunderstood the situation. Our job was to give them better information and better analyses, and they would come to their senses. As we began to learn more about the war, it came to seem less and less like an accident and more and more like a predictable outcome of U.S. foreign policy, ideology, militarization, values, and economic system. The more deeply rooted it appeared, the harder it was to have faith in our strategies for working against it; many of us were periodically paralyzed by the scale of the task we saw before us.

A similar paralysis of scale sometimes affects emergency food providers who genuinely want to go beyond the day-to-day feeding to address the causes of hunger. The more they analyze the pathways that lead to the food pantry door, the bigger the task appears, and the less sure they are that we can do anything to stanch the flow. There are actions that they know are needed: public and private job development and massive investment in education and training; measures that enable parents to work, such as publicly supported day care, family-friendly work environments, and affordable transportation; income protection for children deprived of parental support and dignified income for those unable to work; access to health care for all, including ample and effective treatment for the addictions and community supports for the mentally ill and impaired; a sufficient supply of affordable housing, and policies that redistribute rather than concentrate wealth and income. But these policies seem to have far less support from the bystanders, and even from some of their principal suppliers and donors, than do their emergency food projects. There is no visible and powerful movement for equality and justice with which they can join forces, so their visions seem unattainable.

At the same time, they have become better and better at feeding the hungry. The tremendous inventiveness and extraordinary cooperation that characterize the emergency food system allow them to feel very good about the teamwork they have developed, the social (and material) equipment that enables them to serve more and more meals and distribute more and more pantry bags. They're doing it better, faster, cheaper than they used to; this is one area of American life in which productivity has increased dramatically. "It is a growing industry—if this was a for-profit it would be on the Fortune 500," Fran Ficorelli told me with a mixture of pride and exasperation, describing the whole emergency food approach. Why turn from this arena of success to the frustrations of uncertain politics? If they feel paralyzed in the face of the deterioration at the bottom of our economy and the acceleration of inequality, the growing distance between the poor and the rich, then no wonder they find a sense of relief, a welcome sense of efficacy, in providing nourishing meals to hungry people.

Furthermore, they are only human. There are only twenty-four hours in their days, and they need to spend at least a few of them sleeping. As Madeline Lund told me, "We are tired; we are tired." Upturns in the economy and reductions in unemployment do not seem to reach down to most of the people they help, but each new round of government cutbacks makes their job bigger, sends a new contingent of desperate people to their doors without doing anything to provide better options for the people who were already there. The PRWORA has induced a kind of panic in soup kitchen and food pantry staff members; they were not fully meeting the need before; how will they possibly cope with the avalanche of need to be unleashed as the new legislation takes effect? And each new efficiency plan, each new program to eliminate surplus production, each drought, reduces their supplies, and each hurricane, flood, or earthquake competes for them, so that they have to work harder and harder to maintain their programs, let alone expand them. They cannot realistically afford much time for advocacy and politics if they are to keep feeding the hungry, and who will do it if they stop? Certainly not the Congress that passed the PRWORA nor the president who signed it, and not the Ed Meeses of our society, who don't believe that people are "really hungry" (read "truly needy") in the first place. They are caught in the trap of their own compassion—or the denial and indifference of the people with power.

Attachment

Some of this reluctance to look upstream, however, may come from a quite different source. Return for a minute to the tale of the "Babes in the River." Suppose that the challenge of rescuing babies fits quite neatly into preexisting needs of the community on the riverbank. Suppose, for instance, that much of the work in the town was carried out by individuals working alone, and that it was highly skilled and cerebral in nature, requiring almost no physical exertion and precious little teamwork. Suppose that substantial numbers of members of the community, on the other hand, had little or no work to do, were unemployed or retired and had few meaningful opportunities to contribute to the common good. Suppose that the old village traditions of potluck suppers and volleyball had fallen into disuse, and that the people of this town had spent much of their leisure time, in the months before the discovery of the babes, watching television alone in their rooms. Finally, suppose that the work of rescuing babies required equipment of which the town had an embarrassing oversupply, equipment that had to be stored at some cost if it was not to deteriorate, and that in fact it had been going to ruin with considerable frequency, much to the distress of those who had labored to construct it.

In this amplified scenario, it is easy to imagine that the town might have rallied around the baby rescue project, and in so doing, might have recovered lost pleasures and discovered new ones. The elderly, who, after all, knew better than anyone how to use the old equipment, might have been restored to meaningful, respected, and even central roles. People who had been leading particularly sedentary lives might have discovered the joys, and the health benefits, of vigorous physical exercise. People who had grown isolated might have found new friendships and new social connections, a welcome sense of being a part of a team doing important work. Young people would have been integrated into the project and taught the essential lifesaving skills and, with them, through the example of their parents and grandparents, teachers and scoutmasters, the relevant lessons concerning the importance of human life and the value of cooperation.

Suppose that all or most of the town's religious leaders gave a hearty blessing to the rescue work, and took turns reading scriptures that directed people of faith to save the lives of the drowning, reminding them that each baby was a new incarnation of God. Suppose that celebrities from the entertainment world visited the community and added their support, perhaps leaving behind a donation to cover the cost of a new piece of equipment, or agreeing to spread the word about the effort. Finally, suppose that the town's revered leaders and elected officials joined in encouraging the rescue project, helping out on special occasions when photographers would snap their pictures clad in waders and knee-deep in the river, or cradling a dripping tot under each arm. Suppose they held an annual awards banquet to recognize the accomplishments of those who rescued the most babies or those who cared for them with particular tenderness after their rescue.

Perhaps, then, there is more involved in their reluctance to trek upstream than a feeling of comparative efficacy or the fear that if they shift some of their effort to politics, people will suffer. As suggested in the extended parable above, perhaps the emergency food project meets other needs, serves other functions. What I have found in seven years of studying the growth and institutionalization of the emergency food system is that emergency food has become very useful indeed, and to a very large assortment of people and institutions. The United States Department of Agriculture uses it to reduce the accumulation of embarrassing agricultural surpluses. Business uses it to dispose of nonstandard or unwanted product, to protect employee morale and avoid dump fees, and, of course, to accrue tax savings. Celebrities use it for exposure. Universities and hospitals, as well as caterers and restaurants, use it to absorb leftovers. Private schools use it to teach ethics, and public schools use it to instill a sense of civic responsibility. Churches use it to express their concern for the least of their brethren, and synagogues use it to be faithful to the tradition of including the poor at the table. Courts use it to avoid incarcerating people arrested for Driving While Intoxicated and a host of other offenses. Environmentalists use it to reduce the solid waste stream. Penal institutions use it to create constructive outlets for the energies of their inmates, and youth-serving agencies of all sorts use it to provide service opportunities for young people. Both profit-making and nonprofit organizations use it to absorb unneeded kitchen and office equipment. A wide array of groups, organizations, and institutions benefits from the halo effect of "feeding the hungry," and this list does not even include the many functions for ordinary individuals—companionship, exercise, meaning, and purpose—described in chapter 6. If we didn't have hunger, we'd have to invent it.

These attachments and uses need not detract from the efficacy of the emergency food endeavor. There is nothing inherently *wrong* with meeting personal and organizational needs while doing good; it is just the sort of two-for-the-price-of-one bargain that Americans love. If emergency food is doing a good job of feeding the hungry, then all of these other benefits are net gains. They are an asset to the system, because they provide additional incentives for contribution. But what if emergency food is *not* doing a good job, in fact, *cannot* do a good job? In the terms of our parable, suppose that there are some channels in the river that even the most skilled rescuers cannot reach, and that babies who have the misfortune to enter those troubled waters are seldom rescued. Imagine that, with increasing frequency, the flow of babies exceeds the town's rescue capacity, and some slip by unaided. Or suppose that the equipment suddenly begins to break down, the nets give way, the boats develop leaks, and donations of more up-to-date equipment that had been expected from government or corporate sources fail to materialize. Our villagers improvise, but some babies are not rescued. And finally, suppose that the work of actual rescue takes so much time and energy that the village begins to fall down on its commitment to care for those who are saved from the roaring flood—they lie crowded together in the nursery, waiting for permanent homes, with little attention and virtually no enrichment. The college students who had planned to do an early childhood education project with the toddlers are drafted to help pull the new ones from the river.

Even so, we might argue, the village is doing the best it can with what it has. Our rescue project may not be perfect, but it gets maximum utility out of limited supplies. All things being equal, it appears better to keep as many babies as possible from drowning than to interrupt that work to try to stanch the flow. And in that context, our various attachments to the project are an asset, because they keep us at an increasingly daunting task. All things being equal.

Part of the Problem

But what if all things are not equal? Emergency food programs do not function in a neutral environment in which any charitable activity undertaken is automatically a net addition to the well-being of the poor. They function in an environment in which there is another side, a group working to reduce the public safety net that emergency food was originally created to supplement. In order to assess the impact of this system, and of society's multiple attachments to it, we must consider the possibility that emergency food actually contributes to the problem it tries to solve, for if emergency food programs are, inadvertently, contributing to the underlying causes of hunger, then attachments to this system take on a new significance as obstacles to change.

Reconsider the parable. What if our rescue projects are making it easier for the people who are throwing the babies in upstream? Perhaps the first few tumbled in by accident, because a retaining wall fell into disrepair or the riverbank eroded. At first, perhaps there was denial that there was anything amiss—no need to look too closely if you can count on a rescue operation downstream. And then, when the numbers became too great for plausible denial, perhaps there was a debate between those willing to allocate the funds needed to repair the breach, and those who thought the treasury too depleted to undertake such efforts. Certainly the knowledge that an extensive safety net downstream would rescue most of the casualties from immediate harm would give strength to those arguing against the proposed expenditures. And since the rescue efforts were staffed primarily by volunteers, might not the advocates of inaction argue that rescue was cheaper than prevention? Or perhaps they might argue that the children upstream should not be protected from the risks of life—that they needed to learn to be careful, that retaining walls invite careless behavior—better to let them get a taste of the cold water, and then rescue them. Finally, suppose that a new group takes over, and begins throwing the children into the stream on purpose, hoping that they will learn to swim, and counting on the labors of our villagers if they do not. In this situation, we cannot help but wonder if the rescue project, with its attendant publicity, has contributed to the very problem it seeks to solve.

Is this, too, an analogy for emergency food? Clearly emergency food providers are not responsible for the decline of wages at the bottom of the economic ladder nor for the globalization of the workforce. Certainly they have not contributed much to the rising cost of shelter. But what about the decline of public assistance and the conservative effort to shift the costs of caring for the poor to the voluntary sector? Is the emergency food system, on the whole, a net addition to the well-being of poor people? Or has it occasioned the substitution of charity—unequally distributed, fragile, and unreliable charity—for entitlements? To what extent has all of the hard work and compassion gone unwittingly to further the conservative political agenda?

Kinder, Gentler Help

Several of the more obvious routes by which this has occurred were discussed in chapter 5. The availability of kinder, gentler help at the soup kitchen or food pantry may deter people from exercising their rights to entitlements, and, as a result, they may end up worse off, materially at least. Or, they may be happier in the short run, without the hassles of dealing with a food stamp application and certification process, but left high and dry if the food pantry closes because it runs out of food, or the deaconess who founded it breaks her ankle, or the volunteers go to Florida for the winter. The deterrent style of relief giving has worked, has succeeded in deterring some applicants, in part because emergency food providers have offered more attractive alternatives. Those who want to reduce "dependency" upon public programs, and "drain" on the treasury, have gotten their way.

The Herbert Hoover Doctrine

The Herbert Hoover Doctrine—no one will starve—is another route by which the existence of a visible kitchen and pantry network has contributed to the assault on public assistance: the reassurance that it provides for legislators and presidents engaged in dismantling the New Deal. In the winter of 1932, when the controversy over federal assistance to the unemployed was raging in Congress, a debate arose in the press over the accuracy of President Hoover's assertion that "no one has starved," his insistence that voluntary charities were meeting the need. *Better Times*, a publication of the Welfare Council of New York City, published a summary of convincing evidence showing a substantial number of deaths from malnutrition-related causes, including twenty-two from out-and-out starvation, in the city during the previous year, and included, set off in a box, a quote from journalist Heywood Hale Broun, under the heading "Brutes or Fools!": "It seems to me that the present economic and political temper of the country is to accept anything short of wholesale starvation as good enough. I say it isn't. I say we are not only brutes, but fools if it is our intention to stand by old theories of inaction right up to the time that people begin to drop on our doorsteps." It is possible, I suppose, that the architects of "welfare reform," who have, in very significant ways, returned us to what Broun labeled "the old theories of inaction," are brutes or fools. Perhaps they really do believe that everyone can work and that there will miraculously be jobs for all, and are therefore not concerned about the possibility of acute suffering. Perhaps they anticipate increased privation and just don't care. It seems more likely to me, however, that they believe that the charitable food programs will keep people from dropping on their doorsteps, will prevent severe hunger among those who do not achieve "independence." Certainly organizations that provide food for hungry people believe that they are being asked to take up the slack.

If Congress *is* counting on the emergency food system, then the characterization of our political leadership as "fools" takes on a new meaning. As Bread for the World's David Beckmann said of Newt Gingrich's proposals, "The math just doesn't work." Cuts to the Food Stamp Program over seven years under the 1996 PRWORA are estimated to be in excess of $27 billion, or roughly $4 billion a year. In comparison, Second Harvest estimates that the value of all of the food that passed through its member banks last year was approximately $1 billion. Even in the highly unlikely event that the Second Harvest network could *double* its contributions, the extra billion would still fill only a quarter of the gap created by food stamp cuts alone. Overall, including the block granting and the new TANF restrictions, about $55 billion in savings are expected from the PRWORA. No one but a fool would imagine that the charitable food network, already stretched thin, will be able to miraculously stretch again to cover this abyss, and the leaders of the emergency food movement have been saying so, loud and clear.

The Moral Safety Valve

Maybe, however, Congress just didn't do the arithmetic, and maybe the general public isn't doing it, either. Perhaps the primary function of emergency food, is, after all, symbolic. The New Deal story recounted at the beginning of chapter 5 comes to mind again. The FSRC distributed surplus commodities that, had they reached every family on relief, would have been worth an average of about $.65 per person per month. It wasn't enough to make a big difference in the diets of the unemployed, even at Depression era prices, but it was enough to make a big difference in the discomfort of the well fed, because they didn't ask about the amounts. It was enough that the pigs from the dramatic slaughter, and other visible surpluses, were being given away to the hungry. Food programs, especially food programs that prevent waste of food, operate on a symbolic plane. The same emotional salience that makes them so appealing—to the Cub Scout troop and the Cosmo girl, to the civic organization looking for a good deed to do and the retiree looking for a reason to get out of bed in the morning—makes them effective in relieving guilt and discomfort about hunger, independent of their actual size. Perhaps emergency food, with its ubiquitous collection mechanisms for food and money, its high visibility, its sporting events and canned goods drives and checkout counter options, has reassured the *public* that no one will starve, and thus given Congress and the president tacit permission, if not enthusiastic support, to dismantle the federal guarantee of minimum support for those in need and the newly empowered state governments room to experiment with a variety of time limits, family caps, and other reductions.

Distracting the Advocates

There is a fourth route by which the growth of emergency food may contribute to reductions in public sector provisions for poor people, and that is by absorbing the time and attention of advocates. The debate summarized in the previous chapter over the potential advocacy role of food banks and frontline providers has an obverse side. Where advocates whose main job is the public policy arena have been drawn into emergency food activities, what has been the opportunity cost of their involvement? Running an emergency food program is a demanding, unpredictable, time-consuming task, often fraught with minor but persistent emergencies of its own. Once begun, it cannot easily be put on hold while the agency shifts its energies to rally support for an important bill or to mobilize a campaign to oppose a cut. As advocacy resources are spread thinner than ever by the effects of the PRWORA, the opportunity costs of emergency food grow in significance.

Even where advocates do not get involved in the actual operation of emergency food programs, they have repeatedly been called upon by their allies in the emergency food sector to use their skills and talents—and political bargaining chips—in support of public programs that provide resources for emergency food. New York City advocates, for example, rallied to oppose cuts in the local EFAP budget proposed by the Giuliani administration when it first came into office. The combined efforts of advocates and emergency food providers were successful in the short term, but at what cost? Without raising taxes, not cutting emergency food only meant cutting some other area important for low-income people. Even in its victory statement ("Interfaith Voices Against Hunger Wins Major Budget Victory"),

Interfaith Voices, the clergy arm of the New York City Coalition
Against Hunger, wrote:

> Yet we should not rush to celebrate. This year's budget is grim
> for homeless, hungry and low-income New Yorkers, and the gains
> made by IVAH will be more than offset by losses in other areas, es-
> pecially the Human Resources Administration (welfare programs),
> which was cut by more than $100 million, mostly by permanently
> eliminating 4,000 jobs! Hundreds of millions more were cut from
> the Board of Ed, the municipal hospitals, mass transit, and many
> other services on which the majority of New Yorkers rely, including
> the poor.

The point is not that IVAH and its allies should not have fought the
cuts to EFAP. Once the system was in place serving, as one of the
campaign handouts reported, over 30 million meals annually to destitute New Yorkers, there was little choice; not to have fought the cuts
would have subjected thousands of impoverished New Yorkers to
sudden deprivation. But clearly the ascendant conservatives and the
underlying economy and the structural deficit have the anti-hunger
community fighting over crumbs and otherwise using its energies de-
fensively. In that sort of fight, a well-orchestrated campaign on behalf
of emergency food is quite likely to succeed, precisely because emergency food has so much public appeal. All of the same factors that
make it a prime recipient of casual giving and a magnet for voluntarism make it a poor target for a politician to cut. The symbolism is
too powerful; find something subtler. The Giuliani administration
backed off, and eventually increased funding slightly for supports to
emergency food, but cut other programs essential to poor people.

Ironically, the arguments used to defend the EFAP funding were
precisely the arguments that reinforce and validate the conservative
agenda. In its effort to preserve its public sector resource base, emergency food has begun to provide the architects of smaller government with the ammunition they need to wage their war on more
basic public provisions. In short, by engaging the contributions of
millions of donors and volunteers, emergency food has "proven" the
conservative contention that voluntary sector programs are "cheaper"
than public sector efforts. For example, the Food and Hunger Hot-

line prepared a highly effective flyer called the "Emergency Food Network Efficiency Fact Sheet." It showed that the cost of the average meal served in the city's emergency food network was "below the cost of school lunches and other mass feeding programs," that more than two-thirds of the labor force in the pantries and kitchens were unpaid volunteers, and that EFAP's contributions to the local food bank helped that organization to leverage millions of pounds of private product donations.

These things are all true, but these are also precisely the arguments that conservatives make when they urge increasing voluntary sector efforts—and reducing public entitlements. Are emergency food providers providing them with the facts and figures they need to further undermine public benefits, thus pushing more people into the sea of need that emergency food programs are already unable to drain? *Of course* soup kitchen meals prepared and served by volunteers cost less than school lunches prepared and served by cafeteria workers who not only receive paychecks, but benefits as well (although neither are particularly generous). But be careful, or school lunches will be the next to be "privatized"; and the school food service workers will be competing for jobs with the former hospital workers and the former transit workers, or they will be in the food pantry lines, trying to feed their own families on inadequate unemployment compensation, until it runs out.

Trapped in a Vicious Circle

This has all the hallmarks of a vicious circle. Emergency food providers and anti-hunger advocates are now arguing for the continuation of funds to programs they never meant to start, that they said from the outset they did not want to institutionalize, and that they constantly criticize for being demeaning at worst and mere Band-Aids at best; and they are using as a primary argument their own efficiency (innovation, flexibility, and compassion), which their opponents will use in turn as a justification for cutting back public programs, thus increasing the clientele of emergency food providers, and causing them to become even more efficient, and so on in a potentially endless spiral. Programs that were created largely to com-

pensate for the shortfalls of public entitlements are being used to further undermine them.

And where is the concerned public while advocates are fighting a
rear-guard action to protect emergency food funds and maintain the
integrity of food stamps, WIC, and school meals? As entitlements are
cut and need grows, of course, emergency food providers turn to
their friends and supporters in the public for yet another food drive
or walkathon or benefit concert. The publicity essential for fund-
raising makes the emergency food system even more visible, and thus
reassures the casual observer that the voluntary safety net is alive and
well. That is, like the breadlines of the Great Depression, the visible
emergency food system makes onlookers feel that the situation is under control. With all that activity, of course no one will starve.

The constant resource gathering—fund-raising, food-raising,
friend-raising—at which emergency food has proven itself so successful, is problematic in other ways besides convincing friendly
bystanders that the problem is under control. In the first place, fund-
raising requires emergency food providers to stress their own efficiency, to make a case for how far a dollar contributed to their
program will go, the same arguments used to protect themselves
from the loss of public funds. Few charitable programs overtly compare themselves to public programs when they do this, but the message is implicit: the voluntary sector can do it cheaper. No matter
how many times emergency food leaders declare that they are a
supplement to, not a substitute for, public provision, the residue of
unfavorable comparison remains.

Second, by promoting charitable giving, and by enlisting celebrities to endorse one's charitable activity, the message is loud and clear
that this is an appropriate response to poverty. Actions speak louder
than words. Despite their frequent protestations that they are not,
and have never claimed to be, a solution to hunger, the logic of fund-
raising requires them to stress their successes and achievements.
Even the most creative fund-raising consultants cannot devise appealing solicitations that simultaneously tell donors that charities cannot do the job and that they must hold government responsible and
that they should give more funds so that charities can try to do the
job. When an organization asks people to give money or food to sup-

port an emergency food program, it is implicitly saying that this is a good way to help. This is even more true when we ask our school-children to conduct canned goods drives. It is not reasonable to expect them to absorb the complexities of the context—this is a good thing to do, temporarily, while government fails in its fundamental responsibilities to the people. The people now in young adulthood have grown up with food drives; some have served Christmas dinner in a soup kitchen every year for more than half their lives.

Furthermore, the images of emergency food clients typically used in fund-raising campaigns are generally the images of patient sufferers, humbly waiting. There have been improvements in the visual messages communicated by emergency food fund-raisers since I first began to pay attention to them. There are now fewer pictures of people searching through garbage cans. Just the basic waiting-for-a-handout role in which poor people are portrayed diminishes them, however, and reinforces the public assumption that these are people whose needs are appropriately addressed through charity. Compare the folks lined up for Thanksgiving dinner in the church basement, for example, with the images of poor people that were projected by the civil rights movement or the organizing drives of the farmworkers in the 1960s. The grandchildren of Selma and Delano are in the soup kitchen lines, looking sad and downtrodden before dinner, or smiling and grateful afterward.

The Utility of Hunger

The issue of images of emergency food recipients returns us to the question of attachment to this system. At the Operation Blessing event portrayed in chapter 7, I spoke with a journalist affiliated with the Christian Broadcasting Network and traveling with the Hunger Strike Force Convoy '94. He captured the ambiguity of the hunger publicity shot:

> And I kind of wrestle with, you know, when you give food out and you take the pictures and use them for more promotion, but it seems like you can't have one without the other. I mean, if you're doing social consciousness, this is a way to do it; you've got to show

people results. I guess a lot of people have volunteered their time, and a lot of money has gone into the food, and you have to show the results of that labor. And so the end result is someone receiving a bag of food and a big smile. You know, so it's kind of like a catch-22 there. You don't want to bother them at a vulnerable moment, but you gotta, to keep it going, you gotta raise more consciousness.

And more funds, he might have added. The Operation Blessing staff stressed the educational aspects of the event, calling attention to the problem of hunger, and Pat Robertson himself the evangelical content ("Is the word getting out that the People who love the Lord really care about the poor?" he asked Operation Blessing's New York City director for the benefit of the television cameras). I, however, was impressed with the frequency and sophistication of the fund-raising appeals that were interspersed throughout the *700 Club* broadcast. For just $25 a month, the viewing audience was told, you could "ensure that things like this continue to happen."

Robertson is not alone in making full use of the fund-raising potential of feeding the hungry. In fact, in one sense, the entire emergency food system does it. Many food bankers with whom I talked were quite sure that there would be a role for food banking even if we somehow succeeded in eliminating hunger. The food was important to agencies serving the elderly and to day-care centers and rehabilitation programs, they pointed out. But if you look at their own fund-raising literature, it stresses hunger and the alleviation of hunger; helping agencies stretch tight budgets is a sidelight or an afterthought, if it is mentioned at all. This is not false advertising; with few exceptions, food banks pass the majority of their food along to agencies serving "the hungry" per se. But if you try to imagine the food bankers raising the millions of dollars in contributions that are required to keep the system running, it quickly becomes obvious that thrift and effective social service delivery just don't have the same emotional appeal as hunger. Without hunger, we'd have to go out of business, consigning good food to the dump and further undermining the already thin budgets of underfunded human services.

The repeated emphasis upon *hunger*, however, may also be contributing to a distortion that reduces our ability to confront and solve the underlying problem. By defining the problem as "hunger," the emergency food system is helping to direct our attention away from the more fundamental problem of poverty, and the even more basic problem of inequality. As we saw in chapter 2, poor people use emergency food to ward off acute hunger, when they are "*hungry*, hungry," but they also use it to free resources for other needs—the rent, the shoes, the birthday present. The frequency with which such other needs push a client into the pantry line has everything to do with the extent of inequality in the society. In a rich society, the experience of poverty is inextricably embedded in inequality. The quality of life available at a given absolute level of income and expenditure is intimately related to the distance from the median, the degree to which participation in the normal life of the society is precluded. A mother in a tropical village where few if any children wear shoes will not feel pressured to secure resources for the purchase of shoes at the cost of her dignity. A mother in an American community in 1998 may feel obligated to find a way to buy not only shoes, but shoes of a certain type or brand. If she can get her groceries free by making the rounds of the church pantries, then she may be able to buy those Nikes that her child has been led to believe are an essential prerequisite for social acceptance. Beyond some level of absolute starvation and nakedness, need is a thoroughly relative phenomenon. That is why inequality, rather than simple poverty, is the underlying problem, and no matter how you measure it, inequality has been growing in America.

The rich are richer than they have been since World War II, and the poor are poorer. In fact, a study released last year by the Twentieth Century Fund found that by 1989, inequality in the distribution of wealth had reached a sixty-year high. That means that it was worse—more unequal—than it had been since the onset of the Great Depression. The top fifth held 85 percent of the nation's marketable net worth, leaving only 15 percent for the entire bottom four-fifths. Concentration at the very top is even more pronounced. The top 1 percent of the country held 39 percent of its marketable net worth in 1989. Earnings inequality is not as profound as wealth inequality, of course, but it is substantial, and growing. Economists sometimes measure it by calculating what they call a 90–10 ratio; that is, a ratio of what workers in the top tenth of earners average, compared to workers in the bottom tenth, or decile. In 1995, an adult male in the bottom tenth had to work full-time for more than a month to earn what his counterpart in the top tenth earned in a week. Income inequality has leveled off a bit, because more people are working and they are working longer hours, and because retirees are doing better, but the general trend is toward an ever-increasing inequality that makes us the least equal of nineteen OECD countries. Ironically, the acceleration of inequality coincides substantially with the period of growth in emergency food. As former secretary of labor Robert Reich has recently reported, "From the 1950s through most of the 1970s, the income of the poorest fifth of Americans grew faster than the income of the top fifth. Between 1950 and 1978 the inflation-adjusted family income of the bottom quintile grew by 138 percent, while the real income of the richest 20 percent of families grew by 99 percent." We were "Growing Together." At the end of the 1970s, however, this trend reversed. "Since 1979 the growth of family income has been skewed in favor of the richest; between 1979 and 1995, the inflation-adjusted income of the richest fifth of families grew by 26 percent, while the income of the poorest fifth fell by 9 percent." We have been "Growing Apart."

When I say that the fundamental problem is growing inequality, I do not just mean that the poor are further from the rich, or that they are less well off in absolute terms, and thus more likely to be in need of emergency food assistance, although both of these are true. I mean that our society is coming apart, that we are losing the sense that we are interdependent, all part of the same society. We are becoming the haves and the have-nots, with decreasing prospect of mobility from the have-not group to the have group. We are becoming two societies with quite different interests. All of the solutions that worked to help people out of poverty, and keep people out of poverty in earlier decades are threatened or undermined by this growing inequality.

As the haves and the have-nots move further apart, charity appears more and more appropriate as a response to need. Charity, after all, is typically something we give to people who are *not* like us, and as inequality increases, the poor appear less and less *like* the comfortable. They seem more different because their lives *are* more different. The growing inequality feeds the trend toward charity, but the proliferation of charity feeds our appetite, or at least our tolerance, for inequality as well. That is, as we line up poor people in soup kitchens and food pantries and other programs that are just for the poor, we reinforce the idea that these are people who are fundamentally different from us; and this, in turn, makes it seem more acceptable if they have much less than the rest of us.

Why have we become so attached to the language of hunger and homelessness instead of poverty and inequality? In the first place, we really can't "see" very clearly, the underlying problem of inequality. We read the numbers and the technical words for "rich" and our eyes glaze over. What is "net marketable worth," anyway, and do I know anybody who's got any? We are not, most of us, trained to use or understand the language in which inequality is measured and reported. We *are* trained, however, to look at the symptoms. In fact, the anti-hunger community has invested a great deal of time and talent in teaching us to define and measure hunger. Hunger is so much easier to picture, and to understand, than an abstraction like inequality.

Furthermore, unlike inequality, it is a problem to which we know how to respond. Social workers and psychotherapists have a handy concept called "partialization." When a problem appears too big to solve, they recommend breaking it down into manageable component parts. It is the same advice that parents routinely give teenagers who feel overwhelmed by a demanding school agenda. Study for your chemistry test tonight and write your English paper after school tomorrow. By breaking the fundamental problem of poverty into its symptoms, we make it more manageable. We do what we can. And we know we can do something about hunger: "Hunger has a cure" is the new slogan developed for Second Harvest by the Advertising Council, and other anti-hunger groups are being invited to adapt it to their own efforts. Thus Bread for the World's "Tell Congress: Hunger Has a Cure" offering of letters, and new "Hunger Has a Cure" draft legislation. But by focusing our attention and energy upon the "cure" for hunger, we give it a life of its own, apart from the poverty and inequality of which it is a symptom.

For people who want smaller government and less public assistance for poor people, obviously these subtle but significant effects of the visible emergency food network are not a problem. Ronald Reagan would probably be delighted to learn that the soup kitchens and food pantries inspired by his cheese giveaway have helped to create the climate in which further cuts in food stamps were first imaginable and then obtainable. He would probably be pleased to hear that the flood of kindness unleashed by the "hunger emergency" of the early eighties has contributed to the end of welfare as we have known it. For the thousands of people who participate in emergency food out of a desire to heal the rifts in our society, to build bridges across the widening chasm that separates the poor from everybody else, and to make the lives of poor people a bit easier, however, these are troubling charges. If emergency food really *is* contributing to the creation of hunger and the intensification of inequality, then what can be done?

What to Do

The possible replies to this question can be arranged along a continuum from shutting the emergency food system down, to working actively to harness this vast grassroots endeavor toward more fundamental change, and out there, somewhere, there is probably someone ready to argue for almost any conceivable point along the continuum. Shall we "Close Down the Soup Kitchens" as welfare activist Theresa Funicello once suggested in an Op-Ed piece in the New York *Daily News*? Of course, emergency food is a highly decentralized system, and no one actually *could* shut it down, but people concerned about the network's effects on public provisions could withdraw their support, and that would lead to dramatic shrinkage. They could work actively against further TEFAP-type commodity donations and state and local supports, and they could oppose continued tax credits for businesses that donate. Despite all the flaws described and analyzed in chapters 7 and 8, however, few critics have seriously recommended shutting down the kitchens and pantries. Emergency food clients certainly don't want them closed, although many look forward to a day when they, personally, will not have to rely upon them. Despite the limited nature of the supplements they provide and the indignities that seem to be inherent in such projects, emergency food programs have clearly filled significant gaps in the array of assistance available to people in need, and have brought a measure of kindness and flexibility to the whole national project of helping poor people.

Like Diane Wright, who was quoted in chapter 3 to the effect that she wasn't going to stand by and watch people suffer just to make a political point, almost none of the people involved in providing emergency food on a day-to-day basis can stomach the notion of shutting it down or cutting it back, in hopes of achieving more fundamental reforms for the long run. Remember Herneatha Barbour, who runs the Wednesday soup kitchen at Childs Memorial Baptist Church in Philadelphia, who thought that Bread For the World's anti-hunger agenda was "more of a long-range planning thing," while she felt her group needed "something for right now." As Harry Hopkins once said, "People don't eat in the long run; they eat every day!"

And furthermore, there is all that food: three-quarters of a billion pounds passed through the Second Harvest system last year. Some of the resources that are translated into meals by the emergency food system might be used for other, more adequate or more systematic approaches, but much of the food donated to this effort is unlikely to be made available for other uses. The same might be said for much of the volunteer energy and financial support. Clearly emergency food has enlisted the efforts and contributions of people who are never going to become advocates for a stronger public safety net or a major redistribution of income. The same broad political and social spectrum that gives emergency food much of its staying power means that it attracts people who want to avoid politics altogether and people whose political ideas would not endorse a larger role for government or a downward redistribution of wealth. Many of the people who annually Tee off Against Hunger on their local golf course or Dine Out to Help Out or pay $100 for a ticket to the Taste of the Nation buffet are not likely to join in a campaign to raise the capital gains tax or close loopholes that benefit the rich. Only some of the resources captured by emergency food programs could realistically be transferred to other approaches. Perhaps the broad political and social spectrum reflected in emergency food, and especially in its various resource-gathering strategies, produces the greatest possible assistance to the poor, and we tamper with it at our (their) peril. There is certainly a school of thought among anti-hunger activists that argues that the way to end hunger is to get everyone to do what they can and will, what their politics and their resources permit them to do.

Organize and Educate

Of course, there is always the hope of moving people along, of educating them to see the bigger problems, and many emergency food programs are especially well positioned to work at that task. When I first began this study, Bill Bolling of the Atlanta Community Food Bank summarized the possible role of food banks in such an effort: "I think the food banks have tremendous potential, because they've built the trust in the community, to be change agents in the community, and to educate not only the business community and the foundations and donors, but to educate the people that they're serving." He went on to make clear that the content of that education should be not only entitlement programs but public policy as it relates to jobs and credit and public investments. Perhaps the most crucial group, he concluded, were the volunteers: "This is where we failed in so many ways," he said thoughtfully, "because we brought the people in to volunteer—tens of millions of them in this country—but we haven't taken them that next step. I mean, if a person volunteers in a food box program or soup kitchen, it ought to be a requirement—they volunteer three hours and then they spend an hour reflecting. . . . We have a huge constituency out there that we need to mobilize, and we have the potential to do that."

"I am an incrementalist," Los Angeles FEMA local board director Gene Boutillier told me. "I believe that we make our social progress with lights clicking on over people's heads one at a time or twenty at a time or a hundred at a time," but in order to promote this process, we have to "decrease social distance between the classes. . . . The main political task in dealing with poverty is for people to identify with the poor so they can't be demonized and they can't be discounted and they can't be ignored." And that, he believes, is what happens in emergency food programs. "Food pantries tend to be volunteer operations, and soup kitchens even more. So they do have the effect of putting people into each other's faces, and that can't be anything but good. If it were a more equal equation in the interaction, that would be, of course, much better. But even an uneven interaction is better than no interaction."

Bread for the World has articulated a similar conviction:

> The feeding movement is a first-generation expression of American discontent with domestic hunger. Hunger can be the . . . introduction to larger problems of poverty, powerlessness, and distorted public values. Charities can help educate people from their entry point to a sophisticated understanding of the causes of hunger and its international and national dimensions.

In fact, as we saw in chapter 9, there has been no shortage of efforts to enlist the power and resources of the emergency food community in a broader advocacy. Bread for the World has undertaken its Transform Anti-Hunger Leadership project. Mazon has explicitly tried to link its grantees up with the Food Research and Action Center, and helps frontline providers attend FRAC's advocacy-oriented conferences. Catholic Charities USA, the National Council of Churches, and the Council of Jewish Federations have all taken overtly pro-advocacy stands, urging their affiliated food providers to get involved with efforts to address the underlying causes of hunger. Share Our Strength (SOS) funds advocacy as well as direct service provisions from the proceeds of fund-raisers like the Taste of the Nation. Second Harvest has increased its own emphasis on advocacy, as has Foodchain. World Hunger Year has urged advocacy and helped to replicate projects that help emergency food providers gain advocacy skills. The Center on Hunger, Poverty and Nutrition Policy at Tufts University provides its research findings and policy analyses to food bankers and emergency food providers as well as to scholars, advocates, and government officials.

Furthermore, the advocates and providers have been able to agree on a basic anti-hunger agenda. Almost everyone says that jobs, better-paying jobs, are the first necessity, accompanied by major investment in education and training to equip people to fill such jobs.

Better, fairer, more comprehensive and more generous income support programs for those who cannot work are generally agreed to be the next line of defense, and public food assistance programs like food stamps and school meals to supplement both low wages and cash income supports. Additional emergency food is seen as the last resort by nearly everyone.

And these efforts have paid off. Emergency food providers *have* become increasingly and publicly articulate about the fundamental needs of their clients, and increasingly active in lobbying and related activities. So the problem is not that emergency food providers have not accepted the advocacy challenge, although too few are effectively organized and equipped for such work, and efforts to enlist them need to continue. The problem is that there is not a powerful social movement for justice and equality, for efforts to eliminate poverty in this society and seriously reduce inequality, and without such a movement, what advocates can accomplish, with or without the assistance of emergency food providers, is severely limited. In fact, as we have seen, the contemporary "hunger lobby" was not only not powerful enough to forestall a punitive and damaging welfare reform, it was not even powerful enough to preserve intact the Food Stamp Program, "the safety net under the safety net."

Building a Movement

Suppose, for a moment, that this diagnosis is correct, that little progress in securing more effective and fundamental solutions to poverty, or even restoring the New Deal/Great Society safety net, is likely to be made without a social movement. A certain degree of despair about the prospects for constructive public policy is currently fashionable among liberals and progressives. The twelve years of Republican control of the White House, the failure of the Clinton health insurance initiative, the virulency of the Contract with America, the passage of the PRWORA and the president's willingness to sign it, the general conservative hegemony, make it difficult to imagine a return to vigorous pursuit of an anti-poverty agenda. And a real social movement of the sort that animated the sixties seems out of reach. My experiences in the course of this research, however, make me more optimistic than prevailing fashions dictate.

In the first place, there is an enormous reservoir of good will and compassion out there. I first went to take a closer look at the emergency food network because I was distressed to see a proliferation of charitable programs that I felt were inherently demeaning, and I feared that the spread of charity would undermine the political will necessary to restore and maintain public food assistance and cash supports. In one sense, I found what I was looking for; despite the extraordinary efforts of many providers to make their programs welcoming and dignified, they cannot fully overcome the stigma of charity. But the vigor and creativity of the efforts of emergency food providers to reduce stigma and preserve dignity came as a surprise to me. I did not find nearly as many people as I had imagined who appeared to be in the work for an opportunity to exercise control over others or give themselves a warm, fuzzy feeling. There were some, of course, but they seemed to be greatly outnumbered by energetic and open-minded people who were trying to do the best they could with what they had. I came back to my desk more hopeful about the possibilities for progressive social change in America than I had been when I set out, even as my worst fears for the public safety net were being realized.

The emergency food network has attracted the contributions of people from a particularly wide political spectrum, and not all of them, by any means, are ready to sign on for a struggle for fewer privileges for the rich or greater support for the poor, but there is a great deal of decency, caring, concern. Most people involved with food programs do not have a clear agenda for better public policy or blueprint for building a more caring society, but they want to move in that direction. With a few exceptions, they see the lines at the kitchen and pantry door as evidence that something has gone dreadfully wrong. Just as the polls suggest that "welfare reform" was, on the whole, harsher than what the public wanted, my experience of the emergency food network suggests that both its leadership and its frontline troops are less conservative than their charitable project makes them appear. Furthermore, even though they may not be interested in statistics on inequality, they are concerned about unfairness. When the newspapers print stories of Wall Street year-end bonuses that dwarf the wages of ordinary workers, and report the fabulous salary and benefit packages of CEOs of corporations that are laying off loyal long-term employees, people who pack bags in food pantries and dish up soup talk about unfairness. They make the connection. I believe that many are potential recruits for a movement to challenge unfairness and address the growth of inequality. There is more reason for hope than for despair.

It is likely that the effects of the PRWORA, especially when the current economic expansion exhausts itself and the inevitable "downturn" arrives, will aggravate the situation at the bottom and contribute to an opportunity for action. It is still too soon to know with any certainty what the outcome of the PRWORA will be. Conservatives are predicting a rebirth of individual initiative and independence; liberals are predicting acute suffering; moderates are worrying about the impact of fixed allocations to the states in the event of a recession. I find it easy to imagine that there will be another "emergency," if not when food stamp cuts begin to escalate, then in several years when the "fall off the cliff" provisions of TANF take effect. People who want to build more secure and comprehensive protections for economic security should avoid the temptations of the emergency label. An extraordinary number of the long-term emergency food providers whom I interviewed had been drawn into the project in response to the "emergency" of the early 1980s, and had undertaken programs that in some ways contravened their own values and wisdom, because they thought they would be temporary responses to an emergency situation. Once the programs got started, however, all of the forces of institutionalization began to take effect, and here they are, nearly two decades later, with an enormous system on their hands that requires constant effort and attention. The suffering that comes in the next "emergency" will not be some Act of God or aberration; it will be a predictable outcome of social policy driven by ideology and politics and made without attention to the underlying economic and social realities. People who want a more just and inclusive society, one without a marginalized layer at the bottom, should be thinking now about ways to provide assistance that unite and integrate people rather than separating and segregating them, so that the next time there is an "emergency," we can harness the good will and compassion that will be evoked for a movement for more fundamental reforms.

I am definitely not saying, however, that such a movement should be built around the issue of hunger. The same emotional appeal that makes hunger a magnet for contributions and a common denominator for a broad spectrum of people makes us vulnerable to token solutions and responses that work on a symbolic plane. Hunger makes us uncomfortable, and programs that address hunger relieve that discomfort, independently of their real ability to eliminate the hunger itself. While it is true, as some anti-hunger activists have argued, that fighting hunger can be an entry point, a beginning, that enables people to develop a broader commitment, it can all too easily become an end point, the emotionally gratifying and theoretically winnable struggle that absorbs our attention. We should avoid the lure of hunger, as well as the temptations of "emergency" and the seductions of charity.

There are other reasons, besides its susceptibility to cosmetic solutions, for avoiding the temptation to build a movement around hunger. One is that it distorts and oversimplifies the problem. Although poor people in our society are sometimes "*hungry*, hungry," they live most days in a tangled web of unmet needs and unrealized hopes. We need to avoid getting caught up again in debates like those that characterized the hunger wars of the mid 1980s, about whether people are actually hungry, because it is the wrong question. A program or a policy that tries only to prevent acute hunger is aiming too low. It is not acceptable to have people in our society too poor to participate and contribute, too poor to provide a decent chance in life for their children, too poor to pursue happiness. We need to aim for the creation of a just and inclusive society that taps everyone's potential and makes us all better off in the long run, not just a society where no one starves.

Furthermore, despite its unifying potential, there is a sense in which the hunger issue is divisive, in that it implies work on behalf of the very poor. We need to build our movement around an inclusive vision of fairness and economic security, so that people who enlist will be struggling on their own behalf, and not—in a sort of political counterpart to charity—for someone else's right to dinner. That is, the great majority of Americans are not in any immediate danger of going hungry, but they would benefit from a fairer tax system, campaign finance reform, protections for job security, a cleaner environment, vastly improved public education and job training, access to quality health care and child care, affordable housing, a safer, healthier food system, supports for child rearing and family life, more comprehensive social insurance, better public transportation, a more realistic minimum wage, and a host of other goals that are achievable. And if these goals were achieved, a great deal of contemporary poverty as we know it would be prevented. There would be so many fewer poor people that it would be much easier to contrive ways to help them. We need to imagine and then create a movement that will reduce poverty by helping us all, a movement that will integrate rather than segregate poor people, that will cast them in the role of fellow workers for the greater good rather than grateful recipients of our exertions on their behalf.

Enlisting Kitchens and Pantries in the Movement

Is there a role for the existing kitchens and pantries in this movement-building process? Possibly. If they begin to transform themselves from charitable programs to cooperative endeavors where this integrative process can begin and people can rediscover how much they have in common, then I think there can be a role. If they follow the examples set by the many projects that have already moved beyond the Band-Aid, by the groups that have begun to involve clients in both the work and the decision making, by the SHARE programs that embody a cooperative approach, by the community food security models that have begun to integrate access for poor people into a more inclusive restructuring of local food systems, then I think they can contribute a great deal. "We are moving from being a church bringing in volunteers from somewhere else and serving clients to being a church of the poor, the poor who live in the neighborhood," declared a Lutheran pastor from the South Bronx whose church runs a food pantry, a community meals program, an AIDS luncheon, and an after-school program offering both snacks and dinner. Acknowledging that it can be "a bit frightening" to long-time church members for people from the pantry line or guests at the meals to become members of the church and active in organizing and leading its programs, he went on to assert that

> for those of us who are involved in developing the food program, that becomes an exciting possibility for deepening the roots of our parish in our community. So that the distribution of food no longer becomes a charitable act that makes me feel good because I'm doing something for the other, but the distribution of food becomes the process of organizing . . . a community to become self-determining.

Where emergency food programs take on this challenge, to become a means for organizing people to find their common agenda and pursue it, then I think they can play an important role in bringing about real change.

Just over a decade ago, Sara Evans and Harry Boyte wrote a book entitled *Free Spaces* in which they explored the role of "settings between private lives and large-scale institutions where ordinary citizens can act with dignity, independence, and vision," where they can "experience a schooling in citizenship and learn a vision of the common good in the course of struggling for change." Such free spaces, Boyte and Evans argued, are essential to creating and sustaining social movements. In my most optimistic scenarios, I envision turning our kitchens and pantries into free spaces, places where people can meet and interact across the gulf of social class and the divisions of race and ethnicity, not as givers and receivers in ways that widen the gulf, but as neighbors and fellow citizens in ways that strengthen social bonds. Imagine that we opened community dinner programs in our public schools, where parents picking up their children from after-school programs could share a meal with them, where senior citizens could enjoy an inexpensive night out, where teenagers could learn culinary skills and earn a little spending money, where local artists could display their work and musicians could perform and poets could read. Suppose that churches and synagogues could purchase tickets for such meals and distribute them to the hungry people who now congregate in their soup kitchens and food pantries so that these people would be less isolated, more integrated with the larger community. Imagine that anyone in need could earn dinner tickets by helping with food preparation or with clean-up. Imagine the discussions that might take place around the tables, the new ideas that might be hatched, the gardens that might be planted, the friendships that might be formed, the ideals that might be nourished, and the movements that might be built. Imagine the very different lessons we would be teaching our young people about how to overcome hunger and meet our common human need for food.

I find myself thinking from time to time about the trusty page who accompanied King Wenceslas on his mission of mercy. The tale is constructed, after all, as a lesson to the youthful assistant. When his nerve begins to fail, when his will begins to sag, he discovers the warmth of goodness: "Heat was in the very sod, which the Saint had printed," the mark of divine favor upon his master's labors. What, really, are we teaching the young people whom we enlist to help out with food drives and soup kitchen meals? Like Wenceslas's page, they are learning that *we* are good-hearted if quite saintly, and they are learning important lessons about themselves. We are teaching them that their effort is needed, that their contribution is expected, that helping others can be fun. All of this is good, it is good for them. But what are we teaching them about the people on the other end of the transaction: that they are "downtrodden," and passive, that they must be taken care of, that need is their primary identity. Our young helpers are not experimenting with models for the society we hope they will build. Suppose Wenceslas had turned his attention to mobilizing the poor of his kingdom to assert their rights to a fair share of the fruits of their toil, and to creating structures of mutual aid as a hedge against want. Then his page would have learned about social solidarity, about how much people have in common, about how much we can learn from people who are different from us, how much we need the contributions of everyone if our society is ever to come anywhere near its potential. If we can turn our kitchens and pantries into schools that teach these lessons, then I think they can help us create a future in which we will all have a place at the table.

Notes

Introduction

2 *"Shall yourselves find blessing."* Lyrics to "Good King Wenceslas." *Good King Wenceslas* by John Mason Neale, with Illustrations and Ornaments by Christopher Manson (New York: North-South Books, 1994).

4 *25,970,000 "unduplicated" clients:* VanAmburg Group Inc., *Second Harvest 1993 National Research Study* (Chicago: Second Harvest National Food Bank Network, 1994), 24.

4 *"kinder . . . less just":* Quoted in Nicholas Wade, "Method and Madness: The Vindication of Robert Gallo," *New York Times Magazine*, December 26, 1993, 12.

5 *inequality . . . more pronounced:* Ruth Sidel, *Keeping Women and Children Last: America's War on the Poor* (New York: Penguin Books, 1996), 13, 14.

8 *largest recipients . . . contributions:* Bread for the World Institute, *Hunger 1994: Transforming the Politics of Hunger*, Fourth Annual Report on the State of World Hunger (Silver Spring, Md.: Bread for the World Institute, 1993), 40; *Chronicle of Philanthropy* 8, no. 2 (November 1995): 1, 32, 33; *Second Harvest Update* (winter 1994): 8.

8 *nearly a thousand pantries and kitchens:* Food and Hunger Hotline, *Thirty Million Meals a Year: Emergency Food Programs in New York City* (New York: Food and Hunger Hotline, 1995), 5; Food For Survival, personal communication, June 1997.

9 *150,000 kitchens and pantries:* Bread for the World Institute, *Hunger 1994*, 12, 32.

10 *hunger . . . became news:* Nick Kotz, *Let Them Eat Promises: The Politics of Hunger in America* (Englewood Cliffs, N.J.: Prentice-Hall, 1969), 1–19.

10 *seized on the issue:* Nick Kotz, "The Politics of Hunger," *New Republic*, April 30, 1984, 19–23.

11 *"Hunger is a unique . . . :* George McGovern, "Foreword" to Nick Kotz, *Let Them Eat Promises*, vii, viii.

11 *expenditures . . . grew . . . by 500 percent:* Carl P. Chelf, *Controversial Issues in Social Welfare Policy: Government and the Pursuit of Happiness* (Newbury Park, Calif.: Sage Publications, 1992), 43.

12 *advantages of food stamps . . . clear:* See Janet E. Poppendieck, "Policy, Advocacy, and Justice: The Case of Food Assistance Reform," in *Toward Social and Economic Justice*, ed. David Gil and Eva Gil (Cambridge, Mass.: Schenkman Publishing, 1985), 101–31, for a detailed account of the reform process in the Food Stamp Program.

13 *"sorrow of breadlines . . .":* Barbara Baker Temple, director, Greater Philadelphia Food Bank, in U.S. Congress, House Subcommittee on Domestic Marketing, Consumer Relations and Nutrition, *Emergency Food Assistance and Commodity Distribution Act of 1983*, 98th Cong., 1st sess., March 22, 1983, serial 98-4, 65.

13 *"substitution of cheese lines . . . for bread lines . . .":* Edmond V. Worley, director, Greater Cleveland Community Foodbank, in U.S. Congress, House Subcommittee on Domestic Marketing, Consumer Relations and Nutrition, *Problems of Hunger and Malnutrition*, 98th Cong., 1st sess., February 28, March 25, and April 30, 1983, serial 98-3, 60.

13 *"a 'soup kitchen society' . . .":* Physician Task Force on Hunger in America, *Hunger in America: The Growing Epidemic* (Middletown, Conn.: Wesleyan University Press, 1985), 9.

13 *"Soup kitchens . . . commonplace":* Food Research and Action Center, *Hunger in the Eighties: A Primer* (Washington, D.C.: Food Research and Action Center, 1984), 41.

14 *grog shop and the gaming table:* Viviana Zelizer, *The Social Meaning of Money* (New York: Basic Books, 1994), 126–42.

14 *"the breadbasket . . . and the scrip commissaries":* Helen Hall, *Unfinished Business* (New York, Macmillan, 1971), 51.

14 *"bread line situation"* and *"believed that . . . the needy were receiving adequate relief":* Louis Adamic, *My America, 1928–1938* (New York: Harper, 1938), 296, 297.

15 *assessment of food program use:* Katherine Clancy, Jean Bowering, and Janet Poppendieck, "Audit and Evaluation of Food Program Use: Report of a Random Survey in New York State," submitted to the Bureau of Nutrition of the New York State Department of Health, March 1989; see also Katherine Clancy and Jean Bowering, "The Need for Emergency Food: Poverty Problems and Policy Responses," *Journal of Nutrition Education* 24, no. 1 (1992): 12s–17s.

17 *The historical Wenceslas:* Marvin Kantor, "Wenceslas," in *Historic*

World Leaders, vol. 3: Europe, L–Z, Anne Conmire, ed. (Detroit: Gate Research Inc., 1994), 1320–22.

18 *Children's stories depict:* See, for example, Mildred Corell Luckhardt, *Good King Wenceslas* (New York: Abingdon Press, 1964).

18 *"always pleasing to see a man eat":* Ralph Waldo Emerson, *Essays*, 1st and 2d ser., introduction by Douglas Orase (New York: Vintage Books/The Library of America, 1990), 306.

CHAPTER ONE: *Charity for All*

24 *results were clear:* Vincent Breglio, *Hunger in America: The Voter's Perspective* (Lanham, Md.: Research/Strategy/Management Inc., 1992), 3–6.

24 *"Have you, personally . . .":* Ibid., 14–16.

26 *two-thirds of the hours . . . :* Food and Hunger Hotline, *Thirty Million Meals a Year: Emergency Food Programs in New York City* (New York: Food and Hunger Hotline, 1995), 17, 18.

26 *The median pantry:* VanAmburg Group, Inc., Second Harvest 1993 National Research Study (Chicago: Second Harvest National Food Bank Network, 1994), 72 (calculations mine).

30 *Bill Liddell grows 49,000 pounds:* Kristin Nord, "Bill Liddell's Field of Dreams," *New Choices*, November 1991, 50, 51.

30 *Project Glean:* Carol Taylor, "A Place at the Table," *Mother Earth News*, November/December 1989, 60, 61.

36 *surveys of giving:* See Lester Salamon, *America's Nonprofit Sector: A Primer* (New York: The Foundation Center, 1992), especially pp. 13–31; see also Virginia A. Hodgkinson, Murray S. Weitzman, Christopher M. Toppe, and Stephen M. Noga, *Nonprofit Almanac, 1992–1993: Dimensions of the Independent Sector* (San Francisco: Jossey-Bass Publishers, 1992).

39 *". . . share your bread . . ."* Isa. 58.7 RSV.

39 *"I was hungry . . . did it to me":* Matt. 25.35–40 RSV.

39 *"Food . . . has a spiritual dimension . . .":* Bread for the World Institute, *Hunger 1994: Transforming the Politics of Hunger*, Fourth Annual Report on the State of World Hunger (Silver Spring, Md.: Bread for the World Institute, 1993), 31, 32.

40–41 *". . . the feeding process is the dominant . . ." and "feeding is more than the squirting of nutrients . . .":* Willard Gaylin, "In the Beginning: Helpless and Dependent," in Willard Gaylin, Ira Glasser, Steven Marcus, and David Rothman, *Doing Good: The Limits of Benevolence* (New York: Pantheon Books, 1981), 9.

44 *clean plate milieu:* Hillary Rodham Clinton, *It Takes a Village: And Other Lessons Children Teach Us* (New York: Simon and Schuster, 1996), 116.

44 *The primary strategy:* Amy L. Bently, "Uneasy Sacrifice: The Politics

of United States Famine Relief, 1945–48," *Agriculture and Human Values* 11, No. 4 (fall 1994). (Special Issue: "The Continuing Challenge of Hunger"), 4–18.

45 *a cookbook . . . devoted:* Ruth Moorman and Laila Williams, *The Seven Chocolate Sins: A Devilishly Delicious Collection of Chocolate Recipes* (Brandon, Miss.: Quail Ridge Press, 1979). The book had been through four printings by the time my copy was produced in 1982.

45 *Run Against Hunger:* Denis Hamill, "Help Put the Soup On," New York *Daily News*, November 1, 1995, 6.

46 ". . . *to resolve a glaring paradox . . .*" and ". . . *feelings of emptiness . . .*": Greg Gutfeld, "Mouths to Feed," *Prevention* 45, no. 6 (May 1993): 22.

CHAPTER TWO: Who Eats Emergency Food?

50 ". . . *the individuals most at risk . . .*": Marion Nestle and Sally Guttmacher, "Hunger in the United States: Rationale, Methods, and Policy Implications of State Hunger Surveys," *Journal of Nutrition Education* 24, no. 1 (1992): 20s.

50 *National Research Study:* VanAmburg Group Inc., *Second Harvest 1993 National Research Study* (Chicago: Second Harvest National Food Bank Network, 1994). The study involved both a survey of member agencies by participating food banks, called the "agency survey," and a random survey of clients, called the "client survey." The overall agency survey included shelters that serve meals and non-emergency programs that use food banks, such as day-care centers and drug rehabilitation programs, but most of the results are reported separately for soup kitchens and food pantries as well. A total of 3,182 agencies returned questionnaires reporting on 3,685 programs (an agency may operate more than one program), of which 1,773 responses were from food pantries and 258 were from soup kitchens. The client survey, which consisted of structured personal interviews with randomly selected recipients of services from pantries, soup kitchens, and shelters, what Second Harvest defines as the "emergency" portion of its work, yielded 8,596 completed and usable interviews. See pages 10–18.

50 *"62.9% of adult poor people . . .":* Poverty data for 1993 from United States Department of Commerce, Bureau of the Census, *Income, Poverty, and Valuation of Noncash Benefits: 1993*, Current Population Reports, Consumer Income Series, 60–188, 1994; emergency food use data from VanAmburg Group, *Second Harvest Study*, 107–20, 143. Some calculations mine.

51 *what it costs to eat:* Patricia Ruggles, *Drawing the Line: Alternative Poverty Measures and Their Implications for Public Policy* (Washington, D.C.: The Urban Institute Press, 1990), 32–35.

52 ". . . *poverty thresholds . . .*": Winifred Bell, *Contemporary Social Welfare*, 2d ed. (New York: Macmillan, 1987), 102.

52 *mean family income deficit:* United States Department of Commerce, Bureau of the Census, *Income, Poverty, and Valuation*, xix.

52 *income deficit for . . . people living alone . . . and poor people . . . lived below* half: Ibid.

53 *it is obsolete:* Ruggles, *Drawing the Line*, 39–54.

54 *The Second Harvest study:* VanAmburg Group, 146–48.

54 *top three reasons:* Ibid., 123–26.

55 *in the workforce:* Ibid., 127–41.

55 *Average unemployment rates:* Katherine McFate, "Introduction: Western States in the New World Order," in *Poverty, Inequality and the Future of Social Policy*, ed. Katherine McFate, Roger Lawson, and William Julius Wilson (New York: Russell Sage Foundation, 1995), 3.

56 *images in the press:* See *The Downsizing of America* (New York: Times Books, 1996), 11–18.

56 *"layoffs . . . a durable fixture . . .":* Steve Lohr, "Though Upbeat on the Economy, People Still Fear for Their Jobs," *New York Times*, December 29, 1996.

56 *the proportion of unemployed covered:* Martha Burt, *Over the Edge: The Growth of Homelessness in the 1980s* (New York: Russell Sage Foundation, 1992), 99, 100; and Center on Hunger, Poverty and Nutrition Policy, *Statement on Key Welfare Reform Issues: Empirical Evidence* (Medford, Mass.: Center on Hunger, Poverty and Nutrition Policy, 1995), 17.

58 *long-term unemployment:* VanAmburg Group, *Second Harvest Study*, 134.

58 *"knew nothing . . . interim period.":* Linda Lewis, executive director, Info Line, testifying before the Panetta Committee, April 30, 1983; U.S. Congress, House Subcommittee on Domestic Marketing, Consumer Relations and Nutrition, *Problems of Hunger and Malnutrition*, 98th Cong., 1st sess., serial 98-3, 257.

58 *Of those who lost:* Louis Uchitelle and N. R. Kleinfield, "On the Battlefields of Business, Millions of Casualties," *New York Times*, March 3, 1996, 27.

60 *Real wages . . . dropped: Statement on Key Welfare Reform Issues*, Center on Hunger, Poverty and Nutrition Policy, 14, 15.

60 *the minimum wage has not kept pace:* Burt, *Over the Edge*, 73–75.

60 *". . . federal people":* U.S. Congress, Senate Select Committee on Nutrition and Human Needs, *Hearings*, 90th Cong., 1st sess., part 5B Florida, Appendix, 1835, 1836.

62 *established a benchmark:* Carl P. Chelf, *Controversial Issues in Social Welfare Policy: Government and the Pursuit of Happiness* (Newbury Park, Calif.: Sage Publications, 1992), 59, 60. and Burt, *Over the Edge*, 46–48.

63 *18.1 percent of the clients:* VanAmburg Group, *Second Harvest Study*, 97–99. The figures differed markedly for pantries, kitchens, and

shelters, of course, with the vast majority of shelter clients reporting themselves homeless, while more than three-fifths of kitchen clients and over nine-tenths of pantry clients reported having stable housing. Many pantries, in fact, require proof of domicile before handing out groceries, but the fact that so many people with reliable housing were eating in soup kitchens reinforces what many soup kitchen operators have reported, that the kitchens are becoming a way of life for the house poor as well as the homeless.

64 *The factors that contribute to homelessness:* See, for example, Joel Blau, *The Visible Poor: Homelessness in the United States* (New York: Oxford University Press, 1992); Burt, *Over the Edge*; Kim Hopper and Jill Hamburg, *The Making of America's Homeless: From Skid Row to the New Poor* (New York: Community Service Society, 1984); Christopher Jencks, *The Homeless* (Cambridge: Harvard University Press, 1994); Peter Rossi, *Down and Out in America: The Origins of Homelessness* (Chicago: University of Chicago Press, 1989); and James D. Wright, *Address Unknown: The Tragedy of Homelessness in America.* (New York: Aldine de Gruyter, 1989).

64 *Public assistance is an important source:* VanAmburg Group, *Second Harvest Study*, 136–41. The more than 8,000 clients who were surveyed as part of the Second Harvest study were asked to indicate which of a list of possible income sources had provided income to their household within the previous month. Nearly two-fifths had received payments from AFDC; about a sixth had received income from SSI; more than a fifth had received a Social Security payment; 11.3 percent had received General Assistance, just slightly more than the 10.8 percent who had received help from relatives, and only one in twenty had received unemployment compensation. Asked which of these sources had provided the most income, the top categories were employment (26.1 percent), Social Security (16.5 percent), AFDC (12.0 percent), SSI (8.7 percent), and General Assistance (6.3 percent).

64 *Many states failed:* Burt, *Over the Edge*, 100–105; Center on Budget and Policy Priorities, *General Assistance Programs: Gaps in the Safety Net* (Washington, D.C., Center on Budget and Policy Priorities, 1995), 37–40.

65 *factors associated with homelessness:* Burt, *Over the Edge*, 100–105, 173–78.

65 *benefits . . . have never been ample:* States are permitted to supplement these benefits, and states must supplement them for those covered under the old state-federal programs that SSI replaced in 1974 if the benefits under the old programs were higher than the federal benefit level. The state supplements, however, are not indexed, and inflation has eroded their value. The maximum monthly federal benefit in 1995 was $458 for an individual or $687 for a couple if both are eligible. At the end of 1994, almost 3 million SSI recipients received state supplemental benefits averaging about $110 per month. U.S. General Accounting Office, *Supplemental Security Income: Growth and Changes in Recipient Population Call for Reexamining Program*

(Washington, D.C.: General Accounting Office, July 1995), GAO/HEHS-95-137, 5, 6.

66 *in poor health:* VanAmburg Group, *Second Harvest Study*, 165–71.

67 *AFDC benefit levels had been declining:* Burt, *Over the Edge*, 84, 85.

67 *administrative procedures . . . that deprive:* See Michael Lipsky, "Bureaucratic Disentitlement in Social Welfare Programs," *Social Service Review* 58, no. 1 (March 1984); Physician Task Force on Hunger in America, *Hunger in America: The Growing Epidemic* (Middletown, Conn.: Wesleyan University Press, 1985), 163, 164.

69 *All of these reasons:* These are very similar to what the overall research on Food Stamp non-participation has shown. See Susan Allin, Harold Beebout, Pat Doyle, and Carole Trippe, "Current Perspectives on Food Stamp Participation," in *Food Stamp Policy Issues: Results from Recent Research*, eds. Carole Trippe, Nancy Heisler, and Harold Beebout (Washington, D.C.: United States Department of Agriculture and Mathematics Policy Research, Inc., 1990).

69 *countless opportunities for error:* Physician Task Force, *Hunger in America*, 161–68.

69 *an assets screen:* For this and all other Food Stamp Regulations, see Food Research and Action Center, *FRAC's Guide to the Food Stamp Program*, 9th ed. (Washington, D.C.: Food Research and Action Center, 1994).

72 *paying 60 percent or more:* Burt, *Over the Edge*, 46, 47.

72 *Analysts estimate:* David A. Super, Sharon Parrott, Susan Steinmetz, and Cindy Mann, *The New Welfare Law* (Washington, D.C.: Center on Budget and Policy Priorities, 1996), 17, 18.

73 *the Thrifty Food Plan:* Physician Task Force, *Hunger in America*, 134, 135; Barbara E. Cohen and Martha Burt, *Eliminating Hunger: Food Security Policy for the 1990s* (Washington, D.C.: The Urban Institute, 1989).

73 *The TFP is calculated:* See, for example, Elizabeth G. Crockett, Katherine Clancy, and Jean Bowering, "Comparing the Cost of a Thrifty Food Plan Market Basket in Three Areas of New York State," *Journal of Nutrition Education*, supplement to vol. 24, no. 1 (January/February 1992), 71s–78s.

79 *Researchers at Cornell:* Kathy L. Radimer, Christine M. Olson, Jennifer C. Greene, Cathy C. Campbell, and Jean-Pierre Habicht, "Understanding Hunger and Developing Indicators to Assess It in Women and Children," *Journal of Nutrition Education*, supplement to vol. 24, no. 1 (January/February 1992), 36s–44s.

79 *"Going hungry, hungry . . .":* Ibid., 38s.

79 *the concept of "food security":* See Cohen and Burt, *Eliminating Hunger*, especially 50–53.

79 *"access by all people . . . ways":* Definition developed by the Life Sciences Research Office of the Federation of American Societies for Experimental Biology, quoted in Nancy B. Leidenfrost, "Definitions Concerned

with Food Security," in *Food Security in the United States: A Guidebook for Public Issues Education*, ed. Nancy B. Leidenfrost and Jennifer L. Wilkins (Washington, D.C.: Cooperative Extension System, 1994), 173.

80 *". . . from non-emergency channels."*: Cohen and Burt, *Eliminating Hunger*, 50.

CHAPTER THREE: *The Rise of Emergency Food*

82 *poverty rate:* U.S. Congress, House Committee on Ways and Means, *Overview of Entitlement Programs: the 1990 Green Book* (Washington, D.C.: Government Printing Office, 1990), 1023–25.

82 *Congressional Budget Office estimated:* Physician Task Force on Hunger in America, *Hunger in America: The Growing Epidemic* (Middletown, Conn.: Wesleyan University Press, 1985), 146.

82 *half a million former recipient families* and *"When the General Accounting Office assessed . . .":* Martha Burt, *Over the Edge: The Growth of Homelessness in the 1980s* (New York: Russell Sage Foundation, 1992), 84–86.

83 *The New Poor of the recession:* U.S. General Accounting Office, "Public and Private Efforts to Feed America's Poor," June 23, 1983, 6, 7. Compared to the traditional poor, the GAO study said of those seeking help at emergency food centers, "More of them are members of families, young and able-bodied, and have homes in the suburbs. They now find themselves without work, with unemployment benefits and savings accounts exhausted, and with diminishing hopes of being able to continue to meet their mortgage, automobile and other payments which they committed themselves to when times were better."

83 *A 1983 survey:* Kathryn Porter Bishop, "Soup Lines and Food Baskets: A Survey of Increased Participation in Emergency Food Programs," Center for Budget and Policy Priorities, May 1983, 1.

83 *a sharp increase in the number of programs:* For an account of the outpouring of compassion, and an early caution about the trap represented by emergency food, see Nancy Amidei, "Beyond the Soup Kitchens," *Seeds*, February 1985, 6–11.

83 *"It used to be . . .":* "Churches Form Group to Feed Poor in Bronx," *New York Times*, December 20, 1981.

83 *"As the nation's recession lingers . . .":* Damon Darlin, "America's New Poor Swallow Their Pride, Go to Soup Kitchens," *Wall Street Journal*, January 11, 1983, 1, 20.

84 *"not . . . the creation of Ronald Reagan . . ."* and *"joined the global economy":* Michael Harrington, *The New American Poverty* (New York: Penguin Books, 1984), 7, 8, 9, 10.

85 *"the recognition by a society . . .":* Herbert Blumer, "Social Problems as Collective Behavior," *Social Problems* 18, no. 3 (winter 1971), 302.

85 *"social constructionists"*: See Malcolm Spector and John I. Kitsuse, *Constructing Social Problems* (Hawthorne, N.Y.: Aldine de Gruyter, 1987).

85 *"Claims-makers inevitably characterize . . ."*: Joel Best, ed., *Images of Issues: Typifying Contemporary Social Problems* (Hawthorne, N.Y.: Aldine de Gruyter, 1989), xxi.

86 *an increase in street begging*: See Joel Blau, *The Visible Poor: Homelessness in the United States* (New York: Oxford University Press, 1992), 3–5. See also Mark Stern, "The Emergence of the Homeless as a Public Problem," *Social Service Review*, June 1984, 291–301. Begging continued to be a significant factor shaping the public perception of the problem of homelessness. See, for example, Nancy R. Gibbs, "Begging: To Give or Not to Give" *Time* (cover story), September 5, 1988, 68–74; and Nicholas Dawidoff, "The Business of Begging," *New York Times Magazine*, April 24, 1994, 34–41, 50, 52 (also a cover story).

86 *The same factors*: (causes of homelessness), see notes to page 64, chapter 2.

86 *Partnership for the Homeless*: Blau, *The Visible Poor*, 142. See also editorial, "Hidden resource for the Homeless," *New York Times*, December 22, 1981.

87 *The nutrition cuts*: Physician Task Force, *Hunger in America*, 148.

87 *anti-hunger network*: Bill Keller, "Special Treatment No Longer Given Advocates for the Poor" and "The Poor Lobby: Alliances of Advocates," *Congressional Quarterly Weekly Report*, April 18, 1981, 659–64. See also Editorial Research Reports, "Hunger in America," in *America's Needy: Care and Cutbacks* (Washington, D.C.: Congressional Quarterly, Inc., 1984), 61–80.

87 *The battle lines were drawn*: See Nick Kotz, "The Politics of Hunger," *New Republic*, April 30, 1984. 19–23.

88 *"the Government stores"* and *"America's biggest dairy case"*: "As Big Dairy Surplus Grows, So Do U.S. Wishes to Shed It," *New York Times*, October 4, 1981.

88–89 *"when the new USDA . . ."* and *"So far the Administration . . ."*: James K. Morris, "The Federal Government's Golden Hoard," *Progressive*, October, 1981, 17–18.

89 *". . . turn to waste."*: Ronald Reagan, written statement quoted in "Surplus Cheese Goes to Poor as President Signs Farm Bill," *New York Times*, December 23, 1981.

89 *"Stomping their feet . . ."*: Francis X. Clines, Bernard Weintraub, "Briefing" (Washington Talk), *New York Times*, January 13, 1982.

90 *"As a present . . ."*: "A Mess However It's Sliced" *Time*, January 4, 1982, 63.

90 *cheese distribution had practical consequences*: Michael Lipsky and

Marc A. Thibodeau, "Feeding the Hungry with Surplus Commodities," *Political Science Quarterly* 103, no. 2 (1988), 223–44.

92 *the call for increased voluntary action:* David S. Adams, "Ronald Reagan's Revival: Voluntarism as a Theme in Reagan's Civil Religion," *Sociological Analysis* 48 (spring 1987), 17–29.

92 *"We can be compassionate . . .":* Ronald Reagan, address on spending cuts, text reported in the *New York Times*, September 25, 1981, A28.

94 *leave people hungry:* Elizabeth Wehr, "Congress, Administration Debate Need for More Help to Fight Hunger in America," *Congressional Quarterly Weekly Report*, May 7, 1983, 881–86.

94 *several of the earliest . . . studies:* See lists and summaries of studies in Food Research and Action Center, *Hunger in the Eighties: A Primer* (Washington, D.C.: Food Research and Action Center, 1984), 41–60; and Physician Task Force, *Hunger in America*, 11–24.

94 *"lists three studies . . .":* Marion Nestle and Sally Guttmacher, "Hunger in the United States: Rationale, Methods, and Policy Implications of State Hunger Surveys," *Journal of Nutrition Education* 24, no. 1 (1992): 19s.

94 *all of these studies:* Physician Task Force, *Hunger in America*, Table 1, "Recent Reports Documenting Hunger in America," 13.

95 *"It may seem strange . . .":* Herbert Blumer, "Social Problems," 303.

95 *surveyed its membership:* United States Conference of Mayors, *Human Services in FY82: Shrinking Resources in Troubled Times* (Washington, D.C.: U.S. Conference of Mayors, October 1982), 13, 14.

95 *Several mayors:* Physician Task Force, *Hunger in America*, 13.

97 *". . . didn't eat yesterday"* and *"I don't want anybody to see me . . .":* Johanna Newman, "There's No Famine in America Until the Third Week," second in a series of articles from the Gannett News Service, May 1983, reprinted in Food Research and Action Center, 1984, *Hunger in the Eighties*, 159–62.

97 *". . . it would clear up.":* Emma Williams, quoted in Beverly Stephen, "Fighting Hunger at Home," New York *Daily News*, October 11, 1987.

98 *lack of standards:* See Michael Lipsky and Steven Rathgeb Smith, "When Social Problems are Treated as Emergencies," *Social Service Review*, March 1989, 5–25.

98 *one-time offer:* Lipsky and Thibodeau, "Feeding the Hungry," 225; and Ardith L. Maney, *Still Hungry After All These Years: Food Assistance Policy from Kennedy to Reagan* (Westport, Conn.: Greenwood Press, 1989), 140–43.

98 *virtually no rules:* See Lipsky and Thibodeau, "Feeding the Hungry," for a detailed account of the evolution of standards in the SDDP and its successor, TEFAP.

99 *"The cheese and dairy distribution program . . .":* statement of Barbara Baker Temple, in U.S. Congress, House Subcommittee on Domestic

Marketing, Consumer Relations and Nutrition, *Emergency Food Assistance and Commodity Distribution Act of 1983*, 98th Cong., 1st sess., March 22, 1983, serial 98–4, 63–67.

100 *"You can only go to the well . . ."*: Statement of La Verne Ausman. Ibid., 36–39.

101 *the commercial cheese industry*: Lipsky and Thibodeau, "Feeding the Hungry," 228, 229; and Maney, *Still Hungry*, 141; Elizabeth Wehr, "Food Need Weighed Against Tales of Abuse," *Congressional Quarterly Weekly Report*, July 23, 1983, 1513.

101 *"national scandal"* and *". . . while Americans starve."* Harrison J. Goldin, comptroller, The City of New York, to Lee E. Stambaugh, president, National Association of State Agencies for Food Distribution, March 16, 1983. Letter submitted with testimony by Mr. Stambaugh before the Subcommittee on Domestic Marketing, Consumer Relations and Nutrition, March 22, 1983, ibid., 48.

101 *". . . a stigma associated with accepting any kind of a handout. . . ."*: statement of Walter J. Hoag, and *"any distribution of commodities should be temporary . . ."*: statement of Edmund V. Worley (Cleveland, February 28, 1983), in U.S. Congress, House Subcommittee on Domestic Marketing, Consumer Relations, and Nutrition, *Problems of Hunger and Malnutrition*, 98th Cong., 1st sess., 1983 serial 98-3, 60, 61.

102 *limited in both scope and duration*: Lipsky and Thibodeau, *"Feeding the Hungry,"* 227–29.

102 *". . . not trying to create a new entitlement . . ."* in U.S. Congress, Senate Subcommittee on Nutrition, *Oversight of Nutritional Status of Low-Income Americans in the 1980s*, 98th Cong., 1st sess., April 6, 1983, serial 98-274, 5.

102–103 *six bills . . . under consideration* and *"increase the amount . . ."*: Eric Boyd, "Resource Recovery: The Foodbank Movement," *Environment* 25, no. 7 (September 1983), 4. See also Maney, *Still Hungry*, and Lipsky and Thibodeau, "Feeding the Hungry."

103 *fostered the creation of local organizational structures*: National Alliance to End Homelessness, *Checklist for Success: Programs to Help the Hungry and Homeless* (Alexandria, Va.: Emergency Food and Shelter National Board, 1990), 2–4.

104 *a change of heart*: Maney, *Still Hungry*, 143.

104 *a "no-holds-barred" investigation*: *New York Times*, August 3, 1983.

104 *remarks to wire service reporters*: Elizabeth Wehr, "Hill, White House Settle One Food Dispute," *Congressional Quarterly Weekly Report*, December 24, 1983, 2742.

104 *". . . long soup lines"*: "Banquets and Breadlines," *New Republic*, January 9 and 16, 1984, 7, 8.

104 *alarmed and angered advocates*: Elizabeth Wehr, "Report of Task

Force Draws Mixed Reaction From the Hill," *Congressional Quarterly Weekly Report*, January 14, 1984, 51, 52.

105 "*... no official 'hunger count' ...*": Report of the President's Task Force on Food Assistance, January 1984, excerpted in *World Hunger and Social Justice*, ed. Gary E. McCuen, Ideas in Conflict series (Hudson, Wisc.: GEM publications), 158–64.

105 "*... unattainable scientific precision ...*" Edward M. Kennedy, Statement to the Joint Congressional Oversight Committee Hearings on the President's Task Force on Food Assistance, January 26, 1984, excerpted in McCuen, ed., *World Hunger*, 165–71.

CHAPTER FOUR: *Institutionalization: From Shoestring to Stability*

117 *half of all food used:* VanAmburg Group Inc., *Second Harvest 1993 National Research Study* (Chicago: Second Harvest National Food Bank Network, 1994), 50–57.

121 *more than a billion pounds:* Food Research and Action Center: "Appropriations Update: Immediate Action Needed," May 1994. See also J. William Levedahl, Nicole Ballenger, and Courtney Harold, *Comparing the Emergency Food Assistance Program and the Food Stamp Program*, U.S. Department of Agriculture, Economic Research Service, Agricultural Economic Report no. 698, June 1994, 1–3.

121 *helped to stabilize:* Eric Boyd, "Resource Recovery: The Foodbank Movement," *Environment* 25, no. 7 (September 1983), 4; Jeffrey L. Katz, "Food Program Faces Fight for Its Own Sustenance," *Congressional Quarterly Weekly Report*, November 5, 1994.

122 *state, and local governments together provided:* VanAmburg Group, *Second Harvest Study*, 59–64. Overall, the Second Harvest study found that state governments provide 30.3 percent of income for food programs and all governmental units combined provide 55.3 percent of funding, but these high total averages were influenced by the inclusion of shelters and "other food programs," including drug rehabilitation programs, day care, and senior centers, which tend to have high levels of state and local funding. The averages cited in the text are calculated from tables showing the sources of income for each type of program.

122 *half of the twenty-seven cities surveyed:* United States Conference of Mayors, *A Status Report on Hunger and Homelessness in America's Cities: 1989. A 27 City Survey* (Washington, D.C.: U.S. Conference of Mayors, December 1989), 17.

122 *fourteen different programs:* Office of Food Programs and Policy Coordination, N.Y.C. Human Resources Administration, *A Guide to Resources for Emergency Food Providers* (New York City: Human Resources Administration, rev. ed., 1994).

123 *encouraged the creation of pantries:* Control Systems Research, *EFMS Sampler: A Description of Some Emergency Food and Medical Services Projects* (Washington, D.C.: Emergency Food and Medical Services, Office of Health Affairs, Office of Economic Opportunity, April 1971). See especially pages 4 and 15.

125 *funded Second Harvest:* Community Services Administration, "Background Sheet on Second Harvest," Community Services Administration, Records Relating to Grants, Record Group 381, National Archives and Records Service.

125 *first national donor:* "Foodbanking: A Brief History," *The Clearinghouse*, 1992 update (Phoenix, Ariz.: St. Mary's Food Bank, 1992), 2, 3.

125 *fifteen million pounds:* "A Second Harvest Milestone," *Second Harvest Update*, winter 1994, 4.

125 *285.7 million pounds:* "Meeting the Need," *Second Harvest Update*, summer 1996, 4.

126 *". . . close to maturity . . .":* Lynda V. E. Crawford, "Food Banking: Who Benefits?" *Seeds* 11, no. 12 (January/February, 1989), 14.

126 *Grocery Manufacturers Association:* Ibid. See also "Supermarket Support Triples," *Second Harvest Update*, winter 1994, 7.

127 *innovations such as value-added processing:* See various issues of *Second Harvest Update*, especially "A Look Back at VAP," winter 1994; "Field of Dreams," "A Sweet Deal," and "Home-Style Meals," fall 1995; "Going Fishing," winter 1995; and "Creating a New Life for Unsaleables," summer 1997.

130 *legitimacy:* see Herbert Blumer, "Social Problems as Collective Behavior," *Social Problems* 18, no. 3 (winter 1971), 302–3.

133 *"The sharpest spurs . . .":* Michael Moss, "The Poverty Story," *Columbia Journalism Review*, July/August 1987, 46.

133 *The first to report:* Physician Task Force on Hunger in America, *Hunger in America: The Growing Epidemic* (Middletown, Conn.: Wesleyan University Press, 1985).

134 *a thousand print news reports:* Moss, "The Poverty Story," 46, 47.

134 *Community Childhood Hunger Identification Project:* Cheryl A. Wehler, Richard Ira Scott, and Jennifer J. Anderson, "The Community Childhood Hunger Identification Project: A Model of Domestic Hunger—Demonstration Project in Seattle, Washington," *Journal of Nutrition Education*, supplement to vol. 24, no. 1 (January/February 1992), 29s–35s.

135 *create national projections:* The effort to find a credible method to create the sort of "national hunger count" of which the President's Task Force had noted the absence continued throughout the 1980s and into the 1990s, with researchers in academic, advocacy, government, and for-profit settings all struggling with the task. In January 1994 a "Food Security Measurement and Research Conference" was convened jointly by the Food and Consumer

Service of the United States Department of Agriculture and the National Center for Health Statistics of the Centers for Disease Control and Prevention. Building on the previous work of the nearly one hundred professionals in attendance, the conference took major steps in the direction of a consensus on what should be measured, and how. The result was a food security questionnaire that, after field testing and further revision, was administered by the Census Bureau as a supplement to the regular April 1995 Current Population Survey. For the time being, at least, a "national hunger count" with wide credibility does exist. See William L. Hamilton and others, *Household Food Security in the United States in 1995*, Summary Report of the Food Security Measurement Project (Washington, D.C.: Office of Analysis and Evaluation, Food and Consumer Service, United States Department of Agriculture, September 1997), 1–65, for a brief history of the development of the instrument and the results of its first major use.

135 *"Harry always believed . . .":* quoted in Joe Morgenstern, "The Inside Story: Planning the Greatest Participatory Event in History," *The Official Record Book, Hands Across America* (New York: Pocket Books, Hands Across America, 1986), 2.

136 *". . . he was invited":* Ibid., 26.

137 *"Hands certainly succeeded . . .":* Ibid., 25.

138 *made a virtual "civil religion":* David S. Adams, "Ronald Reagan's Revival: Voluntarism as a Theme in Reagan's Civil Religion," *Sociological Analysis* 48, spring 1987, 17–29. Quotes from Reagan are taken from this source.

138 *federally sponsored volunteer programs:* Susan M. Chambre, "Kindling Points of Light: Volunteering as Public Policy," *Nonprofit and Voluntary Sector Quarterly* 18, no. 5 (fall 1989), 249–68.

139 *A Points of Light Initiative: The Points of Light Movement: The President's Report to the Nation* (Washington, D.C., Government Printing Office, 1993).

CHAPTER FIVE: *The Uses of Emergency Food*

141 *Congress finally changed:* Jeffrey L. Katz, "Food Program Faces Fight for Its Own Sustenance," *Congressional Quarterly Weekly Report*, November 5, 1994, 4.

141 *". . . continue it forever . . .":* U.S. Congress, Senate Subcommittee on Nutrition, *Oversight of Nutritional Status of Low-Income Americans in the 1980s*, 98th Cong., 1st sess., April 6, 1983, serial 98-274, 5.

143 *slaughter generates outrage . . . "I'll take a whole pig . . ." "Why, oh why . . .":* For a more detailed account, see Janet Poppendieck, *Breadlines Knee Deep in Wheat: Food Assistance in the Great Depression* (New Brunswick, N.J.: Rutgers University Press, 1986), especially chapter 7, pages 108–28.

143 *threaten dire consequences:* see Poppendieck, *Breadlines Knee Deep*, 116–17.

143 *public relations nightmare:* Ibid., 113–14.

144 *"Swift Roosevelt Blows . . .":* Turner Catledge, "Swift Roosevelt Blows Deal with Discontent," *New York Times,* September 24, 1933.

144 *. . . relieve our minds . . . :* "Plenty and Want," *New York Times,* September 23, 1933.

144 *". . . go to the unemployed.":* Henry Wallace, *New Frontiers* (New York: Reynal and Hitchcock, 1934), 183.

145 *"take the curse off":* Kathleen McLaughlin, "Mrs. Roosevelt Goes Her Way," *New York Times Magazine,* July 5, 1936.

145 *". . . a mighty fine thing.":* Roy Anthon, Underwood Fruit and Warehouse Company to the Federal Surplus Relief Corporation [FSRC], October 8, 1935, FSRC Files, Record Group 124 (Records of the Surplus Marketing Administration).

146 *". . . an accepted outlet . . .":* Jonathan Garst to Henry Wallace, January 29, 1935, Secretary of Agriculture's Files, Record Group 16, NARS.

146 *". . . physical destruction of any surplus . . ."* and *". . . dribbles . . . and gluts . . .":* Food Survey Committee, "Preliminary draft of a report of Department of Agriculture to the national Emergency Council," March 1935, AAA Legal Division Files, Record Group 16, NARS.

146 *"to something which includes the word 'commodities' . . .":* FSRC Memorandum of a Meeting of the Board of Directors, October 24, 1935, Harry Hopkins Papers, Franklin D. Roosevelt National Library, Hyde Park, New York.

147 *When surpluses mounted:* for a summary of the subsequent history of surplus commodity distribution, see Poppendieck, *Breadlines Knee Deep*, 204–55.

148 *". . . action on the stockpile . . .":* "Surplus Cheese Goes to Poor as President Signs the Farm Bill," *New York Times,* December 23, 1981.

149 *Dairy Herd Buyout:* "Beef Glut," *Time,* April 28, 1986.

149 *end in April.:* Testimony of John W. Bode, assistant secretary for Food and Consumer Services, U.S. Department of Agriculture before the Subcommittee on Domestic Marketing, Consumer Relations and Nutrition, House Committee on Agriculture and the Domestic Task Force of the House Select Committee on Hunger, February 24, 1988 (typescript supplied by USDA).

150 *less money for commodities:* Katz, "Food Program Faces Fight."

151 *". . . sport of hunting.":* Hunters for the Hungry, Virginians Helping Virginians, "Take Aim Against Hunger" organizational brochure distributed by the Society of Saint Andrew. Similar organizations exist in many other states.

151 *". . . store the stuff.":* George F. Will, "Why Not Use Food as Food?" Op-Ed, *Washington Post,* September 25, 1983.

153 *". . . as true volunteers."*: Carol Taylor, "A Place at the Table," *Mother Earth News*, November/December 1989, 61.

155 *". . . barriers to participation,"*: J. William Levedahl, Nicole Ballenger, and Courtney Harold, *Comparing the Emergency Food Assistance Program and the Food Stamp Program*, U.S. Department of Agriculture, Economic Research Service, Agricultural Economic Report no. 698, June 1994, 3, 4.

156 *establish their eligibility:* Katherine Clancy, Jean Bowering, and Janet Poppendieck, "Audit and Evaluation of Food Program Use: Report of a Random Survey in New York State," submitted to the Bureau of Nutrition of the New York State Department of Health, March 1989.

157 *error rate standards:* Physician Task Force on Hunger in America, *Hunger in America: The Growing Epidemic* (Middletown, Conn.: Wesleyan University Press, 1984), 168–70. See also pages 159–68 for a compelling discussion of bureaucratic intimidation, procedural denials, and the creation of an adversarial climate in food stamp administration.

157 *more willing to risk a wrongful denial:* New York City Interfaith Hunger Policy Task Force, "1987–88 Public Policy Agenda" (New York: Interfaith Hunger Policy Task Force, n.d.).

158 *a greater role:* David S. Adams, "Ronald Reagan's Revival: Voluntarism as a Theme in Reagan's Civil Religion," *Sociological Analysis* 48 (spring 1987): 19–23.

161 *"All companies agreed . . ."* and *"the tax benefits . . ."*: "Second Harvest Report on Donor Interviews," May 1994, 2 and 3; typescript supplied by Second Harvest.

161 *an incentive for donation:* Eric Boyd, "Resource Recovery: The Foodbank Movement," *Environment* 24, no. 7 (September 1983), 3; also Second Harvest, *The Benefits of Donating* (Chicago: Second Harvest, 1987).

164 *In a random survey:* Leo J. Shapiro and Associates, "Second Harvest, Benchmark Survey of the Public, Summary of Key Findings," revised June 8, 1994, 20; typescript supplied by Second Harvest.

167 *"What these groups are experiencing . . ."*: Liz Spayd, "Food Banks Are Going Hungry," *Washington Post*, April 17, 1994.

169 *". . . a lot more running around"*: *Chronicle of Philanthropy*, December 2, 1989.

169 *". . . a lot of local hustle . . ."*: Ibid., 195.

171 *a good source of high-protein foods:* "A Drive for Nutrition," *Second Harvest Update*, spring 1995, 8.

171 *"enough food to feed . . ."*: Conference announcement, distributed by USDA.

172 *"relieve our minds . . . :* "Plenty and Want," *New York Times*, September 23, 1933.

CHAPTER SIX: *The Seductions of Charity*

178 *". . . That COSMOPOLITAN GIRL":* Ad from the *New York Times*, reprinted in Freda Garmaise, "Oh *That* Cosmo Girl . . . ," *The Village Voice*, May 3, 1989, 42.

191 *"If you pour . . .":* Isaiah, chapter 58, verses 10 and 11, Revised Standard Version.

191 *other major text:* Leviticus, chapter 19, verses 9 and 10.

192 *"Give food to the hungry . . .":* One Hundred Graces, selected by Marcia and Jack Kelly with calligraphy by Christopher Gausby (New York: Bell Tower, 1992), 42.

200 *". . . meaning in our individual lives . . .":* Hillary Clinton, quoted in "37 Million Poor Americans—If They Don't Know Their Place, They're Learning It," *The Washington Spectator* 20, no. 10 (May 15, 1994).

CHAPTER SEVEN: *What's Wrong with Emergency Food?*

201 *". . . donated and reduced-cost items . . .":* "Questions Frequently Asked About Operation Blessing/Hunger Strike Force Convoy '94" and "Operation Blessing's 'Hunger Strike Force Convoy '94' to Fight Hunger Coast-To-Coast," news releases provided in press kit supplied by Operation Blessing, Virginia Beach, Virginia.

211 *more than a third:* Nutrition Surveillance Program, Division of Nutrition, New York State Department of Health, "Fact Sheet: 1992 Census of Emergency Food Relief Organizations in New York State," 3.

212 *family of four:* See, for example, a list recommended by a nutritionist, a food pantry director, and an agricultural extension agent to pantries in Knoxville, Tennessee, and reproduced in a guide to starting a food pantry:

dry orange drink mix, 8.8 oz.	pork and beans (2 cans), 16 oz.
dry milk, 5 qts.	mixed greens, 15 oz.
cream of wheat, 14 oz.	spaghetti with meat sauce (2 cans), 16 oz.
tomato soup (2 cans), 10 oz.	
chicken noodle soup (2 cans), 10 oz.	applesauce (3 cans), 16 oz.
vegetable soup (2 cans), 10 oz.	fruit cocktail, 16 oz.
peanut butter, 18 oz.	peaches, 16 oz.
saltines, 1 lb.	corn bread mix, 8 oz.
macaroni dinner, 7 oz.	tuna, 12 oz.
cut green beans (2 cans), 16 oz.	

Gail Olsen, "Start a Food Pantry," *Seeds Magazine's Hunger Action Handbook*, ed. Leslie Withers and Tom Peterson (Decatur, Ga.: Seeds Magazine, 1987), 33, 34.

213 *". . . standing here for some cheese,"*: Francis X. Clines and Bernard Weintraub, "Briefing" (Washington Talk), *New York Times*, January 13, 1982.

215 *soup kitchen meals in the state of New York*: Gayle Kelly, Barbara S. Rauschenbach, and Cathy C. Campbell, *Private Food Assistance in New York State: Challenges for the 1990's* (Ithaca: Cornell University, 1989), 21.

215 *A national study*: Martha Burt and Barbara Cohen, *Feeding the Homeless: Does the Prepared Meals Provision Help? A Report to Congress on the Prepared Meals Provision* (Washington, D.C.: Urban Institute, 1988).

216 *only meal of the day*: Legal Action Center for the Homeless and New York University Metropolitan Studies Program, "Below the Safety Net: A Study of Soup Kitchen Users in New York City" (New York: Legal Action Center for the Homeless [now the Urban Justice Center]: 1987).

218 *"Only a small fraction . . ."*: Food and Hunger Hotline, *Thirty Million Meals a Year: Emergency Food Programs in New York City* (New York: Food and Hunger Hotline, 1995), 17.

218 *contributed by volunteers*: Ibid., 17.

218–19 *a paid staff person*: Kelly, Rauschenbach, and Campbell, *Private Food Assistance*, 21.

219 *"Reliance on volunteer labor . . ."*: Food and Hunger Hotline, *Thirty Million Meals*, 18.

220 *". . . misleading and dangerous . . ."*: Kelly, Rauschenbach, and Campbell, *Private Food Assistance*, 22.

220 *1992 Census of Emergency Food*: Nutrition Surveillance Program, "Fact Sheet: 1992 Census," 2.

220 *programs were "threatened."*: VanAmburg Group Inc., *Second Harvest 1993 National Research Study* (Chicago: Second Harvest National Food Bank Network, 1994), 73, 74.

221 *"a wide disparity . . ."*: Edmund V. Worley, *Report on the Conclusion and Recommendations of the Planning Study of the Emergency Food System in Cuyahoga County, Ohio* (Cleveland: The Greater Cleveland Committee on Hunger, December 1992), 3, 34–36.

221 *two wealthiest city council districts*: Food For Survival, *Who Feeds the Hungry? Mapping New York City's Emergency Food Providers* (New York: Food For Survival, 1995), 35, 36.

222 *". . . large differences in access . . ."*: Beth Osborne Daponte, Gordon Lewis, Seth Sanders, and Lowell Taylor, *Food Pantries and Food Pantry Use in Allegheny County* (Pittsburgh: H. John Heinz III School of Public Policy and Management, Carnegie-Mellon University, 1994), 4.

222 *"Poor whites and poor blacks . . ."*: Ibid., 3.

222 *". . . transportation difficulties. . . ."*: U.S. Congress, House Subcommittee on Domestic Marketing, Consumer Relations, and Nutrition, *Hunger in Rural America*, 101st Cong., 1st sess., May 17, 1989, serial 101–15, 38.

224 *". . . most in need of a food bank . . ."*: "Obstacles to Domestic Food

Security: The Ambiguous Role of Food Banks in Supplementing Government Programs," paper presented at the 1991 annual meetings of the Association for the Study of Food and Society, Tucson, Arizona, June 14, 1991, 9, 10.

224 *". . . misperceive the ability of voluntary organizations . . .":* Ibid., 10, 11.

228 *measures for evaluating social programs.:* Winifred Bell, *Contemporary Social Welfare,* 2d ed. (New York: Macmillan, 1987), 166, 167. See also, David Gil, *Unravelling Social Policy* (Cambridge, Mass.: Schenkman Publishing Co.,), *passim.*

CHAPTER EIGHT: *Charity and Dignity*

232 *". . . more charity food'":* Betty Smith, *A Tree Grows in Brooklyn* (New York: Harper Perennial, 1943, 1968), 267.

232 *". . . it wounds.":* Mary Douglas, "Introduction," in Marcel Mauss, *The Gift: the Form and Reason for Exchange in Archaic Societies,* translated by W. D. Halls, Foreword by Mary Douglas (New York: W. W. Norton, 1990), p. vii.

234 *"Welcome to Angels House! . . .":* quoted in David A. Snow and Leon Anderson, *Down on Their Luck: A Study of Homeless Street People* (Berkeley: University of California Press, 1993), 85.

235 *". . . easier than paying for it.":* quoted in "Banquets and Breadlines," *New Republic,* January 9 and 16, 1984, 7, 8.

236 *Will you serve . . . :* Susan McCarter, "Start a Soup Kitchen," in *Seeds Magazine's Hunger Action Handbook,* ed. Leslie Withers and Tom Peterson (Decatur, Ga.: Seeds Magazine, 1987), 38.

238 *". . . searching for handouts.":* Gail Olsen, "Start a Food Pantry," ibid., 31.

240 *"It is an indignity . . .":* Willard Gaylin, "In the Beginning: Helpless and Dependent," in Willard Gaylin, Ira Glasser, Steven Marcus, and David Rothman, *Doing Good: The Limits of Benevolence* (New York: Pantheon Books, 1981), 30.

243 *"'. . . that far down.'":* Kathy Radimer, "Understanding Hunger and Developing Indicators to Assess It" (Ph.D. diss., Cornell University, 1990), 364.

244 *". . . a meal of his soup . . ."* and *"Soyer's new model soup kitchen . . .":* Cecil Woodham-Smith, *The Great Hunger: Ireland 1845–1849* (New York: Signet Books, 1964), 174.

245 *"the popular image . . .":* Irene Glasser, *More Than Bread: Ethnography of a Soup Kitchen* (Tuscaloosa: University of Alabama Press, 1988), 14.

247 *"The atmosphere is sedate . . .":* Linda Ashman, Jaime de la Vega, Marc Dohan, Andy Fisher, Rosa Hippler, and Billi Romain, *Seeds of Change:*

Strategies for Food Security for the Inner City (Los Angeles: Southern California Interfaith Hunger Coalition, 1993), 29.

247 *". . . like a human being.":* Don Terry, "Cafe Plies Homeless with Hope," *New York Times*, September 6, 1993.

248 *"Eat it and beat it.":* Carol Cohen, "Multiple Case Study: Soup Kitchens," 11; paper prepared in the doctoral program of the Hunter College School of Social Work; typescript provided by Dr. Cohen.

250 *". . . being Mr. Kind!":* Robert Coles (text) and Jon Erikson (photographs), *A Spectacle Unto the World: The Catholic Worker Movement* (New York: Viking Press, 1973), 48.

251 *dishonor, guilt, and shame.:* Richard Titmuss, *The Gift Relationship: From Human Blood to Social Policy* (New York: Pantheon Books, 1971), 72.

251 *charity "wounds":* Mary Douglas, in Mauss, *The Gift*, vii.

255 *". . . the charitable relation . . .":* Jane Addams, *Democracy and Social Ethics*, ed. and with an Introduction by Anne Firor Scott, The John Harvard Library (Cambridge, Mass.: The Belknap Press of Harvard University Press, 1964), 13, 14.

CHAPTER NINE: *The Ultimate Band-Aid*

263 *Reinvesting in America program:* Robin Garr, *Reinvesting in America: The Grassroots Movements That Are Feeding the Hungry, Housing the Homeless, and Putting Americans Back to Work* (Reading, Mass.: Addison-Wesley, 1995).

269–70 *". . . brand name protection"* and *". . . to end poverty."* and *". . . solution to hunger.":* Lynda V. E. Crawford, "Food Banking: Who Benefits?" *Seeds* 11, no. 12 (January/February, 1989), 13, 14.

270–71 *"agencies work daily . . ."* and *". . . service to citizenship.":* Bread for the World Institute, *Hunger 1994: Transforming the Politics of Hunger*, Fourth Annual Report on the State of World Hunger (Silver Spring, Md.: Bread for the World Institute, 1993), 16, 17.

271 *". . . advocacy as a program activity."* and *". . . this type of activity.":* Ibid., 17.

279–80 *integrate poor people into systems:* see Laura DeLind, "Celebrating Hunger in Michigan: A Critique of an Emergency Food Program and an Alternative for the Future," *Agriculture and Human Values* 11, no. 4 (Fall 1994).

280 *a press conference:* Press packet with press releases provided by the Food Research and Action Center.

281 *capacity and obligation:* For an excellent overview of this issue, see Julian Wolpert, *What Charity Can and Cannot Do* (New York: The Twentieth Century Fund, 1996).

284 *". . . safety net under the safety net.":* Peter Edelman, "The Worst Thing Bill Clinton Has Done," *Atlantic Monthly*, March 1997, 48.

284 *advice to providers:* "So many of God's children," in *News & Views*, A Hunger Action Coalition Publication for the Emergency Food Providers Network, January/February 1997. Distributed as an insert in *Breadlines* 17, no. 1 (January/February, 1997).

Conclusion

297 *". . . drop on our doorsteps."*: Heywood Hale Broun, "Brutes or Fools!" from an editorial in the *New York World* reprinted in Eleanor Flexnor, "Yes, There Is Starvation in New York City," *Better Times*, April 11, 1932, 4.

298 *$.65 per person:* Janet Poppendieck, *Breadlines Knee Deep in Wheat: Food Assistance in the Great Depression* (New Brunswick, N.J.: Rutgers University Press, 1986), 146, 147.

300 *". . . including the poor."*: New York City Coalition Against Hunger, "Interfaith Voices Against Hunger Wins Major Budget Victory," *NYCCAH Newsletter*, July 1994.

301 *school food service workers:* If we had more school aides and cafeteria workers, paid at a decent rate—if, for example, we were finally to follow in the footsteps of many of our European trading partners and institute universal free school meals, we would have fewer people in the pantry lines—and we would need less EFAP. Clearly, however, this is not the direction in which public policy is evolving. As we back away from entitlements and publicly funded social services, we are also backing away from the forms of employment that have been most available to poorly educated women, the group that is overrepresented in the pantry lines, and the group that the PRWORA wants to force off public assistance and into the workforce.

305 *A mother:* "One woman cut herself back to a meal a day to buy her son a pair of $50 sneakers," Jason DeParle reported in an article that featured the work of sociologist Katherine Edin. Jason DeParle, "Learning Poverty Firsthand," *New York Times Magazine*, April 27, 1997, 34.

305 *rich are richer:* "Income Disparity Between Poorest and Richest Rises," *New York Times*, January 20, 1996.

305 *sixty-year high:* Edward N. Wolff, *Top Heavy: A Study of the Increasing Inequality of Wealth in America,* A Twentieth Century Fund/Century Foundation Report (New York: Twentieth Century Fund Press, 1995), 13.

305 *90–10 ratio:* Office of the Chief Economist, U.S. Department of Labor, "The Unfinished Agenda, Technical Appendix" January 9, 1997. Technical appendix to accompany Robert B. Reich, "The Unfinished Agenda" address to the Council on Excellence in Government, January 9, 1997, 1, 13.

306 *"Growing Together"* and *"Growing Apart."*: Ibid., 3, 4.

308 *"Close Down . . ."*: Theresa Funicello, "Close Down the Soup Kitchens," New York *Daily News*, December 3, 1989.

309 *". . . eat every day!":* Harry Hopkins, quoted in Edward Robb Ellis, *A Nation in Torment: The Great American Depression, 1929–1939* (New York: Capricorn Books, 1971), 506.

311 *"The feeding movement . . .":* Bread for the World Institute, *Hunger 1994: Transforming the Politics of Hunger,* Fourth Annual Report on the State of World Hunger (Silver Spring, Md.: Bread for the World Institute, 1993), 19.

311 *basic anti-hunger agenda.:* See, for example, the Medford Declaration to End Hunger in the United States, which most of the major national anti-hunger organizations signed in 1990. The Declaration is available from the Center on Hunger, Poverty, and Nutrition Policy at Tufts University, Medford, Massachusetts.

317 *". . . struggling for change.":* Sara M. Evans and Harry C. Boyte, *Free Spaces: The Sources of Democratic Change in America* (New York: Harper & Row, 1986), 17, 18.

317 *Imagine that we opened . . . :* This is a lively fantasy that I have cherished for many years, one that has been enriched by the imagination of others, especially the staff and board of directors of the Community Food Resource Center in New York City. It was prompted, originally, by Kathy Goldman's vision of the project that grew into the Community Kitchen of West Harlem, and it is an image that is at least partially realized by the intergenerational project and the Senior Dinner Program directed by CFRC staff member Pat Caldwell at the Harriet Tubman Elementary School in Harlem.

Selected Bibliography

Abramovitz, Mimi. *Under Attack, Fighting Back: Women and Welfare Reform.* New York: Monthly Review Press, 1996.

Amidei, Nancy. "Beyond the Soup Kitchens." *Seeds.* February 1985.

Bently, Amy. "Uneasy Sacrifice: The Politics of United States Famine Relief, 1945–48." *Agriculture and Human Values* 11, no. 4 (1994).

Blau, Joel. *The Visible Poor: Homelessness in the United States.* New York: Oxford University Press, 1992.

Blumer, Herbert. "Social Problems as Collective Action." *Social Problems* 18, no. 3 (1971).

Bread for the World Institute. *Hunger 1994: Transforming the Politics of Hunger.* Fourth Annual Report on the State of World Hunger. Silver Spring, Md.: Bread for the World Institute, 1993.

Breglio, Vincent. *Hunger in America: The Voters' Perspective.* Lanham, Md.: Research/Strategy/Management Inc., 1992.

Burt, Martha. *Over the Edge: The Growth of Homelessness in the 1980s.* New York: The Russell Sage Foundation, 1992.

Chambre, Susan M. "Kindling Points of Light: Volunteering as Public Policy." *Nonprofit and Voluntary Sector Quarterly* 18, no. 5 (1989).

Chelf, Carl P. *Controversial Issues in Social Welfare Policy: Government and the Pursuit of Happiness.* Newbury Park, Calif.: Sage Publications, 1992.

Citizens Board of Inquiry into Hunger and Malnutrition in the U.S. *Hunger U.S.A.* Washington, D.C.: New Community Press, 1968.

Clancy, Katherine, and Jean Bowering. "The Need for Emergency Food: Poverty Problems and Policy Responses." *Journal of Nutrition Education* 24, no. 1 (1992).

Cohen, Barbara, and Martha Burt. *Eliminating Hunger: Food Security Policy for the 1990's.* Washington, D.C.: The Urban Institute, 1989.

Coles, Robert. *The Call of Service: A Witness to Idealism*. Boston: Houghton Mifflin, 1993.

Curtis, Karen A. "Combatting Hunger in Delaware." Paper delivered at meetings of the American Anthropological Association, December 1992.

Daponte, Beth Osborne, et al. *Food Pantries and Food Pantry Use in Allegheny County*. Pittsburgh: H. John Heinz III School of Public Policy and Management, Carnegie Mellon University, 1994.

DeLind, "Celebrating Hunger in Michigan: A Critique of an Emergency Food Program and an Alternative for the Future." *Agriculture and Human Values* 11, no. 4 (1994).

Edelman, Peter. "The Worst Thing Bill Clinton Has Done," *Atlantic Monthly*. March 1997.

Field Foundation. *Hunger in America: The Federal Response. 2nd Report of the Physicians Task Force on Hunger*. San Francisco: Greenhaven, 1977.

Food and Hunger Hotline. *Thirty Million Meals a Year: Emergency Food Programs in New York City*. New York: Food and Hunger Hotline, 1995.

Food For Survival. *Who Feeds the Hungry? Mapping New York City's Emergency Food Providers*. New York: Food For Survival, Inc., 1995.

Food Research and Action Center. *Hunger in the Eighties: A Primer*. Washington, D.C.: Food Research and Action Center, 1984.

Gans, Herbert. "Positive Functions of the Undeserving Poor: Uses of the Underclass in America." *Politics and Society* 22, no. 3 (1994).

Garr, Robin. *Reinvesting in America: The Grassroots Movements That Are Feeding the Hungry, Housing the Homeless, and Putting Americans Back to Work*. Reading, Mass.: Addison-Wesley, 1995.

Gaylin, Willard, Ira Glasser, Steven Marcus, and David J. Rothman. *Doing Good: The Limits of Benevolence*. New York: Pantheon Books, 1978.

Glasser, Irene. *More Than Bread: The Ethnography of a Soup Kitchen*. Tuscaloosa, Ala.: University of Alabama Press, 1988.

Harrington, Michael. *The New American Poverty*. New York: Penguin Books, 1985.

Kelly, Gayle, Barbara Rauschenbach, and Cathy Campbell. *Private Food Assistance in New York State: Challenges for the 1990's*. Ithaca, N.Y.: Division of Nutritional Sciences, Cornell University, 1989.

Kotz, Nick. *Let Them Eat Promises: The Politics of Hunger in America*. Englewood Cliffs, N.J.: Prentice-Hall, 1969.

———. "The Politics of Hunger." *New Republic*. April 30, 1984.

Lipsky, Michael, and Marc Thibodeau. "Feeding the Hungry with Surplus Commodities." *Political Science Quarterly* 103, no. 2 (1988).

Lipsky, Michael, and Steven Smith. "When Social Problems Are Treated as Emergencies." *The Social Service Review* 63, no. 1 (1989).

Maney, Ardith L. *Still Hungry After All These Years: Food Assistance Policy from Kennedy to Reagan*. Westport, Conn.: Greenwood Press, 1989.

Marcuse, Peter. "Neutralizing Homelessness." *Socialist Review* 18, no. 1 (1988).

Nestle, Marion, and Sally Guttmacher. "Hunger in the United States: Rationale, Methods, and Policy Implications of State Hunger Surveys." *Journal of Nutrition Education* 24, no. 1 (1992).

Physicians Task Force on Hunger in America. *Hunger in America: The Growing Epidemic*. Middletown, Conn.: Wesleyan University Press, 1985.

Poppendieck, Janet E. *Breadlines Knee Deep in Wheat: Food Assistance in the Great Depression*. New Brunswick, N.J.: Rutgers University Press, 1986.

———. "Policy, Advocacy, and Justice: The Case of Food Assistance Reform." In David Gil and Eva Gil, eds., *Toward Social and Economic Justice*. Cambridge, Mass.: Schenkman Publishing, 1985.

Radimer, Kathy L. "Understanding Hunger and Developing Indicators to Assess It." Doctoral dissertation, Cornell University. Ann Arbor, Mich.: University Microfilms, 1990.

Radimer, Kathy L., Christine M. Olson, Jennifer C. Greene, Cathy C. Campbell, and Jean-Pierre Habicht. "Understanding Hunger and Developing Indicators to Assess It in Women and Children." *Journal of Nutrition Education* 24, no. 1 (1992).

Riches, Graham. *Food Banks and the Welfare Crisis*. Ottawa: Canadian Council on Social Development, 1986.

———, ed. *First World Hunger: Food Security and Welfare Politics*. London: Macmillan, 1997.

Ruggles, Patricia. *Drawing the Line: Alternative Measures of Poverty and Their Implications for Public Policy*. Washington, D.C.: Urban Institute Press, 1990.

Salamon, Lester. *Partners in Public Service: Government-Nonprofit Relations in the Modern Welfare State*. Baltimore: Johns Hopkins University Press, 1995.

Sidel, Ruth. *Keeping Women and Children Last: America's War on the Poor*. New York: Penguin Books, 1996.

Stern, Mark J. "The Emergence of the Homeless as a Public Problem." *Social Service Review*. June 1984.

Titmuss, Richard. *The Gift Relationship: From Human Blood to Social Policy*. New York: Pantheon Books, 1971.

VanAmburg Group Inc. *Second Harvest 1993 National Research Study*. Chicago: Second Harvest National Food Bank Network, 1994.

Wolpert, Julian. *What Charity Can and Cannot Do*. New York: The Twentieth Century Fund, 1996.

Wuthnow, Robert. *Acts of Compassion*. Princeton, N.J.: Princeton University Press, 1991.

Zelizer, Viviana. *The Social Meaning of Money*. New York: Basic Books, 1994.

Index